For Janie

SOUTHEAST ASIA
A Region in Transition

*A thematic human geography of
the ASEAN region*

Jonathan Rigg

Department of Geography
School of Oriental & African Studies
University of London

London and New York

First published 1991
by Unwin Hyman Ltd

Reprinted 1994
by Routledge
11 New Fetter Lane, London EC4P 4EE
29 West 35th Street, New York, NY 10001

© 1991 Jonathan Rigg

Typeset in 10 on 11 point Bembo
Printed in Great Britain at the University Press, Cambridge

British Library Cataloguing in Publication Data
A catalogue record for this book is available from the British Library

Library of Congress Cataloging in Publication Data
A catalog record for this book is available from the Library of Congress

ISBN 0-415-11938-3

LIBRARY

Tel: 01244 375444   Ext: 3301

UNIVERSITY COLLEGE
CHESTER

This book is to be returned on or before the
last date stamped below. Overdue charges
will be incurred by the late return of books.

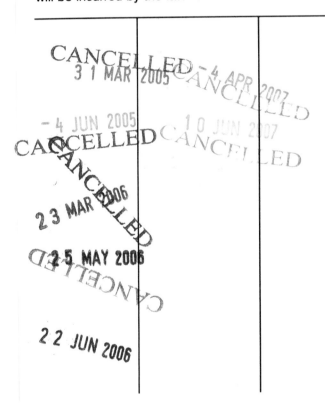

Preface

This book is a thematic contemporary human geography of the Association of Southeast Asian Nations (ASEAN) and has been written to fulfil two main objectives. First, to present an up-to-date statement covering some of the changes that are currently affecting the countries of the area. And second, to provide an account that gives greater detailed discussion than would normally be found in a general, regional geography. It is for this reason that a thematic approach has been adopted. In addition, and arising from the objectives that have been set and the approach selected, the book focuses only on the countries of ASEAN, namely Brunei, Indonesia, Malaysia, the Philippines, Singapore, and Thailand.

Eight 'themes' have been selected, most of which are illustrated with detailed reference to the experience of a single country. Although the specifics of each discussion may not apply across the ASEAN region, the essence usually does, and in each case lessons and implications can be drawn that have wider application. An inevitable danger with any book of a thematic nature is that no one will be satisfied with the themes that are chosen. There are good reasons, for example, to include chapters on the development of marine resources, on population growth and family planning, and on regional development, to name but three. However, it is felt that the disadvantages of following a thematic approach are more than counterbalanced by the greater detailed discussion that is possible. The themes selected in part reflect a personal preference, although the purpose is also to cover a range of issues and debates. Thus there are chapters covering such topics as rice cultivation and agrarian change, urbanization and primacy, natural resource development, plural societies, and land settlement.

Each of the chapters stands on its own and reference need not be made to other sections of the book. But that said, the intention is that the book should build up a patchwork of understanding in which the perspectives of one chapter link up with those of another. In addition there are two introductory chapters that deal briefly with the physical environment and with the history of the area. Although not exhaustive, which would be an impossible task, it is hoped that the book will provide a broad framework without sacrificing too much of the detail that is so crucial to building an understanding as well as an appreciation.

Jonathan Rigg
London,
Spring 1990

Acknowledgements

I am very grateful to the following people who kindly offered their advice and encouragement while I was writing this book. In the Department of Geography at the School of Oriental & African Studies I would like to thank Richard Edmonds, Keith McLachlan and, especially, Philip Stott for their suggestions and their time, and Catherine Lawrence who drew all the maps. And in the Department of Economics and Political Science, Peter Ayre and Robert Taylor. I am also grateful to Richard Barry, who offered a number of insights into the oil industry in Indonesia.

A substantial portion of the book was written while I was a British Academy Research Fellow at SOAS and I am very grateful for the support of the British Academy during that time.

Finally, I would like to thank my wife, Janie, who put up with a great deal.

Contents

List of figures

List of tables

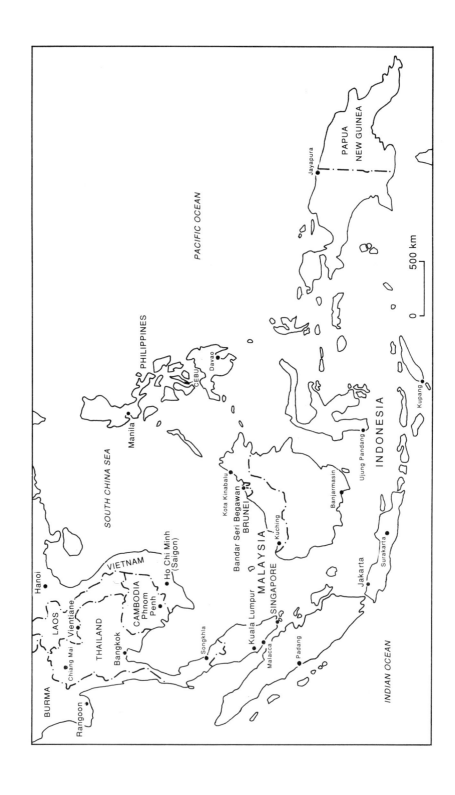

A note on names

The spellings of the countries and towns mentioned in this book in the main follow the *Times Atlas* standard. However, the American spelling of the term Southeast Asia is used. In addition, Southeast Asia is used in some places to mean the countries of ASEAN, and in others the entire geographical region of Southeast Asia (i.e. also including Burma, Cambodia, Laos, and Vietnam). The context in which the term is used will indicate to which group of countries reference is being made.

Burma officially changed its name to Myanmar on 18 June 1989 (the capital, Rangoon, also had its name changed, to Yangon). Throughout the book, Burma will be used. In addition, Cambodia is used rather than Kampuchea, Malacca rather than Melaka, and Java and Sumatra in place of Jawa and Sumatera.

1

Southeast Asia: physical and historical threads

Introduction

The market economies of Southeast Asia are among the most vibrant in the developing world. Indeed, as a group, Brunei, Indonesia, Malaysia, the Philippines, Singapore and Thailand are often regarded as developmental success stories. In 1970 the value of their exports amounted to US$6.11 billion, which was a mere 2.18 per cent of world trade. By 1988 they had increased to US$104.73 billion (3.91 per cent of world trade), and the region is now widely considered to be in the vanguard of countries that will make the 21st century the century of the Pacific. Admittedly, this perspective of economic success tends to gloss over the poverty, corruption, inefficiency, and inequality that continue to be a feature of the area, but progress has nonetheless been remarkable, and in the main the perspective is justified.

Yet following the end of the Second World War, the governments of Thailand, and of the newly independent countries of Indonesia, Malaysia, the Philippines, Singapore, and (later) Brunei hardly found themselves in an enviable position. They were confronted with the task of continuing the reconstruction of their war-ravaged infrastructures. They had to create a sense of nationhood where previously none had existed. They had to appease groups who were less than satisfied with the terms of independence. They lacked skilled personnel in government and industry. And they were without sufficient financial resources. This makes the transition from underdeveloped, to developing and – in some cases – newly industrializing all the more striking. To take the point one step further, it could even be argued that the market economies of Southeast Asia are the first group of developing countries to escape from underdevelopment.

The Southeast Asian region as a whole consists of ten countries. These are the mainland countries of Burma, Cambodia, Laos, Thailand, and Vietnam, and the island states of Brunei, Indonesia, Malaysia, the Philippines, and Singapore. As will be discussed shortly, such a regional formulation does have some geographical legitimacy. This extends from a certain physical unity in terms of climate and geological evolution, combined with common historical and cultural threads. It is these common features that have led numerous geographers to claim that Southeast Asia has a distinct identity that sets it apart from the regions surrounding it (e.g. Fisher 1966). However, although there may be some very good physical, historical, and cultural reasons for studying the ten countries as a unit, their recent economic and political development has served to divide the region into at least two competing subregional blocs.

On the one hand there are the countries of Indochina. Since 1975, Cambodia, Laos, and Vietnam have embarked upon strategies of communist reconstruction and development, and their respective governments have aligned themselves with the Soviet Union or the People's Republic of China. Burma is also a command economy, although its government has studiously avoided developing close relations with any of the superpowers. On the other hand, there are the six remaining countries, which make up the Association of Southeast Asian Nations (ASEAN): Brunei, Indonesia, Malaysia, the Philippines, Singapore, and Thailand. These are market economies following outward-looking, export-oriented strategies of economic development. They have also aligned themselves, to varying degrees, with the USA and the West. And, as if to emphasize their economic and political links, Indonesia, Malaysia, the Philippines, Singapore, and Thailand signed the Bangkok Declaration in 1967, so creating ASEAN. Brunei became the sixth member in 1984.

This book, above all, is a thematic contemporary human geography of the ASEAN countries. The exclusive focus on ASEAN countries is because of the divergent recent experiences of the market and command economies. As a result there is little to unite the two groups of countries in terms of their contemporary human geography, and there are few themes that span the political and economic divide. This is reflected in a number of books (including this one) that claim to deal with 'Southeast Asia', but use the term only to denote the countries of ASEAN (e.g. Higgot & Robison 1985, Robison *et al.* 1987b, Clad 1989). The tendency is becoming increasingly prevalent in academic, diplomatic, and business circles.

However, although ASEAN is gaining its own regional identity, which to a limited degree has begun to supplant older geographical divisions, it should always be borne in mind that ASEAN remains a subregional bloc within a larger geographical region, and it is only recent political and economic developments that have served to divide the region. Should there be a political and economic convergence between the two competing groups of countries, a prospect that is discussed towards the end of the book, then the wider Southeast Asia may achieve greater coherence.

Geology, climate, relief and soils

Geology and structure

The countries of the wider Southeast Asia have a combined land area of 4 492 820 square kilometres, while those of ASEAN cover 3 068 920 square kilometres (Table 1.1). However, it is not so much the land as the sea that dominates the region. At its core are the shallow waters of the Sunda Shelf, which are less than 200 metres in depth and extend from the Gulf of Thailand to the Java Sea (Figure 1.1). During much of the Pleistocene,

Table 1.1 Population and land area of Southeast Asia, 1600–1989

	Land area (square km)	Population (millions) 1600	1800	1989
ASEAN				
Thailand	513 100	2.2	3.5	55.6
Malaysia[1]	330 400	1.2	1.5	17.4
Singapore	620	—	—	2.7
Brunei	5800	—	—	0.3
Indonesia	1 919 000	9.1	12.3	184.6
Philippines	300 000	1.0	2.0	64.9
ASEAN	3 068 920	13.5	19.3	325.5
Indochina and Burma				
Vietnam[2]	329 600	4.7	7.0	66.8
Laos	236 800	—	—	3.9
Cambodia[3]	181 000	1.2	1.5	6.8
Burma	676 500	3.1	4.6	40.8
Total Southeast Asia	4 492 820	22.4	32.4	443.8

Sources: Reid 1988, p. 14, Asia Yearbook 1990

Notes: 1) The population figures for 1600 and 1800 include Patani and all of Borneo. 2) The population figures for 1600 and 1800 include only north and central Vietnam. 3) The population figures for 1600 and 1800 include Champa (now part of southern Vietnam).

which extended over 2 million years and ended approximately 15 000 years ago, sea levels were 200 metres lower than they are today. During these glacial periods the entire Sunda Shelf would have been exposed, linking the mainland with the islands of Sumatra, Java, Borneo and possibly the Philippines, and in this way providing a land bridge for the dispersal of plants and animals (see Morley & Flenley 1987). Although the Sunda Shelf was subsequently submerged, its rich seas have made the region uniquely accessible, and it is no accident that the early history of the archipelago focuses on sea-based empires and maritime trade.

Intense research by geologists, palaeontologists, and others has done much to further our knowledge of the geological origins of Southeast Asia (see Audley-Charles 1981, 1987, George 1987). Nevertheless, new evidence and perspectives are continually coming to light, and much of the story has yet to be told. It seems that Southeast Asia took shape through a long and complex process of rifting during which sections of the region separated from the southern supercontinent, Gondwanaland, and drifted northwards to eventually collide with the other supercontinent, Laurasia (Figure 1.2). First to break away were eastern Thailand, Laos, Cambodia, and Vietnam (together with north Tibet and Iran), which possibly separated during the Permo-Carboniferous (345–225 Ma [=megayear, 1 000 000 years]). Next, during the Jurassic (200–160 Ma), Burma, western Thailand, Malaya, and Sumatra (together with south Tibet) broke away. And later still, New Guinea, east Sulawesi, and Timor drifted northwards. It was not until relatively recently that the present configuration of the region was finally attained. The collision of the eastern and western sections of Sulawesi,

3

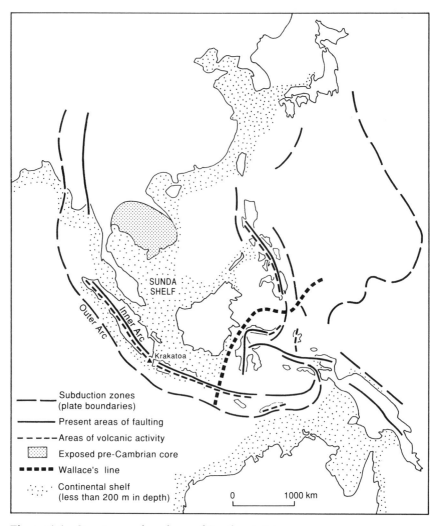

Figure 1.1 Structure and geology of Southeast Asia

for example, did not occur until the Miocene (15 Ma), while Timor collided with the Banda volcanic arc only 3 Ma during the mid-Pliocene (3 Ma). Interestingly, it has only been since the theory of plate tectonics (or continental drift) has been developed that Alfred Russel Wallace's observations on the striking changes in the fauna of the archipelago between his 'Indo-Malayan' and 'Austro-Malayan' zoological regions (Wallace's line marking the interface between the two) have been understood in terms of the Tertiary geological history of the region (Figure 1.1) (Whitmore 1981). That said, it should be borne in mind that although the general process of successive riftings of fragments of Southeast Asia northwards from

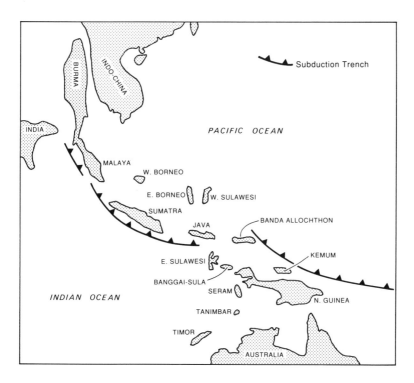

Figure 1.2 Tectonics and the rifting of Southeast Asia: late Eocene (40 Ma) (adapted from Audley-Charles 1987)

Gondwanaland now seems firmly established, the details and the dates of separation remain far from settled.

Despite Southeast Asia's complex geological and tectonic origins, its present configuration shows a surprising surface coherence. The region forms the south-eastern section of the Eurasian plate, and is clearly demarcated from the regions that surround it. Running from western Burma southwards past Sumatra and Java, and then northwards to Sulawesi and the Philippines, the region is bounded by a series of deep-sea trenches where the Australian, Pacific, and Philippine plates plunge beneath the Eurasian plate (so-called subduction zones) (Figure 1.1). These trenches consist of an outer, earlier (mid-Miocene) arc, and an inner, later (late-Pliocene) arc. The inner arc is a zone of intense volcanic activity, which was most dramatically displayed when Krakatoa exploded in 1883 (Figure 1.1). The sound of the explosion was heard over 3000 kilometres away in Sri Lanka, and the seismic wave that it produced led to a noticeable two-inch surge in the English Channel (Furneaux 1965). Within these deep-sea ocean trenches lies the stable Sunda Shelf, which dates from the Triassic, and an even more ancient partially exposed section of Cambrian rock covering most of Cambodia, and parts of Thailand and southern Vietnam (Figure 1.1). This older, inner core is heavily weathered, and characterized by rather more subdued relief compared with the younger, active, rugged rim. Finally, and less clearly, Southeast Asia is bounded to the north by the highlands of Burma, Thailand and Vietnam which were uplifted during the Tertiary mountain-building phase. The surface geological unity of Southeast Asia, and the central focus of the region on the Sunda Shelf, was recognized as long ago as 1847 when Logan in his paper 'The present condition of the Indian Archipelago', wrote:

> That there is a real and not merely fanciful connection between the Archipelago and Asia is demonstrable. . . If [the region] was raised but a little, we should see shallow seas dried up, the mountain ranges of Sumatra, Borneo, and Java become like those of the Peninsula, and great rivers flowing not just in the Straits of Malacca . . . but through the wide valley of the China Sea, and by the deep and narrow Strait of Sunda, into the Indian Ocean. Thus the unity would become geographical, which is now only geological (Logan 1847, p. 2).

Climate and vegetation

Climatically, all of Southeast Asia lies within the humid tropics and, as has been observed on numerous occasions, it differs from its neighbours in being considerably wetter than India and warmer than China.[1] However, this generalization masks an unusual degree of climatic complexity, particularly as it relates to rainfall. At sea level, temperatures are fairly uniform, both across the region and through the year, and it is altitudinal differences which have the greatest influence. But temporal and spatial patterns of rainfall are more varied and complex. Thus seasonality in Southeast Asia is a function not of temperature but of rainfall, and it is the pattern and timing of rainfall that is of fundamental importance to human activity.

Rainfall is intimately associated with the advance and retreat of the major air streams that converge on the region. Two broad climate types can be identified:

(a) Equatorial monsoon climates (Köppen's *Af* classification, Trewartha's *Ar*).
(b) Dry and wet monsoon climates (Köppen's *Am* or *Aw* classifications)

Over much of island Southeast Asia, extending ten degrees north and south of the equator, an equatorial monsoon climate prevails. This accounts for nearly all Indonesia, the southern portion of the island of Mindanao in the Philippines, and all of Malaysia, Singapore, Brunei and the southern provinces of Thailand (Figure 1.3). Annual rainfall in equatorial monsoon Southeast Asia is in excess of 2000 mm, and close to the equator it is evenly distributed through the year, there being no marked dry season (Figure 1.4). However, moving north and south from the equator, the dry season becomes more pronounced, and rainfall becomes concentrated in one or two seasonal peaks (Figure 1.5). The pattern of rainfall is determined by

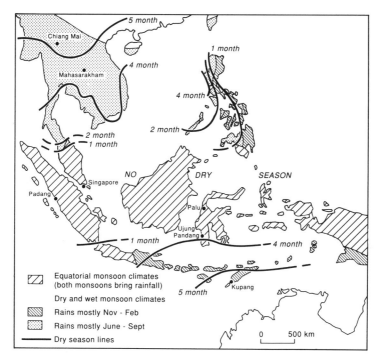

Figure 1.3 Climate and rainfall

the north-east and the south-west monsoons, which in turn are affected by the advance and retreat of the air streams which converge on the area.

The north-east monsoon, which south of the equator is often referred to as the west monsoon, prevails during the months from November and December to February and March, and forms the wet season over much of the archipelago. During this monsoon the Northern Equatorial Air

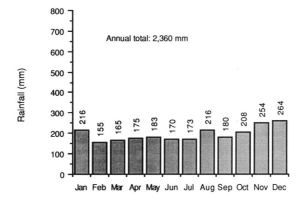

Figure 1.4 Rainfall: Singapore

7

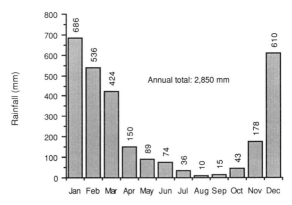

Figure 1.5   Rainfall: Ujung Pandang, Sulawesi

Stream boundary lies across the equator, having been pushed southwards by the advance of the Siberian and Pacific dynamic highs. The south-west monsoon, which in Java is referred to as the east monsoon, prevails from June to August and September and brings dry conditions to the area. During this monsoon the Northern Equatorial Air Stream boundary retreats northwards along with the Siberian and Pacific dynamic highs, and the Southern Equatorial Air Stream Boundary advances from the south to reach a position in which it lies in a line from Central Sumatra, through Singapore, to the Philippine island of Palawan. The periods from March to May and from September to November mark transitional periods between the north-east and south-west monsoons during which the air stream boundaries are advancing and retreating across the region.

Although the south-west and north-east monsoons are central to under-standing the pattern and timing of rainfall in the region, there are a number of pockets of reduced and increased rainfall across the equatorial zone. These areas of pronounced rainfall variations are linked to the effects of local wind systems and climates, which in turn are influenced by topography and convection. For example at Palu in Sulawesi, just one degree south of the equator, the shadowing effect of the surrounding highlands means that annual rainfall is only 530 mm (Figure 1.3). In comparison, Padang on the west coast of Sumatra, and also one degree south of the equator, has an annual rainfall in excess of 4500 mm because of rainfall caused by orographic lifting of the monsoon winds which are laden with water vapour (Figure 1.3). In addition to the effects that mountains can have on local climates, convectional rainfall – caused by the heating of the land during the day – can also produce heavy local thunderstorms.

Dry and wet monsoon climates prevail over mainland Southeast Asia, the Philippines and eastern Indonesia (Figure 1.3). In these areas rainfall tends to be both lower (less than 1500 mm) and more seasonally pronounced, with a dry season often extending over between four and five months. In the mainland, the north-east monsoon (November to March) brings cool, dry air to Thailand, Burma, and much of Indochina, and during these months rainfall may be very low indeed. For example, during the three months from November to January, Mahasarakham in Northeastern Thailand receives an average of only 14 mm of rainfall, 1.1 per cent of the annual figure (Figures 1.3 and 1.6). Before the onset of the south-west monsoon in June, the heating of the land may lead to convectional thunderstorms of some intensity. In Thailand and Burma these are referred to as the 'mango rains'. The south-west monsoon itself corresponds with the period of heaviest rainfall, and the town of Mahasarakham receives 93 per cent of its average annual rainfall of 1240 mm between April and October (Figure 1.6).

Again, however, although the pattern of summer rainfall in mainland Southeast Asia is determined largely by the south-west monsoon, it needs to be emphasized that relief can play a decisive role in determining local conditions. For example, the significantly lower totals over much of Thailand are linked to the shadowing effect of the Tenasserim highlands, which run north–south down the border between Thailand and Burma. Sittwe (Akyab) in western Burma, receives an annual average of 5180 mm of rainfall. In contrast, Chiangmai in Northern Thailand has only 1220 mm (Figure 1.3).

Rainfall patterns in the Philippine islands are even more complex, and local variations in climate are numerous. By the time the north-east monsoon has crossed the South China Sea and reached the Philippines, it is moisture-laden and any orographic lifting can bring large amounts of rainfall to localized areas. As the north-east monsoon weakens, and before the onset of the south-west monsoon in May, the Philippine islands come under the influence of the North Pacific Trades which bring little rainfall. The south-west monsoon itself represents the season of heaviest rainfall and prevails from May through to September.

Finally, eastern Indonesia (east Java, Bali, Lombok, Timor and the other islands of Nusa Tenggara) is affected by two monsoons: the west monsoon from December to March, and the east monsoon from May to September. The west monsoon, which is a continuation of the Asian north-east monsoon after it has changed direction on crossing the equator,

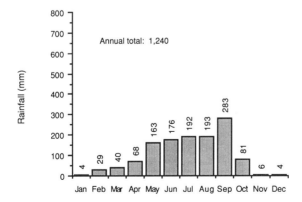

Figure 1.6   Rainfall: Mahasarakham, Northeastern Thailand

9

brings large quantities of rainfall to the area (the monsoon by then having picked up moisture over the seas of the Indonesian archipelago) (Figure 1.7). During May the hot and dry South Pacific Trade winds again prevail and rainfall can be very low during a dry season that may extend over six months (Nieuwolt 1977, pp. 143–4).

As should have become apparent from this brief discussion of climate, the pattern and timing of rainfall in the region are highly complex. Indeed, in many respects such a short account can barely begin to explain this complexity. However, the seasonality of rainfall is the point to stress so far as the impact of climate on human activity is concerned. For it is the variability in rainfall, rather than total rainfall, that is of paramount importance. As will be discussed later in the chapter, the need in many areas of the region to design agricultural strategies that deal with, and in some cases harness, the variable rainfall regime has led to striking and ingenious solutions.

The seasonality and pattern of rainfall in Southeast Asia determines the natural vegetation. The dominant forest type is tropical rainforest, which extends in its distribution from northern Burma southwards through the islands and into New Guinea. The heart of these tropical rainforests, which are second in size only to those of the Americas, is centred in the archipelago, where once they would have clothed virtually the entire area. But the rainforests of the region are not uniform in character, consisting of 13 different and distinctive formations (Whitmore 1989, pp. 203). Perhaps the best known are the two lowland climatic climaxes represented by tropical lowland evergreen rainforest and semi-evergreen rainforest. In addition, however, there are also formations related to soil conditions (e.g. heath forest and forest over limestone), to other habitat characteristics (e.g. coastal mangrove forest), and to altitude (montane rainforests).

In mainland Southeast Asia, because rainfall totals are generally lower and the dry season longer, there exists a mosaic of savanna forests, monsoon forests and tropical rainforests that often reflects local climate variations. However, it should be emphasized that human activity has done much to alter and to destroy these natural formations. In many areas, logging,

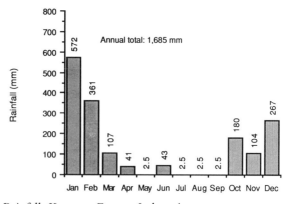

Figure 1.7 Rainfall: Kupang, Eastern Indonesia

the removal of trees for fuelwood and for agriculture, grazing, and fire have degraded the natural formations, causing anthropogenic climaxes to arise. In some areas the forest has been replaced by grassland, perhaps the best, although still contentious, example being the spread of the fire climax dominated by the grass *Imperata cylindrica*.

Relief and soils

Southeast Asia's relief offers relatively few favourable areas for human settlement. In general terms, a distinction can be made between the mainland and the archipelago. On the mainland, mountains and valleys run north to south, and within the valleys flow the great rivers of the region: the Irrawaddy, Sittang, Salween, Chao Phraya, Mekong and the Song Koi or Red river (Figure 1.8). It is here that there has been the greatest human settlement with exploitation of the abundant nutrient-rich water and alluvium to develop rice culture to its highest state. Much of the rest of the mainland is upland, and although the narrow valleys within these highlands have also been used for wet rice cultivation (e.g. in Northern Thailand), in the main the land is best suited to shifting cultivation. Beyond the alluvial lowlands the soils of the mainland are generally poor. Although they may support impressive stands of tropical forest, this is no indicator of fertility. Nutrients tend to be stored in the forest biomass rather than in the soil, and soils are usually moderately to severely leached, low in cation exchange capacity, and prone to rapid degradation should the forest cover be removed.

Favourable niches for human settlement in island Southeast Asia are even more limited. Ironically, the Sunda Shelf – the zone that might have offered the greatest opportunities – is now covered by sea, and the process of flooding has left large areas of the remaining lowland as swamp (e.g. eastern Sumatra and southern Borneo) (Figure 1.8). This is not to say that the archipelago is devoid of areas with significant agricultural potential. In particular, the fertile azonal volcanic soils of central Java support some of the highest agricultural population densities in the world (more than 1000 per square kilometre), while the volcanic soils of Luzon in the Philippines are also particularly suited to intensive wet rice cultivation. As on the mainland, however, the rich tropical forests of the archipelago are supported on soils that are generally infertile. The failure to take proper account of this has sometimes caused development projects to perform poorly, and land to become degraded, sometimes to the point where it has had to be abandoned (see Chapter 5).

Social and commercial intercourse: water for communication

Of the environmental elements, water has possibly been the most instrumental in forging Southeast Asia's distinctive personality. The degree to which the region is interpenetrated by waterways has made it remarkably

1 Irrawaddy River
2 Sittang River
3 Salween River
4 Chao Phraya River
5 Mekong River
6 Song Koi River

Highlands - Land above 500 m
Plains
Swamps

0   500 km

Figure 1.8 Southeast Asia: relief

accessible. Winds tend to be moderate and predictable, and this, coupled
with an abundance of wood available close to the shooreline for shipbuilding,
has made 'the region uniquely favourable to maritime activity' (Reid 1988,
p. 2). Extensive trade, both within and beyond the region, was in evidence
as early as the end of the 14th century (Reid 1990). Southeast Asia's
accessibility has had two effects. On the one hand it has meant that the
region has experienced successive seaborne invasions. It has also meant,
however, that despite what appears to be a bewildering array of languages
and cultures, its inhabitants have been in relatively close contact with one
another and as a result exhibit certain common features. It is notable, for
example, that in 1521 Magellan's Sumatran slave could immediately be

understood in the Central Philippines, over 3000 kilometres distant (Reid 1988, p. 7).

In prehistory, waves of migrants from the north filtered southwards through the valleys of Burma and Thailand, and hence to the islands of the archipelago and on to the Pacific and Australasia. In some cases those early migrants intermingled with the indigenous Negrito groups. More often, though, they either pushed them into the mountains or farther southeastwards. Next, at the beginning of the 1st century AD, Southeast Asia experienced an infusion of Hindu-Buddhist culture when Indian traders ventured to the region in search of gold and spices. This 'Indianization' of Southeast Asia led to the evolution of the cult of the god-king (*deva raja*) that saw its apogee in the magnificent empires and temples of Srivijaya and Angkor (Keyes 1977). Subsequently, at the start of the second millennium, Arab and Indian traders introduced Islam into island Southeast Asia, while monks from Sri Lanka disseminated Theravada Buddhism to the mainland. In the face of these popular religions, the corrupt, degenerate *deva raja* cults of the aristocracy were quickly displaced. Finally, in the modern era, the colonial powers brought yet another influx of technology and culture. Their activities also created the conditions that encouraged the settlement of Chinese and Indians in the region from the late 19th century onwards.

Scholars of the colonial period, no doubt reflecting the atmosphere of the time, tended to emphasize the degree to which the inhabitants of Southeast Asia had been moulded and influenced by these external cultural influences. More recently, however, the emphasis has shifted to stress the extent to which foreign cultural forms have been assimilated and adapted to meet the needs and preferences of the inhabitants of the region. Reid (1988) notes that although some of the common features of Southeast Asian life can be linked to the demands of the environment, others are clearly tied to the degree of commercial interaction *within* the region. He points to the wide dispersal of the finger knife (*ani ani*) (used for rice harvesting) and the piston bellows; the universality of betel chewing[2]; the significance of musical patterns dominated by the brass gong and of similar patterns of body decoration; the widespread concept of spirit or 'soul stuff'; the prominence of women in descent, ritual, and marketing; and the importance of debt as a determinant of social obligation:

> What I wish to stress here is that maritime intercourse continued to link the peoples of Southeast Asia more tightly to one another than to outside influences down to the seventeenth century . . . What did *not* happen (with the possible exception of Vietnam) was that any part of the region established closer relations with China or India than with its neighbors in Southeast Asia (Reid 1988, p. 6).

Wet rice cultivation: water for life

Water not only made Southeast Asia uniquely accessible; it is also the central element in the cultivation of wet rice, the pre-eminent crop of the region (Figure 1.9). Two agricultural systems are particularly characteristic of Southeast Asia: shifting cultivation and wet rice cultivation. The former is concentrated in the forested highlands and is an extensive subsistence system. Land is cleared by burning and then cultivated for only a short period of time (two to five years), after which the soil is exhausted. It is then abandoned until it recovers its fertility (see Figure 4.1). This form of cultivation, together with hunting and gathering, was the basis of the earliest subsistence systems. Today, as population pressure grows, systems of shifting cultivation are slowly being replaced in most areas by permanent field agriculture (see Chapter 4).

At a broad level of generalization it is safe to assume that rice culture spread southwards from a core area in the piedmont zone running eastwards from Assam to north Vietnam, displacing in the process the older tuber-based cultures (Watabe 1985, p. 35, Hill 1977, p. 1). At first it was concentrated in the lowland areas of mainland Southeast Asia, and from there spread to the Malay Peninsula and into the archipelago. However, as with many aspects of the prehistory of Southeast Asia, the evidence for the evolution and dissemination of rice cultivation is fragmentary, and the conclusions drawn from it often highly tendentious. The earliest date for use of rice grains in the region is 7000 BC, from Spirit Cave in Northern Thailand. However, although some archaeologists (e.g. Gorman) have argued for a similarly early date for rice domestication, this seems unlikely. Rice was probably not cultivated until the fourth or third millennium BC (Glover 1979, Sørensen 1986, Higham 1989). Whatever the doubts over the origins and dispersal of rice in Southeast Asia, by the 15th century,

Figure 1.9 Water for life: Lua' rice terraces, Mae Hong Son, Northern Thailand (photograph: Philip Stott)

when Europeans arrived in the region, rice culture had evolved into a complex system adapted to a variety of environments and incorporating a range of technological, cultural, and biological characteristics. Wherever it could be cultivated it had displaced other staple crops; only in such areas as the dry islands of Timor, and the northern Moluccas did the inhabitants continue to rely on other subsistence crops. Bray (1986, p. 11) has noted that 'once people became accustomed to eating rice they were loath to change back to other foods', and that staples such as taro and sago were, and are, widely regarded as 'poor man's food'. By the 15th century rice was both the pre-eminent staple crop of the region and its most important item of bulk trade.

Although there are numerous variants and subvariants of wet rice cultivation – rainfed wet rice, floating rice, irrigated rice, transplant rice, broadcast rice – they all depend upon an ample and fairly constant supply of water (see Chapter 3). To the wet rice farmers of the region, water is a necessity, and indeed there is probably no other staple crop so dependent upon the environment for its successful cultivation. This is reflected in the number of rice varieties that exist (some 120 000), and in the rituals and songs that honour the 'gift of water' and dwell upon the vagaries of the monsoon. Water-throwing festivals, designed partly to induce abundant rainfall, are widespread and should the rains be delayed villagers will often resort to magic. In Thailand, for example, images of the Buddha with claimed powers will have water thrown at them, and female cats (the personification of dryness) are carried in procession and drenched while villagers chant 'Hail Nang Maew [Lady Cat], give us rain, give us holy water to pour on Nang Maew's head' (Phya Anuman Rajadhon 1955, Demaine 1978).

In parts of Northern Thailand, Bali, the Philippines, Java and Sumatra sophisticated irrigation systems have been constructed to overcome the vagaries of rainfall and to ensure a stable water supply. In some cases these systems have made it possible for farmers to grow two or even three crops of rice each year. Over much of the region, however, the nature of the terrain requires that rice be grown in 'rainfed' conditions, relying upon natural rainfall. In such areas, farmers are dependent upon the seasons for their survival, and complex strategies of cultivation have evolved to maintain a stable level of production through periods of flood and drought. Songs and stories make clear the link between rice, water, happiness, and wealth. Perhaps the best-known example is contained in a famous late 13th century inscription of King Ramkhamhaeng of the Sukhotai kingdom of Thailand: 'During the lifetime of Ramkhamhaeng, this city of Sukhotai is prosperous. In the water there is fish, in the fields there is rice' (Coedès 1968, p. 207).

Land and forests

Although water is of paramount importance in forging a distinctive Southeast Asian 'personality', there is a second environmental element worthy of special note: the forests (Figure 1.10). As an Indian king is reported to have said to a Siamese boasting about the greatness of the lands ruled by Siam: 'It is true, I admit, that they are greater in extent than mine, but then the King of Golconda is a king of men, while your king is only king of forests and mosquitoes' (quoted in Stott 1978, p. 7). Why this should have been so relates not only to the tropical climate, but also to the human impact on the region. Outside a few areas of high population density, such as Java and the Red River Delta of Vietnam, Southeast Asia was a low pressure area when compared with its neighbours, India and China. Although estimation of the region's historical population is very much an exercise in guesswork, it has been calculated that in 1600 the total population was about 22.4 million, a density of 5.55 persons per square kilometre. By 1800 this had increased to approximately 32.4 million, a modest annual growth rate of 0.2 per cent (Reid 1988, p. 14). In contrast, between 1800 and 1989 – approximately the same span of time – the population increased by more than 410 million, to 444 million (Table 1.1).

The low population density of Southeast Asia before the expansion of the last two centuries meant that land in most areas was abundant and much of it remained forested. Wood, bamboo, and other forest products were plentiful and the dominant building materials. Even in the largest cities, and for the dwellings of the most wealthy and powerful nobles and merchants, wood was used for construction. Only temples and other religious buildings were built of brick and stone, and as a result it is only these that have survived from this period. Temples in

Figure 1.10 A land of forests: undisturbed monsoon and savanna forest, Uthai Thani, Western Thailand (photograph: Philip Stott)

ancient cities such as Sukhotai and Ayutthaya in Thailand, Angkor in Cambodia, and monuments such as Borobudur and Prambanan in Java bear testament to the construction skills of the pre-colonial empires of the region.

As land was an abundant resource it tended not to be valued particularly highly. The converse was that people were scarce, and consequently had a high value. This becomes clear in the pattern and purpose of warfare in Southeast Asia. Battles did not usually result in great numbers of casualties, and armies were rather used to intimidate opponents (Reid 1988, p. 121–9). La Loubère (1691, p. 90), in his account of Siam, writes: 'Kill not is the order, which the King of Siam gives his troops, when he sends them into the field'. The principal objective of waging war was to extend an empire's influence over greater numbers of people, not over greater expanses of land, for it was the control of manpower that was the paramount indicator of power and status. La Loubère (1691, p. 90) notes of the tactics of the Siamese (Thai) armies:

> They busie themselves only in making slaves. If the Peguins [Burmese], for example, do on one side invade the lands of Siam, the Siameses will at another place enter on the lands of Pegu, and both parties will carry away whole villages into captivity.

Southeast Asia: unity and disunity

This chapter has brought together a number of threads of evidence – mostly historical and physical – that are indicative of the unity of the wider Southeast Asian region. It is on the basis of such evidence that scholars have argued that the region is distinctive and coherent, and that it has an identity that sets it apart from surrounding regions. However, there is also a strong argument for ignoring such geographical generalizations. There is always a danger when looking for unifying features that patterns that do not exist are identified, and that too much weight will be given to elements of environment and of life that are, in the end, of little consequence. It is interesting that many geographers consider Southeast Asia's distinctiveness to reside 'in its common diversity rather than in any closely-knit unity' (Fisher 1966, p. 9). This view leads us back to the perception that Southeast Asia represents a residual region: it owes its regional identity not to internal coherence, but to external incoherence. India and China are sufficiently different from the region to warrant its identification as a separate unit, irrespective of the characteristics that might bind the region internally.

The remaining chapters of this book will focus on the countries that make up the Association of Southeast Asian Nations (ASEAN). However, although its structure and purpose demand that Indochina and Burma be largely excluded from the analysis, it is important to begin by seeing the countries of ASEAN in the context of the wider Southeast Asia.

Notes to Chapter 1

1 For short accounts of Southeast Asia's climate see Lockwood 1976, pp. 82–5, Trewartha 1981, pp. 199–206, Ooi Jin Bee 1976, pp. 29–69. See also Nieuwolt 1977, Oldeman and Frère 1982.
2 Reid (1988, p. 6) makes the point that the three ingredients – areca nut, betel leaf and lime – have to be combined in a fairly complex operation before their stimulating effects can be experienced.

2
Colonization, decolonization, and the impact of the colonial period in Southeast Asia

The colonization of Southeast Asia

To understand the colonial impact on Southeast Asia, it is first necessary to appreciate that the European powers were not on a civilizing mission. The *raison d'être* for colonialism was economic: it was profitable. The desire to take up the 'white man's burden' and to evangelize also played a role, but it should not disguise the fact that most governments, companies, and individuals were in Southeast Asia for money. For it to have been otherwise would have been remarkable.

Southeast Asia first became important to Europe as a source of spices. These were used to flavour an otherwise monotonous diet, particularly during the winter months when even the wealthy had to exist on pickled and salted fish and meat. Of the spices, cloves and nutmeg originated from just one location, the Moluccas (Maluku) or Spice Islands of eastern Indonesia (Figure 2.1). It was widely believed that these spices could be grown nowhere else and they commanded a high price (Savage 1984, p. 77). In order to break the monopoly of the spice trade held by Venetian and Muslim traders the Portuguese began to extend their possessions eastwards during the latter part of the 15th century. This culminated in 1511 in the capture by Alfonso Albuquerque of the port of Malacca, which became the first European possession in the region. From there, the Portuguese sent an expedition to open up trading relations with the Moluccas (Figure 2.1). The only other European power to impose itself on the region at this time was Spain. Magellan, in a remarkable feat of seamanship sailed from South America across the Pacific to the Philippines, where he made landfall in the Visayas in 1521. The Spanish, like the Portuguese, were attracted by the wealth of the Spice Islands, but found themselves unable to compete and quickly withdrew. Because the Portuguese aimed to monopolize the trade in spices they were not concerned with territorial expansion. Their presence in the region consisted only of a string of fortified ports – Malacca, Bantam (Banten), Flores, Ternate, Tidore, Timor, and Ambon (Amboyna) – and so far as most people in Southeast Asia were concerned, life remained unchanged (Figure 2.1). By the middle of the 16th century, estimated annual exports of Moluccan cloves, nutmeg, and mace to Europe were averaging 143 000 kilograms (Reid 1990, p. 7).

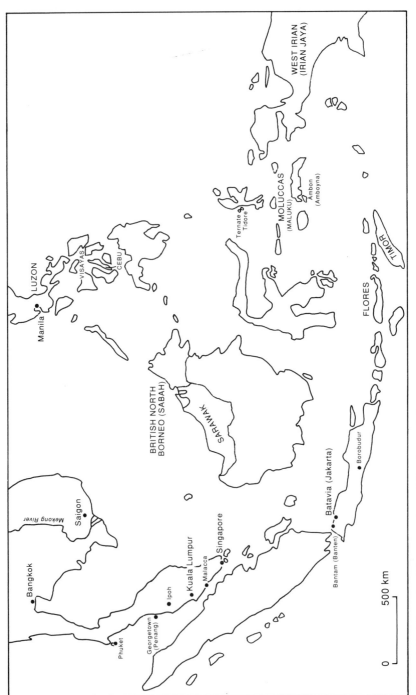

Figure 2.1 The colonial penetration of Southeast Asia

It was not until the late 16th century that the European powers began to intensify their presence in the archipelago. Miguel Lopez de Legazpi established a settlement on the island of Cebu in the Philippines in 1565; in 1571 he captured Manila, which became the capital of the Spanish Philippines. In extending their control over the Philippines, the Spanish halted the northward spread of Islam so that today it is the only predominantly Christian country in the region. In Indonesia, the Dutch supplanted the Portuguese, who were weak and overextended, and began to establish their own bases across the region and to take control of the spice trade (by 1616 they had 15 trading posts). This culminated in the acquisition of Malacca from the Portuguese in 1641.

Although the Dutch and the Spanish extended their territorial control rather more than had the Portuguese, the impact of the European powers remained superficial. Although, for example, the Dutch, controlled the western third of Java (centred on Batavia, now Jakarta), they remained unaware of Borobudur, possibly the greatest Buddhist monument in the world (Figure 2.1). At the same time, the Spanish could only claim firm control of central Luzon, and they had to await modern technology, in particular the steam gunboat and modern field artillery, before the rest of the country could be subjugated.

If the European impact in island Southeast Asia remained peripheral until the 19th century, their contacts with the mainland were even less significant. They amounted to the establishment of trading relations with the various kingdoms and sultanates, and the sending of a handful of missionaries. There were three principal reasons for this state of affairs. First, the mainland did not have the allure of spices to attract Europeans. Second, the geography of the area made colonization more difficult. And third, the mainland states were stronger and more united and so posed a greater military challenge.

During the course of the 17th and 18th centuries Southeast Asia lost some of its attractiveness from a European perspective. Alternative sources of spices were developed and exploited, and fortunes could no longer so easily be made. Thus the economic basis for European involvement in the region was eroded, and the expansion and intensification of the colonial experience slowed and in some areas stagnated. However, in the early part of the 19th century a series of economic, political, and technological changes served to transform and reinvigorate the region in the eyes of the European powers. To begin with, the Industrial Revolution in Europe and North America greatly increased the demand for raw materials such as tin, timber, sugar, and coffee. In addition, the rapidly expanding industries that were central to Europe and North America's industrial growth required ever larger markets for their finished products. Second, the Caribbean, where much European commercial interest had been focused in the 18th century, was in decline. The abolition of slavery in the 1830s and 1840s undermined the slave labour system, and land was also becoming increasingly scarce and expensive. Third, a number of technological innovations brought Southeast Asia into closer contact with Europe. The development of the steam engine and the steamship substantially reduced the risks and costs of trading with the region, while the opening of the Suez Canal in 1869 considerably shortened the journey. Fourth, increasing interest in China meant that Southeast Asia once again became important as a maritime crossroads between west and east. Finally, the end of the 18th century saw a rise in missionary zeal in Europe and a corresponding increase in missionary activity in the region. Public opinion demanded that the missionaries be protected, and this in some instances necessitated a more direct involvement of the Western powers in the area.

The upshot of these developments was that in the space of less than half a century – from about 1825 to 1870 – most of Southeast Asia was formally to fall under European control. There is not space here to detail the final European subjugation of the region. Suffice it to say that there were two sets of major rivalries: between the United Kingdom and the Netherlands in the archipelago during the first half of the 19th century, and between the United Kingdom and the France in the mainland during the second half of the 19th century. Although the colonial powers suffered minor military setbacks, the sultanates and monarchies of the region lacked the organization, manpower, and military might to withstand colonization. Quickly, and with relatively little loss of life, the colonial powers extended their control over Southeast Asia; by the end of the 19th century the political map with which we are familiar today had been drawn. The only country to maintain its independence, albeit in a reduced state, was Thailand (formerly Siam) which was fortunate in two respects. First, it benefited from having successive kings (Mongkut and Chulalongkorn) who were both perceptive and realistic, and who recognized that they would have to compromise if their kingdom was to survive. Secondly, it appears the United Kingdom and France felt it was in their mutual interest to maintain Thailand as a buffer between their respective spheres of influence. In the Philippines, Spain ceded control to the USA in 1898 following the Spanish–American War. In Borneo, Raja Brooke, a romantic English adventurer, managed by a combination of diplomacy, skill, and manipulation to become governor or raja of Sarawak.

Although the process of colonization is a fascinating issue in itself, the primary purpose of this chapter is to examine the impact of the colonial period, and to assess the colonial legacy that was left to the countries of the region when they gained self-government following the end of the Second World War.

The impact of colonization and the colonial period

Attempts to assess the impact of the colonial period on the subsequent development of Southeast Asia have been a source of much heated debate. Balance sheets of costs and benefits vary according to the period, country, and locale under consideration, and according to the ideological perspective that the analyst brings to bear on the issue. To the colonial powers and many of their representatives the mere fact that these 'backward' lands were being incorporated into the modern, 'civilized' world was a force for positive change. The construction of a modern infrastructure, the provision of schooling and health facilities, the extension of Western concepts of justice, and the termination of local conflicts were, and are, highlighted as evidence of the benefits of the colonial period. These benefits are also felt to have aided the progress and development of the region since the colonial era. On the other side of the debate, there was a handful of commentators writing during the colonial period, and considerably more since, who have emphasized the costs of colonization to the indigenous population. They have drawn attention to the manner in which the process engendered dependency, undermined local subsistence production, eroded traditional structures, and alienated the populations from their own countries. In the end, however, drawing up a balance of the costs and benefits of colonization must always contain a large element of value judgement. All that can safely be said is that the colonial period did have a significant effect, and that this remains in evidence today. It is also worth noting at this point that the length of time that Europe and the USA had colonial interests in the region spanned a relatively short period – a single lifetime.

Economic impacts

COMMERCIALIZATION

Arguably the most pervasive impact of colonialism was the penetration of capitalism and attendant commercialization. Peasants throughout Southeast Asia began to grow crops for sale. In some cases this merely involved producing a surplus of a traditional crop, such as rice or coconuts; in other instances farmers took up the cultivation of new crops, such as rubber and tea. This process entailed the clearance of large areas of previously uncultivated land, and although it was often achieved without Western technology or capital it was in response to the new economic environment created by the presence of the colonial powers. The rapid expansion of rice cultivation into the Mekong, Irrawaddy, and Chao Phraya deltas, for example, was a process pioneered by large numbers of individual peasants responding to the increase in global demand for rice in the latter part of the 19th century. However, the process of incorporation of the peasantry into the market economy was not always entirely voluntary. In Indonesia, the 'Culture System' established by the Dutch East India Company and then developed by the Dutch colonial authorities required that every farm household allocate one-fifth of its landholding to the cultivation of a cash or export crop. Although the system worked relatively well in the sugar-growing areas of Java, elsewhere it was sometimes abused, and proved enormously burdensome to some families. Local officials received a commission for the production that they delivered, and in order to increase their incomes and ingratiate themselves with the higher authorities some would insist that greater areas of land than were necessary be planted to cash crops. When rice was added to the list of export crops in the early 1840s, it resulted in a widespread famine in the Residency of Cheribon in Java in which hundreds died of starvation and thousands fled the area (Tate 1979, p. 44).

23

The commercialization of traditional agriculture and, by association, of traditional life, led to an increasing use of cash inputs in production: seeds and fertilizers had to be purchased, labour paid, and equipment bought or hired. This required that farmers borrow money, and in order to meet this demand for credit, as well as for agricultural inputs and marketing outlets, middlemen, moneylenders, and merchants began to establish themselves in the countryside. Many were immigrant Chinese and Indians, although there were also a few indigenous entrepreneurs. These individuals played a central role in financing and provisioning the dramatic expansion of commercial production. In Lower Burma, for example, the area under rice cultivation increased from 400 000 hectares in 1855 to 4 million hectares in 1930, while over the same period the population rose from 1.5 million to 8 million (Steinberg *et al.* 1987, pp. 230–1). This would have been impossible had it not been for the willingness of the Burmese smallholder to respond to the new economic conditions and to pioneer rice cultivation in the delta, and entrepreneurs of various nationalities to finance the process.

RUBBER AND TIN
In addition to an expansion and intensification of rice cultivation – the traditional staple crop of the region – the presence of the colonial powers also encouraged the cultivation and production of new commodities. Rubber, the most important of these, was planted over large areas of Malaya, Sumatra, and Java, transforming the landscape. In Malaya, the area under rubber increased from 137 hectares in 1897 to 1.4 million hectares in 1939, and as early as 1916 had overtaken tin as the Peninsula's most valuable export (Courtenay 1981, Barlow 1985). Although Malay and Chinese smallholders played an important part in the expansion of the rubber industry, accounting for 24 per cent of the area under rubber in 1910 and 39 per cent by 1939, it was the establishment of plantations owned and operated by Europeans that spearheaded and dominated the process. Plantations were capital- and labour-intensive. Capital was provided by investors in the United Kingdom, but labour was more difficult to secure. Most Malays were not enthusiasticc about wage labour, while the Chinese in Malaya tended to remain in the tin industry or enter into commerce and exchange activities. To meet the growing labour shortage, companies began to import large numbers of indentured Indian and Ceylonese workers. Between 1907 and 1917 some 700 000 Indian labourers entered Malaya (Steinberg *et al.* 1987, p. 228).

The tin industry was also centred on Malaya, but in this case it predated the colonial period, the metal having been mined and exported from Malacca during the 15th century (Reid 1988, p. 115). For much of the 19th century the tin industry in Malaya – and also in Indonesia (formerly the Dutch East Indies) and Thailand – was dominated by Chinese mining enterprises that utilized cheap Chinese immigrant labour. From the 1860s, however, European mining interests began gradually to introduce new technology – drilling methods, more efficient furnaces, steam pumps – that slowly undermined the cheap labour advantage that the Chinese held. The culmination of this process was the introduction of the steam chain-bucket dredge early in the 20th century. Dredges were highly efficient; they were also such massive capital investments that they lay beyond the scope of the relatively small Chinese clan-based tin mining enterprises. By the late 1930s, Malaya, Thailand and Indonesia were supplying approximately 60 per cent of world trade in tin.

COMMUNICATIONS

The economic changes described above were predicated upon an improvement in transportation. Before the 19th century, overland communications were slow, difficult, and expensive. The colonial authorities, and those of Thailand, set about providing a network of roads and railways and also substantially improving river transport. This brought previously isolated, peripheral areas into contact with the core, and allowed economic activities geared to the export market to develop and expand. However, the nature and the purpose of the colonial presence – to secure raw materials to fuel the industrial growth of the West – gave the transport networks a characteristic pattern. Roads and railways were constructed to link the areas of export commodity production with the outside world. The colonial port cities of Georgetown (Penang), Jakarta, Manila, Singapore and, in the case of Thailand, Bangkok served as entrepôts funnelling manufactures from the metropolitan nations into the colonial dependencies and raw materials and other basic commodities outwards (Figure 2.1). In Malaya for example, the road and rail network was built to service the tin mines of the west coast, and it was also there that the principal focus of plantation agriculture was located. By contrast, the east coast of the Peninsula is even today far less well served. The pattern of selective transport development in the region, meant that some areas were quickly and pervasively incorporated into the modern capitalist economy while large areas elsewhere remained relatively unaffected by the changes and developments under way at the centre.

The importance of Southeast Asia as a source of raw materials can be judged from the fact that by the late 1930s the region – including Indochina and Burma – was contributing more than 90 per cent of world trade in rubber, teak, abaca, rice, pepper, Manila hemp, cinchona (for quinine) and kapok, 75 per cent of copra and tapioca, 60 per cent of tin, and 55 per cent of palm oil. As a consequence, the possessions of the colonial powers in the region became a source of great revenue and wealth.

DUALISM AND DEPENDENCY

One effect of the pattern of colonial development was the emergence of dual economies. This refers to the existence of two economies – one the modern, western capitalist economy, and the other the pre-modern traditional economy – which existed in the same geographical space but did not interact. The notion of the dual economy has come under close and critical scrutiny, particularly in so far as it has been argued by dualists that the modern sector represented an enclave economy, but it is useful to note the differences between the two. One depended upon Western technology and capital, immigrant labour, and imported inputs, and was geared to the export market; the other used indigenous labour and technology, was organized traditionally, and produced for domestic consumption.

A second effect of the process of colonial development was the dependency that it engendered. Whereas traditionally demand could be met almost entirely from domestic production, colonial economic development brought with it greater dependency upon imported capital, skills, and technology. Even more important, the closer integration of the inhabitants of Southeast Asia into the market economy rendered them increasingly vulnerable to fluctuations in international trade, be it for rice, tin, rubber or any of the other export commodities. The degree and implications of dependency were placed in stark perspective during the 1930s when the economic recession in the industrialized nations led to a sharp global decline in the demand for, and therefore the price of, many of Southeast Asia's exports. The rubber price, for example, had fallen to a quarter of its 1929 value by 1932 (Pluvier 1974, p. 28). Restrictions were placed on the production of rubber, tin and sugar in an attempt to maintain prices, but these could do little to protect either the large Western-owned enterprises or the small producer and indigenous smallholder. Many who had borrowed money on the expectation that returns would remain buoyant were ruined, and farmers were forced to return to subsistence cultivation, using traditional technology.

The social and political impact

SOCIAL CHANGE AND DISINTEGRATION

Although economic change was the most visible impact of the colonial period, it also had far-reaching social implications, an issue that was hinted at in the previous section. Peasants became landless, the incidence of tenancy and landlordism rose, and inequalities in rural areas widened. The process of impoverishment and proletarianization was most marked in areas where population densities were highest and where commercialization had proceeded furthest: the Chao Phraya delta of Thailand, Java, Malaya, and Luzon in the Philippines. Families that previously might have been able to assure their subsistence either by farming communal lands or by clearing forest at the frontiers in farmland expansion were forced to provide wage labour for the farms of larger landowners or on commercial plantations. Peasant discontent rose accordingly and was expressed in a series of riots and disturbances in Java, Malaya, Sarawak, and the Philippines.

Not only were individual peasants marginalized in this way, in some cases whole societies came under pressure and occasionally disintegrated. However, it is important not to see the inhabitants of the region merely as victims. They also contributed to the economic changes outlined above. Malay smallholders took up rubber cultivation with alacrity and against the wishes of the colonial authorities, while peasants in Thailand took advantage of the more open, liberal trading regime and actively cleared lands in the Chao Phraya delta to plant rice for sale. In addition to these changes in traditional society, the colonial period also saw the incorporation of some entirely new cultural elements. In particular, plural societies emerged and urban centres grew.

26

PLURAL SOCIETIES AND URBANIZATION

Although Southeast Asians became involved in new economic activities, not everywhere were they willing to respond on a sufficiently large scale to meet the demand for labour in mines, plantations, and cities. To meet the shortfall, the colonial authorities allowed (and sometimes actively encouraged) the immigration of large numbers of Chinese and, to a lesser extent, Indian labourers. This influx reached its height in the late 19th and early 20th centuries. In the ten years between 1890 and 1899, for example, almost 165 000 Chinese labourers were arriving each year in the Straits Settlements of Singapore and Penang alone (Yip Yat Hoong 1969, p. 68). Some arrived with a degree of wealth and established themselves as merchants, middlemen, and moneylenders – occupations the Chinese had traditionally filled for many years. Most, however, landed with nothing, and took up jobs as coolies, road and railway construction workers, tin miners, rubber tappers, and in the multitude of new activities that colonial economic development had spawned. In this way, the countries of Southeast Asia became plural societies, comprising a number of distinct ethnic groups – Chinese, Indians and, of course, Europeans – who interacted with one another but did not combine (see Chapter 6). Furthermore, even though it is unlikely that the Chinese and Indians were ever more than 6 per cent to 8 per cent of the population, their significance far outweighed their numbers. The immigrants were concentrated in urban areas and zones of commercial agriculture and mining, and they were predominantly employed in the key modern sectors of the economy. In 1901 in the Federated Malay States of Perak, Selangor, Negeri Sembilan and Pahang, the Chinese population actually outnumbered indigenous Malays, the figures being 299 739 and 285 278 respectively (Heng Pek Koon 1988, p. 11). The Chinese and Indians were, quite simply, indispensable to the economic development of Southeast Asia, filling the roles of commercial intermediaries and providing a source of cheap labour.

It was in the towns and cities of Southeast Asia that the immigrant communities were concentrated. Although urban centres fulfilling ceremonial and trading functions existed in the pre-colonial period, the presence of the Western powers substantially increased their rate of growth and their relative significance. Moreover, the new cities had a different *raison d'être* from their indigenous precursors: they were founded on money, on new economic activities, and on new immigrant classes, and were dominated – with the exception of Bangkok – by external powers. Examples include the port cities of Manila and Batavia (Jakarta), and the tin and plantation towns of Phuket, Ipoh and Kuala Lumpur (Figure 2.1). They created new conditions and with it a new culture. This was based on imported ideas and fashions, and was financed through external trade. Possibly nowhere else would a Southeast Asian from a rural area have felt so removed from his or her native culture and land. That said, it was still true that Southeast Asia remained a region of villages and hamlets, not of cities and towns. Only perhaps 10 per cent of the total population lived in urban areas and they were in many respects uncharacteristic of the whole.

EDUCATION, HEALTH AND POPULATION GROWTH
Changes in the provision of education and health facilities also occurred during the colonial period. Education for rural inhabitants of the region was in the main not felt to be necessary, and it was rudimentary, occasionally building upon traditional vernacular education structures (e.g. temple schools). Some financial assistance was provided but it was minimal. The only exception to this was the Philippines, where far more emphasis was placed upon providing an adequate education to the population. By 1938 there were over 2 million pupils there, with 7000 in local universities (Steinberg *et al*. 1987, pp. 264–5). However, modern Western-style education was made available to an élite group in all the territories. Such an educated class was necessary to help in the running of the colonies and its members went to schools in the newly created and fast growing urban centres, or were occasionally sent abroad to study. There, in the metropolitan nations, many of the men who were to lead the nationalist movements in the region received their first introduction to revolutionary politics and first appreciated the fallibility of the colonial powers. Their education also led to the emergence of an indigenous intelligentsia that was to guide and to govern the countries when they gained their independence after the end of the Second World War.

Perhaps slightly more impressive were advances made in health provision and medical techniques during the colonial era, and particularly during the inter-war years. It appears that the 'health' of the region has progressed cyclically. Prior to the intensification of European control, it seems that Southeast Asia was a relative healthy region. Reid reports that longevity there was apparently substantially greater than in Europe at the same time, and that the inhabitants were in relatively good health, benefiting from a good diet, adequate levels of hygiene, and a reasonable level of medical care (Reid 1988, pp. 45–61). By the 19th century, however, conditions had deteriorated considerably and Tate (1979, p. 13) believes that at that time Southeast Asia was one of the unhealthiest areas of the world, a situation that persisted into the 20th century. This change in fortunes seems to have been associated with population growth and concentration, and the greater contact between groups. It was not until the inter-war years that the colonial authorities introduced general, systematic policies to improve public health and reduce epidemics, and began looking for medical solutions to local health problems.

This, however, raises something of a paradox, for during the 19th century annual population growth in the region increased considerably, from perhaps 0.2 per cent to well over 1 per cent in many areas (Reid 1988, p. 14, Owen 1987) (see Table 1.1). If it was not due to improvements in health, how can this increase be accounted for? The underlying reasons remain unclear, although a number of possible explanations have been raised, each of which relates in some way to the colonial presence. To begin with, there may have been a change in patterns of fertility. It seems, for example, that the spread of Christianity in the Philippines increased birth rates substantially. In addition, the expansion of settled agricuulture may have provided couples with the opportunity and the security to raise large families. Second, there

28

was the influence of the *pax imperica* which eliminated local, low-intensity conflicts. This not only meant fewer deaths in battle; more importantly it also meant less disruption to agriculture. This led to improvements in nutrition, thus providing long-term stability for child raising. Third, the expansion of cities and the introduction of new economic activities may have led to couples marrying earlier and having greater numbers of children. But in spite of this wealth of explanation – cultural adaptations, improvements in nutrition, changes related to health and hygiene, the influence of the *pax imperica* – it still remains unclear why there was such a dramatic increase in population growth rates during the 19th century.

BUREAUCRACY AND ADMINISTRATION

The colonial powers also brought about changes in the way in which the region was governed. There arose a bureaucratic élite that administered each colony. Initially this elite was largely foreign (except of course in Thailand), but by the 20th century it had been augmented by large numbers of Western-trained Southeast Asians who acted as intermediaries between the colonial authorities and the local populations. Thus not only did the colonial powers build an administrative framework that was to carry through to the modern era, but also trained a cadre of men (and a handful of women) who were to become the new élite – an élite, incidentally, that was somewhat divorced from its Southeast Asian roots.

The strengthening of administrative control over the population enabled more efficient taxation systems to be put in place. In general, these were iniquitous, taxing the indigenous population to a degree that was out of proportion to their wealth and income. The Culture System introduced in Indonesia represents just one of a number of examples. By contrast, immigrant (both Chinese and European) communities and the industries that they controlled were relatively lightly taxed, although it should be borne in mind that this was one of the reasons why the region was so attractive to foreign investors. Allied to more efficient taxation, the colonial and Thai administrations introduced standardized currency systems, a development that was a concomitant of the commercialization, and by implication monetization, of life in the region. Western legal methods and systems were also introduced. All these developments served to rationalize the economic networks that were evolving, thus enabling the economic integration of Southeast Asia into the metropolitan and world economies.

The rise of nationalism, the Japanese occupation of Southeast Asia, and independence

The rise of nationalism

The presence of the colonial powers in Southeast Asia, rather ironically, did much to further the nationalist cause in the region. To begin with, the processes of social and economic change outlined in the previous sections brought the population into contact with the wider world while simultaneously upsetting traditional modes of life. Peasants were incorporated into the market economy, and partly as a result large numbers lost their land and were forced to become tenant farmers or cash wage earners. The uneven pattern of economic development, and the subordinate position of the local populations, engendered a great deal of bitterness. In addition, the paternalistic attitude of many colonial administrators and their occasionally harsh treatment of the local inhabitants created a reservoir of resentment that nationalist leaders were only too happy to exploit in order to achieve their aims.

For an élite group of Southeast Asians, the presence of the colonial powers gave an opportunity to study abroad. Here they were introduced to notions of nationhood, independence, and freedom, and read works by Marx, Lenin, Locke, Rousseau, and other European and American writers. It was these individuals, men such as Sukarno of Indonesia, who formed the vanguard, and provided the inspiration and the impetus to the nationalist movements. Although much of the intellectual vigour that underlay the rise of nationalism in the region was European in origin, developments elsewhere in Asia also encouraged its growth. The anti-Western Boxer rebellion in China in 1899, the Chinese revolution of 1911, the rise of Japanese military and industrial power following the Meiji Restoration in 1869, and the Japanese defeat of Tsarist Russia in 1905 all demonstrated that the West did not have a monopoly of industrial might and military prowess.

From the beginning of the 20th century many groups were formed that embraced nationalist ideals. In Indonesia, for example, the Budi Utomo (Noble or Glorious Endeavour) was established in 1908, Sarikat Islam (Islamic Union) in 1911, the Social Democratic Union of the Indies in 1914, the Communist Party in 1919, and the Indonesian Nationalist Party (which Sukarno helped to organize) in 1927. These formed the foundations on which postwar nationalist movements could build. Even Thailand experienced a bloodless revolution mounted by sections of the educated élite and the army in 1932 that led to the introduction of a constitutional monarchy.

The Japanese invasion and occupation

Following the defeat of France by Germany in 1940, Germany's ally Japan secured access to all ports and airfields in French Indochina, and took control of the colonies' exports. Ultimate power rested with Tokyo, but the French colonial administration was allowed to remain in place. The true role of Japan's informal rule was illustrated by its intervention to ensure that Thailand regained control of the Cambodian provinces of Battambang and Siem Reap, and Laos west of the Mekong river.

In December 1941, the invasion proper began. In a remarkably short time, and with fewer men under arms than its opponents, the Japanese overran virtually the entire Southeast Asian region, save for small areas on the island of New Guinea. On 11 January Kuala Lumpur fell, on 15 February Singapore surrendered, and on 8 March the Dutch capitulated in Indonesia.

Resistance in the Philippines was slightly stiffer; the US and Filipino forces there did not surrender until 8 May 1942. Nevertheless, less than six months after the initial landings in northern Malaya on 8 December the Japanese had managed to establish control over the region.

The Japanese endeavoured to gain the support of the local populations. With slogans such as 'Asia for the Asiatics' and talk of organizing a Greater East Asia Co-prosperity Sphere they tried to stress the common purpose they shared with the inhabitants of Southeast Asia. In addition, the Japanese gave support and encouragement to nascent nationalist movements and transferred some power to local leaders. In Malaya the Chinese were brutally treated, but the Malay sultans were shown considerable respect and were given prominent positions in the new administration. In Indonesia, the nationalist leaders imprisoned by the Dutch (among them Sukarno) were released and allowed the freedom to pursue their aims. 'Independence' inauguration ceremonies were given wide coverage, and new national anthems were written and flags designed. However, although the initial victory of the Japanese was greeted with some enthusiasm, in general the euphoria did not last. The new occupying force proved to be little different from the ones it had replaced, and in many cases was considerably worse. In the Philippines, in spite of the fact that the élite co-operated with the Japanese, the mass of the population was often viciously treated and an effective resistance movement developed with considerable local support. Likewise, the Chinese in Malaya established a resistance movement to fight the Japanese.

The Japanese interregnum between 1941 and 1945 was important in paving the way for subsequent independence. First, the spectacular defeat of the colonial forces was demeaning for the European powers and the USA, ending the illusion of colonial invincibility. It was also achieved by fellow Asians. Second, the positions of responsibility given to local leaders meant that some experience in administration was acquired. This demonstrated to the inhabitants of the region that they had the human resources to organize their own affairs. Third, the nationalist movements became far stronger numerically, ideologically and militarily. The colonial powers returned to find that they were not negotiating with loose and ill-defined groups of radicals, but with nationalist movements that had enjoyed some power and had widespread support. Only in the Philippines and Malaya did the return of the former colonial powers elicit some enthusiasm. In the Philippines, the USA had already in 1934 laid down a ten-year timetable towards independence that was interrupted by the war, while Malaya had probably the least developed nationalist movement in the region, and that which did exist was largely Chinese-based.

Independence and the legacy of the colonial period

The Second World War undoubtedly served to quicken the introduction of self-government in Southeast Asia. The Philippines gained independence in 1946, Indonesia in 1949, Malaya along with British North Borneo and Sarawak (as part of the Federation of Malaya) in 1957, and Singapore in 1963. Brunei did not achieve full self-governing status until 1984.

The main elements of the legacy of the colonial period should already be clear. First, there was the all-important economic legacy. An industrial and agricultural base centred on export commodity production. An uneven, although significant, economic infrastructure that focused on the extraction of primary products and their export to the West. A population that had been increasingly drawn into the market economy, and whose way of life was becoming commercialized. These economic changes also left their imprint on the physical landscape: the clearance of land for plantation crops, the irrigation and cultivation of the great rivers and plains, and the rapid growth of towns and cities. Economic changes were the most dramatic, pervasive and decisive of the transformations wrought by colonial rule.

The colonial period also left its mark on Southeast Asian culture and society. Economic changes tended to undermine traditional structures of authority and to replace them with modern, Western frameworks. At the same time Western culture and education began to impinge on the region, first in urban areas and among the indigenous élite, but later increasingly in the countryside and among the population as a whole. In addition, the migration of large numbers of Chinese and Indians introduced an entirely new cultural element. The plural societies that resulted have confronted the governments of the region with heightened ethnic tensions and the task of assimilating (or at least accommodating) immigrant communities.

Finally, the colonial period left an institutional and ideological legacy. The educated men who led the nationalist movements in Southeast Asia and later formed the governments of the newly independent nation states were Western-educated. Legislative and executive institutions were established that mirrored those of the colonial powers, and although they were sometimes abolished or had their powers undermined, the administration and functioning of the countries followed the Western mould. The values that the new indigenous élite brought with them were those of democracy, socialism and communism. Even when leaders attempted to develop national ideologies – such as Sukarno's *Pantjasila* or five basic principles[1] – these were not free from the influence of Western thought.

However it is important to stress that the changes outlined above would have occurred even if the countries of the region had maintained their independence. As the experience of Thailand makes clear, colonization was not a prerequisite for rapid economic and cultural change. The triumph of the West dictated, and continues to dictate, that all countries, whatever their legacies, adopt a similar framework. The point is that the colonies of Southeast Asia did not even have the facade of independence.

Note to Chapter 2

1   Belief in one supreme God, just and civilized humanity, the unity of Indonesia, democracy which is guided by the inner wisdom in the unanimity arising out of deliberation among representatives, and social justice for the whole of the people of Indonesia.

3
Rice cultivation, the Green Revolution and agrarian change in Southeast Asia

Introduction

Southeast Asia is one of the fastest urbanizing, industrializing and, in general, modernizing regions of the world. Industry expanded at an annual average rate (weighted according to population) of 10.7 per cent between 1965 and 1980, and 2.1 per cent between 1980 and 1987, and in 1987 the proportion of GDP generated by industry averaged 32 per cent (weighted) (see Table 9.1). The service sector generated 41 per cent of GDP. In contrast, agriculture contributed only 27 per cent of GDP. However, these figures, and the continual talk of the region's bright economic prospects, have served to obscure one very important fact: that the lives of the great majority of the population are still centred on agriculture, and will remain so for some time to come. Agriculture may not generate the returns or growth rates of industry, and particularly manufacturing, but if we think of the economy in terms of the sectoral allocation of the labour force, rather than in terms of output, then Southeast Asia is a region where agriculture predominates. For 50 per cent of the labour force are employed in the agricultural sector.

A second point to emphasize is that 'traditional' agriculture, in the pure sense of the term, scarcely exists. Remnant pockets, or outliers, do remain in the more remote areas such as Irian Jaya, on the island of Borneo, and in Mindanao, but these should be viewed as exceptional (see Chapter 4 for an account of shifting cultivation and hunter-gathering in Sarawak and the Philippines). Agriculture has for the most part adapted and changed, incorporating new technologies and becoming increasingly commercialized. In turn, the social structures that underpin agriculture have also changed. Land and labour are owned, allotted, and paid in new ways, and the village has become more closely integrated into, and dependent upon, the wider national and international economies. Visually, the landscape may appear to have changed little since before the colonial impact; but the social, economic and, indeed, biophysical, frameworks that underlie the visual impression are often fundamentally altered. This chapter will highlight some of these changes, examine the processes at work, and offer suggestions as to their origins and implications. The discussion will focus on rice cultivation for four principal reasons. First, because rice is the pre-eminent crop of the region – it is grown on nearly half of the cultivated land – and is the staple food for much of the population (Table 3.1). Secondly, because wet rice farming is one of the most complex

Table 3.1 Rice cultivation in Southeast Asia

	Riceland as percentage of total cropland 1986	Percentage of riceland planted MVs 1981–4	Area irrigated (hectares) 1987	Percentage harvested rice area irrigated 1981	Estimated chemical fertilizer application (kg/ha rice) 1961–5	1976–9	1985/6
Brunei	28.6	—	1 000	—	—	—	—
Indonesia	47.1	81.8	7 400 000	38	8	57	107
Malaysia	14.7	53.5	338 000	62	47	97	—
Philippines	43.7	85.1	1 480 000	40	8	29	—
Thailand	46.3	13.0	3 996 000	25	2	11	67

	Paddy yields (tonnes/ha)					No. of tractors per thousand hectares arable		
	1955	1965	1973	1983	1988	1978	1984	1987
Brunei	—	—	—	—	1.3	—	—	—
Indonesia	2.0	2.1	2.7	3.8	4.1	0.2	1	1.1
Malaysia	2.1	2.5	2.9	2.7	2.7	—	2	11.3
Philippines	1.2	1.3	1.6	2.5	2.7	0.2	3	4.4
Thailand	1.6	1.9	1.9	2.0	2.0	2.1	6	7.6

Sources: various.

agricultural systems in the world. Thirdly, because the rice societies of Southeast Asia represent one of the finest and best researched examples of human–land interaction. And, finally, because rice has received enormous scientific and 'developmental' attention, best exemplified in the technology of the Green Revolution.

However, although this chapter will concentrate on the way in which rice farmers and rice farming have adapted to changing conditions, the same forces for change are affecting every agricultural system in the region. Population growth, the changing pattern of needs, the 'intrusion' of the market economy and new technologies, and the growing influence of the state have all served to force, or to encourage, the modification of traditional systems. The point, of course, is that different systems respond to change in different ways. As is discussed in Chapter 4, systems of shifting cultivation, and hunting and gathering break down very quickly should they come under stress, and the tribal groups in question may undergo cultural impoverishment in the process. In contrast, wet rice agriculture – at least superficially – responds favourably to change and the rice farmers of Asia have proved to be both innovative and resilient.

This chapter will concentrate on changes in rice production in Southeast Asia, stressing the experience of Thailand. Thailand has the longest tradition of rice cultivation in the region and is also the world's biggest rice exporter. Riceland accounted for 46 per cent of total crop land in

1986 (Table 3.1), rice is grown in all the regions of the country, and the majority of the population depend upon rice production for their subsistence.

Systems of rice cultivation

Commercial rice cultivation in Southeast Asia is dominated by *Oryza sativa* L. (Asian or common rice) which consists of two major ecogeographic races, japonica and indica[1] (Dalrymple 1986). Japonica is mainly grown in temperate locations (Taiwan, Korea, Japan, and northern China), while indica is suited to tropical or subtropical areas. Not surprisingly, indica rices predominate in Southeast Asia. However, this distribution has been complicated in recent years by the breeding of crosses between indica and japonica that are designed to harness the desirable characteristics of each race. Five types of rice cultivation, whose relative importance in the region is illustrated in Figure 3.1, can be identified.

(a) *Upland, hill, or dryland rice* Hill rice was the first type of rice cultivated in the region. It was only later, after selection and genetic differentiation, that rices suited to the flooded paddy field were grown (Watabe 1978, pp. 6–10). Today, hill rice is grown mainly by shifting cultivators who clear the land, burn the residue, and cultivate the crop in dry conditions. Yields tend to be low in comparison to those achieved with wet rice systems, averaging approximately one

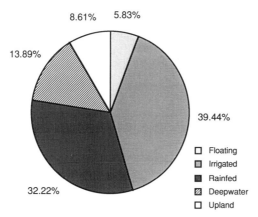

*Note: 'Asia' excludes India, China, Japan and Korea

Figure 3.1 Major rice culture systems, Asia (by area)

35

tonne per hectare, and if fertilizers are not utilized the land must be abandoned or left fallow in order to regenerate.

(b) *Irrigated wet rice* As the name suggests, wet rice is grown in flooded conditions, and is the more 'advanced' form of cultivation. Fields are bunded (surrounded by embankments) and water is added to the paddy until it is inundated to a depth of approximately 50 centimetres. Although the quality of irrigation varies considerably across the region, in general the farmer has a fair degree of control over water conditions in his fields.[2] Rice seedlings are grown for about a month in carefully prepared nursery beds before being transplanted into the puddled paddy field. Using new rice varieties, fertilizers and irrigation, yields of over six tonnes per hectare are possible, although two to three and a half tonnes is more usual.

(c) *Rainfed wet rice* An important distinction within the broad category of wet rice is that between irrigated wet rice and rainfed wet rice. In rainfed cultivation, water collects in the paddy through natural rainfall, and the farmer has less control over conditions in his fields. As a result, yields tend to be lower and more variable, with typical levels of production of two tonnes per hectare.

(d) *Deepwater rice* Deepwater rice is another variant of wet rice. It is grown in deeply flooded conditions where maximum water depth may be up to one metre. The rice seed is usually broadcast into the dry field, although it may be transplanted into a prepared paddy. Yields are low, averaging approximately one and a half tonnes per hectare.

(e) *Floating rice* This form of rice cultivation, which was extensively practised in the Chao Phraya and the Mekong Deltas, is becoming less common. The crop is broadcast before the onset of the flood, and when the flood is at its peak the depth of water may reach between three and four metres (Fukui 1978, pp. 247–8). The rice plant grows as the waters rise and highly elongated internodes result. Such is the degree of inundation that the crop is sometimes harvested from boats. Yields tend to be low (one tonne per hectare), and as the low-lying areas of Southeast Asia are developed and flooding is better controlled so floating rice cultivation is being superseded by the more common wet rice system.

The traditional rice-growing community

The importance of rice, and the degree to which culture and crop have become intermeshed, is reflected in the mythology and ceremony associated with its cultivation and in the central place it occupies in rural life. In Thailand, for example, there are numerous rituals associated with rainmaking, the preparation of the seed bed, heading, harvesting and the period prior to threshing (see deYoung 1966, pp. 141–3, Klausner n.d., Phya Anuman Rajadhon 1961). deYoung (1966, p. 141) describes the intimate relationship that existed between the rice farmer and his crop in a village he studied in Central Thailand in 1948–9:

He [the farmer] reverences the crop he grows as a sentient being; he marks its stages of growth by ceremonies; and he propitiates the spirit of the soil in which it grows and the good or evil spirits that may help or harm it. He considers rice to possess a life spirit (*kwan*) and to grow much as a human being grows; when it bears grain, it has become 'pregnant' like a mother, and the rice is the seed or child of the Rice Goddess.

Rice production was mainly oriented towards meeting the subsistence requirements of the household growing the crop. Moral economists such as Scott and Wolf maintain that communities also set social controls in order to redistribute production from the better-off to the poor, so that the entire community could survive and prosper (Scott 1976, 1985, Wolf 1967, Geertz 1963). Villages in pre-capitalist societies, in the view of the moral economists, were both 'closed' and 'corporate', and as a result were more humane, benevolent and egalitarian. This notion has not gone unchallenged. Most notably, Popkin has argued that in traditional village society it was the individual, not the group, who was of paramount importance, and it was on the family unit that people depended to guarantee their subsistence (Popkin 1979, and see Chovanes 1986).

Whatever the case, and doubtless different environments, histories and times entail and lead to different levels of co-operation, the concerns of traditional communities were focused inwards. In general, strategies of cultivation were primarily aimed at the minimization of risk, not the maximization of profit. The essential guiding principle was that each and every year a certain minimum critical level of production would be achieved. Beyond that, however, peasants might be just as experimental, adventurous, and risk-taking as a capitalist businessman (see Alexander & Alexander 1982, pp. 598–601).

In addition to being oriented towards subsistence needs, the resources for rice cultivation – and indeed for all production – were mobilized locally. This mobilization tended to be centred on the household or family, although for certain functions it extended up to the level of the village or even to a group of villages. Rice seed was selected at harvest (and also sometimes at seeding and transplanting) and huge numbers of locally 'bred' rice varieties were developed, often being distinct not only between villages but also between households within a village (see Bray 1986, pp. 19–26, Lambert 1985, pp. 55–72). The fertilization of the crop was achieved through the use of manures, mulches, composts and the burning of the crop residue. Irrigation, where it was possible, often entailed co-operation at the level of the village in order to ensure the successful functioning of the system. A fine example of such co-operation is to be found in the *muang fai* of Northern Thailand where the responsibility for the upkeep of the wood, brushwood, and stone dam (*fai*) is allocated to a *pan meng* (sometimes called a *hua naa muang fai*) or dike headman (Ishii 1978, p. 20, Lando n.d., pp. 69–80). The dike headman is elected or appointed by all the users of the system who belong to an irrigation association, and each year the *fai* and associated ditches and canals are repaired or replaced. Likewise, in Bali, all farmers owning land which is irrigated from a single water source form themselves into *subak* (irrigation societies) that often incorporate households from more than one village. A chief, or *klian subak*, is elected by the members of the *subak*, and the society is collectively responsible for the maintenance of the system (Geertz 1967, pp. 260–2, Liefrinck 1969).

The nature of rice farming also means that at certain peak periods during the cultivation cycle – particularly transplanting and harvesting – more labour is required than can be provided by any single household (Figures 3.2 and 3.3). As a result, reciprocal labour exchange has developed in almost every society where wet rice is grown: *gotong-rojong* in Java, *long khaek* in Thailand, and *berderau* in Malaysia. Labour was pooled, to be used on each field as and when it was required. As far as the 'marketing' of the crop was concerned, this was pursued on a limited basis. In the main, production was not sufficient to generate much of a surplus, and in any case the general lack of marketing facilities restricted the ability of farmers to benefit should a surplus be produced. In the main, production over and above subsistence was stored to meet future shortfalls. Admittedly, local barter was common, and farmers regularly exchanged crops and livestock with one another. In some areas, villages within a particular location would specialize in the production of certain commodities (often reflecting ecological variations, e.g. salt, lime, and pottery) and these were traded in exchange for another village's speciality. Even trade outside the vicinity of the village was not unknown. In the Northeast region of Thailand, during the dry season, villagers would often sell or barter buffalo and cattle to herders who would then drive caravans of cattle to the Central Plains for sale.

A similar pattern of production and consumption applied to the cultivation of crops other than rice, the raising of livestock, and the manufacture

Figure 3.2 Transplanting rice, Khon Kaen, Northeastern Thailand (photograph: author)

Figure 3.3   Threshing rice, Mahasarakham, Northeastern Thailand (photograph: author)

of such goods as cloth and tools. Resources for production were obtained locally, consumption was invariably centred on the household or village, and trade was limited. Those few goods that could not be manufactured locally (e.g. metal implements) were obtained from travelling traders who also brought news about the wider world. Marriages were concluded between men and women living in the same village, or in villages in close proximity to one another. Occasionally, a particular headstrong or adventurous young man might leave to travel more widely, perhaps becoming a wandering monk such as existed in Thailand (Tambiah 1970, pp. 68–76, Bunnag 1973, p. 184), but such actions were rare. It is also true that at times the state might impose itself on the community. Taxes were levied, although often intermittently, and young men were sometimes required to work for the king or sultan, or were conscripted into his army. However, the important point is that for much of the time these external institutions had only a marginal impact on the village and on village life (see Sungsidh Piriyarangsan 1983, pp. 23–8, Chattip Nartsupha 1986 on pre-capitalist Thailand). Villages in pre-colonial Southeast Asia were closed institutions that lay 'within the territorial boundaries claimed by the state . . . [but were] largely outside the institutional boundaries of the central regime' (Hirsch 1989, p. 35). In general, life was not too far removed from the subsistence 'ideal' described by Wharton (1969b, p. 13):

> Pure 'subsistence production' refers to a self-contained and self-sufficient unit where all production is consumed and none is sold and where no consumer or producer goods and services from sources external to the

unit are purchased. Pure subsistence production is characterized by the total absence of commercialization and monetization. The interesting feature of a pure subsistence unit is the close relationship between farm and home or production and consumption; they are inherently a unified process.

This admittedly simplified, and to an extent idealized portrait of the traditional rice-growing village has almost entirely disappeared in Southeast Asia. Production technologies and methods have changed, strategies of production have altered, the nature of co-operation has been distorted, the needs and desires of villagers have radically changed, available opportunities have diversified, and inequality has intensified. Before turning to examine some of the forces that have been instrumental in promoting these changes, it is worth pointing out that views of traditional life in Southeast Asia are often overly romantic (e.g. Cederroth & Gerdin 1986, p. 124). 'Subsistence affluence', and the egalitarianism[3] that is sometimes thought to have existed in the region before the commercialization of production gloss over the fact that, for many villagers, trying to maintain an existence was a struggle. Periods of plenty were few, and the margin between subsistence and starvation was narrow. This is clear in novels such as Kampoon Boontawee's *Luuk Isan* (Child of the Northeast), which describes life in the Northeast of Thailand during the 1930s and is based on the author's own childhood experiences. The concerns of villagers revolved around rain, or the lack of it, and health was poor, education limited, malnutrition the norm rather than the exception, tools and technology were primitive, and agricultural production was highly variable (Kampoon Boontawee 1988). The picture painted is not one of smiling peasants, living in harmony with nature, enjoying the bounty of a munificent land (Figure 3.4).

Agents of change

The changes that have occurred in the rural areas of Southeast Asia have been driven and moulded by three principal agents or forces: population growth, commercialization and the influence of the 'state'.

The most influential theoretical statement on the relationship between population growth and agricultural change has been the book by Ester Boserup, *The conditions of agricultural growth: the economics of agrarian change under population pressure* (1965). Boserup's central assertion is that population density explains geographical variations in farming practices, and population growth stimulates change in those farming practices. In her view, when population growth begins to outstrip the productive potential of a particular agricultural system, the society in question will be encouraged to innovate and to change rather than suffer from famine and starvation. Out of this will evolve a new or adapted agricultural system, more productive than the one that existed previously. In this way, population growth – although it may lead to some short-term hardship – will in the long term encourage the 'advancement' of agriculture. Boserup's optimistic view of mankind's

Figure 3.4 A farmer and his house, Khon Kaen, Northeastern Thailand (photograph: author)

ability to meet the demands of an increasing population is often contrasted with the Malthusian perspective, which holds that population will always press upon the limits of subsistence and that an underclass, malnourished and poor, will always exist (Malthus 1970).

In parts of Southeast Asia Boserup's theoretical predictions have apparently been fulfilled. In Java, the wet rice system has been honed and developed to the extent that agricultural population densities in excess of 1000 persons per square kilometre are supported. From a population of approximately 28.5 million in 1900 (Mantra 1985, p. 170), which was even then regarded as dangerously high by Dutch colonial officials, the population has increased to almost 110 million. Far from suffering famine, the island of Java is almost self-sufficient in rice production (the staple crop) and this has been achieved by continually improving the wet-rice system of agriculture so that yields have increased from 2.1 to 2.2 tonnes per hectare at the turn of the century to more than 4.75 tonnes today (Booth 1985, 1988, p. 123, see also Mears 1984).

Although Java provides an instance of dramatic yield increases, it should be recognized that in much of Southeast Asia the need to raise output has until recently been met through an *extensification*, not an *intensification*, of production. In most areas there was abundant virgin land that could be cleared for cultivation, and the response of farmers to population growth was to extend the land frontier. But although there still exist locations where there is considerable scope for further extensification of production (the basis of the transmigration programme examined in Chapter 5), land is a resource in increasingly short supply in most areas of Southeast Asia.

41

...refore have to be achieved through higher yields,
...creases in the area of land cultivated. Indeed, as urban
... expand, so there is the likelihood that the stock of
...hay begin to decrease in some areas. This, in turn, will
...sure on the agricultural systems in use in a particular area,
... the sorts of changes envisaged by Boserup.

...although population growth is clearly important in under-
stan... why agriculture should change, especially historically, in recent
years, it has been overshadowed by another, arguably more powerful agent
of change: commercialization. The notion that levels of production are
based upon subsistence needs has always been rather suspect. Production
over-and-above subsistence, Brookfield's 'social production', has often
meant that the true pressure of needs has been substantially above that
which would be required should we take a pure subsistence view of village
requirements (Brookfield 1972). As Adam Smith (1930, p. 354) wrote so
eloquently as long ago as 1776 in *The wealth of nations*:

> By necessities I understand not only the commodities which are indis-
> pensably necessary for the support of life, but whatever the custom
> of the country renders it indecent for creditable people, even of the
> lowest order, to be without.

Today, the subsistence perspective is even less applicable. Rural households have to meet greater cash demands from the state in the form of taxes,
and in addition a far wider array of goods and services are felt to be necessary
if a family is to lead a 'creditable' existence. As I noted with reference
to Northeastern Thailand: 'Children have to be educated and books and
uniforms paid for; medicines bought; soap, radios and cigarettes purchased;
and ultimately a motorcycle or pick-up acquired' (Rigg 1986a, p. 34, see also
Turton 1988) (Figure 3.5). In Thailand, the increase in agricultural output
has been largely driven by the need for farmers to secure (cash) incomes.
A surplus of rice is now grown for sale wherever possible, and if farmers
do not have access to suitable land, then alternative crops such as cassava
(*Manihot utilissima*), kenaf (*Hibiscus sabdariffa, H. cannabinus*, an inferior jute
substitute) and maize (*Zea mais*) are cultivated instead. These last crops are
rarely grown for domestic consumption. They are export commodities,
grown for cash (Rigg 1987).

The third agent of change is the state. The state, very broadly speaking,
has the power to create the conditions that favour change in agriculture or,
for that matter, hinder change. And further, the actions of the state are likely
to mould agriculture in particular ways. These actions may extend from
the institution of land reform programmes, to improvements in communications, to the provision of technology and credit, to the imposition of
tariffs and quotas on imported agricultural equipment, to the direction and
emphasis of national agricultural research programmes, to state perspectives
on family planning. In no country of Southeast Asia can the pattern and
nature of agriculture be portrayed as 'natural'. It is extensively moulded by
the state, and in this sense the form that agriculture takes is 'artificial'.

Figure 3.5 The commercialization of the countryside: a countryman and his taxi, Thailand (photograph: author)

Perhaps the most obvious, and pervasive, way in which the state has moulded agriculture is through the ideology that it embraces. Among the ASEAN countries, a broadly 'capitalist' or 'market' approach has been adopted. In pursuing a capitalist path, and promoting the ideology of consumerism, the state has done much to alter the farmer's view of his place in the world, and what he should seek to achieve with his life. As Turton (1988, p. 207) points out: 'Time (clock time, money time) and money have become the measure, if not of all things, then of much that they formerly had no power to control'.

The state has not only provided the ideology; it also sets barriers, constraints, hurdles, and encouragements to farmers as they strive to meet their (and the state's) objectives. A case in point is Thailand's Rice Premium. This was introduced in 1955 and is a levy imposed on the export of rice with the dual objectives of raising revenue and placating the politically powerful urban population by lowering the price of rice. It has been estimated that between 1955 and 1966 the Premium represented a tax, on farmers, of slightly more than 80 per cent (Bertrand 1980). It created a disincentive to the cultivation of rice, and promoted the diversification of agricultural production by making other crops relatively more profitable than paddy (see Holtsberg 1982, Rigg 1987).

The final point to stress is that all environments and agricultural systems do not have the same potential for change. The environment, although it does not determine the actions of people, certainly sets the limits of the possible. For it is in agriculture that people and land interact most closely and in Southeast Asia climate, topography, and soil play a considerable

43

role in influencing the form that agriculture will take (see, for example, Rigg 1985). Man is not omnipotent and able to impose his will on a pliant earth.

Changes in rice cultivation with special reference to Thailand

Technological change

Much of the enormous literature on rice cultivation in Southeast Asia has focused on the so-called Green Revolution in rice production. The term Green Revolution refers to the use of High Yielding Varieties (HYVs) or Modern Varieties (MVs) of rice, their cultivation under optimum water conditions, the application of chemical fertilizers, and the protection of the rice plant through the use of chemical pesticides and herbicides. This application of modern agricultural methods may seem fairly innocuous. However, the dissemination of the New Rice Technology (NRT) has been a greater source of dispute and dissent, not to mention misrepresentation and confusion, than any other development (see Chambers 1984, Rigg 1989b, Lipton & Longhurst 1989). For the Green Revolution has been felt by many to be the primary source and agent of change in rice agriculture in the region and, more to the point, many of these changes have been viewed as undesirable (e.g. Cederroth & Gerdin 1986, p. 124). They include the mechanization of production, the rise of wage labour in the place of community labour, and the widening of inequalities in rural communities as the rich exploit the new technology and harvest its benefits. These changes are common to all the countries of the region and will be dealt with shortly. However, as Cederroth and Gerdin (1986), Feder (1983) and others maintain that the Green Revolution has been instrumental in causing these changes to occur, it is necessary to ask whether such an overt link between the Green Revolution and the broader issue of agrarian change in Southeast Asia actually exists. This is no simple question, and for many it remains an article of faith rather than something that can be decided on the basis of the evidence. In the view of this writer, the NRT has been blamed for a far wider range of negative developments than is reasonable.

The first point to stress in any assessment of technological change in rice cultivation is that change did not begin with the Green Revolution of the mid-1960s. Farmers have always experimented with new techniques and tools, and they have been involved in developing new strains ever since the first wild-rice plant was cultivated, perhaps as long as 10 000 years ago. Using Richards' (1985) phrase, Southeast Asia has been experiencing a long-term 'indigenous agricultural revolution', and the current Green Revolution only represents a continuation of this process, albeit one worthy of special attention (Bray 1986, pp. 25–61). Improved varieties (IVs)[4] were disseminated as long ago as 1000 AD when early maturing (60 to 100 days after transplanting) Champa rices from present-day Vietnam were introduced into Fujian province, China (Dalrymple 1986, p. 15), and both pre-colonial and colonial administrations in the region have concerned themselves with improving the methods and technology of rice production.

Although rice production has being undergoing a constant process of evolution and adaptation, when the International Rice Research Institute (IRRI) at Los Baños in the Philippines 'released' the first of the MVs in 1966 (IR-8), so heralding the onset of the Green Revolution in rice, there did occur a dramatic quickening in the pace of change. It was only in the 1960s that governments in the region began to invest large quantities of money and manpower in rural and agricultural development, and this was supported with substantial funds and expertise from foreign governments, and international aid and research organizations. The release of IR-8 also coincided with an acceleration in the commercialization and commoditization of life and production, a process that was given added impetus by the Green Revolution, but which would have occurred even had the new rice varieties never been developed. As I have (Rigg, 1989b, p. 378) noted:

> The commercialization of rice production, the use of cash inputs, and the pressure to increase yields already existed as part of a wholesale and fundamental process of agrarian change. It is this that represents the 'revolution' in rural areas, and it would have occurred (albeit at a slower rate) even if the Ford Foundation and the Rockefeller Fund had never allocated funds to establish the International Rice Research Institute in the Philippines.

Table 3.1 gives details of the extent to which the new technologies, encapsulated in the Green Revolution, have spread through Southeast Asia. It is clear from the table that the majority of rice farmers now use modern varieties of rice, that chemical fertilizers are being used at increasing rates of application, and that yields are rising. In addition, the use of chemical pesticides and herbicides is becoming more widespread, and the benefits of irrigation are becoming available to greater numbers of farmers. It is also worth pointing out (although the details will be discussed later) that mechanization is spreading. Farmers use tractors, rotavators, diesel–electric rice mills, and even combine harvesters to assist in crop production and processing.

The new rice technology and equity

Although some observers regret the passing of the old ways in favour of the new rice technology, often one feels for overly romantic reasons,[5] the central issue that has concerned researchers is the extent to which the NRT has been monopolized by richer peasants. Many of the early studies argued that the Revolution, far from being 'scale-neutral', as claimed by its proponents (i.e. being adopted by all, irrespective of farm size), was only benefiting certain areas and, more pertinently, certain (richer) farmers (see Pearse 1977, 1980, Feder 1983). Poor households could not afford to purchase the new inputs, and, because the Green Revolution was felt to be an indivisible package, there existed no chance for farmers to adopt the technology gradually. It was a case of all or nothing. This tendency for the technology to be monopolized by the rich was termed the *talents-effect* by Pearse, quoting from the Parable of the Talents in St Matthew's Gospel: 'For to every person who has something, even more will be given, and he will have more than enough; but the person who has nothing, even the little that he has will be taken away from him' (St Matthew 25. 29).

To the governments of Southeast Asia, this perspective on the distributional effects of the new technology was a source of some concern. The countries of Indochina were in the process of 'turning' to communism, Burma was following its own idiosyncratic road to socialism, and communist parties and insurgencies were gaining increasing support within the ASEAN nations. Much of the appeal of the communist alternative lay in its claim that wealth would be redistributed from the rich to the poor, and that development would benefit all sections of society. If the Green Revolution really was causing inequalities to widen in rural areas, it might lend additional support to the communist cause and further alienate the people. For this reason, many academics and officials in the 1960s saw the revolution in rice production not as the cornucopia it was touted to be, but as a Pandora's Box (see Wharton 1969a).

There are many who still support this perspective. Cederroth and Gerdin (1986, p. 128), for example, state: 'it has been repeatedly observed that it is the wealthy farmers, as a group, who have been able to take full advantage of the new technology, and that consequently existing economic cleavages have rapidly widened. As a general conclusion such statements are obviously true'. In recent years, however, this rather gloomy view has to some extent been superseded by a rather more optimistic view of the distributional effects of the NRT. This holds that the technology has attractions for *all* classes of farmer (e.g. Lipton 1987, Lipton & Longhurst 1985, 1989, Hayami 1981, 1984, Barker, Herdt & Rose 1985, Herdt 1987, Schweizer 1987). Indeed, some maintain that the widening inequalities visible in rural areas are in fact due to the *insufficient progress* of the Green Revolution in offsetting the effects of population growth when land is in short supply (Hayami 1984, p. 394, Lipton 1987, p. 522). There are a number of points that help in the understanding of the pattern of adoption of the NRT in Southeast Asia and the diverging views noted above:

(a) Not all environments are suited to the new rices. Where rainfall is uncertain and irrigation is absent, the MVs often prove to be too 'generalized'. In these environments, for example in Northeastern Thailand (see Rigg 1985, Grandstaff & Grandstaff 1987) and south Sulawesi (Deuster 1981), farmers often continue to cultivate traditional or improved varieties.

(b) Related to point (a), if the environment is such that yields are highly variable, then farmers tend to be reluctant to invest their scarce financial resources in cash inputs such as chemical fertilizers and pesticides (see Rigg 1985). This is only good economics.

46

(c) The Green Revolution is a continuing revolution. Between 1966, when IR-8 was first disseminated, and 1985, IRRI conducted over 50 000 crosses and 'released' 29 IR varieties (Dalrymple 1986, p. 20). These have often overcome the shortcomings of the earlier releases (e.g. suceptibility to pest attack and improved grain stability). Thus the problems highlighted in the earlier studies are not, necessarily pertinent to the MVs of today. Further, the technology, as it develops, is becoming increasingly 'smallholder friendly' (Lipton & Longhurst 1985, p. 28).

(d) The governments of Southeast Asia have had rather different attitudes to the NRT, reflecting the availability of funds and manpower, the perceived need to promote the technology, the suitability of the environment, and each country's approach to development. This is clear when a comparison is made between Thailand and the Philippines. In the former case, land was in plentiful supply until fairly recently so that the extensification of production remained a possibility, a substantial surplus of rice is always produced, and in many areas the environment is unsuited to the cultivation of the new varieties. The importance of rice exports also caused many officials to worry that the poor eating quality of the early MVs might jeopardize the reputation of Thai rice in its export markets. In the Philippines however, rice shortages had been common since the turn of the 20th century, the assistance of IRRI (located in Los Baños in central Luzon) was close at hand, and suitable land was in short supply (Barker 1985). Largely as a result of these differences, in Thailand the Green Revolution received rather a tepid response from the government and MVs account for only 13 per cent of the planted area; while in the Philippines it has been enthusiastically embraced and MVs cover 85 per cent (Table 3.1).

(e) Villages in Southeast Asia have never been as egalitarian as is sometimes suggested. Inequalities existed long before the arrival of the colonial powers, and by the time the new rice technology was first disseminated in the mid-1960s, cleavages had deepened. The political and economic structures (or class structures) that arose gave certain households superior access to the new technology which, it should be remembered, was in short supply during the early years of dissemination (see, for example, Husken 1979). Moreover, those families living on the edge of subsistence often found that they could not risk adopting rice varieties whose potential they knew little about. Their precarious position gave them little room for manoeuvre and experimentation.

In those areas of Southeat Asia where environmental conditions favour the use of the new rice technology, it is common today to see almost all farmers, whatever their standing, planting MVs and using chemical fertilizers and pesticides. A series of surveys conducted in Luzon and Laguna in the Philippines revealed that by 1981/82 virtually all rice fields were planted to MVs, well over 90 per cent of plots had fertilizers applied to them, and most farmers protected their crops using chemical pesticides and herbicides (Herdt 1987) (Table 3.2). Since the technology was first

Table 3.2 Changes in rice production technology, Luzon and Laguna, the Philippines, 1965–82

Central Luzon	1966	1970	1974	1979	1982
Parcels growing MVs (%)	0	63	76	95	96
Area planted to MVs (%)	0	67	63	94	92
Parcels with fertilizers (%)	60	90	90	95	94
Fertilizers applied (kg/ha)	20	42	58	82	78
Parcels with insecticide (%)	31	53	84	90	92
Insecticide expenditure (p/ha)	2	9	38	90	111
Parcels with herbicides (%)	12	37	57	56	74
Herbicide expenditure (p/ha)	1	2	4	32	45
Laguna	1965	1970	1975	1978	1981
Parcels growing MVs (%)	0	0	100	98	100
Area planted to MVs (%)	0	94	97	98	99
Parcles with fertilizers (%)	81	98	97	100	98
Fertilizers applied (kg/ha)	19	52	88	111	83
Parcels with insecticide (%)	46	88	88	98	97
Insecticide expenditure (p/ha)	2	13	65	95	95
Parcels with herbicides (%)	94	96	84	88	96
Herbicide expenditure (p/ha)	3	8	27	36	56

Source: Herdt 1987, p. 334.
Note: MV = modern variety.

introduced there has occurred a process of catching–up in which smaller, poorer farmers have also enjoyed the benefits of the new rices. Indeed fertilizer use is sometimes higher among small landowners than it is among large ones (e.g. Shand 1987, Handoko 1983, Rigg 1985). This merely reflects the fact that small farmers are under greater pressure to raise their yields, as they invariably have to support each family member on a smaller area of land. Variation is often most significant at the macro–scale. In other words between regions and countries, rather than between households in individual villages.

However, it is not just the technology of rice cultivation that has changed in Southeast Asia. So too have many elements in the social and cultural framework of rice cultivation.

Land ownership and land tenure

Traditionally in Southeast Asia, the 'ownership' of land was determined through use, although ultimately it belonged to the king, the sultan, or God (see Hill 1977, p. 196, Tan 1981, p. 9–10). There was little purpose in cultivating an area larger than that required to satisfy each household's subsistence needs and, in general, land was an abundant resource. It was labour that was invariably the limiting factor of production. Reflecting this, property rights were often loose and ill–defined and 'ownership' remained an alien concept until relatively recently.

Two processes have changed this state of affairs. On the one hand, the growth of population has led to land scarcity in many areas. On the other, the commercialization of rural life has encouraged farmers to cultivate larger areas of land and, in some cases, to accumulate land. Land has become a resource, with a value, that can be bought, sold, and rented. Restrictive rules of access now apply and this is even true, and increasingly so, of village common land. The effects of these two processes can be seen in the fragmentation of landholdings, in the spread of tenancy, and in the increase in the area of land owned – although not necessarily cultivated – by large landowners (often referred to in the literature as *kulaks*).

In Thailand, the Central Plains region has the highest levels of tenancy. It is here that population densities are among the highest in the kingdom, and it is here that commercialization has been under way for longest (see Ingram 1971). In the provinces of Ayutthaya, Pathum Thani and Nakhon Nayok for example, the land rented amounts, respectively, to 56 per cent, 60 per cent and 48 per cent of total farmland (Figure 3.6). For the Central

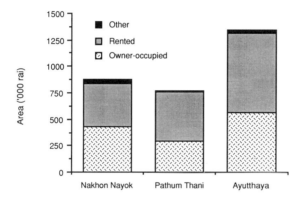

Figure 3.6 Land tenure in three provinces of Central Thailand, 1985

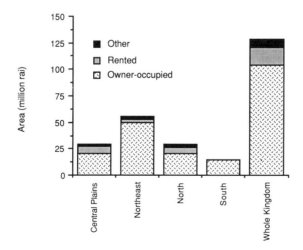

Figure 3.7 Land tenure in Thailand, by region, 1985

Plains region as a whole the figure is 25 per cent, while for Thailand it is 13 per cent (Figure 3.7). At the same time, the area of land cultivated by each farm household has begun to decline, although not nearly as dramatically as in the more densely settled areas of Southeast Asia. In Java, for example, the area of *sawah* (riceland) per capita declined from 0.070 hectares in 1940, to 0.059 hectares in 1955, to 0.038 hectares in 1980 (Booth 1985, p. 123).

One important aspect of land tenure status is the extent to which it inhibits the use of the new rice technology (this point links back to the last section). It is widely felt that insecurity of land ownership 'deprives the owners of both the means (credit) and the incentive to undertake the investments and purchase the inputs necessary for agricultural intensification' (Panayotou 1984, p. 44). 'Security' refers not only to whether the land is owned or rented, but also to the type of ownership. In Thailand, for example, there are four types of ownership certificate, of which only two – *nor sor saam* and *chanot thii din* (the full title deed) – are acceptable to institutional sources of credit as proof of ownership when farmers wish to use their land as collateral. Panayotou (1984, pp. 48–9), quoting World Bank data, states that only 50 per cent of agricultural land in Thailand may be considered to have 'secure' land ownership rights, and as a result farmers are often constrained in their attempts to intensify production. Supporting this, Feder (1987, p. 26), in his assessment of land security and productivity in three provinces in the Central Plains and Northeastern regions of Thailand, conclude that the results indicate that the provision of secure, legal ownership to untitled farmers can significantly increase their productivity. When untitled farmers do decide to borrow money to purchase agricultural inputs, they are forced to go to informal sources such as merchants and middlemen, where annual interest rates may exceed 100 per cent (Rigg 1986b, p. 77).

The increase in tenant farmers and the fragmentation of land holdings has been accompanied by a rise in the number of landless agricultural labourers. These individuals have sometimes been pushed off their land, having gone into debt and had their land repossessed, or have been unfortunate enough never to have inherited land. Whatever the case, they today constitute an army of dispossessed, and often dissatisfied rural inhabitants who represent a potential political opposition and a possible security risk. The rationale for land settlement schemes in Indonesia and Malaysia has been to provide land to the landless and land poor so as to prevent political disorder (see Chapter 5). In the 1970s, the rise in tenancy in the Central Plains was used by the Communist Party of Thailand to generate support for its policies, while in the Philippines it currently helps to fuel the insurgency there. Although overall rates of landlessness remain manageable in Thailand, the twin pressures of time and population growth will cause the problem to become increasingly serious in the years to come. The solution must be a combination of further increases in output per unit area, coupled with the creation of jobs in the urban–industrial sectors of the economy so that the 'excess' rural population can be absorbed.

The first of these solutions raises something of a dilemma, as many analysts equate the rise in tenancy and landlessness with precisely these attempts to raise output – through the Green Revolution. Would not the further promotion of the technology therefore serve simply to create an even larger army of land poor and landless agriculturalists? This remains an area of considerable dispute, but increasingly the new technology is being seen as a means to ameliorate the effects of population growth and commercialization when land is scarce (Hayami & Kikuchi 1981, pp. 39–63, 211–25). For the Green Revolution 'augments' land in two ways. First, it saves land by increasing yields; and, secondly, through irrigation and the use of quick-maturing rice varieties and mechanization, it 'creates' land by enabling the cropping ratio (the number of crops grown on each unit of land per year) to rise. Some analysts also feel that the NRT raises real wage rates and so benefits landless labourers by increasing the demand for labour (Hayami & Kikuchi 1981, p. 212, and see Herdt 1987, pp. 339–43).

With respect to changes in land ownership and tenure, it is important to see that the process is multi-dimensional. Among the influencing factors are commercialization, land resources, the Green Revolution, and the state. These factors are not discrete influences, without links to one another, and the notion that there is a simple cause and effect relationship is erroneous. Land tenure and land ownership may undergo change for a range of reasons, and the balance between the various forces will also vary between countries and through time. If one factor is to be highlighted, however, it is the availability of land.

Labour relations and mechanization

Changes in labour relations have accompanied changes in land ownership associated with commercialization of rural production in Southeast Asia. In many areas of the region, traditional forms of reciprocal labour exchange have been superseded by wage labour or adapted forms of labour exchange (see Hart 1986, Palmer 1977, Luechai Chulasai *et al.* 1986). As, in the view of the moral economists, it was just these community obligations that guaranteed the subsistence of even the poorest members of village society, their replacement by wage labour has been seen by some analysts as another example of the triumph of the individual over the community. This triumph is also felt to be to the detriment of the poor who, in the process, have lost their traditional rights and the means to secure a livelihood.

As with landownership and tenure, the issue of changing labour relations, and its causes and effects is highly complex. Perhaps the best indication of the degree of complexity (and disagreement) does not come from Thailand, but is illustrated in the work that has been conducted on rice-harvesting systems in Java (see Antlov 1986, Hart 1986, Hayami & Hafid 1979, Collier *et al.* 1973, Collier *et al.* 1974, Collier 1981, Palmer 1977, Husken 1979, Alexander & Alexander 1982).

In Java, rice harvesting was traditonally a community activity in which everybody had a right to participate. Landowners were not able to limit the number of harvesters and there have been reports of 500 villagers harvesting a single hectare (Collier *et al.* 1973, p. 37). Depending on each harvester's relationship to the landowner, the share of the crop or *bawon* (hence, the *bawon* system) that they received might vary from one-half to one-twenty-fifth of the rice they had personally harvested. Although the *bawon* system was not the only form of rice harvesting to be practised in 'traditional' Java, it has been set up as the traditional ideal.

In many areas the *bawon* system has now been replaced by the *tebasan* system, a harvesting arrangement with which it is usually unfavourably contrasted. In the *tebasan* system the rice crop is sold to a *penebas* (middleman) who then organizes the harvest himself. If the *penebas* originates from the same village as the landowner, he will select a group of harvesters from the local community. These tend to be relatives and friends. If he is from another village, as is usually the case, he will invariably bring in outsiders to harvest the crop. By selling the standing crop, the landowner is freed from his community obligations, while the *penebas*, as a 'foreigner', is unconstrained and is free to organize the harvest as he desires. The *bawon* and *tebasan* systems are often presented as in opposition to one another; the former representing the egalitarian and corporate nature of the pre-capitalist village, the latter as exemplifying all the undesirable consequences of modernization. As Hayami and Hafid have written (1979, pp. 94–6), the substitution of the *bawon* system with the *tebasan* system has virtually acquired the status of a paradigm.

It is the papers of Collier and Collier *et al.* that have argued the case against the *tebasan* system most cogently (see especially Collier *et al.* 1973). In brief, it is contended that the changes in rice harvesting have conferred gains on landowners, middlemen, and village leaders, while worsening the position of harvesters and, particularly, landless labourers. The traditions of community and mutual help and assistance have been undermined and inequalities have widened. These changes are seen to be a response to Java's worsening human : land ratio on the one hand, and the spread of technologically (i.e. Green Revolution) induced commercialization on the other. However, although the arguments are convincing, as with the previous section on landownership, there exist a complex of influences, and teasing out those that are important and those that are subsidiary (or merely associated) is far from straightforward.

To begin with, the *tebasan* system of harvesting was in widespread use in Java in the late 1960s, sometime before the introduction of the first MVs, and there appears to be no clear-cut association between technological change and the spread of exclusionary labour practices (Hayami & Hafid 1979, p. 102, Hart 1986, p. 187, Antlov 1986, pp. 156–7). Indeed in some areas where riceland is exclusively planted to MVs, and where the *tebasan* system is widely employed, community obligations still exert a significant influence (Schweizer 1987, p. 58–61). Second, the *bawon* system might not be quite as selfless, nor as redistributive in its effects, as is sometimes argued. Alexander and Alexander point out that from the landowner's point of view, costs are muuch the same with 500 harvesters as they are with 50. Further, landless households, who receive a far smaller share of the harvest, have to work considerable longer in the fields than do those with whom the landowners have reciprocal rights. 'Javanese explain the high *bawon* paid to neighbours and kinsmen in terms of moral obligations and generosity, but it is generosity without cost, for members of the landowner's family also receive high *bawon* when they assist in the harvest on their friends' and neighbours' lands' (Alexander & Alexander 1982, p. 610). Thirdly, there exist considerable variations in the form that the *tebasan* system, and other labour arrangements, take. Schweizer, for example, found that in spite of the fact that MVs were cultivated and the *tebasan* system was in widespread use, there was still a tendency for the rice crop in his research area to be harvested with the finger knife, or *ani ani*, an implement that is widely reported to have been supplanted by the sickle as a result of the adoption of the new rice varieties. In addition, gleaning by one or two children or old women (often related to the harvesters) was also still permitted (Schweizer 1987, 1989).

Although changes in rice harvesting in Java have possibly received the most attention from scholars, the same processes, and the same academic disputes, arise in the other countries of Southeast Asia. Community arrangements, be they for harvesting or transplanting, are being replaced by more exclusive systems in which workers are paid in cash rather than kind. Poor landowners and landless labourers are felt by many to be becoming increasingly marginalized. And the forces driving this process are widely perceived to be linked to the scarcity of land resources and commercialization encouraged by the dissemination of the new rice technology.

Mechanization

Even more dramatic than changes in labour practices has been the spread of mechanization. Once again the central debate has revolved around the issues of whether the Green Revolution 'package' includes mechanization, whether the package is divisible, and whether mechanization selectively benefits only larger landowners. The mechanization of rice production has certainly been concomitant with the spread of the other elements of the new technology and, in general, inequalities have also widened. For those who believe that the Green Revolution package is indivisible, the implications of mechanization are clear. Land poor and landless farmers who depend on farmwork for their livelihoods will be forced into subordinate and increasingly unfavourable positions relative to other landowners. Husken (1979, p. 146), discussing the impact of the mechanization of rice hulling and the spread of other labour-saving devices, techniques, and 'rationalizations' in Gondosari, Central Java, writes:

> The landless are now almost completely at the mercy of the land-
> owners, and can do little more than complain about their fate (*wong
> cilik dipateni kabeh*: the little men are all beaten to death); or about the
> way the odds are stacked against them (*kebo gede menang berik*: the big
> water buffaloes can win because they use their horns).

Although it is tempting to see the relationship between the mechanical and biochemical elements of the NRT as clear cut, with the two spreading across the region in association, there are numerous reasons to assume that the package is far from being indivisible. In addition, it is not always the case that mechanization decreases demand for labour; and nor is it true that mechanization is attractive and available only to larger farmers.

Regarding the first point, it seems to be the case that most important in determining the degree of mechanization is the extent to which machinery is subsidized and the price of capital reduced. Governments in Southeast Asia have provided numerous incentives to the mechanization of production, introducing such mechanisms as overvalued exchange rates (which make imports relatively cheap), concessionary credit facilities, special tariffs and taxes, and subsidized energy prices (Hayami 1981, pp. 174–5, Binswanger 1984, p. 15). As a result, in some areas where MVs are widely cultivated, mechanization may have made few inroads, while in others, where traditional forms of rice cultivation are still preferred, mechanization may be widespread. As Barker *et al.* (1985, pp. 118–19) conclude in a general discussion on the mechanization of rice production: 'Adoption of machinery has been independent of the adoption of modern rice varieties'.

The second point concerns the impact of mechanization on labour demand. Although it is usually the case that mechanization of production decreases labour demand, there are some instances in which it has improved 'timeliness' – by easing production bottlenecks – and so actually resulted in an increase in the need for workers. Ramsay's (1985) study of mechanization, population pressure, and landlessness in the Central Plains of Thailand concludes that the increased use of mechanical pumps, tractors, and improvements in irrigation enabled the spread of double cropping to occur. This in turn, substantially increased the demand for labour. Reflecting this, the real wage rates of agricultural workers were rising throughout the 1970s, an indication that shortages of workers were becoming more severe just at the time when mechanization was spreading.

The third point addresses the question of whether the mechanical element of the NRT, like the biochemical element, is also 'scale neutral'. In this instance it would seem fairly clear that tractors and other forms of mechanization would only be available to richer, larger landowners. However, in Thailand, the demand from large and small landowners alike for the mechanization of some aspects of cultivation, particularly land preparation, has led to the proliferation of entrepreneurs who own tractors and hire out their services to farmers. The going-rate for ploughing a *rai* of land in the Northeastern region in 1988 was 100 baht (= £14.30 per hectare – author's own research). Further, Binswanger (1984, pp. 13–14) reports that this service is also widely available in many other countries of Asia, while at the same time machinery is increasingly being developed for smaller farms.

Finally on this issue of mechanization, it is important to appreciate that agriculture is not isolated from developments occurring in other sectors of the economy. In Malaysia, for example, serious agricultural labour shortages have arisen because of the migration of the rural population to urban areas in search of better paid work in the industrial and service sectors. Rural wages have therefore been pushed upwards and there exist considerable incentives for farmers to mechanize production. Even so, in

1987 it was estimated that two million acres of agricultural land (810 000 hectares) in the smallholder sector were left idle because of labour shortages (Courtenay 1987).

Summary

It is indisputable that the lives of rice farmers in Southeast Asia have changed TRADITIONAL significantly. Traditional rice varieties, manures, and animal traction have been replaced across the region by modern (high-yielding) rices, chemical fertilizers, pesticides, and the increasing use of machinery. Further, traditional labour arrangements and forms of landownership and transfer have been supplanted by wage labour, tenancy, and new, exclusionary systems. Farmers are no longer isolated from the wider national, and international, economies and the forces that mould and drive their lives are fundamentally different from those that existed in rural areas even as recently as 20 years ago. If these changes were to be summed up in a single word, it would be commercialization or, perhaps, commoditization. Land and labour have become commodities that are bought and sold; inputs for rice production must be purchased from the market, with cash; money must be borrowed to finance cultivation; and a surplus, over and above subsistence must be produced, and then marketed. As Turton (1988, p. 209) notes, even the 'supernatural itself has become commoditized'. At the same time as farmers have found themselves inexorably drawn, although rarely reluctantly, into the market economy, so there has occurred a widening in the disparities between rich and poor. Some landowners have found that they have been able to accumulate land, while others have either become landless labourers or have been pushed into increasingly unattractive tenancy arrangements. Conditions have worsened to the extent (relatively if not absolutely) that many rural inhabitants have been encouraged to abandon farming altogether and migrate to urban areas. This migration has led to the burgeoning of Southeast Asia's capital cities which, in turn, has raised a new set of problems and challenges (see Chapter 7). The fact that widespread and pervasive change has occurred is not disputed. What is disputed are the causes and effects of these changes. Central to the debate has always been the Green Revolution and the role that the new technology has played in the process.

During the 1970s, the Green Revolution gained an unenviable reputation: the technology was seen by many scholars to be causing the widening of inequalities in rural areas and although, in some çases, high yields were being obtained, overall it was felt to be doing more harm than good. Cross (1987, p. 45) has equated the technology with tower block architecture, writing: 'Both were technical fixes of the 1960s, discredited 20 years on'. However, not only is the view that the Green Revolution only holds attractions for the richer and larger farmers increasingly debatable, but the link between the new technology and the negative changes that have occurred in the region seems not to be as transparent as many have argued. It now seems that the technology holds attraction for all classes

55

of farmer. There are, moreover, those who believe that the widening inequalities visible in rural areas, the growing incidence of landlessness, and the quickening of migration flows as agriculturalists escape to the cities is not because of the Green Revolution, but in spite of it: 'Contrary to popular belief', argues Hayami (1984, p. 394), 'we see a real danger of growing inequalities in rural communities not because of the MV technology but because of insufficient progress in the technology under the strong population pressure on land'. This is not to say, of course, that all is well. There are still hurdles to be overcome, perhaps the most challenging of which is to develop MVs and associated technology for the marginal, rainfed areas of Southeast Asia. A growing concern is also the ecological and environmental implications of high input–high output farming methods that use large applications of chemicals (Glaeser 1987). The new technology must be sustainable, and this demands that high yields are attained today, tomorrow, and indefinitely.

Notes to Chapter 3

1   There is a third, less important race – javanica.
2   The extensive flood and gravity irrigation that predominates in the Central Plains region of Thailand, for example, is less precise than the storage systems available to farmers in many areas of Java.
3   Best exemplified in Geertz's notion of the 'shared poverty' (we are poor, but at least we are *all* poor) that he felt existed in pre-colonial Java (Geertz 1963). This view has since been widely challenged on historical grounds (e.g. in Nørlund, Cederroth & Gerdin 1986, pp. 119–21, Hart 1986, Alexander & Alexander 1982).
4   Rice varieties are often referred to as TVs (traditional varieties), IVs (improved varieties) or MVs (modern varieties). The rices associated with the Green Revolution are MVs.
5   For example, Cederroth and Gerdin (1986, p. 124) write in their study of change in Lombok (Indonesia): 'In the villages, the familiar and homely sound of rice threshing had been silenced and in the distance the loud, shrieking voice of the diesel-powered electric rice mill could be heard'.

4

Development and environment: the impact of development on the forest dwellers of Sarawak, East Malaysia, and the Philippines

Environment and development: opposing objectives?

'Development' is a much used and much abused word. So for that matter, and increasingly so, is the word 'environment'. Both are highly evocative and emotive but at the same time are difficult to define adequately. To some, development is an increase in national output, narrowly interpreted; for many others, it should also incorporate general welfare concerns (e.g. education and health), human rights, and equality. The environment, meanwhile, is usually thought to encompass the 'natural' environment – soils, forests, climate, water, and wildlife – although there are those who would also wish to include the indigenous human inhabitants of that natural environment. Not only is the definition of the two terms somewhat fraught, but their relationship to one another has elicited much, and growing attention.

Development and environment are often viewed as antithetical. Specifically, it is argued that the promotion of development will adversely affect the environment and *vice versa*. In short, there is a trade-off between the two. As Goldsmith (1985a, pp. 211–12) puts it: 'The real cause of all environmental destruction becomes clear if one considers what sort of policies Third World countries must adopt in order to develop and how such policies must affect their environment'.

However, the above perspective on the relationship between development and environment is dependent upon the definitions that are employed. And even when definitions are broadly comparable there may be sharp differences in opinion. In an exchange of articles with Goldsmith (quoted above), Botafogo (1985, p. 207) of the World Bank states: 'Perhaps the most unfounded allegation is that development *per se* is antithetical to the aspirations and interests of poor nations [and] is automatically destructive of the environment'. This difference of opinion is not merely semantic – although semantics certainly have a role of play. The following points need to be borne in mind:

(a)   Environmental degradation is conjunctural (see Blaikie & Brookfield 1987, p. 239, Blaikie 1985). There is invariably a combination of

57

circumstances that contribute to degradation in any one instance; and these will differ between cases. As Blaikie and Brookfield (1987, p. 239) explain: 'The bewildering complexity produced by inter-relating environmental variability in resilience and sensitivity with social and economic variations in agricultural production. . .must point to conditional and multiple hypotheses, not universal nor single ones'.

(b) Tropical environments are markedly different from temperate environments, particularly in terms of the speed that processes occur. If development models and methods are transplanted from temperate to tropical zones, with no account being taken for the differences that exist, it is probable that they will either fail or perform below expectations (Bunting 1988, p. 10). In particular, they are unlikely to be sustainable and will promote a deterioration in the environment.

(c) Even within the tropics, different localities and systems will embody different characteristics, and will vary in terms of their susceptibility to environmental deterioration. While the wet rice field, for example, is remarkably resilient and stable, the swidden (shifting cultivation field) breaks down rapidly if a particular ecological threshold is exceeded (Geertz 1963). The same is true of natural ecosystems.

(d) Market forces can be used to promote the conservation of the environment. Although 'worshipping at the altar of economic pragmatism' – putting resources to their best economic use – is commonly perceived to be opposed to the demands of conservation (e.g. Goldsmith 1985b, pp. 146–8), recent work indicates that the environment will be best protected when the interests of conservation and economic development coincide (Pearce *et al.* 1989). That said, developing countries often suffer from a dearth of accurate information on the status of their forests (and other facets of the environment), making planning and policy formulation, let alone implementation, difficult (see Barbier 1989 on Indonesia).

(e) Finally, development (like environment) is not monolithic in character. Obvious as it may seem, there is 'good' development and 'bad' development. Where policies and programmes have promoted environmental deterioration, they are invariably of the latter kind.

It is gradually being recognized that the protection and preservation of the environment is not only far from being in opposition to development, but that it is indeed part of development and intrinsic to the process: they are interdependent. The fact that the World Bank has recently established an environmental department employing a number of ecologists and other environmentalists to vet all its development projects is indicative of this change in view, and the environmental input into project identification, design, implementation, and management is now significant (see Warford & Partow 1989). 'Sustainable development' is a term that not only crops up in a great deal of United Nations literature but is also in widespread everyday use, and many of the issues that it embraces concern the promotion of sound management of the environment (see, for example, Tolba 1987). Judging by the quantity of literature extolling the virtues of sustainable development –

perhaps matched in size only by the number of definitions of the term that have been coined – it is likely that the principle will become increasingly important in determining the pattern of development in both the developed and developing worlds.[1] However, this is no reason to be complacent. It is still the case that many of those in authority in Southeast Asia regard the demands of conservation as a luxury that they can ill-afford. At the same time, environmentalists question whether the World Bank and other multilateral agencies are committed fully to the need to preserve and protect the environment.

This chapter will examine the impact of development on the indigenous shifting cultivators and hunter-gatherers of Sarawak, East Malaysia, and the Philippines. Necessarily, therefore, the discussion will be fairly narrowly focused. However, the points that are raised do have general applicability across the region, and much of the debate can be reduced to a handful of central questions that repeatedly crop up. These are:

- Equity; who benefits from development?
- How do we assign a value to the natural environment and quantify the unquantifiable?
- What is the balance between short-term benefits and long-term costs?
- Is the system sustainable?
- What are the externalities of individual projects, and how can they be accounted for and controlled?
- What do we mean by development and by progress, and does it vary between countries, and between groups within countries?
- How can the pressures for development be met while minimizing the costs of such development for the environment?
- Are there any viable environment-friendly alternatives?

Forests: a dwindling resource

Although there is considerable debate about rates of deforestation in Southeast Asia and the amount of land that remains forested,[2] it is not disputed that encroachment by commercial loggers and agriculturalists is severe, and that in some instances it is accelerating. The World Resources Institute, for example, has released figures – themselves rather dubious – showing that between 1981 and 1985, 1.2 million hectares of land was being deforested each year in the ASEAN countries (Table 4.1). It is also not disputed that the core areas of tropical lowland evergreen rainforest – located for example on the islands of Borneo and New Guinea, and in Peninsular Malaysia – are among the richest ecosystems in the world. Research has shown that in a single hectare of Malayan rainforest there may exist 176 species of tree with a diameter of ten centimetres or more (Whitmore 1989, p. 199). The world's tropical forests, of which those found in Southeast Asia are possibly the most diverse, are thought to support half the known species of plants and 80 per cent of insects (Jeffries 1989, p. 38). Malesia (the archipelago plus the Malay penninsula) alone contains 25 000 species of

Table 4.1 Forest resources of Southeast Asia

Country	Closed forest area (1980) hectares (WRI)	Closed forest area (1985) hectares (WRI)	Forest and woodland (1985) (ESCAP)	Annual rate deforestation 1981–5 (%) (WRI)	Area deforested annually (1981–5) hectares (WRI)
Brunei	325 000	290 000	275 000	2.2%	7 000
Indonesia	113 895 000	110 895 000	121 494 000	0.5%	600 000
Malaysia	20 996 000	19 721 000	20 061 000	1.2%	255 000
Philippines	9 510 000	9 055 000	11 350 000	1.0%	91 000
Singapore	—	—	—	—	—
Thailand	9 235 000	8 015 000	15 000 000	2.6%	244 000

Note: WRI = World Resources Institute; ESCAP = Economic and Social Commission for Asia and the Pacific.

flowering plants, 10 per cent of the world's flora (Whitmore 1984, p. 5). Not only is their destruction opposed on moral grounds (the 'guardians of the earth' argument), but the genetic and chemical resources that they contain, most of which remain undocumented, are also felt to be economically invaluable. In the 17th century, Peruvian Indians told Jesuit priests that the bark of the cincona tree contained a drug (quinine) that would protect against malaria. Cocaine, which is derived from the leaf of the coca plant, is the basis of all local anaesthetics, while a derivative of the Madagascan periwinkle is the only treatment available for childhood leukaemia. More than 10 per cent of prescription drugs are derived from tropical forest products. Complementing these reasons for preserving Southeast Asia's tropical forests is the growing acceptance that they are a non-renewable resource. Even when selectively logged, on a carefully managed basis, the removal of economically valuable trees is likely to lead to a decline in species diversity; and if forests are clear-felled, the norm throughout the region (Scott 1989, p. 35), the poverty of the soils invariably means that secondary growth is highly degraded. Attempts at reafforestation have in general been both intermittent and unsuccessful, and in some cases the removal of forest cover has led to the formation of large areas of *Imperata cylindrica* grasslands.

Although it is the protection and preservation of tropical rainforests from exploitation by humans that has dominated recent debate – a debate given additional prominence because of growing fears that their destruction may be contributing to the 'greenhouse effect' – this is not to imply that the 'natural' tropical forest ecosystem excludes people. The true indigenous inhabitants of Southeast Asia, tribal Negrito (in Spanish, 'small, black') people such as the Semang of Peninsular Malaysia, the Ilongot of Luzon, and the Batak of Palawan, have evolved subsistence systems that utilize, and even manipulate, the forest. They are also part of the total forest resource, and no less than the forest itself – perhaps even more so – have been affected by development. Indeed, the dominant thinking among professionals (Chambers' 'first thinking') tends to exclude people, and especially the poor, and to stress physical resources and processes. A solution to forest destruction in Southeast Asia will not be found if the search is restricted to finding a technical remedy that is then imposed on the marginalized poor. It must begin, Chambers (1987, p. 7) argues, with the poor:

> Normal professional thinking does not start with people or categories of people like these [forest dwellers, small farmers, etc.], least of all with the poor. People come later, if at all, and often as residuals and problems after technical solutions have been sought and found to physical problems.

This chapter will examine two facets of the debate over the impact of development on the forest dwellers of Southeast Asia. To begin with, the discussion will focus on the shifting cultivators of Sarawak, East Malaysia, before then turning to investigate the hunter–gatherers of the Philippines. Although the chapter will therefore have two distinct sections, it will become clear that the problems and pressures facing the two groups are in many respects remarkably similar. In particular, the unsustainability of shifting cultivation and hunting and gathering as subsistence systems; the corrosive cultural effects of contact and conflict between tribal groups and lowlanders, and their incorporation into the cash economy; and the powerlessness of forest dwellers in the determination of their futures.

The Dayaks and development in Sarawak, East Malaysia

Sarawak is the largest of the Malaysian states, with a land area of 124 450 square kilometres (Figure 4.1). In comparison, the population of 1 542 800 (1985) is small (9.8 per cent of Malaysia's total population) and the state remains land rich. The Fifth Malaysia Plan (1986–90) records that 69.6 per cent of the population are *bumiputra* ('sons of the soil'). This, however, includes both Malays and the Dayaks (indigenous tribal groups), the collective name for the natives of Sarawak.[3] As of 1984, the Dayaks made up 43 per cent of the total population, of whom the Iban, numbering some 439 000 were the most numerous.

The Dayaks of Sarawak are in the most part shifting cultivators, many of whom grow hill, or dry, rice as their staple crop (Figure 4.2). Land is cleared through firing, cultivated for a few seasons, and then abandoned so that it can regenerate. In the case of settled shifting cultivators, an extensive form of rotation is practised in which swidden plots are shifted as they lose fertility but where the settlement itself is usually permanent. Migratory shifting cultivators, however, shift both swidden and settlement, moving to an entirely new location when the land has been exhausted. The latter system is characteristic of steep-sloped locations in the remote interior of Sarawak (see Majid 1983, Hose 1988).

Numbering approximately 36 000 households (216 000 individuals),[4] shifting cultivators live in communal long houses and land is utilized

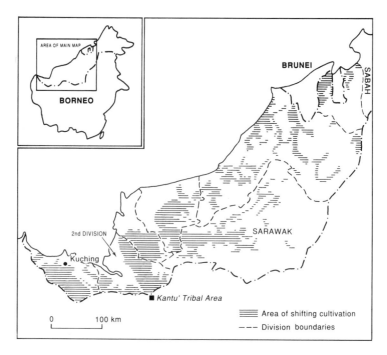

Figure 4.1 Sarawak: areas of shifting cultivation (adapted from Cramb & Dixon 1988)

through customary, or *adat*, law (Figure 4.3). In addition to the shifting cultivators, there are smaller groups of hunter-gatherers such as the Penan, Ukit, and Bukitan (Hong 1987, p. 3). Although 77.4 per cent of Sarawak's land area remains forested, of which over a third is primary forest (Hong 1987, p. 74, Ngau, *et al.* 1987, p. 175), the Dayaks have not been insulated from the process of development. Between 1981 and 1985, an estimated 1 207 111 hectares of forest were logged in Sarawak and the rate of logging has been accelerating (Figure 4.4, see also Hong 1987, p. 129). Indeed some commentators have been reported as saying that Sarawak's commercial forest resources will be exhausted in 20 years if logging continues at current rates (King 1988a, p. 272). In addition to logging, land is being cleared for agricultural use (the two usually go hand-in-hand), roads are being built and dams constructed (such as the Batang Ai dam). Dayaks are also being encouraged to engage in commercial farming, to send their children to school, to take advantage of modern health facilities, and to become generally integrated into modern Malaysian society (Figure 4.5). Given the dependence of the Dayaks on the forests for their physical and spiritual well being, what have been the effects of development and what has been their role in the process of change? As Hong (1987, p. 3) observes on the relationship between the Dayaks and their environment:

Table 4.2 Sarawak: population and ethnic composition

Population: 1985

Bumiputra	1 080 800
Chinese	442 900
Indians	4 000
Others	15 100
Total	1 542 800

Population by tribal group

Bumiputra	1980	1984
Iban	368 208	439 000
Bidayuh	104 885	123 000
Kenyah	15 557	
Kayan	13 368	
Kedayan	10 669	
Murut	9 473	
Punan/Penan	5 600	
Bisayah	3 837	
Kelabit	3 672	
Other Dayaks	4 555	78 000
Malays	247 972	300 000
Melanu	69 578	85 000
Total Bumiputra	857 374	1 025 000
Chinese	359 884	434 000
Indians	3 293	
Indonesians	7 040	
Others	5 512	18 000
Total	1 233 103	1 477 000

Sources: Government of Malaysia 1986, p. 129, Hong 1987, p. 2, Colchester 1989, p. 12.

To all these Dayak peoples, the land, the waters, and the forests have provided them their livelihood and daily needs ever since they can remember. Their communities have thrived on a complex system of rights and obligations towards the land, the forests and the resources of nature.

Development planning in Malaysia is highly centralized and, in general, the states are expected to 'conform to the aims, directives, pronouncements, policies and guidelines emanating from Kuala Lumpur' and contained in the national five-year development plans (King 1988b, p. 13). Thus development in Sarawak is predicated on development priorities for the country as a whole and, in particular, those of the Peninsula. Whereas some analysts believe that on balance the planning experience in the Peninsula has been appropriate and relevant to the conditions found in Sarawak and the neighbouring state of Sabah (Figure 4.1) (e.g. Lim 1986), many others feel insufficient attention has been paid to those factors that are distinctive to

Figure 4.2 Iban rice swidden, Sarawak (Second Division) (photograph: Judy Tice)

Figure 4.3 *Tanju* (open veranda) outside an Iban longhouse, Sarawak (Second Division). The longhouse accommodates approximately eight families (50 individuals) (photograph: Judy Tice)

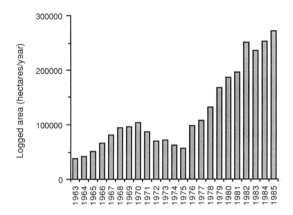

Figure 4.4 Sarawak: estimate of area of forest logged, 1963–85

Figure 4.5 A resettlement longhouse for Iban displaced following the construction of the Batang Ai Dam, Sarawak (Second Division) (photograph: Judy Tice)

East Malaysia (e.g. King 1988a, 1988b, Ngau, *et al.* 1987). Many of these factors relate to the interests of the Dayaks.

Sarawak's role in Malaysian national development is as a source of primary products, notably petroleum and timber. Between 1981 and 1985, Sarawak yielded 35 per cent of Malaysia's petroleum, 59 per cent of natural gas, and 31 per cent of log production (Government of Malaysia 1986, pp. 170–1). The primary sector as a whole accounted for 53 per cent of the state's GDP (1985), while manufacturing represented a mere 9.5 per cent (Government of Malaysia 1986, pp. 174–5). The major benefits of such natural resource exploitation for Sarawak come in the form of additional employment and the revenue that it generates for the state government. However, employment opportunities tend to be for low-skilled, temporary workers, and government expenditure is primarily targeted at infrastructural developments in urban, rather than rural, areas (King 1988a, pp. 273–4). Even when expenditure has been directed at the agricultural sector, it has predominantly favoured commercial farmers and land settlement schemes. Little attention has been paid to improving the traditional agricultural systems, as practised by the Dayaks.

It is no doubt true that the small voice that the Dayaks have in federal and state government plays a large part in restricting their input to the planning and policy formulation process. They are geographically dispersed, and are politically, economically, and educationally ill-equipped to compete with the established Malay and Chinese élites. It is those élites rather than the Dayaks, who dictate the form that development will take. As a result, there has never been a concerted effort to challenge the official view that the development of Sarawak implies economic growth Peninsula-style. Nor has there been sufficient consideration of whether such development is suited to Sarawak's physical and cultural resources. This is clearly reflected in the view that is held by those in authority of the modern versus the traditional sectors. As King (1988a, p. 296), in his account of East Malaysian development planning and problems, states:

> This dualistic approach [to the 'modern' and the 'traditional'] . . . tends to denigrate what it perceives to be 'traditional'; it is the backward, undesirable sector, in comparison with the dynamic, advanced, commercialised, preferred 'modern' sector. This notion of dualism certainly goes a long way to explaining the differential evaluation by politicians and planners in Sarawak of, on the one hand logging activities, and on the other shifting cultivation.

Shifting cultivation and the environment

As King hints in the above quotation, an allegation that may be strongly contested is the view, purveyed by many government officials, and also by some academics, that shifting cultivation is a 'primitive' system of agriculture that is a primary cause of forest loss and soil erosion, and is insufficiently productive to raise household incomes much above subsistence level (King 1986, pp. 78–80, Hurst 1987, pp. 172–3, Nicolaisen 1986, p. 111). The implications of this view are significant: if deforestation is to be reduced, erosion and soil degradation minimized, and if the general welfare of the Dayaks is to be improved and poverty alleviated, then shifting cultivators must be settled in modern communities, encouraged to take up commercial, permanent field agriculture and bound more tightly into the cash economy and the Malaysian state. A recent paper by Masing (1988, pp. 63–4), who is a member of the state legislature and who has worked as a research officer for the Sarawak Electricity Supply Corporation, illustrates the 'official' view of the Dayaks and their traditional system:

> I have presented a grim picture of people living in the rural areas of Sarawak. They are economically backward, lacking in basic amenities and infrastructure, far behind in education and haunted by the spectre of malnutrition, and under current development trends they have little chance of bettering their present living conditions.

However, this view may be challenged on a number of grounds. First, and perhaps most importantly, it is arguable that shifting cultivation, far from being primitive and ecologically unsustainable, is an agricultural system that is complex and utilizes the tropical forest environment rationally (for a defence of shifting cultivation as a rational system see Hong 1987, pp. 19–32). As Geertz (1963, p. 16) explained when comparing wet rice cultivation with shifting cultivation, while the former is a 'bold reworking' of the environment, the latter is a 'canny imitation' of the natural system. It mirrors the forest in terms of species diversity and vertical stratification, and the methods that are used – partial clearance, multiple cropping, and shallow cultivation – often help to reduce erosion and promote forest regeneration. Nonetheless, it should be noted that it is primarily the small size of plots and their location within the forest that serves to limit and localize erosion. Some groups, such as the Senoi of Peninsular Malaysia, purposefully clear steep slopes as firing is made easier, and on such swidden fields soil loss may be high (Rambo 1988, p. 284). Work by numerous ecologists, ethnologists, soil scientists, geographers, and others (e.g. Nye & Greenland 1960, Conklin 1957, Dove 1985, Hong 1987, Spencer 1966) has demonstrated that shifting cultivators have an intimate knowledge of tropical soils and the plants that they cultivate. Dove, who worked among the Kalimantan Kantu', on the borders with Sarawak, records that a household would plant an average of 17 different rice varieties each year, and 20 to 21 non-rice cultigens (Dove 1985, pp. 160, 173) (Figure 4.1). Conklin, meanwhile, in his classic study of the Hanunóo of southeastern Mindoro, the Philippines, notes that in distinguishing general and specific soil types, the Hanunóo use eight different selection criteria[5] and refer to ten basic and 30 subtypes of rocks and minerals associated with different soil formations (Conklin 1957, pp. 36–7). The crops grown and cultivation systems used vary according to the soils and topography of each site. These two examples give a lie to the assertion that shifting cultivation is a primitive and simple agricultural system in which the forest is exploited regardless of its ecological capacity and resilience.

Not only is the system highly complex, it is also productive in labour terms and ecologically sustainable. Although productivity per unit area – i.e. yield – is low, output per unit of labour is high (Hong 1987, pp. 22–4, Dove 1985, pp. 377–9). Shifting cultivation is an extensive system, but this should not disguise the fact that it is efficient given the relative scarcity of factors of production. For land is a resource in abundant supply, and the system that has evolved reflects this fact. In addition, many official assessments ignore the important contribution that forest products, exploited through hunting and gathering, make to general nutrition. Moreover, shifting cultivation will not cause excessive soil erosion if properly managed. Depending upon conditions, the swidden field will be left for between 15 to 30 years before being recultivated, during which time the forest, and the soil, will have regenerated (Jackson 1968, pp. 81–5).

But although shifting cultivation is a productive, sustainable, and rational system given certain conditions, if these conditions should change, then the integrity of the system may quickly become undermined. Most important in Southeast Asia is decreasing available land and the expanding 'pressure of needs' in the region (see Chapter 3). In Sarawak, the Land Code recognizes native customary land rights and has afforded some measure of protection to the Dayaks by preventing the 'substantial alienation of land to non-natives, private companies and commercial interests' (King 1988a, p. 287). However, the 'protection' of Native Customary Land is under threat. Increasing numbers of officials regard the system as a constraint on Sarawak's development and a 'problem' that needs to be circumvented (e.g. Bugo 1988, p. 54, see also King 1988a, pp. 287, 291). But even with land legislation as it stands today, the Dayaks are still experiencing a growing shortage of available land. Primary forest cannot be freely cut to create additional swidden plots, which then become customary land (Cramb & Dixon 1988, p. 10), and the intensification of land use, usually reflected in the shortening of fallows, is causing the system to break down in some areas (e.g. in the Second Division; see Figure 4.1), and erosion and soil degradation to set in (King 1986, pp. 78–80, Cramb 1988, pp. 122–3). The growing pressure of needs among the Dayaks is also promoting the partial commercialization of production. Rubber is being planted on hill sides, and the area cultivated by each family is increasing as their needs grow (Cramb 1988, pp. 123–4). This has compounded the pressures imposed by the growing population.

The point to stress is that shifting cultivation is only sustainable given certain conditions. Where land resources are limited, the system may indeed appear rapacious. In addition, Rambo (1984, p. 155) makes the point that although the system deserves its reputation for labour productivity and stability (when practised in situations of low population pressure), 'it does not merit . . . the acclaim that it has received as a farming system that utilizes energy with extraordinary efficiency'. Past studies have tended to ignore the huge amounts of energy expended in burning to create a swidden site, and as the forests of Sarawak are cleared, the shifting cultivator is faced with an energy crisis that is essentially little different from that confronting commercial farmers (Rambo 1984, pp. 159–60). It is also true that although shifting cultivators may have the knowledge and expertise to deal with the 'traditional' problems they face, the process of development and the decline in available land is confronting some groups with entirely new challenges they may be ill-equipped to overcome (see Hadi & Lung 1988).

It is important to distinguish between different types of shifting cultivation. Where partially commercialized systems have evolved, or where groups who are not traditionally shifting cultivators have taken up incipient forms, erosion and forest destruction may be severe. The 'ideal' described by Conklin and others is becoming increasingly rare, so when criticisms and blame are directed at the system (e.g. Ooi Jin Bee 1987 with reference to the *kaingineros* of the Philippines) they are normally referring to bastardized forms of the original.

Effects of development on Dayak society

Among shifting cultivators, culture, society, economy, and environment are inseparably wedded to one another. Dove (1985, p. 382), referring to the Kantu', writes:

> The Kantu' adaptation to their environment involves not merely their subsistence but, in more general terms, their entire society. The local environment and the nature of their adaptation to it is the dominant, independent variable in Kantu' life . . . This characterization of Kantu' reality is reflected in the cognitive schema of the Kantu' themselves. For example, there is no distinction within this schema corresponding to that between the analytical categories of 'production' and 'ideology'. Most of the Kantu' belief system is bound up with swidden related ritual, and all such ritual is glossed by the Kantu' as integral steps in *bumai* 'making swiddens', with no ontological differentiation from slashing, felling, burning, and so on.

As many studies have made clear, when the environment or the economy is forced or encouraged to change and to adapt, so too do the underpinnings of society and culture. In more resilient societies this may be possible without excessive tension; among many shifting cultivators it has left them 'in a state of paralysis and considerable psychological strain' (Nicolaisen 1986, p. 12). Established frameworks of authority and class relations are undermined; traditional forms of production are regarded as inferior and to be avoided; and a process of cultural alienation is set in train (Hong 1987, Nicolaisen 1986, Colchester 1989, Sarawak Study Group 1989). Although some Dayaks regard their integration into modern society and economy as wholly a desirable outcome of development (see Masing 1988, p. 67) – and there is certainly a degree of romanticism in some reports about the need to protect tribal groups – others have actively campaigned and fought against the commercialization that is forced upon them, and particularly the impacts of logging. In March 1987, several tribal groups in Sarawak, mainly Penan but also Kelabit and Kayan, began to blockade logging roads and to sabotage logging camps (Apin 1987). They complained that the logging industry was encroaching upon their land, destroying their livelihoods, polluting their rivers and eroding their soils. For the most part, however, and this will be returned to at the end of the chapter, the Dayaks have been relatively powerless to restrict logging operations and to influence the form that development takes in the state.

Hunter-gatherers and development in the Philippines

The Negrito hunter-gatherers of the Philippines were originally distributed throughout the upland forested areas of the three major island chains of Mindanao, the Visayas and Luzon (Figure 4.6). Although these upland peoples managed to preserve their autonomy for far longer, and to a far greater degree than the indigenous lowland groups, subsistence hunting and gathering is today rare as a primary means of survival. This also applies to the other countries of Southeast Asia. In most cases, hunter-gatherers have made the transition to agriculture, and it is difficult to draw a distinction between their subsistence strategies and those of the more numerous shifting cultivators. In total, and excluding the Muslim populations of Mindanao, the tribal population of the Philippines numbers approximately 5 million, or 8 per cent of the total population (extrapolated from Anderson 1987, p. 258). There are 72 tribal ethnolinguistic groups, 34 in Luzon, 33 in Mindanao and 5 in the Visayas (Anderson 1987, p. 258) (Figure 4.6).

The decline in the population of hunter-gatherers has closely paralleled the destruction of their habitat: the forests of the Philippines. When the Spanish colonized the archipelago in the 16th century, an estimated 90 per cent of land was under forest. By the end of the Second World War this figure had declined by a comparatively small amount, to perhaps 75 per cent (Headland 1986, p. 4). However, deforestation subsequently accelerated dramatically. Between 1952 and 1970, 190 000 hectares of additional agricultural land came into production each year, with most being derived from the legal and illegal conversion of forest land.[6] Although at the beginning of the 1980s the Philippine government still classified 16.7 million hectares (56 per cent of the country's total land area) as public forest, a significant proportion of this officially designated forest land is heavily denuded, and in some cases has been converted to grassland (Fujisaka 1986a, p. 2). Of 5.5 million hectares of 'timberland', only 2.7 million hectares is classified as old growth. The remainder consists of impoverished secondary growth (Sajise 1986, p. 15). These figures indicate that by the beginning of the 1980s, undisturbed primary forest had been encroached upon to the extent that it accounted for only 9 per cent of the land area of the Philippines. With a rate of deforestation approaching 100 000 hectares per year in the 1980s (Table 4.1), we can speculate that this figure has declined still further, to perhaps 6 per cent. It has been calculated that at present rates of destruction, the forests of the Philippines will have disappeared entirely by the beginning of the next century, or soon thereafter (Headland 1986, p. 5).

The factors underlying this dramatic reduction in the Philippines' forests are not hard to identify. In particular, the tripling of the country's population between 1948 and 1989, from 19.2 million to 64.9 million, has greatly increased pressure on the land, encouraging farmers and *kaingineros* (shifting cultivators) to clear the forest and convert it to agricultural use. Allied to land clearance for agriculture, timber exploitation has also significantly increased. Before the Second World War, annual output of logs and lumber averaged 770 000 cubic metres (1908–35). In 1969 alone, output

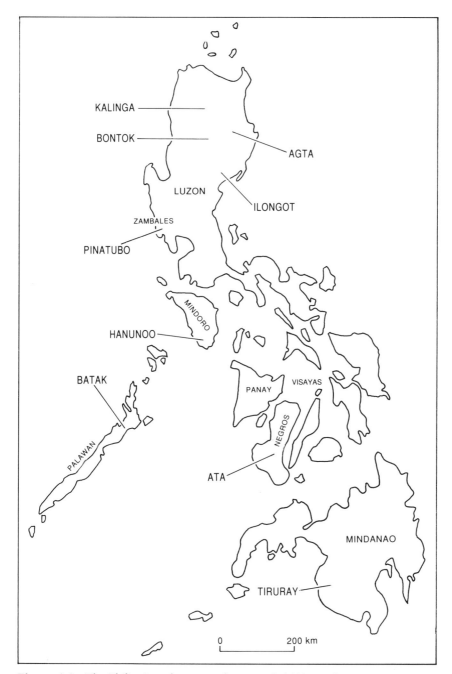

Figure 4.6 The Philippines: hunter-gatherers and shifting cultivators

of logs and lumber was 11.5 million cubic metres (Ooi Jin Bee 1987, p. 14). Most of the Philippines' remaining forests are located on the islands of Luzon (40 per cent), Mindanao (37 per cent), in the Visayas (16 per cent) and on Palawan (7 per cent) (Sajise 1986, p. 16) (Figure 4.6). This reduction in forest area has had great implications for the hunter–gatherers of the country, a way of life that is on the verge of extinction.

Hunter-gatherers as they were

Southeast Asian Negrito hunter-gatherers have been unevenly studied. In the Philippines, some groups such as the Negritos of Zambales (west central Luzon) attracted scholarly attention at a fairly early date (e.g. Reed 1904). Most others, however, such as the Batak of Palawan, were not studied until after the Second World War. In spite of this paucity of information, however, there does exist enough ethnographic and other evidence to construct, or at least reconstruct, a picture of the hunter-gathering way of life.

Traditionally, hunter-gatherers lived in small (perhaps two to five households) groups and were highly mobile. Depending upon resource availability, groups would move to a new camp site between 15 and 30 times every year (Eder 1987, p. 32). From these camps, small parties would venture into the forest on foraging and hunting expeditions to collect tubers, honey, fruit, insects, and other forest products, and to hunt a variety of animals. If a task required greater numbers of participants, for example communal pig hunts and fish-stunning[7] expeditions, all camp members might become involved. Hunter-gatherers exploited a number of ecological zones and a wide range of flora and fauna were hunted and gathered. Eder (1987, pp. 34–7), in his account of traditional Batak resource utilization, records that the principal plant and animal foods that his informants said they, and their ancestors, once used included wild pigs, porcupines, wild cats, monkeys, bats, pheasants, turtles, pythons, molluscs, fish, bee larvae, honey and a large number of different tubers, fruits, greens and fungi.[8]

There is a tendency to regard hunting and gathering as a primitive system, a system one step below shifting cultivation in the progression to settled agriculture. Although it is difficult not to think in such evolutionary terms, three points need to be made. First, hunter-gathering, from what we can tell, was a successful subsistence strategy. Certainly, the rather Rousseauian notion that there existed such an abundance of food that no one went hungry is overly romantic, and hunter-gatherers did periodically run short. However, for much of the time food was available and sufficient, and it has been calculated that only four hours' work per adult was necessary each day to meet a group's subsistence requirements (Endicott 1984, Eder 1987, pp. 44–5). Second, there is evidence to indicate that many hunter-gatherers *have* practised agriculture in the past. Rai (1982, pp. 165–6) maintains that the Agta have been engaged in horticulture for 200 years, while Eder (1987, pp. 45–51, 1988, pp. 49–54) and Headland (1986) make the point that hunting and gathering did not exclude the possibility that agricultural activities of various types, however subsidiary, might also be undertaken. And third, and this returns to the point made in the discussion of shifting

72

cultivation, hunting and gathering is not a primitive and simple system. In 1952 Fox wrote the following about the Pinatubo Negritos of Zambales (Figure 4.6):

> the acute observation of the pygmies and their awareness of the interrelationships between plant and animal life [gives] them an ecological picture of their environment . . . Most Negrito men can with ease enumerate the specific or descriptive names of at least 450 plants, 75 birds, most of the snakes, fish, insects and animals and of even 20 species of ants (quoted in Brosius 1983, p. 138).

Hunter-gatherers, development and change

As the forests of the Philippines have been cleared, communications improved, and as the market economy has penetrated deeper into the uplands, so the hunter-gatherers have found it increasingly difficult to pursue the traditional way of life outlined above, or to protect their traditional culture from change. Whether such Negritos have had change thrust upon them, a view strongly argued by Bodley in his book *Victims of progress* (1982), or whether they have willingly accepted change is an area of continuing debate. However, Eder makes the point that although it is the more dramatic instances of land having been aggressively expropriated and rapidly cleared by mining, logging, and plantation enterprises that have tended to receive the greatest attention, the less visible processes of social, political, and economic change are far more pervasive and important. These processes – 'market incentives, cultural pressures, new religious ideologies – permeate the fabric and ethos of tribal societies and motivate their members to think and behave in new ways' (Eder 1987, p. 6). It is useful to classify these new ways as consisting of new or adapted subsistence strategies, and new or adapted cultural frameworks. That said, it should be remembered that dismembering the lifestyle of hunter-gatherers in this way distorts an integrated system in which culture and production are inseparably wedded.

LAND PRESSURES AND AGRICULTURAL CHANGE

In much the same way that the shifting cultivators of Sarawak are facing an increasing shortage of land, so too are the hunter-gatherers of the Philippines. Settlement of the uplands by lowland migrants, and the failure of both the government and the migrants to respect customary land ownership has resulted in land grabbing and the alienation of hunter-gatherers from their principal resource, the forest. Those forests that do remain are often impoverished. Large mammal populations have declined due to overhunting and have been driven away by increased levels of human activity. Aquatic resources are polluted, and logging has reduced the richness of the tropical forest ecosystem (Rai 1982, pp. 177–82). When population begins to outstrip resources, hunter-gatherer strategies can, in fact, seriously damage those resources. Rambo (1982, p. 277) writes of the Semang of central Peninsular Malaysia that contrary 'to popular ideas about primitive men living in some sort of wonderful harmony with nature, the Semang take whatever they feel they need, without sentimentality and often with considerable ruthlessness'.

In response to the loss and impoverishment of their forest resource, hunter-gatherers have either given up their land claims and moved to new virgin areas (a response that is becoming increasingly difficult), or they have adapted their subsistence strategies. In many instances this second response has involved a decrease in mobility and an increase in the importance of agriculture. Some hunter-gatherers have become entirely settled (e.g. the Ata of Negros); others have adapted to a cyclical lifestyle, moving from a central fixed settlement out to temporary forest and swidden camps (e.g. the Batak of Palawan) (Cadeliña 1988, Eder 1987) (Figure 4.6). As these groups have become increasingly settled, so they have become more reliant on agriculture. The level of dependence varies considerably: while the Batak still remain 50 per cent dependent upon hunting and gathering (Cadeliña 1988, p. 62), the Negritos of Zambales are today totally committed to swidden agriculture (Brosius 1983, p. 139), and the Ata have gone to the extent of taking up plough agriculture using *carabao* (buffalo) and cattle (Cadeliña 1988, pp. 61–2) (Figure 4.6). This transition is one which all hunter-gatherers will in the near future have to undergo, for the population and resource realities of the Philippines demand it.

UPLAND–LOWLAND INTERACTIONS
The settlement of upland areas by lowland migrants has brought hunter-gatherers into contact with other Filipinos and with the market economy. They have responded by entering into trade relationships with the lowlanders, exchanging such forest products as wild pig, copal resin, rattan, orchids, and honey for cash, alcohol, soap, canned foods, and other consumer goods. In many cases hunter-gatherers assume a subordinate role in these trading relationships and may receive only 10 per cent to 30 per cent of the true value of the products they sell (e.g. Rai 1982, pp. 189–94). The exploitation of the forest (and the forest dweller) for the market has often reduced the productivity of the hunter-gatherers' traditional subsistence strategy, so making them increasingly dependent upon the market for survival. In some instances such trading contacts have even led to Negritos buying consumer goods and thereby becoming indebted. Should they have taken steps to register their land, this in turn raises the possibility that it will be taken from them (Rai 1982, p. 193).

Contact with lowlanders has also led to Negrito depopulation. Often this has been seen in terms of cultural extinction, an issue that will be returned to shortly. However, intermarriage with lowlanders and disease have also taken a toll. Coutts *et al.* (1981, p . 109) note that the number of Negritos on the island of Panay (Figure 4.6) declined from 14 000 in 1849 to less than 1000 by 1900, to a mere handful of individuals of dubious ethnicity by the 1980s. Ironically, although epidemics such as cholera and measles may no longer be the scourge of tribal populations that they were in the past, the settled lifestyle that many Negritos now follow has introduced them to a new range of diseases and illnesses. Contaminated drinking water and unhygienic cooking conditions, for example, have led to a rise in gastrointestinal diseases. Such new diseases, coupled with a poorer diet linked to growing resource scarcity, may help to explain the low fertility of some groups and the continued high rates of mortality (Eder 1987, pp. 159–61).

DECULTURATION

The impact of development on the cultures of hunter-gatherers is the area of change that had received the greatest attention from commentators. Terms such as cultural extinction, deculturation, acculturation, detribalization, cultural impoverishment, cultural erosion, and cultural disruption are all employed to describe the process. Many researchers believe that there now exists a crisis in tribal life, a crisis largely brought about by the increasing contact between hunter-gatherers and the modern world. Dorall and Regpala (1984, pp. 254–5), for example, recall that:

> For both authors, those years spent in joint fieldwork among the tribal peoples of the Central Cordilleras on Northern Luzon, Philippines were indeed a time of crisis: both researchers had to radically adapt that which they had learnt in the comparative quiet and safety of the university seminar room to the crisis-ridden realities of tribal-life facing wave-upon-wave of economic, political, cultural and social intrusions, each coming in the name of 'development' and 'modernization'.[9]

Deculturation involves the loss or erosion of cultural beliefs and prac-ices without their replacement by functional equivalents. In addition to this loss of culture, there also invariably occurs a cultural gain (accul-turation) of new beliefs and practices. For example, traditional means of barter and exchange have been superseded by monetization, animist beliefs by Christianity. Finally, hunter-gatherers and other tribal groups are also being confronted with new challenges and opportunities with which they are often ill-equipped to deal. This results in the political and economic subordination of hunter-gatherers to wider Philippine soci-ety, a position often reflected in their being viewed as second-class citi-zens.

In the past many hunter-gatherers have been sufficiently mobile to escape or minimize cultural stress brought on by contact with other groups. However, as they have been forced to become less mobile and more settled, so contact with lowlanders and the cash economy has increased. This has led to rapid cultural change.[10] Anthropologists generally believe that culture is adaptive, and that most beliefs and traditions are functional. If so, then the loss of these beliefs and traditions without replacement by functional equivalents (deculturation) is likely to render groups less able to operate. Eder, for example, is of the opinion that the erosion of Batak belief systems has made it more difficult to mobilize social support, and has also undermined their traditional herbal and supernatural curing system (which, he writes, is 'virtually moribund') (1987, p. 202). He concludes:

75

The Batak are caught between increase and diversification in the total amount of stress on their social environment and reduction in the efficiency of their traditional ways of coping with stress. Both social resources and ego resources for coping with the exigencies of life have been disrupted by the deculturation attending incorporation of Batak society into lowland Philippine society (1987, pp. 219–20).

As the culture of hunter-gatherers has become eroded, so there has arisen the possibility, in some cases the reality, of culture extinction. Some tribal groups have – culturally – disappeared entirely.

Conflicts, priorities, and power in Sarawak and the Philippines

Traditional forms of shifting cultivation, and hunting and gathering are under severe pressure in Sarawak, the Philippines, and elsewhere in Southeast Asia. They are perceived by those in authority to be incompatible with the demands and nature of a modern state. The priorities of development, which are invariably formulated by the central authorities, go much of the way to ensure that upland minorities remain marginalized economically, politically, and culturally. Implicit in many government policies is a denial of common time. 'Primitive' indigenous groups, these policies assert, 'live in the past' and need to 'advance' before they can achieve equality with other 'developed' groups. Empowerment of these groups will have to go a long way if they are to play a significant role in dictating the form that development in the forests of Southeast Asia should take. The dominant thinking is that forest land must be cleared to settle landless lowlanders, that it must be made available to the logging industry to generate valuable foreign exchange and additional revenues, and that it must be made more accessible to secure and maintain the integrity of the state.

In the Philippines, the rights of indigenous groups are *de jure* (if not always *de facto*) protected by the state. The Ancestral Land Decree (1974), the Public Land Act, the Presidential Assistant on National Minorities (PANAMIN) – which was dissolved in 1981 to be replaced by a new office of Muslim Affairs and Cultural Communities – all have clauses or have been provided with powers to assist tribal groups in the Philippines (see Fujisaka 1986b, pp. 28–9, Makil 1984, Eder 1987, p. 170). In reality, however, while forestry policies have been generally accommodating towards commercial users such as logging enterprises, they have often failed in their task of protecting the interests of tribal groups: 'At best [cultural minorities] have been treated like second class citizens, objects of policies which are, more often than not, baffling for their ambiguities and contradictions. At worst, they have been treated like criminals' (Makil 1984, p. 47). An example of such a contradiction is the fact that although the Ancestral Land Decree enables 'cultural minorities' to register their land, the Revised Forestry Code (1975) states that no land in the public domain (i.e. with a slope of over 17 per cent) can be alienated. A significant proportion of traditional tribal uplands falls into this category. In addition, Presidential Decree 1559

(1978) provides for the ejection and relocation of tribal peoples 'whenever the best land use of the area so demands' (Lopez 1987, p. 236, Anderson 1987, pp. 256–60).

Not only are the policies, as they stand, often ambiguous and contradictory, but the corruption and 'cronyism' that is endemic in Philippine public life has meant that even the policies that ostensibly protect minorities can often be ignored or circumvented by the economically wealthy and politically powerful. In 1969, for example, PANAMIN attempted a forcible resettlement of the entire Batak population of Palawan. This appears to have been linked to the furtherance of the personal and political ambitions of PANAMIN's director, not the furtherance of the interests of the Batak. Eder (1987, p. 169) believes that although the resettlement attempt was ultimately unsuccessful, it was the 'single most stressful event affecting the Batak since World War II'. Although PANAMIN has since been discredited and disbanded, corruption and political patronage mean that logging interests in Palawan still enjoy the freedom to act much as they wish. It has been calculated that Palawan's 780 000 hectares of forests will be reduced by 60 per cent over the next 20 years if current rates of deforestation are maintained (Clad & Vitug 1988, Clad 1988). Hunter–gatherers and other tribal groups lack the necessary political influence to do much to prevent the imminent destruction of their primary subsistence resource.

A similar scenario of corruption, political patronage, and powerlessness, applies to the position of the Dayaks in Sarawak. The logging industry, which is dominated by local Chinese (Foochow) contractors (Leigh 1988) and backed by powerful national and state interests, wields considerable power, to the extent that companies are sometimes able to operate outside the law with little fear of reprisal (Apin 1987, p. 188, Scott 1989, p. 38, Ngau, *et al.* 1987, p. 177). Leigh noted that politics in Sarawak is 'concerned essentially with the control of land, timber, and minerals' (Leigh 1979, p. 371) and Cramb and Dixon (1988, p. 11) concur, stating that 'it is thus in the nexus between politics and economics that an understanding of the nature of development in Sarawak must be sought'. Power lies with the logging industry and its supporters, rarely with the shifting cultivators.[11] Thus, although indigenous groups in Malaysia have been equated with Malays since the 1971 constitutional amendment, and should in theory enjoy the same privileges as Malays (as enshrined, for example, in the NEP see Chapter 6), their marginalization has meant that they are more often than not in a poor position to exploit fully these privileges.

Although the balance of power clearly does not lie with the tribal shifting cultivators and hunter–gatherers of Southeast Asia, a discernible shift in the debate has occurred. Environmental groups such as Sahabat Alam Malaysia (Friends of the Earth, Malaysia) and the Manila-based Haribon Foundation are beginning to have an impact on public opinion.[12] No longer is it always true that development can be carried on irrespective of the effects that it may have on the natural environment and the peoples who inhabit that environment. Levels of education are rising in Southeast Asia, and the public are becoming increasingly aware of the preservation of their environment and are placing a greater value on it. With these developments in mind, the state of the environment in Southeast Asia can be viewed as both a cause for concern and for limited optimism. Development since the end of the Second World War has definitely been environmentally destructive. The drive for growth and modernization has been, understandably, the first priority of governments in the region. Their very stability has often depended upon it, and in the process there has sometimes been a reckless disregard of the effects that such development has had upon the natural and the human environments. Pesticides have been used despite the evidence that they are persistent and cause birth defects; logging has continued apace even though it is now widely acknowledged that serious erosion and flooding may result; and the interests of minority groups have been ignored despite the fact that they may be recognized and protected by law.

However, there is a contradiction in the desire to conserve the tropical forests of the region while simultaneously preserving the tribal way of life. Shifting cultivation, and hunting and gathering are extensive subsistence systems that function well in conditions of low population pressure. Rapid population growth and the expansion of settled agriculture have rendered such systems unsustainable in many areas. Although the transition to settled agriculture and the incorporation of tribal peoples into the modern Southeast Asian state could certainly be achieved with far greater cultural sensitivity than has so far been shown, it is difficult to ignore the fact that in most cases such a transition is inevitable and imminent. If at least the forests are to be conserved, then the shifting cultivators and hunter–gatherers of Southeast Asia will have to adapt their lifestyles.

Notes to Chapter 4

1 See for example: Pearce, Markandya and Barbier 1989, World Commission on Environment and Development 1987, Brookfield 1988, Barbier 1989.
2 In Thailand, for example, the Royal Forestry Department claims that in 1985 29 per cent of the country was forested. This, however, includes large areas of rubber trees and is regarded by many commentators as an overestimate. Estimates of the area of natural forest range from 19 per cent (see Paisal Sricharatchanya 1989c, p. 40, Hirsch 1987) to as low as 15 per cent, while the area of undisturbed forest (i.e. excluding degraded forest) may now account for only 9–10 per cent of Thailand's land area (personal communication P. A. Stott).
3 The tribal groups are also often referred to as *Orang Ulu* or 'peoples of the interior'. This, however, excludes the Iban and Dusun (Hong 1987, p. 3).
4 This official figure may be an underestimate. Colchester records that some other estimates are as high as almost 500 000 (1989, p. 48).
5 For example: moisture content, sand content, rock content, general texture, firmness, structure in dry season, stickiness in wet season and colour.
6 Officially, 106 000 hectares of forest land was released each year for agriculture between 1952 and 1970. The remaining 84 000 hectares was illegally cleared, mostly by *kaingineros* (shifting cultivators) (Ooi Jin Bee 1987, p. 20).
7 The bark of the croton oil plant (*Croton trigilum*) is pounded and then soaked in streams releasing a stunning agent which immobilizes the fish, allowing them to be collected from the surface (see Eder 1987, pp. 40–1, Rai 1982, pp. 95–6).

8 Among these, yams and honey, together with palm shoots, rattan pith, and various greens, were the most important as sources of carbohydrate; rivers and streams as sources of animal protein; while wild pigs were the culturally (and also possibly nutritionally) the most important mammal (Eder 1987, pp. 38 45).

9 Although this comment is directed at all tribal groups, the authors were working among the Igorots, a group of shifting cultivators/settled agriculturalists.

10 Headland (1986, p. 293) describes an celebration among a group of Agta as follows: 'When we arrived at the camp, at 9.30 that morning, 12 of the 24 Agta adults in the camp were roaring drunk. This in itself was no surprise . . . One of their former trading partners, a Casiguranin townsman, had recently returned from a two-year employment stint in Saudi Arabia. He was sharing his homecoming with his former Agta clients with a complete 'blowout' – a feast, liquor, and especially a night of watching hard core pornographic video tapes on his Betamax TV set, which he and his cronies had carried up to the camp along with a generator! Such is an example of culture change among Philippine tribal people today'.

11 It is significant that Datuk Amar James Wong, the owner of the largest logging company in Sarawak (Limbang Trading), is also the state Minister for Environment and Tourism.

12 So much so that in October 1987 Harrison Ngau, the head of the Sarawak branch of Sahabat Alam Malaysia, was arrested – along with other logging protesters – under the provisions of the Internal Security Act. He has been active in promoting the interests of the Dayaks and many feel that his arrest reflects his success in highlighting the plight of the shifting cultivators and hunter-gatherers (Colchester 1987, p. 189).

5
Land settlement in Southeast Asia: the Indonesian transmigration programme

Land settlement schemes in Southeast Asia: an overview

Land settlement schemes *per se* in Southeast Asia are usually traced back to 1905, when the Dutch implemented their colonization programme in what is now Indonesia. However, the process of land clearance and settlement, with varying degrees of government encouragement and involvement, has been under way for considerably longer. De Koninck and McTaggart (1987, p. 343), for example, claim that 'there have been many instances where centralized political systems have acted to promote the establishment or amelioration of agriculture under their control', and cite the extension of control by the Thai (Siamese) state over the Central Plains of Thailand. However, although the actions of both pre-colonial and colonial states in the region often facilitated and encouraged the settlement of new lands, it was the process of spontaneous land clearance and settlement that was (and remains) far more important (Uhlig 1984). This 'natural' process, in which the cultivated area was gradually extended to new lands with 'daughter' villages being established as communities grew too large, has a fairly low profile historically and as a result has received relatively less attention. Indeed, even contemporary spontaneous settlement has been somewhat neglected (see Uhlig 1984, Rigg 1987). The problem is that there is a fairly thin and indistinct line between 'spontaneous' and 'sponsored'. For example, although the Thai state was involved in the agricultural development of the Central Plains of Thailand, it was the peasant, acting independently of the state, who was of paramount importance. The canals constructed in the Central Plains during the Ayutthaya and early Bangkok periods (*c.* 1350–mid–19th century) were built largely to improve transport and communications for military and trade reasons. They were then used by farmers to exploit the agricultural potential of the area (see Tanabe 1978, Sharp & Hanks 1978, Ingram 1971). Indeed, it was not until 1870 that the Thai state fully appreciated the link between canal construction and the reclamation of ricelands in the delta.

Contemporary planned land settlement schemes in the morre rigorous sense of the term – implying the officially sanctioned and sponsored movement of people into previously underutilized areas – can be viewed as beginning in Southeast Asia with the Dutch colonization programme of 1905. Since that date, all the ASEAN countries (apart from Singapore and Brunei) have implemented such projects as have Vietnam, Laos, Cambodia, and Burma

(Table 5.1). The rationale for planned land settlement programmes is clear. Southeast Asia has areas where agricultural population densities are high and increasing, for example, the Central Plains of Thailand, much of Java, and the Visayas in the Philippines. At the same time, there are also large areas of underdeveloped and sparsely populated land with considerable agricultural potential. Therefore, it is 'not surprising that . . . most Southeast Asian governments [should have] developed programs to settle people into areas with development potential' (Jones & Richter 1982, p. 3).

   MacAndrews (1982, pp. 9–10), in his overview of land settlement schemes in the region, identifies four main categories of settlement, examples of all of which can be found in Southeast Asia (see Table 5.1):

Type 1 Settlements created by spontaneous migration, with the state providing virtually no inputs or assistance apart from the provision of land.

Type 2 Settlements created by spontaneous migration but in which settlers are provided with a wide range of inputs and services as well as land.

Type 3 Government-sponsored settlements in which settlers are selected according to specific criteria, and where they receive full assistance and support.

Type 4 Settlements created by compulsory relocation in response to natural disasters (e.g. volcanic eruptions) or large-scale development projects (e.g. dam construction). Such settlements may also be created for strategic reasons to settle sensitive and unstable areas.

Although these schemes and programmes obviously vary, the parallels between them are more striking than the differences. This extends from the objectives and rationales underlying the schemes to the problems they have faced. To simplify, three objectives have been of paramount importance, while the problems facing the schemes can be classified under four main headings. Objectives include:

(a) Development of previously un/underutilized land to increase national output.
(b) Easing of social, political and economic pressures in densely populated areas.
(c) The strengthening of national security in sensitive border areas.

Problems facing the schemes include:

(a) Those linked to migrant selection and suitability.
(b) Those linked to site selection and suitability.
(c) Those linked to the productivity and sustainability of agricultural systems.
(d) Those linked to conflicts with local/indigenous groups in the settlement area.

Table 5.1 Land settlement in Southeast Asia

Type of scheme	Numbers settled (persons)	Dates	Comments
Malaysia			
4	543 000	1950–52	Forced relocation of rural population in 'New Villages' during the Malayan Emergency (communist insurgency).
3	130 523	1957–70	Heavily capitalized with considerable
3	68 088	1971–80	government investment. Largest is
3	190 000	1981–5	the FELDA programme; also FELCRA and KEJORA. Generally regarded as the most successful of the land settlement schemes in the region.
Indonesia			
3	26 821	1905–31	Dutch colonization scheme (see text).
3	248 458	1932–41	
1, 2, 3, and 4	412 366	1951–68	Indonesian transmigration
	5.99 million	1969–87	programme. For period 1969–87 includes both 'general' and 'spontaneous' transmigrants (see text).
Thailand			
3 and 4	1.2 million	1935–79	Many settlements performed poorly with high turnover of settlers. 'The settlements have tended to be used as a dumping ground for any family offering a political or social problem, sometimes even against their own inclination' (Demaine 1984, p. 5). Some recent improvements and movement towards 'self-help'.
Philippines			
3	8 000	1913–17	Government-sponsored settlement of
3	31 408	1918–34	Mindanao begins in 1913: poor
3	11 016	1939–41	results and high costs. In 1918, migrants with sufficient funds to finance themselves are actively encouraged. In 1939 the programme is expanded and National Land Settlement Administration established. Loans reintroduced, greater government investment in settlements. Programme cut short by the war.

Note: The land settlement scheme 'types' refer to those noted in the text. The table is adapted from MacAndrews 1982, p. 12 using various other sources.

Indonesia's transmigration programme is by far the most significant of the land settlement schemes that have been undertaken in Southeast Asia. This is true in terms of numbers moved, length of operation, degree of international support, scope of academic enquiry, and degree of criticism.

The Indonesian transmigration programme

Introduction

Indonesia, with 185 million inhabitants, is the world's fifth most populous country. It also has substantial land resources extending over 1.92 million square kilometres. However, the distribution of Indonesia's population is highly uneven, and almost 60 per cent (107.5 million) (Bank Indonesia 1989, p. 186) are concentrated on the four 'metropolitan' islands of Java, Madura, Bali and Lombok, which account for only 7 per cent of the total land area (Figure 5.1). To put these figures into perspective, were the United Kingdom to be settled as densely as Java, then its population would approach 200 million. Over large areas Java's population density exceeds 1000 per square kilometre, and the island supports among the highest agricultural population densities in the world (Hugo *et al.* 1987, pp. 55–6). In contrast, the Indonesian province of Irian Jaya (Figure 5.1) supports only three persons per square kilometre. This uneven distribution of population, to some a maldistribution, is no historical accident. The fertile neutral-basic volcanic soils that cover much of Java and Bali, coupled with a warm and humid climate, provide an enormously attractive agricultural environment. Through the cultivation of wet rice (*sawah*) the islands have supported high population densities and impressive empires for thousands of years. The ancient civilizations, such as the Sailendra dynasty of central Java, owed much of their success to the agricultural wealth that Java and Bali had to offer.

Despite Java's formidable natural advantages,[1] by the end of the 19th century fears were emerging that even these advantages were insufficient to support a population that reached 28.5 million by 1890 (Mantra 1985, p. 170). These fears, coupled with reports that land holdings were shrinking and general welfare declining, gradually filtered through to the Dutch colonial authorities. Crucial in heightening awareness was the publication in 1899 of a famous article, 'A Debt of Honour', written by C. Th. Van Deventer which was instrumental in the formulation of the so-called Ethical Policy adopted in 1901. This policy explicitly recognized that it was the duty of the Dutch to improve the lot of the native population. Van Deventer was commissioned to propose ways of achieving the aims of the Ethical Policy and arrived at a formulation of 'education, irrigation, and emigration'. The third element envizaged the movement of the 'surplus' population of Java to the underpopulated Outer Islands. Interestingly, Thomas Stamford Raffles, the British governor of the Dutch East Indies during the years of the Napoleonic wars when Holland was annexed by France (1811–16), had predicted just such an outcome in his *History of Java* published in 1817.

83

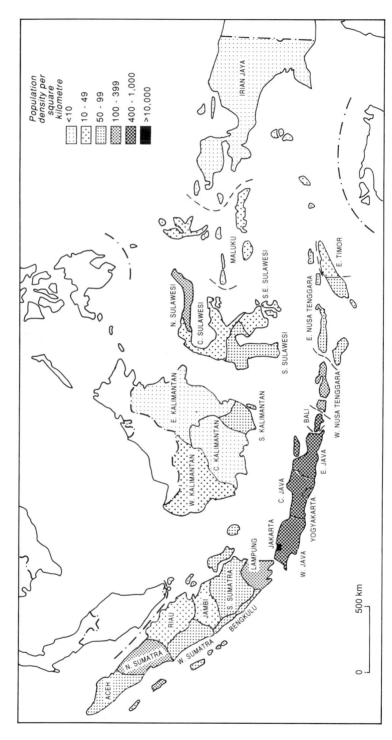

Figure 5.1 Indonesia: population density, 1985

He felt that after Java's land resources had been exploited to the full, 'the immense tracts of unoccupied or thinly peopled territories of Sumatra, Borneo and the numerous islands scattered over the Archipelago, may be ready to receive colonies, arts and civilization from the metropolis of the Indian seas' (Raffles 1978, p. 71).

The Dutch colonization programme

The Dutch authorities responded to Van Deventer's suggestion by implementing a 'colonization' (*kolonisasi*) programme in 1905.[2] This began with the transfer of 155 families to Gedong Tataan district in the residency of Lampung, South Sumatra (Figure 5.1). From 1905 through to the Japanese occupation of the Dutch East Indies in 1941, 275 279 migrants from Java were settled, mostly in southern Sumatra. It should be stressed that although the ethical policy, with its determination to improve the general welfare of the Javanese population, is usually seen as instrumental in causing the Dutch to initiate the colonization programme, there were other, less humanitarian motivations. Foremost among these was the desire to provide labour for the plantations that were being established in Sumatra (Hardjono 1977, p. 16). Initially, the programme was somewhat experimental in nature and suffered from delays and deficiencies. For example, some of the early settlements were abandoned because of poor soils and maladministration (Suratman & Guinness 1977, p. 78), the bank established to finance the colonization efforts (the Lampoengs Credit Bank) went into liquidation in 1928 (Pelzer 1983, p. 198), and the cost to the colonial authorities was proving too high. It was not until the early 1930s that the programme really took off when a dramatic worsening in the international economic climate and a new approach to colonization led to a substantial increase in the number of migrants being settled each year (Figure 5.2).

Perhaps the most significant feature of the colonization programme is the extent to which the problems it faced have afflicted the later transmigration programme. These problems include poor survey work, management and administration; financing difficulties; the identification and promotion of suitable agricultural systems; appropriate migrant selection; and the lack of social services and infrastructure.

The origins of transmigration in Indonesia

The Japanese invasion of the Dutch East Indies in 1941 effectively halted the colonization programme and it was only shortly after independence that it was resumed, under a different name. Sukarno, the president of the newly independent Indonesia, did not support family planning, which he viewed as unnecessary given the country's abundant land resources, but was enthusiastic about transmigration. He perceived the problem to be one of underproduction rather than overpopulation and considered that the answer was the exploitation of more of Indonesia's underutilized land resources. His comment that the transmigration programme was 'a matter of life and death for the Indonesian nation' has been quoted countless times

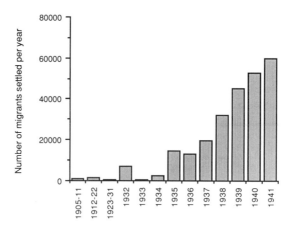

Figure 5.2 The Dutch colonization programme, number of migrants settled, 1905–41

(e.g. Suratman & Guinness 1977, p. 82, Caufield 1985, p. 188) and it does emphasize the importance placed upon land settlement by the 'father' of the nation. The adoption of a new name reflected a desire to disassociate the programme from its colonial antecedent, while the prefix 'trans' indicated that the migration was to be over water – from the metropolitan islands of Java, Madura, Bali, and Lombok to the Outer Islands.

Since the transmigration programme proper was introduced in 1950 it has been an enduring and important feature of Indonesia's development plans. During the course of the third five-year development plan (Repelita III, 1979–84) for example, it consumed 6 per cent of the development budget (Arndt 1984a, p. 40).[3] As Arndt has observed, it 'has grown into a social engineering project of monumental proportions – the largest voluntary land settlement scheme in the world', and since 1950 well over 5 million people have been settled in the Outer Islands (Arndt 1983b, p. 50). This is not to imply that the scheme has enjoyed uninterrupted progress; there have been great fluctuations in the numbers of migrants settled and a succession of phases can be identified in terms of objectives, methods, and outcomes as well as in quantitative terms (Figure 5.3).

Stages in the evolution of the transmigration programme

MacAndrews (1978, pp. 462–3) identifies three 'distinct' stages in the evolution of the transmigration programme, and we can now add a fourth stage that has evolved since his paper was published. The first coincided with the Sukarno presidency and ran from 1950 to 1965; the second covers the period of confusion that followed the attempted coup of 1965, and lasted until 1969; and the third ran from 1970 to 1986 when the programme was experiencing steady growth. The fourth stage began in 1987 and is characterized by retrenchment and consolidation. However, although it

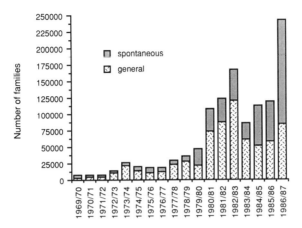

Figure 5.3   The transmigration scheme: numbers of families settled, 1969–87

is handy to think of the scheme in terms of stages, it should be noted that more than one such set can reasonably be made. For example, we could examine the scheme's evolution, since 1969 at least, with reference to each of the five-year development plans or Repelitas; or we could use the changing philosophy and objectives underpinning the scheme as our yardstick; or, indeed, the changing location of the settlement sites.

The first transmigration plan was formulated by Ir. A.H.O. Tamboenan the first head of the Transmigration Bureau. Over a 35-year period (1953–87) he planned to move 48.675 million people from Java to the Outer Islands. The intention was to settle one million plus the natural rate of increase in the first five years; two million and the natural rate of increase during the second five years, and so on. In this way Tamboenan aimed to reduce Java's population from 54 million to 31 million (Mantra 1985, p. 173, Suratman & Guinness 1977, p. 82). The plan was highly unrealistic and the figures, to say the least, fantastic. At no time did the actual number of migrants even begin to approach the targets that Tamboenan had set.

The second transmigration plan was incorporated in the Eight Year National Development Plan (1961–9). In spite of the fact that its targets were far more realistic – the intention was to settle 'only' 390 000 families (almost 2 million people) within the eight year planning period – they again proved to be highly over-optimistic. Only 38 591 families were settled (Oey 1982, p. 31). This can be explained by the fact that during this period Indonesia was experiencing growing social, political, and economic instability, culminating in the attempted coup d'état of 1965. The coup and its aftermath, led to a considerable drop in migrant numbers and it was not until 1969 that order returned to Indonesia as the new president, Suharto, established his authority. This period of confusion (1965–9) is the second stage in MacAndrews' three-stage evolution of the transmigration programme.

By 1969 Suharto had gained firm control, and his New Order government could resume planning the development of Indonesia. These development objectives have been contained in a series of five year plans – Repelita I (1969/70–1973/74) to Repelita V (1989/90–1993/94) – and within each the transmigration programme has been prominent, aiming to move more migrants with each successive plan (Table 5.2). Although targets have had to be revised, and have even so still occasionally proved to be too ambitious, the period from the beginning of Repelita I to 1987 has been one in which the programme has continuously expanded. During Repelita III (1979/80–1983/84) an average of more than 73 000 families were settled each year, while in the first four years of Repelita IV (1984/85–1988) the figure was more than 146 000 (Table 5.2). As will be discussed in Chapter 8, it was the rise in oil prices and hence revenue during the 1970s that made such an expansion financially feasible (Arndt 1984a, p. 40).

The targets set for Repelita IV envisaged a further growth of the programme to 750 000 families settled over the five-year plan period (Table 5.2). However, the plan failed to anticipate the sharp fall in oil prices in 1986 and the consequent fall in government revenue. The budget allocation to finance the transmigration programme was cut, sharply by 42 per cent in 1986/87, and this, together with increasingly vocal opposition, and growing doubts and criticism on the part of the World Bank, has led to an extensive reappraisal of the programme (Vatikiotis 1987, p. 28). Since

Table 5.2 Transmigration: numbers settled and targets, 1951–88

	Numbers settled (individuals)	
	Total	Per year
1951–5	111 595	22 319
1956–60	134 371	26 874
1961–65	141 844	28 369
1966–68	24 556	8 185

	Numbers settled (families)		Targets (families)			
	Total	Per year	Total (original)	(revised)	Per year (original)	(revised)
Repelita I (1969/70–73/74)	46 100	9 200	40 959	38 141	8 192	7 628
Repelita II (1974/75–78/79)	87 800	17 560	250 000	82 959	50 000	16 592
Repelita III (1979/80–83/84)	365 977	73 195	500 000		100 000	
Repelita IV (1984/85–88)	584 342	146 086	750 000		150 000	

Sources: Suratman & Guinness 1977, p. 83, Arndt 1983b, p. 52, Hardjono 1986, pp. 29, 40, World Bank 1988, p. 15, Hardjono 1988, p. 434.

1987, the scheme has effectively been on hold and emphasis has shifted to the improvement and consolidation of existing settlements rather than further expansion. The reasons why there should have been this apparent reversal, or at least setback, will be discussed at length in the second half of the chapter. There are three elements in the evolution of the programme that need to be reviewed first, however. First, the objectives and rationale underpinning the programme; second, the types or categories of migrant that are selected for settlement; and, third, the location of the settlements themselves.

Objectives and rationale

During the early years of transmigration the principle objectives of the scheme were demographic. The intention was to solve Indonesia's perceived population imbalance and, in particular, the overpopulation of Java (Kebschull 1986, p. 35). Soon after the programme had got under way, however, it became clear that such an objective was entirely unrealistic and at most the rate of increase of Java's population could be only marginally reduced. During the course of Repelita III, when approximately 1.8 million 'general' transmigrants were settled, this represented only 22 per cent of the increase in Java and Bali's population (Hardjono 1986, p. 29, Hugo *et al.* 1987, pp. 42–3).[4] With the recognition that transmigration could not solve Indonesia's population imbalance, so the rationale that underlay the scheme changed. Increasingly, documents stressed regional development, security, food production and general welfare objectives (Kebschull 1986, pp. 35–37, Otten 1986a, pp. 39–44; Hardjono 1988, p. 430). It was hoped that the standard of living of the rural and urban poor of Java would be improved if they were settled in the Outer Islands. At the same time, it was hoped to promote the development of these frontier areas, boosting agricultural, and especially food, production, and helping to unify the country and strengthen national security. Today, transmigration is seen as a means of achieving multiple goals, of which correcting the distribution of the country's population is only one. That said, it remains true that the demographic justification of the programme is deeply rooted and remains attractive among Indonesia's politicians and also within the Ministry of Transmigration (Jones 1979, p. 29). Indeed, Hardjono (1988, p. 433) believes that by Repelita IV 'policies had come full circle, back to the days of the 1950s, when demographic goals had been given top priority'.

Categories of migrant

Transmigrants are grouped into a number of categories. Most important in terms of numbers are *transmigrasi umum* or 'general' transmigrants. These receive full government sponsorship and support: they are transported free-of-charge, are given land (currently between two and five hectares), a house, farming implements and agricultural inputs, and are supported during the first 8 to 12 months with basic rations and a cash allowance. The second category are *transmigrasi spontan* (spontaneous transmigrants) or now, more commonly, *transmigrasi swakarsa* (self-initiative transmigrants). This group consists of both partially assisted and completely unassisted migrants, and due to confusion between the two terms are now referred to as *swakarsa murni* (unassisted) and *swakarsa berbantuan* (partially assisted). Members of this latter subgroup travel independently (although may receive some travel assistance), but receive land, equipment and agricultural inputs upon arrival (Hardjono 1986, pp. 41–3). The third category is *transmigrasi lokal* or 'local' transmigrants. These are families that move within a single transmigration district or island, sometimes from one transmigration site to another (Otten 1986a, pp. 40–1). The great majority of transmigrants are ostensibly voluntary,[5] the exception being those moved because of natural disasters (e.g. the eruption of Mount Galunggung in Java in 1982) or relocated because they have lost their land as a result of dam construction (e.g. Saguling dam in West Java in 1984). Even then, those affected are not always required to move and many opt to stay in the area (Hardjono 1986, pp. 40–1). During the course of the programme the relative importance of spontaneous migrants has gradually grown, the proportion rising from 27 per cent of all transmigrants in Repelita I, to 59 per cent in the first three years of Repelita IV (Table 5.3) (Otten 1986a, p. 124, Hardjono 1986, p. 40, World Bank 1988).

Location of settlements

Another change that has occurred during the course of the programme is in the location of the settlements. At first, as in the Dutch colonization scheme, the transmigration programme concentrated upon developing sites in Sumatra – between 1969 and 1982 approximately 60 per cent of all migrants were settled there (Figures 5.4 and 5.5) (Arndt 1983b, pp. 52–3). However, as suitable sites have become fewer, so other locations have been exploited. First Sulawesi, then Kalimantan and finally, Irian Jaya, as the programme has extended eastwards (Table 5.4; Figure 5.6). In Repelita IV, Irian Jaya and Kalimantan have been targeted to receive 167 739 and 317 255 families respectively (spontaneous plus general transmigrants), 22 per cent

Table 5.3 General and spontaneous transmigrants, 1969–87 (families)

	General	Spontaneous	Percentage spontaneous
Repelita I (1969/70–73/74)	46 100	17 000	27
Repelita II (1974/75–78/79)	87 800	35 000	30
Repelita III (1979/80–83/84)	365 977	169 497	32
Repelita IV (1984/85–end June 1987)	195 750	281 100	59

Sources: Hardjono 1986, pp. 29, 40, Otten 1986a, p. 124, World Bank 1988, p. 15.

Figure 5.4 Ketenong Satu (Ketenong '1') transmigration site showing rice fields surrounded by 'forest reserve' land (photograph: Tim Forsyth)

Figure 5.5 Ketenong Satu (Ketenong '2') transmigration settlement, Bengkulu province, Sumatra (photograph: Tim Forsyth)

Table 5.4 Transmigrants and destination areas, 1969–87

	Sumatra	Kalimantan	Sulawesi	Other		
		(percentages)				
1950–5	86.2	5.7	2.8	5.3		
1956–60	90.4	7.8	1.4	0.4		
1961–5	81.4	14.9	3.5	0.2		
1966–8	62.6	10.8	20.3	6.3		

	Sumatra	Kalimantan	Sulawesi	Irian Jaya	Maluku	Other
			(percentages)			
Repelita I	57.9	14.6	26.3	0.3	0.9	—
(1969/70–73/74)						
Repelita II	59.0	19.4	20.0	1.1	0.2	0.3
(1974/75–78/79)						
Repelita III	62.0	19.3	11.7	4.5	2.1	0.4
(1979/80–83/84)						
Repelita IV	61.1	26.1	9.8	3.1	—	—
(1984/85–end June 1987)						
Repelita IV	27.0	42.3	4.4	22.3	1.9	2.1
(Planned, 1984/85–88/89)						

Sources: Arndt 1983b, pp. 52–3, Hardjono 1986, pp. 26, 31, 42, World Bank 1988, p. 15.

and 42 per cent of the total to be settled during the plan period (Hardjono 1986, p. 45). It should be emphasized that although settlements in Irian Jaya have received the greatest criticism and thus have the highest profile, the province is still relatively unimportant when the programme is viewed as a whole (Figure 5.6). Indeed, during the first three years of Repelita IV only 14 550 families were settled in Irian Jaya, a mere 3 per cent of total transmigrants settled during that period (see Table 5.4). This may change if Irian Jaya, the least populated region in Indonesia, is developed further as an area of settlement.

The process of selection, migration, and settlement

Migrants are selected for transmigration with two objectives in mind. First, they are selected to ensure that the scheme has the maximum effect upon poverty, unemployment, and overcrowding in Java and Bali. Highest priority is given to areas prone to natural disasters or affected by development projects, and areas where population pressure is severe and home and landlessness rife. Secondly, migrants are selected with the rigours of settlement in mind. Officially, the following criteria should be applied (Hardjono 1986, p. 40, Kebschull 1986, p. 42, Guinness 1982, p. 64, Otten 1986a, p. 45):

(a) Migrants should be Indonesian citizens.
(b) They should be voluntary migrants.

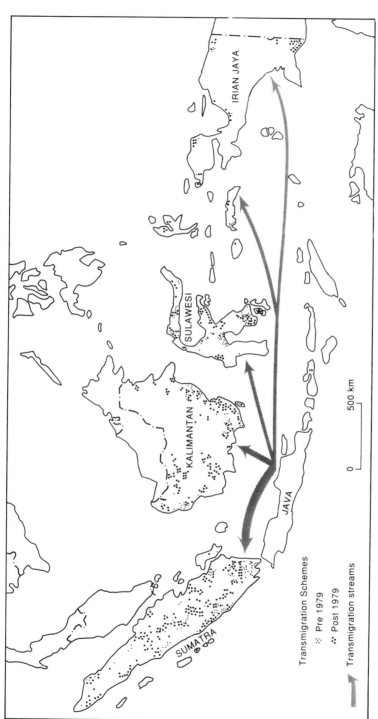

Figure 5.6 Location of transmigration settlements (adapted from World Bank 1988)

(c)   The household head and his family should be in good health.
(d)   The household head should not be younger than 20 nor older than 40 years of age.
(e)   The household head should be legally married.
(f)   The youngest member of the household should not be less than six months old, nor the oldest member more than 60 years.
(g)   The household should not have more than five members.

Other prerequisites are some knowledge of farming or another skill, the absence of a criminal record, the ability to read, adherence to a religion, support for the state philosophy of Pantjasila, and low income.

On selection and registration, migrants may have to wait several months before they are taken to the point of transshipment. Guinness (1982, p. 65) reports that 20 per cent of the transmigrants he questioned had to wait more than six months before they departed. As they were under the impression that they would leave immediately, many had sold their land and other assets and repaid their debts. They therefore had to eat into their savings, which had been intended to support them in their new life in the Outer Islands (Guinness 1982, p. 65). From the point of transshipment, where they may also have to suffer a delay (Suratman & Guinness 1977, pp. 91–2), they are taken, usually by boat but increasingly by plane, to the settlement site (see Figure 5.5). On arrival at the settlement they are allotted a piece of partially cleared land of between two and five hectares, and given a house, agricultural tools and inputs, rations, and other requirements. The settlement should already have schools, health centres, water facilities, and all other social services and the elements of a basic infrastructure. The settlement then proceeds through a number of developmental stages in which land is cleared, food production increased and self-sufficiency achieved, and local institutions (e.g. co-operatives) established and strengthened (see Figure 5.4). After an average of five years, the settlements are released from the control of the Ministry of Transmigration and become independent communities under the overall administration of the local district authorities.

This, then, is the broad framework of the transmigration programme: numbers moved, history, migrant selection and classification, and settlement development. But the scheme has not elicited so much discussion merely because it happens to be the largest voluntary resettlement scheme in the world. There has also been a continuing and heated exchange between the proponents and the critics of the programme, particularly concerning the balance between overall costs and benefits. In 1986, for example, the *Ecologist* magazine published an open letter to the World Bank strongly urging that 'the Bank carefully reviews its present policy of supporting the project . . . [and] take immediate steps to halt funding the programme' (*Ecologist* 1986, p. 60). It is to this debate and the arguments that characterize it, to which this chapter will now turn.

Arndt (1983b) reviews the transmigration programme under three main headings: achievements, problems, and options. This framework will also be used to structure the following analysis (see also Babcock 1986).

Achievements

It is difficult to measure the achievments of the transmigration programme because objectives, and their relative priority have changed over time. The scheme has clealy failed as a solution to Indonesia's population imbalance. It has only been possible to move a fraction of the increase in the population of the metropolitan islands since 1950 and the targets set have often proved, in retrospect, to be unrealistic. Between 1969 and 1984 (Repelitas I–III), approximately 2.5 million general transmigrants settled in the outer islands, while the population of Java and Bali increased by 24 million. Even taking account of spontaneous migrants who have been encouraged to move as a result of the programme,[6] the total number of migrants, sponsored and unsponsored, is still small in comparison to what would be needed to decrease Java's population. Interestingly, since the introduction of Repelita IV in 1984 *transmigrasi swakarsa* have been incorporated into the official transmigration statistics in plotting the achievement of the targets set (Hardjono 1986, World Bank 1988). However, as Jones (1979, p. 212) points out: 'underachievement in relation to unrealistic targets does not necessarily imply failure, and it can be argued that measured against more modest objectives . . . the programme has been moderately successful.' What are these more modest objectives? Three are central to the programme: the promotion of regional and agricultural development, the improvement of migrants' welfare, and securing Indonesia's borders and strategic areas.

Regional and agricultural development

In so far as transmigration has led to the clearance of large areas of forest in the Outer Islands and the extensification of agricultural land, the programme has had the effect of promoting regional and agricultural development. During Repelita III (1979–84), for example, 25 581 kilometres of roads were constructed and 448 696 hectares of land brought into cultivation as part of the scheme (Hardjono 1986, p. 38). Much of this land was, admittedly, of poor quality (an issue that will be discussed shortly), and critics of the scheme note that food production in many settlements has failed to reach planned levels; indeed in some instances the communities are unable to provide for their own needs (Otten 1986a, pp. 133–6, Caufield 1985, p. 197). Moreover, surplus production sometimes cannot be marketed because of infrastructural constraints. These criticisms need to be addressed, but it should also be borne in mind that since many migrants were landless before settlement, the land being cleared in the Outer Islands is a supplement to land in Java, not a replacement for it. Thus any level of production, however small and disappointing, is an addition to total Indonesian output and is a step on the way to food self-sufficiency, a principal policy objective of the New Order government (Arndt 1983b, p. 58, Mears 1984).

Opening up and settling previously unoccupied or sparsely populated areas in order to boost agricultural output are not the only objectives of transmigration. The promotion of industrial development and the exploitation of natural resources have also been integral objectives, with the aim of promoting equitability (*pemerataan*) in spatial terms (Hardjono 1988). On this score however, the evidence is rather less convincing. For in spite of the fact that settlements are now designed as growth poles with larger populations, tree crop estates (see below), oil refineries, and fertilizer plants (Otten 1986a, pp. 29–30), there is little evidence that any process of self-sustaining industrial growth has been set in train through other industries being attracted to the sites. Although there have been some spin-offs, 'the major industrial developments of the past decade in the outer islands, chiefly based on oil and gas, mineral processing and plywood production, have occurred entirely independently [of the transmigration programme]' (Arndt 1983b, p. 59). Whether this will change in the future is a moot point, but Arndt (1983b, p. 58) notes that the programme may have laid the foundations on which the long-term development of the Outer Islands can be based.

The improvement of migrant welfare

The second issue demands an assessment of the success of the scheme in providing transmigrants with a better standard of living. Has it improved their general welfare? Critics argue that since average incomes and conditions in the settlements are similar to those in Java, the effect has merely been to transplant the poverty of Java to the Outer Islands (Otten 1986b, p. 74). For example, a 1985 survey conducted in 110 transmigrant settlements by the Ministry of Transmigration, with the help of the Central Bureau of Statistics, found that average monthly household incomes were 59 000 rupiahs (US$53). Average incomes in areas supplying migrants were then 67 000 rupiahs (US$61) (World Bank 1988, p. 18). Certainly, a handful of sites have failed dismally. Settlers in many areas have had to look for additional work to supplement their incomes, and in some cases migrants have actually abandoned the settlements and returned home, a process known as *remigrasi* (Otten 1986a, p. 105, 1986b, p. 74, Guinness 1982, pp. 68–9). It seems that the government's main emphasis in the 1970s and the early 1980s was 'overwhelmingly on moving people to the outer islands rather than on developing those settlements as viable sites' (Guinness 1982, p. 70) and as a result a considerable number are now in need of further investment and rehabilitation. Moreover, in those settlements established some time ago, so-called 'second generation' problems are beginning to manifest themselves. The growing population of these sites is particularly important since it has caused landholdings to become subdivided into uneconomically small units, and is forcing settlers' children to look elsewhere for work. Overcrowding and landlessness are now so severe in some areas that they themselves have been declared transmigration source areas. Lampung, for example, was so designated in 1986 (Hugo *et al.* 1987, p. 354). Ironically, a different second generation problem is most pronounced in those settlements that are most successful. In these communities, rising aspirations that cannot be met on-site are causing the young to look beyond the settlements for work, encouraging them in some cases to leave altogether and even to return to Java.

But, in spite of these problems, it it important to keep in mind that transmigrant families are not average Javanese families. Before the migration they were the urban and rural poor, without land or work, living at the very margins of subsistence. Indeed, the Ministry of Transmigration and Central Bureau of Statistics survey quoted above showed that whereas virtually all transmigrants were drawn from households living below the poverty line, in the transmigration settlements themselves 'only' 50 per cent were living in poverty. Two-thirds reported that they were better-off than they had been previously (World Bank 1988, p. 20). Even if incomes and welfare reach only the average levels of Java, they may therefore represent a considerable improvement in living standards, and a considerable achievement.

Strategic objectives

The third central objective of the transmigration scheme is the strengthening of national defence and security. To some commentators this objective is of overriding importance and 'explains why the programme is not likely to be abandoned, however damaging it may be' (Budiardjo 1986, p. 111). The settlement of the Papua New Guinea–Irian Jaya border, for example, has helped to secure the area and restrict the movement of secessionist rebels belonging to the Free Papua Movement (OPM) (Colchester 1986b, pp. 102–3),[7] while its is also claimed that the 'colonization' of East Timor ('occupied' by Indonesia since 1975) has been used to undermine resistance by the Revolutionary Front for Independent East Timor (Fretilin). At the same time, the remote Outer Islands have been incorporated more tightly into the Indonesian state, fostering national unity. As the inhabitants of Borneo (Kalimantan), New Guinea (Irian Jaya), and East Timor are racially, linguistically, religiously, and culturally distinct, this process has been termed the 'Javanization' of the Outer Islands (Caufield 1985, pp. 197–8, Pérez-Sainz 1983, p. 201). Critics consider that the government is involved in a process of 'ethnocide' in which local initiative is being suppressed and a nationwide, hierarchical political organization, imposed (Colchester 1986c, p. 92).

The perspective that each writer adopts on the security aspect of the transmigration scheme depends very much upon his or her political and ideological preconceptions. For some, for example Hardjono (1986) and Kebschull (1986), the main analytical concerns are site location, preparation, costs, and other 'non-political' points. Javanization of the Outer Islands is not considered to be particularly insidious, but merely as an attempt to promote national unity. For other analysts, for example Colchester (1986c), the political dimension is paramount.

Two points need to be borne in mind when evaluating the transmigration programme. First, what are the opportunity costs? Could the US$2.3 billion allocated to the programme during Repelita III, and the US$2.6 billion budgeted for in Repelita IV (World Bank 1988, pp. 9–13), have been used to greater overall effect in some other way? The problem with this question is that it inevitably involves costs and benefits that are extremely difficult to quantify, especially for the outsider. What is the value, for example, of securing frontier areas? Foreign researchers and correspondents can scarcely appreciate the 'worth' of such an objective to the Indonesian government. The second point concerns the variability in the success or failure of settlements. Some sites have been unmitigated disasters and settlers have been forced to abandon them (Otten 1986a, pp. 109–13); others (e.g. some in South Sumatra) have suffered from outbreaks of disease and from crop shortfalls, and have been officially classified as 'failures' (Secrett 1986, pp. 81–2). More still have required 'rehabilitation'. Hardjono reports, for example, that 67 village units were identified in 1982/83 as requiring rehabilitation, that is 8 per cent of all units under the responsibility of the Transmigration Bureau at that time (Hardjono 1986, p. 38). In addition, however, to the sites that have suffered from various degrees of failure, there are also prosperous communities (e.g. in Central Sulawesi and South Sumatra) that have done well (Arndt 1983b, p. 57, Hardjono 1986, p. 38). The great variation in the experiences of transmigration settlements is an important reason for the sharply opposing perspectives in the literature.

Problems

Migrant selection, suitability, and preparation

In spite of the fact that the selection of migrants is supposed to follow tight guidelines (as noted previously), so that only families prepared and suited to the harsh life that awaits them are chosen, there have been frequent reports that a significant proportion do not meet the criteria set. One survey conducted in South Sulawesi and South Kalimantan in 1976 revealed that a third of household heads were over 40 years of age on departure, over a third of the families had more than five members, and 41 per cent had never attended school (Guinness 1982, p. 64). Another, more recent survey among transmigrants in East Timor discovered that far from being the 'model' Balinese farmers they were claimed to be, many were 'high school graduates who thought they could get jobs as businessmen or civil servants in East Timor' (Budiardjo 1986, p. 115). The poor performance of some settlements is partly due to the unsuitability of the migrants selected. Those over 40 years of age find it difficult to carry out the arduous work of clearing land; those with families of more than five may discover that their rations are insufficient to meet their needs; while those without agricultural experience require extensive training before they can cultivate their land to its full potential (Suratman & Guinness 1977, p. 91, Guinness 1982, p. 64). Otten (1986a, p. 79) claims that the failure to select suitable candidates is, in turn, 'one of the causes of the failure [as she perceives it] of the transmigration programme'.

If candidates who do not meet the selection criteria are registered for transmigration, then clearly there must be deficiencies in the selection process. It seems that in some areas local officials, forced to meet escalating provincial and *kapupaten* (subdistrict) targets, especially during Repelita III, have been both less selective (Caufield 1985, p. 191) and more 'persuasive' (Arndt 1983b, p. 63). The result is that the settlers often lack the initiative, skills, and enthusiasm to make a success of their new lives. There are also reports that village headmen, wishing to be rid of troublemakers and the poor, have collaborated with local officials to have those undesirables placed on the transmigration register while at the same time discouraging landowners who might wish to migrate from doing so (Suratman & Guinness 1977, p. 90). In spite of these widely reported instances of excessive persuasion and propaganda on the part of those in positions of authority, it still remains true that the supply of voluntary migrants tends to exceed the demand (Arndt 1983b, p. 63). More serious perhaps are the growing number of poor migrants from urban areas who lack the necessary skills and knowledge. To counteract this problem, the preparation of migrants becomes crucial. Here too, however, there have been deficiencies: migrants have received little or no guidance and training, agricultural extension services are sometimes unavailable, and families are forced to learn from one another, rather than from a trained and experienced agent (Kebschull 1986, p. 23, Guinness 1982, p. 65).

Site selection, suitability, and preparation

These issues of selection, suitability, and preparation apply not only to the migrants but also, and equally importantly, to the sites. The selection of suitable sites for transmigration settlements relies on careful and effective survey work. This has often not occurred: the quality of the land has been overrated, sometimes because of the absence of a suitable and accurate data base (Caufield 1985, p. 193); survey work has been cursory so that problems are only identified after the sites have been developed (Suratman & Guinness 1977, p. 90); and analyses have often proved to be inadequate to the task (Secrett 1986, p. 86). The problem is essentially two-sided. On the one hand, the demands of a burgeoning programme have outstripped the ability of the administrative framework to perform satisfactorily. There has been constant pressure to meet targets and partly as a result the scheme has fallen into a 'plan-as-you-proceed' approach (Hardjono 1986, p. 33). This is not conducive to effective survey work. On the other hand, and in opposition to the need to establish more and more settlements, it is becoming increasingly clear that there is a shortage of suitable sites.

That there should be a shortage of sites when Indonesia's Outer Islands are so sparsely settled may seem contradictory, but it is at the heart of the problems currently afflicting the programme. For the image of Indonesia as a nation with virtually limitless resources of land – an image that Sukarno, among others, fostered – is a false one:

The basic reality, that large tracts of good land are no longer available, is reflected in the fact that one expatriate firm of consultants carrying out feasibility studies in southern Sumatra had a rejection rate of 80%

of all sites proposed by local provincial authorities for transmigration projects during Repelita III (Hardjono 1986, p. 34).

The absence of good agricultural land in the Outer Islands means that transmigration sites are now being established in areas that are increasingly marginal. The red–yellow podzolic soils that characterize much of the remaining forested areas are infertile, and quickly degrade if the land is cleared and subjected to annual cropping. The indigenous inhabitants have always recognized this fact and cultivate the land using various forms of shifting cultivation (or swiddening) in which small areas of forest are partially cleared, cultivated for a few years, and then left to regenerate (see Chapter 4). In addition to the generally poor soils of the Outer Islands, other limitations include large areas of *alang-alang* (*Imperata cylindrica*) which are notoriously hard to clear and cultivate (Donner 1987, pp. 218–25) and also the growing shortage of flatlands, which has forced settlements onto hillsides where steep gradients promote soil erosion. Recognizing the problems inherent in developing the remaining forested areas in Indonesia, during Repelita III the authorities increasingly turned their attention to the large areas of swampland in Sumatra and Kalimantan, intending to convert them into ricelands. These cover more than 10 million hectares (Hanson 1981, p. 226), but once again the image of limitless agricultural land waiting to be developed is somewhat removed from reality:

> the accumulating information on soils and existing landuse patterns suggests that only a very small fraction is likely to have potential for rice cultivation. Thus an expansion of ricefields onto at most, one million hectares, may be an eventual upper limit to development (Hanson 1981, p. 26).

Even Hanson's estimate now seems to be over-optimistic. Hardjono reports that 'most' of the Repelita III *pasang-surut* settlements (tidal swamplands) are experiencing difficulties, in particular because of marginal swamp soils and sea-water infiltration, and in spite of the fact that during Repelita IV 400 000 hectares of such land was due to be developed this has not been achieved (see Hardjono 1986, p. 47, Abdoellah 1987).

The selection of poor sites for transmigration settlements is therefore a reflection of inadequate survey work compounded by the simple truth that good sites are becoming increasingly scarce. In addition, there has also been the problem of poor site preparation. Land has been cleared using heavy earth-moving equipment, thereby aggravating problems of erosion by destroying the top soil (Hardjono 1986, p. 35). In some cases, contractors, partly due to inexperience, but also because of the need to meet deadlines and keep costs to a minimum, have only partially cleared the land (Otten 1986a, pp. 89–92). And there have been frequent complaints that migrants have either arrived to find their settlements incomplete (Caufield 1985, p. 192) or, occasionally, completed for so long that 'the roofs . . . were rotting and the houses hidden in thick undergrowth' (Guinness 1982,

p. 65). Moreover, processing facilities have sometimes been lacking, social services inadequate, and infrastructure poorly developed (Otten 1986b, pp. 71–72, Pérez-Sainz 1983, p. 204).

Agricultural problems

As the economic mainstay of the settlements is agriculture, this needs special attention, for if agriculture fails or performs below expectations, then the settlements fail. A widespread problem with many of the earlier settlements was that a single farming system, wet rice cultivation, was promoted, ignoring the variations in conditions that exist between Java and the Outer Islands, and between different areas within the Outer Islands. The programme was apparently trying to recreate the Javanese wet rice based farming system, irrespective of the ecological realities of the Outer Islands. Furthermore, until the 1970s the quantity of land allotted, in addition to the use of that land, was fixed at two hectares per family (Arndt 1983b, pp. 61–2). Given that transmigration settlements have been established in areas of fire-disturbed upland grassland, upland forest, lowland forest, and swamp forest, it is perhaps hardly surprising that in many areas the Javanese wet rice system should have performed below expectations when such a rigid planning framework has been imposed. Studies have shown that the red–yellow podzolic soils that dominate the Outer Islands cannot support intensive wet rice agriculture. They are generally too infertile and deteriorate rapidly under continuous cultivation (Perry 1985, Hardjono 1986, p. 34, Arndt 1983b, p. 60, Donner 1987, pp. 249–62). Aggarwala reports a settler at Rimbo Bujang, West Sumatra as saying: 'The first year we moved here in 1979 we got seven tons of rice from two and a half hectares of land. This year [1983?], I would be lucky to get three tons despite the use of fertilizers' (Aggarwala 1984, p. 75). Other problems include difficulties in clearing the land, deficiencies in, or absence of, irrigation systems, inappropriate technology, and lack of training and advice (Guinness 1982, p. 66, Kebschull 1986, p. 26, Oey 1982, p. 37). The inadequacies of agriculture in the settlements have had the effect of forcing settlers to look for work elsewhere. Sometimes this is in the vicinity of the sites, but there have also been reports that transmigrants have had to travel great distances in the search for work (Otten 1986a, pp. 105–7, Abdoellah 1987, pp. 83–6), a process that the transmigration programme has been in part designed to halt.

During Repelita II, the recognition that the system based on wet rice was inappropriate to many areas in the Outer Islands led to the establishment of settlements based on tree crop agriculture and on dryland farming. In addition, where land was less fertile and suited to more extensive systems of cultivation, the allocation of land was increased considerably, to four to five hectares per family (Hardjono 1986, p. 34). The development of tree crop estates in the Outer Islands began in the early 1970s with World Bank support and although initially they were planned for local settlers, they have gradually become increasingly oriented towards the transmigration pro-gramme (Arndt 1983b, p. 62). The most recent form of tree crop-based settlements are the so-called Smallholder Nuclear Estates (or PIR – *Perkebunan Inti Rakyat* – People's Nucleus Estate) the first of which was established in 1981 (Hardjono 1986, p. 47). As the name suggests, at the core of each settlement is a commercially run plantation that provides guidance and processing and marketing facilities to the smallholders that surround it. The PIR programme is an attempt to marry the economic and managerial advantages of a large commercially run plantation with the social and political attractions of smallholder production. The system provides transmigrants with a cash income and also the means to meet their own consumption needs (a portion of the land is planted to food crops). Further, because perennial tree crops more closely mirror the natural ecosystem, erosion and fertility loss are kept to a minimum. Like the Smallholder Nuclear Estate programme, the dryland farming model with larger plots (up to five hectares) allotted to each family also represents an attempt to promote an agricultural system that is more in tune with environmental conditions in the Outer Islands. But although both models represent an advance on the transplanted Javanese wet rice system, there still remain enormous difficulties in promoting agriculture which is both productive and viable in the long term.

The low inherent fertility of many sites and their susceptibility to erosion continues to retard progress and there remains the simple fact that there are now few suitable areas of unoccupied land left to be settled. Hardjono (1986, pp. 32–3) catalogues the types of conditions that migrants face: 'barren soil full of stones . . . soils less than 10 cm in depth . . . swamp soils that cannot be used for farming . . . heavily dissected terrain where erosion is already advanced . . . poor drainage', and so on. Environmental constraints are not the only problems, however. The location of settlements in remote areas and the failure to construct sufficient roads and other means of communication has meant that even when settlements have been fairly vibrant agriculturally, and have produced a surplus for sale, the marketing of this surplus has been difficult, if not impossible, especially during the wet season (Hardjono 1986, pp. 37–8, Perry 1985, pp. 109–11, Abdoellah 1987, pp. 78–80). Processing facilities have also often proved to be inadequate, while transport limitations have made the supply of inputs, as well as the marketing of output, difficult and intermittent (Perry 1985, pp. 109–11, Kebschull 1986, p. 27). Poor transport facilities are a further reflection of the paucity of suitable sites, for as these become fewer, so the authorities are forced to establish transmigration settlements in increasingly remote locations.

Finally on this issue of agricultural problems, special mention needs to be made of the difficulties currently facing the development of coastal swamplands. These areas have been specifically targeted in Repelitas III and IV and it is clear that the difficulties of development have generally been underestimated. As Caufield notes (1985, p. 200), 'swamps are among the least well-understood ecosystems for agriculture', and many of the proposed sites in Kalimantan, Riau, Jambi, and South Sumatra have proved to be unsuitable for rice farming (Figure 5.1). The location of such tidal settlements in inaccessible coastal areas also means that communications, and hence supply and marketing, are also made more difficult (Hardjono 1986, p. 33).

Conflicts with indigenous groups and the demands of conservation

It has already been noted that the Outer Islands contain far fewer suitable locations for settlement than was originally thought. In addition, of those that have been identified, however, many are far from being unoccupied and 'free' for development, being already in use by indigenous peoples. These claim customary title to land through *adat* law and communal ownership through the *marga* (clan). In the past, the lack of legal records and the imprecise nature of ownership – as well as a lack of regard for the rights of indigenous groups on the part of the authorities – has meant that such claims have not always been honoured and transmigration settlements have been sited on land that is already in use as part of a system of shifting cultivation (Arndt 1983b, pp. 60–1, Colchester 1986b, pp. 100–6, Monbiot 1989).

The problems of identifying 'unoccupied' land, and also in distinguishing between 'unoccupied' and 'unclaimed', are clear in the literature. Hardjono (1986, p. 46), for example, maintains that: transmigration 'does not involve the taking of land from local people but rather the utilization of unoccupied land for sedentary agriculture'. Conversely, Colchester (1986, p. 100) argues that: 'the idea that there are vast areas of unclaimed lands available for settlers is completely false'. 'In fact', he continues, 'it is possible to find examples of the fact that *all* [emphasis in original] land is owned, throughout Melanesia as a whole'. Not only is land utilization and landownership often hard to gauge and to define,[8] but land law in Indonesia is also somewhat unclear as to the status of *adat* law. The 1960 Basic Agrarian Law recognizes existing *adat* law, but only 'as far as it is not adversary to the interests of the nation and state' (quoted in Colchester 1986b, p. 104, see also Oey 1982, p. 42–4). As transmigration is a national policy, it may be argued that the establishment of settlements is indeed in the interests of the nation and state.

The failure to recognize traditional forms of land ownership, to provide adequate compensation, or to be sensitive to the needs and feelings of indigenous peoples has sometimes led to conflict, and even to murder (Otten 1986a, pp. 147–50, Colchester 1986b, p. 109). However, pressure from the World Bank and from groups both within and outside Indonesia, and better management of the programme, has meant that conflicts between transmigrants and local inhabitants are less common today (Hardjono 1986, p. 39). More care is taken over site selection and the delimitation of project boundaries, and local groups are encouraged to take an active part in the settlements. Since 1982, places in settlements have been reserved for locals as part of the APPDT quota (*Alokasi Pemukiman Penduduk Daerah Transmigrasi* or Resettlement Allocation for Inhabitants of a Transmigration Region) and from 20 per cent to 25 per cent of settlement land is now allocated to them (Budiardjo 1986, p. 113, Hardjono 1986, p. 39, Manning, 1987c, p. 43). In addition, schools, health centres, and other services are now open to the local inhabitants; the fact that in the past they were not was a source of some resentment (Suratman & Guinness 1977, p. 98). Even with these advances, however, the perception remains that 'the major share of benefits from the larger government presence [in terms of roads, education etc] has gone to newcomers' (Manning 1987a, p. 41). The development strategy that has been adopted is set in a Javanese framework, with little attention paid to the special conditions that apply to the Outer Islands, and particularly to Irian Jaya and Kalimantan (see Vatikiotis 1989).

To critics of the transmigration programme, these attempts at integration are not as desirable as they might appear to be, for at their core they are felt to have nothing less than an 'ethnocidal' intent (e.g. Colchester 1986a, p. 68). The charge is that they aim to destroy the identity of the ethnically distinct groups in the Outer Islands and to subsume them within a unitary Indonesian state. It is no doubt true that at times the authorities have been rather heavy-handed in their dealings with local peoples, but to see behind every trannsmigration policy directive some insidious attempt at ethnocide is taking tthese fears to extremes. That said, with the intention in Repelita IV to target increasingly Kalimantan and Irian Jaya – the two islands that are furthest removed in cultural terms from Java – the implementing bodies have had to be even more aware of the sensitivities of the local inhabitants and to take account of them in the planning, construction and management of sites. It is notable that the Repelita IV target to settle 167 739 families (approximately 840 000 people) in Irian Jaya[9] already seems an impossibiility. In the first three years of the plan period, only 14 550 families were settled in the province, and this is a reflection of the heightened awareness of the authorities to the special status of Irian Jaya (see Arndt 1986 on transmigration to Irian Jaya).

Linked to this question of ethnic relations is the associated issue of tropical forest conservation. The opening-up and settlement of the Outer Islands has inevitably led to the clearance of large areas of tropical moist forest, one of the world's most diverse and valuable ecosystems. Until recently, forest conservation came fairly low on the Indonesian government's list of priorities and, as a result, environmental concerns have received little attention (Secrett 1986, p. 85). But pressure from the World Bank and others, and a growing appreciation within the administration that the country's forests are a valuable resource have led to a growing concern with conservation in official circles. In 1979, President Suharto banned the clearance of primary tropical rainforest for transmigration settlements, and although this ban has not always been respected there is a discernible move in the direction of paying greater heed to the demands of conservation (Caufield 1985, p. 190, Secrett 1986, p. 80). Nevertheless, it should always be borne in mind that when the welfare of Indonesians and the security of the state are at issue, these factors inevitably override all other considerations.

Problems of management and administration

With a programme as large and complex as the transmigration scheme, involving the co-ordination of government departments and ministries ranging from agriculture to health and public works, it is clearly important that the management of the programme should be efficient. An indication that this has not always been the case is the succession of changes that have occurred in the administrative structure and focus of the scheme. Between 1974 and 1984, for example, the status of the overall co-ordinating body changed on no less than five occasions. During Repelita I there existed a Department of Transmigration; during Repelita II a directorate-general responsible for transmigration was created and the programme was administered from within the Department of Manpower, Transmigration and Cooperatives; in 1978 a junior minister of transmigration was appointed and project implementation was transferred to individual departments; and in March 1983, for the first time, the directorate-general became a department in its own right (Arndt 1983b, pp. 64–5, Hardjono 1986, pp. 49–50). Finally, just prior to Repelita IV, a Ministry of Transmigration was created to administer the programme (World Bank 1988, p. 13).

The effects of poor general administration can be seen in virtually all aspects of the scheme. As Arndt (1983b, p. 64) notes, 'a recurring theme in every report . . . is failure or breakdown due to administrative weakness in some part or other of the huge and complex bureaucracy [nearly 10 000 officials] involved in the programme'. This extends from the failure of crop intensification efforts (MacAndrews 1978, p. 467) to delays in the transfer of migrants after registration (Oey 1982, p. 40). The administrative weaknesses have been further compounded and accentuated by corruption within the relevant bodies. However, given the size and complexity of the programme, it might be argued that the most remarkable fact is not that such problems should have arisen, but that even with these problems the co-ordinating bodies should still have managed to settle such large numbers of migrants. This is no mean organizational achievement.

Options

At the core of the transmigration programme is an implicit, and sometimes explicit, assumption that Indonesia suffers from an imbalance in the distribution of its population. Although the reduction of Java's population is no longer the central objective of the scheme, the settlement of the 'underpopulated' and 'underutilized' Outer Islands is. However, it should be clear from the preceding discussion that the imbalance is more apparent than real. The Outer Islands are generally infertile and there are few areas that can be successfully developed agriculturally. The failure of the authorities to appreciate this fact is reflected in the number of settlements that are performing below expectations, are in need of rehabilitation, or have been abandoned.

However, a lack of suitable sites is not the only reason why the programme is likely to be entering a period of contraction. The costs of settlement have continually risen as more remote areas have had to be exploited and as the limitations of existing settlements have encouraged the authorities to invest more funds in site identification, planning, preparation, management and maintenance. Costs per family have risen from approximately US$600 in 1970 to between US$5000 and US$8000 by 1985 for food crop-based settlements (the difference in cost relating to the remoteness of the site) (World Bank 1988, p. 42). And for some types of settlement, for example, the Smallholder Nuclear Estates, costs per family are even higher, ranging from US$7900 to US$9200 (World Bank 1988, p. 61, and see Arndt 1983b, pp. 62, 66). These ever-rising real unit costs have to be set against falling oil revenues which have put a ceiling on the funds available for the programme. The transmigration budget for 1986/87 was cut by 42 per cent over the previous year and as a result the settlement targets also had to be reduced, from 100 000 to 36 000 families (Vatikiotis 1987, p. 28, Hugo *et al.* 1987, p. 353). In fact, the Ministry of Transmigration has been reported as saying that only 2000–3000 families would be moved in 1987 and no new sites developed (Vatikiotis 1987, p. 28).

The two issues of forest conservation and conflicts with indigenous groups, despite their high profile in the international press, are very much of secondary importance when set against the financial constraints that the programme currently faces and the shortage of suitable sites. Nonetheless, pressure from conservation and human rights groups has made an impression on the Indonesian government and, perhaps more significantly, on the World Bank, and this has also helped to reduce the rate of transmigration both directly and indirectly through, for example, raising costs.

What then are the options open to the authorities? to begin with, and this is clear in the decisions taken since the mid-1980s, the programme will concentrate not on establishing new settlements but on the consolidation and, where necessary, rehabilitation, of existing settlements and the improvement of settler welfare (Hardjono 1986, pp. 51–2, Hugo *et al.*1987, p. 319, Vatikiotis 1987, p. 28). In addition, increasing attention is being paid to spontaneous settlers and the promotion of 'chain' migration in which relatives and friends of transmigrants move to the settlements. This is for two reasons. First, cost: spontaneous settlers, for obvious reasons, demand financially less of the authorities. And, secondly, there is evidence that such spontaneous settlers are also more successful (Otten 1986a, pp. 34–36, Hardjono 1986, p. 44). As Guinness (1982, p. 71) notes in his case study conducted in Binuang, South Kalimantan:

> The settlements of spontaneous settlers are a lesson for transmigration planners. Personal links with established settlers provided the new-comers with a basic knowledge and security, and with their high motivation and independence they discovered ways to succeed in the virgin areas.

But although it is in these two directions that the scheme currently seems to be moving – towards a consolidation of existing settlements and greater reliance on spontaneous migrants – the key to improving conditions in Java does not lie in the Outer Islands, but in Java itself. Too many studies of transmigration examine the programme in isolation, divorced from other developments and opportunities in the Indonesian economy, and as a result present a rather myopic view of the problems currently facing the scheme, and the solution to those problems. Given that the Outer Islands cannot easily absorb Java's surplus population, it is necessary to assess what possibilities exist within Java.

In the agricultural sector the potential for growth is limited, although perhaps not as limited as commonly perceived. The frontiers of farmland expansion were reached in the 1960s (Booth 1985, p. 121) and yields in many areas are already high. Nonetheless, the Green Revolution in Java has not reached its limits and there is still room for a further intensification of production through increasing the cropping ratio (i.e. the number of crops per year on a given piece of land) and raising yields (Booth 1985, 1988). In addition, rural incomes have been boosted through an expansion in off-farm employment opportunities, and this diversification of the rural economy will continue to absorb labour and help to meet the growing pressure of needs in the countryside. 'Rural economic strategy,' Hugo *et al.* (1987, p. 359) argue, 'should focus on the development of such activities [fishing, trading, the manufacture of tiles, bricks, footwear, mats, etc.] through increased capitalization and technical assistance'.

Even with greater dynamism in agriculture and in rural non-agricultural activities, the countryside will still not be able to absorb fully Java's expanding labour force, and the urban industrial sector will need to provide the additional employment opportunities. The rate of rural–urban migration and the growth of Java's cities already indicate the ability of urban centres to absorb surplus rural labour. Between 1971 and 1980, Java's annual urban growth rate averaged 3.7 per cent per year and, more to the point, urban employment grew by 6.2 per cent per year as against 1.1 per cent in rural areas in Java (Hugo *et al.* 1987, pp. 94–9). This rapid rate of expansion of urban areas has actually accelerated since 1980, with the annual rate of urban population growth averaging 5.0 per cent between 1980 and 1987 (World Bank 1989). Admittedly, many of the jobs created in urban areas are poorly paid and conditions for migrants from rural areas are unsatisfactory, but it is the urban-industrial sector in which the greatest potential for labour absorption lies. As Hugo *et al.* (1987, p. 354) note, 'urbanization is not a prospect to be feared'. Finally, and in the long term, the key to the population issue must lie in the success of Indonesia's family planning programme[10] and in the reduction of population growth rates.

Notes to Chapter 5

1   That said, the widely held belief that all of Java is highly fertile is simply untrue. The basic, azonal, volcanic soils are concentrated in eastern Java.
2   For more detailed accounts of the Dutch colonization programme see: Pelzer 1983, Mantra 1985, Suratman and Guinness 1977, Otten 1986a, and Pérez-Sainz 1983.
3   In fact the effective budget allocation has been even higher, as this does not include the added costs of providing schooling, health facilities, and other services in remote areas such as Kalimantan and Irian Jaya.
4   In fact the transmigration figures cover the years 1979/80–1983/84 while the population figures are for the years 1980 and 1985. The increase in population

between 1980 and 1985 was 8.4 million (excluding those transmigrants who left the island between those years).

5 Some researchers disagree with the use of the term 'voluntary' to describe the scheme, arguing that a significant proportion are settled against their will (e.g. Otten 1986a, pp. 63–71).

6 This assumes that there is a causal connection between the programme and the rate of spontaneous migration. No doubt, a portion would have moved even had the scheme not existed (see Arndt 1983b, pp. 54–5, Hardjono 1986, pp. 42–3).

7 Also see Otten (1986a, pp. 203–12) and Budiardjo (1986, pp. 115–16) on the 'colonization' of East Timor which was occupied by Indonesia in 1975.

8 Land rights and land utilization are not the same. Colchester (1986b, p. 100) notes that land rights in the Outer Islands 'extend far beyond the areas actually used for swidden agriculture; they include the areas of swamp and virgin forest which are used for hunting, collecting wild produce, and as a reserve for future swidden sites'.

9 The accusations of ethnocide are often based upon the Repelita IV targets. The intention to settle over 800 000 transmigrants in Irian Jaya during the plan period would have considerably 'diluted' the local population, which in 1985 numbered only 1.357 million (Hugo *et al.* 1987, pp. 42–3).

10 Recent evidence indicates that the government target – to reduce fertility by 50 per cent by 1990 – is on course to being met. Indonesia's total fertility rate declined at an annual rate of 2.4 per cent between 1969 and 1980; and at 5.4 per cent between 1980 and 1985 (Hull & Dasvarma 1988, p. 119).

6
Immigrant communities and plural societies: the New Economic Policy and the Chinese in Malaysia

Introduction: plural societies and the Chinese in Southeast Asia

All the countries of Southeast Asia are plural societies. This usage of plural was coined by Furnivall in 1948 with reference to the Netherlands Indies (now Indonesia) and Burma to describe the 'medley' of peoples that lived there. He noted that they are:

> in the strictest sense a medley, for they mix but do not combine. Each group holds by its own religion, its own culture and language, its own ideas and ways. As individuals they meet, but only in the market–place, in buying and selling. There is a plural society, with different sections of the community living side by side, but separately, within the same political unit. Even in the economic sphere there is a division of labour along racial lines (Furnivall 1948, p. 304 and see Furnivall 1980).

Although the term plural is in no sense ethnically specific, in the case of Southeast Asia it has often come to be principally associated with the relations that exist between the ethnic Chinese and the indigenous population. For the Chinese are both the most numerous minority group and the most successful, and they form an element in the population of every country in the region (Table 6.1). This ranges from 76 per cent in Singapore, which is in effect a Chinese city state, to 31 per cent in Malaysia, to a low of 1.5 per cent in the Philippines. Overall, the Chinese make up some 6 per cent to 8 per cent of the region's population. However, it should be stressed that these figures are only rough estimates and there exist considerable difficulties in measuring accurately the numbers of Chinese in Southeast Asia. This is clear, for example, in the case of Thailand, for which various authors for the years between 1955 and 1962 have provided estimates of the proportion of the total population who are Chinese ranging from 8.7 per cent to 15 per cent (Table 6.2).

This is principally because plurality is not absolute. Through the course of time, the Chinese and other ethnic groups have settled in the region and have been variously assimilated into the local cultures. In Thailand, many Chinese have married ethnic T'ais, taken Thai names, adopted Thai

Table 6.1 The Chinese in Southeast Asia

	Number of Chinese	Percentage of total population	Date	Source
Singapore	2 038 000	75.9	1989	Department of Statistics 1989, p. 3
Malaysia	4 882 300	30.9	1985	Government of Malaysia 1986, p. 129
Indonesia	4 116 000	2.8	1980	Suryadinata 1985b, p. 16
Thailand	3 500 000	8.5	1974	Limlingan 1986, p. 3
	6 000 000	13.0	1980	Asia Yearbook 1981
Philippines	699 000	1.5	1981	Suryadinata 1985a, p. 6
Brunei	54 150	25.4	1980	Asia Yearbook 1981
ASEAN	16 939 170	6.6	1981	Suryadinata 1985a, p. 6

Table 6.2 Estimates of the Chinese population of Thailand

Date	Number of Chinese	Total population	Percentage Chinese	Source
1955	2 315 000	20 480 000	11.3	Skinner 1957, p. 183
1956	3 000 000	20 000 000	15	Fisher 1966, p. 181
1960	2 670 000	26 257 911	10.2	Purcell 1965, p. 3
1962	2 500 000	28 800 000	8.7	Hunter 1966, p. 15

citizenship, embraced Theravada Buddhism, and have been fully absorbed into Thai society. The same is also true of many Chinese in the Philippines (Osborne 1979, pp. 97–8). The Babas or Peranakan Chinese of Malacca, meanwhile, have evolved a culture that is a synthesis of Chinese and Malay elements, and is distinctive in terms of language, dress, food, mannerisms, and habits (Clammer 1986, p. 57). As a result, there exists a sharp distinction between the Babas, the Malays, and the Orang Cina (non–Baba Chinese), who tend to regard the Babas as inferior. The Orang Cina, in both Malaysia and Indonesia, have tended to preserve their ethnic identity, partly because most are fairly recent immigrants – arriving in the late 19th and early 20th centuries – and partly because intermarriage and assimilation into a Muslim society pose greater problems than does such absorbtion into a Buddhist society (Tan Chee Beng 1984). Not only does the degree of assimilation and acculturation, and hence plurality, vary, but even on arrival in Southeast Asia the Chinese were hardly the homogeneous ethnic group they are commonly perceived to be. In Malaysia, the Chinese community comprises a number of linguistic and provincial groups, including, among others, Chaozhou, Fujian, Guangdong, Hainan, Kejia, Fuzhou, and Guangxi (Tan Chee Beng 1987, p. 102, Daud 1985, p. 125). However, although the Chinese in Southeast Asia are far from being ethnically monolithic, the reaction of governments in the region to them has often been in a similar vein and taken a similar course. This reaction could be summed up in two terms, 'economic nationalism' and 'political discrimination', and it has grown out of the dominant position that the Chinese are perceived to enjoy in certain economic activities and, in particular, in trade and commerce.

Why the Chinese should fill these two economic niches, and with such success, is an area of considerable and continuing debate in which there has always been a tendency to draw upon cultural stereotypes. Lim, in her assessment of Chinese economic activity in Southeast Asia, highlights the position of the Chinese as recent immigrants. She notes that they rarely had access to land and in most cases were intending to return to their homeland after having made their fortunes. As a result, they were reluctant to invest their savings in enterprises with a long lead time and preferred to enter into activities in which capital could be kept liquid and profits could be rapidly accrued. Trading was the obvious answer and in this way, 'Chinese dominance in exchange activities evolved as the obverse of indigenous dominance of [primary] production.' (Lim 1983b, pp. 2–3). The reasons used to explain the success of the Chinese in the region include their high motivation (which is linked to their status as migrants), their Confucian work ethic and business acumen, and the role of Chinese business networks.

The position of the Chinese as middlemen in Southeast Asia – to the extent that the very word middleman has become synonymous with 'Chinese' – has given the Chinese great visibility and also opened them up to charges of exploitation. In Thailand in 1914 King Rama VI (1910–25) under the *nom de plume* Atsawaphaahu, wrote an essay entitled 'The Jews of the East' in which he accused the Chinese of being unpatriotic and unethical. Subsequently, there have been numerous attempts, particularly following the revolution of 1932, to control Chinese economic activity (Rigg 1986b, pp. 68–69). In Indonesia the Chinese were prohibited in 1959 from involvement in the retail business in rural areas (Lee Yong Leng 1982, p. 130; Suryadinata 1985b, p. 22), while in the Philippines the Retail Trade Nationalization Act of 1954 similarly restricted Chinese participation (Lee Yong Leng 1982, p. 127). The Chinese have been discriminated against politically as well as economically. There remains an enduring distrust of them that is founded on the belief that their political and cultural allegiances still lie with their motherland rather than with their adopted lands. It is significant, for example, that the government of the Republic of China (Taiwan) still maintains seats for overseas Chinese in its National Assembly. The Chinese in the region are felt to represent a security risk, a potential fifth column, and as a result they have had to deal with periods of persecution and have often found it difficult to secure citizenship and other rights accorded to the indigenous population (see Suryadinata 1985b, pp. 17–19, Coppel 1980, Lee Yong Leng 1982). At times of particularly severe intercommunal tension, this latent distrust has escalated into violence. In 1965, after the abortive coup d'état by the Partai Komunis Indonesia (PKI, the Indonesian Communist Party) which was thought to have been inspired and supported by the People's Republic of China, considerable numbers of Chinese were killed, with estimates ranging from several hundreds to several hundreds of thousands (Coppel 1983, p. 58).

Malaysia is the most glaring example of pluralism in the region. Almost 31 per cent of the population are Chinese, and a further 8 per cent, Indian (Government of Malaysia 1986, p. 129). In addition, assimilation is slight and the Chinese are perceived by the Malays to enjoy a dominant position in the economy. However, before turning to discuss the case of the Chinese in Malaysia in detail, it is necessary to review briefly the historical background to their presence in the region as a whole.

The Chinese in Southeast Asia: historical background

Although the large-scale immigration of Chinese to Southeast Asia is a relatively recent phenomenon dating from the second half of the 19th century, contacts between China and the region can be traced back to well before the 1st century BC. Nevertheless, the overall impact of the Chinese during this early perriod was superficial. Few established themselves in the region, much of the trade was carried by Arab and Indian seafarers, and the influence of Chinese culturee, religion, and politics was minimal. In the 5th century AD, however, the Jin dynasty in China lost access to the central Asian caravan routes which brought luxury goods from the West. In response, maritime trading routes through the Southeast Asian archipelago were developed and ports, depots, and commercial centres in southern Sumatra, northwestern Java, and southwestern Borneo all grew in significance (Hall 1985, pp. 39–41). Tribute-bearing missions from the states of Southeast Asia to the Chinese court became more common and the settlement of Chinese in the region increased as it grew in commercial importance. In turn, the cultural impact of China became more pronounced: Chinese medical theory, technology, cloth, games, music, and calligraphy were all assimilated to a greater or lesser degree (Reid 1988). The Chinese diplomat Chou Ta-kuan, who visited the city of Angkor (Cambodia) in 1296, noted in his journal the large number of his countrymen who had arrived in the city, often as sailors, and had then married local women, become involved in commerce and were gradually being absorbed into the social fabric of the kingdom:

The Chinese who follow the sea as a profession take advantage of their being in this country to dispense with wearing clothes. Rice is easy to obtain, women are easy to find, the houses are easy to run, personal property is easy to come by, commerce is easy to engage in. Thus there are constantly those who direct themselves towards this country (quoted in Purcell 1965, p. 14).

Elsewhere, the degree of assimilation was often not as pronounced. In Malacca, for example, members of the Chinese, Arab, and Indian communities generally maintained their ethnic distinctiveness, possibly because they saw themselves as temporary visitors who would be returning home.

Although the presence of the Chinese in Southeast Asia can be traced back many years, it was not until the European powers colonized the region that favourable conditions for large-scale immigration arose. The primary stimulus was economic. The southeastern Chinese provinces of Guangdong, Fujian, and Guangxi, from where the great majority of the migrants originated, were overpopulated and fraught with internal strife, encouraging people to look for opportunities elsewhere. At the same time, the colonial authorities were finding it difficult to recruit the necessary cheap labour to manage and run their possessions. In addition, as a result of the growing contact between China and Europe, communications between Chinese ports such as Fuzhou and Guangzhou and Southeast Asia were significantly improved, providing the means by which potential labourers could reach the region. The irony, as Fisher (1966, p. 179) has pointed out, is that just at the time when emigration of Chinese to Southeast Asia was growing, so the European powers were undermining Imperial China's influence in the region.

The role of the colonial authorities in this massive immigration of Chinese – reaching up to 150 000 annually in the case of Singapore in the 1890s (Yip Yat Hoong 1969, p. 68) – varied from the case of the British in Malaya where migration was actively encouraged, to the Americans in the Philippines, which came under US immigration laws and where consequently numbers were restricted. In general, the colonial governments were happy to see the Chinese filling the economic roles that had been spurned by the indigenous population and placed few obstacles in their way, at least up until the Depression of the 1930s.

The Chinese in Malaysia

Colonial origins and development

Although the origins of the Chinese in Malaysia are pre-colonial, the degree of pluralism that exists today – some 31 per cent of the population are officially classified as Chinese, 8 per cent Indian, 60 per cent Bumiputra[1] or 'indigenous' and 1 per cent 'other' (Government of Malaysia 1986, p. 129) – is a product of the colonial period and in particular the last decades of the 19th and the first of the 20th century. The expansion of the tin industry on the west coast of the Peninsula from the 1850s, the growth of Singapore and Penang into thriving entrepôts, and the development of rubber estates at the beginning of the 20th century led to a considerable demand for cheap labour that could not be satisfied domestically. Initially, the immigration of Chinese was voluntary and unassisted, but as the demand for labour rose, so the so-called credit-ticket system came into force in which a 'Chinese coolie-broker would pay the expenses of the immigrant but would hold him on arrival in the Straits settlements (Singapore, Malacca and Penang) until the debt so incurred was paid off by an employer in exchange for a lien on the immigrant's services for a specific period' (Yip Yat Hoong 1969, p. 71). Conditions in the coolie ships were often appalling, and suicide and mutiny were common (Gullick 1981, pp. 52–3, Purcell 1965, pp. 286–9). Even on arrival, conditions of work could be extremely hazardous and death rates were high. In the tin mines, for example, the death rate among miners sometimes reached 50 per cent (Yip Yat Hoong 1969). The scale of immigration that the British encouraged was such that between 1909 and 1940 some 16 million Chinese and Indians arrived in Malaya (Abraham 1986, p. 8). As early as 1911, the Chinese population of the Federated Malay States (Perak, Selangor, Negeri Sembilan, and Pahang) as well as in the Straits Settlements exceeded that of Malays (Sidhu & Jones 1981, p. 3). In short, the entire demographic character of Peninsular Malaysia was transformed over a period that spanned barely 20 years.

The Chinese who arrived in Malaya to take up jobs as coolies, plantation workers, clerks, miners, merchants, and servants did not regard themselves as permanent settlers nor, indeed, were they so regarded by the authorities. For the great majority, the intention was to make their fortunes and then to return to China, and many did just that. For example, during the years of the Depression (1931–4) Malaya suffered a net migration loss of 400 000, most of whom were Chinese (Sidhu & Jones 1981, p. 4). Many who had intended to leave, however, stayed in Malaya, some because they were too poor, but many because they were too rich and wished to remain to protect and to manage their new-found wealth (Daud 1985, p. 125). The concentration of Chinese in a fairly narrow range of activities – tin mining, rubber production, marketing, and retailing – was not only due to their status as temporary migrants. The Malay aristocracy was in general agreement with the British authorities that the indigenous Malay peasant needed to be protected from 'economic competition, ugly commercialism, and the deleterious effects that modern urban life was considered to pose for their culture' (Milne & Mauzy 1986, p. 20). Thus the Malay peasant, living in a *kampong* (village) and growing wet rice, was restricted in various ways from entering the modern economy – through, for example, creation of Malay reserves, restrictions on land sales, and limits on their education – so perpetuating the distinction between the indigenous and immigrant populations. This pluralism, which the British, with the tacit support of the Malay élite, helped to preserve, dominates and lies at the very heart of the Malaysian political economy today.

In the long and arduous negotiations between the British, Malays, and non-Malays before Malaysia achieved independence on 31 August 1957, the racial issue came to the fore. The solution that was finally arrived at has been termed the 'racial bargain':

> The essence of the Bargain was the acceptance by the non-Malay leaders that the Malays, as the indigenous race, were entitled to political dominance, while in return the Malay leaders recognized that the socio-economic pursuits of the non-Malays should not be infringed upon (Milne & Mauzy 1986, p. 28).

The Constitution incorporated articles designed to protect the non-Malays, the most important of which was a fairly liberal citizenship provision.[2]

But there were also numerous provisions whose object was preservation of Malay cultural and political dominance, and which gave them special rights and economic safeguards (see Cham 1977, Milne & Mauzy 1986, Milne 1970).

Economic and political developments: 1957–1970

Between independence in 1957 and 1970, the political and economic status quo encapsulated in the racial bargain was, to a large extent, maintained. It is true that the Federal Land Development Authority (FeLDA) which administered Malaysia's land settlement programme was geared primarily towards the demands of the Malays, as also was the Council of Trust for the Indigenous People (MARA or Majlis Amanah Raayat), which was reorganized and strengthened in 1960. Nevertheless, these policy initiatives designed to foster the development of the (Malay) rural sector were not sufficient to alter the 'double dualism' that characterized Malaysian society and economy. In this framework of double dualism the usual sharp division between the modern and traditional sectors was further compounded by an ethnic division in which the Malays dominated the traditional agricultural sector and the Chinese the modern urban and industrial sector (Othman 1984, p. 137).

During the years from independence to 1970, the distribution of income worsened, the incidence of poverty remained unchanged, and the absolute difference in incomes between Malays and non-Malays widened to the advantage of the latter (Pang Eng Fong 1983, p. 317, Jomo 1986, p. 249–52). This deterioration in the economic fortunes of the poorer sections of Malaysian society was in large part due to the 40 per cent fall in rubber prices between 1957 and 1970 (Othman 1984, p. 131). By 1970, 65 per cent of rubber smallholders were living in poverty and they accounted for 29 per cent of the total number of households living below the poverty line (Government of Malaysia 1986, p. 86) However, as the Malays dominated smallholder rubber production, and it was smallholders who were finding it most difficult to replant with new high-yielding varieties, the effects of the decline in prices fell disproportionately upon Malays. In fact, Chinese smallholdings were approximately twice the size of those operated by Malays (Selvadurai 1979, p. 27). It has been calculated that the fall in rubber prices, coupled with domestic inflation, caused real incomes of smallholders to decline by approximately half (Othman 1984, p. 131). During the 1960s, some of the more radical Malay politicians, responding to what they saw to be a worsening in the economic position of Malays, began to demand that the government introduce policies more directly targeted at the needs of the indigenous population. This was not, however, to happen until 1969, a watershed year in Malaysian politics.

The 1969 race riots and the New Economic Policy

The general election of May 1969 was a prelude to the race riots of July. The opposition parties, most notably represented by the essentially Chinese

Democratic Action Party (DAP), had for the first time organized themselves
so as not to split the anti-Alliance vote.[3] Morover, the Alliance, in response
to the Parti Islam se-Malaysia's (PAS, previously called the Pan-Malayan
Islamic Party) strategy of stressing Islam and Malay interests, had itself
adopted a more starkly communal stance. Although the Alliance won the
election, its percentage of the vote declined to 48 per cent (from 58 per
cent in 1964) and it won 23 fewer seats (Strauch 1981, p. 32). During the
celebrations by the Chinese opposition parties that followed their 'victory',
insults were exchanged between Malays and Chinese. The following day,
a counter-demonstration was held by Malay groups, many of whom were
armed, 'it quickly degenerated into an uncontrolled battleground of racial
violence, mindless murder, and widespread arson' (Milne & Mauzy 1986,
p. 41). The government declared a State of Emergency, but even so 235
people were officially recorded as dead or missing between 13 July and
31 July, with the true figure probably being considerably higher (Strauch
1981, pp. 33–4).

The July 1969 race riots persuaded the Alliance that a clear programme
of restructuring designed to narrow the differentials between the Malay
and the Chinese populations would have to be implemented. As Milne and
Mauzy (1986, p. 132) put it, 'ambiguities were no longer to be tolerated'.
This resulted in the formulation of the New Economic Policy (NEP),
which was incorporated as the central element of the second five-year
national development plan (Second Malaysia Plan, 1971–5). Although the
riots of 1969 undoubtedly precipitated the adoption of the NEP, most of the
elements contained in the programme had already been widely discussed,
and even if racial disturbances had not occurred it is likely that something
similar would have been adopted. The NEP was designed to eradicate the
double dualism of the Malaysian economy in which it was possible to
identify race with economic function and geographical location. In 1970,
when the NEP was formulated, the incidence of poverty among Malays
was over double that among Chinese, mean incomes were less than half, the
ownership of share capital was 7 per cent that for the Chinese, and whereas
almost half the Chinese population was living in urban areas, only 15 per
cent of Malays were (Table 6.3).

The New Economic Policy

The New Economic Policy, as laid out in the Second Malaysia Plan, had
two prongs:

> (a) 'to reduce and eventually eradicate poverty, by raising income
> levels and increasing employment opportunities for all Malaysians,
> irrespective of race'.
> (b) To restructure 'Malaysian society to correct economic imbal-
> ance, so as to reduce and eventually eliminate the identification of
> race with economic function' (Government of Malaysia 1971, p. 1).

Table 6.3 The Chinese, Malays, and Indians in Peninsular Malaysia: employment, wealth, and education, 1970–88

	1970	1985	1988
Population of Peninsular Malaysia by ethnic group (percentages)			
Malays/Bumiputras	52.7	56.5	57.7 (1989)
Chinese	35.8	32.8	31.8 (1989)
Indian	10.7	10.1	8.0 (1989)
Mean household incomes (M$ per month)			
Bumiputras/Malays	172	384	
Chinese	394	678	
Indian	304	494	
Incidence of poverty (percentage of households)			
Malays	64.8		23.8
Chinese	26.0		7.1
Indian	39.2		9.7
Total	49.3	18.4	17.0
Ownership of share capital in limited companies (percentages)			
Malays and Malay interests	2.4	17.8	24.0[1]
Bumiputra individuals		10.1	16.0
Bumiputra trust agencies		7.7	8.0
Other Malaysian residents	34.3	56.7	
Chinese		41.0	41.0
Indian		1.5	1.5
Employment by sector[2] (as percentage of total employed in sector)			
Primary			
Malays	67.6	73.2[3]	
Chinese	21.4	16.3	
Secondary			
Malays	30.8	44.3	
Chinese	59.5	46.1	
Tertiary			
Malays	37.9	50.3	
Chinese	48.3	40.3	
Enrolment in degree courses[4] (as percentage of total enrolment)			
Malays	39.7	63.0	
Chinese	49.2	29.7	
Degree of urbanization (percentage of population in urban areas)			
Malays	14.8	30.0	
Chinese	47.6	59.2	
Whole population	28.8	41.1	

Notes: 1) The 1985 data on share ownership relates to the whole country, not just the Peninsula. 2) Primary sector = agriculture; secondary sector = mining, manufacturing, construction, utilities and transport; tertiary sector = wholesale and retail trade, banking, public administration, education, health and defence. 3) The 1985 and 1988 data on employment by sector relates to the whole country, not just the Peninsula. 4) The data on enrolment on degree courses relates to the whole country, not just the Peninsula.

The first of these two objectives, poverty reduction, was not explicitly aimed at any particular ethnic group, although as the majority of the poor were Malay they were the group most likely to benefit. The second objective, the restructuring of society, was ethnically specific, however, and was to be accomplished through meeting two central targets. The first was the achievement of an ethnic composition of the labour force that mirrored the ethnic commposition of the population as a whole. The second target was the restructuring of business ownership so that Malays and other indigenous groups controlled or managed at least 30 per cent of the share capital of the corporate sector. The NEP was set to run over the 20 years from 1971 to 1990, at the conclusion of which period these targets were to have been met. Although these economic elements of the NEP are stressed in most accounts of Malaysian development since 1970, for the Chinese the fundamental and all-embracing change in approach to Malaysia's communal 'problem' had much more far-reaching implications. These extended from the promotion of the Malay language at the expense of Chinese and English, to the equation of Malaysian with Islamic, to the calls for the Chinese lion dance to become Malayanized by replacing the lion with a tiger. All these actions on the part of the politically dominant Malays were perceived as a chipping away at the ethnic integrity of the Chinese, a process that many of them believe continues to this day. For the New Economic Policy was far more than a sterile programme of economic restructuring; it was first and foremost a political programme.

It is important to note, however, that the economic objectives of the NEP were expected to be achieved through following a growth-oriented strategy rather than a redistributive one (Lim 1983a, p. 4). This would mean that the NEP was not a zero-sum game in which one group would benefit at the expense of the other, but rather one in which the Malays (or the Bumiputras) would merely benefit to a greater extent than non-Malays. The economy, so it was hoped, would expand at a rate sufficient to allow all racial groups to feel satisfied and so suppress the communal tensions that are latent in Malaysian society.

The means by which poverty was to be alleviated and society restructured were, and are, numerous. With respect to poverty alleviation, the Malaysian government promoted numerous schemes directed at helping smallholders, a group amongst which much of the poverty was concentrated (Table 6.4). The government's Guaranteed Minimum Price scheme raised the purchase price of padi (unmilled rice) from M$16 per pikul in 1970, to between M$36 and M$40 by 1980 (Shari & Jomo 1984, p. 333). Simultaneously, Green Revolution technology was assiduously promoted, as best exemplified in the Muda irrigation project in the states of Perlis and Kedah. Meanwhile, rubber smallholders benefited from a comprehensive replanting scheme and greater government support in the shape of the Rubber Industry Smallholders Development Authority (RISDA) which was established in 1973 (Stubbs 1983, p. 101), while FeLDA and other land development schemes were provided with additional resources.

A criticism of these policies as far as the Chinese were concerned was that although poverty alleviation was ostensibly to be pursued 'irrespective of

Table 6.4 Incidence of poverty in Peninsular Malaysia by economic group, 1970 and 1984 (households)

	1970		1984	
	Total poor households	Incidence of poverty (percentages)	Total poor households	Incidence of poverty (percentages)
Rural	705 900	58.7	402 000	24.7
Rubber smallholders	226 400	64.7	67 300	43.4
Rice farmers	123 400	88.1	67 300	57.7
Estate workers	59 400	40.0	16 000	19.7
Fishermen	28 100	73.2	9 500	27.7
Coconut smallholders	16 900	52.8	6 600	46.9
Other agriculture	128 200	89.0	158 800	34.2
Other industries (rural)	123 500	35.2	76 500	10.0
Urban	85 900	21.3	81 300	8.2
Agriculture			8 900	23.8
Mining	1 800	33.3	300	3.4
Manufacturing	19 700	23.5	11 300	8.5
Construction	5 900	30.2	5 300	6.1
Transport and utilities	13 100	30.9	2 700	3.6
Trade and services	45 400	18.1	21 900	4.6
Services not adequately defined			30 900	17.1
Total	791 800	49.3	483 300	18.4

Sources: Government of Malaysia 1976, Government of Malaysia 1981, Government of Malaysia 1986, Aznam & McDonald 1989c, Aznam & McDonald 1989b.

race', most of the programmes were targeted at the rural Malay poor, not at the poor in general, and particularly not at the urban, Chinese poor. Under the FeLDA scheme, for example, 96 per cent of those given land have been Malays (Seaward 1986a, p. 77). In contrast, the New Villages created during the Malayan Emergency of the 1950s where many of the Chinese poor are concentrated have been comparatively ignored. It has also been claimed that the methods used to measure poverty have favoured Malays, and that the Economic Planning Unit, which determines levels of poverty, is overly politicized (Aznam & McDonald 1989a, p. 29). The use of cash incomes to assess poverty ignores the value of subsistence agricultural production; this works to the advantage of those engaged in agricultural pursuits, who are mostly Malays. Again, the use of the household as the unit of measurement fails to take account of the larger size of Chinese households (Seaward 1986c, p. 80–1). The poverty line (which has never been revealed) also makes no distinction between rural and urban areas. It thus fails to take account of the higher costs of urban living. Partly as a result of the concentration upon rural areas and bias towards them, while the number of rural poor declined rapidly between 1970 and 1983, both absolutely and as a proportion of the total rural population, the number of urban households living in poverty actually increased in that period (Figures 6.1 and 6.2).

The policies connected with the second prong of the NEP, restructuring society were, however, far more overtly dicriminatory. The policy centred on achieving employment composition targets based on ethnic group, for it was felt that if more Malays entered higher-paying employment in the modern sectors of the economy, then there would also be a narrowing in income differentials. A number of policies were introduced to promote this, of which the most significant was the Industrial Co-ordination Act (ICA) of 1975. The ICA stipulated that all companies over a certain size would have to apply to the Ministry of Trade and Industry for a licence to operate (Bowie 1988, p. 56). If the company in question was deemed to be failing to meet the employment and ownership targets of the NEP – for example that every firm had to employ a minimum proportion of Bumiputras – this licence could be revoked (Lim 1983a, pp. 11–12, Milne & Mauzy 1986, p. 137, Bowie 1988, pp. 56–7). In addition to the ICA, Malay higher education was promoted and training courses were provided

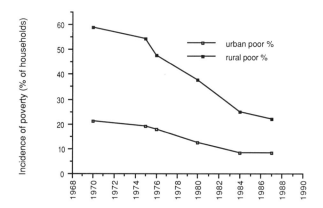

Figure 6.1   Incidence of poverty in Peninsular Malaysia 1970–87

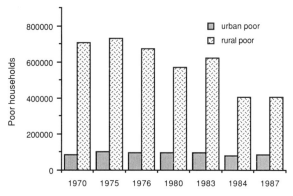

Figure 6.2   Households living in poverty in Peninsular Malaysia, 1970–87

by such agencies as MARA and the Bank Negara Malaysia; credit was made easily available to Malay entrepreneurs; and a proportion of all government contracts were reserved for Malay businessmen, who also received price preferences of between 2 per cent and 10 per cent (Othman 1984, p. 200). Finally, in order to achieve the target of Bumiputras owning or controlling 30 per cent of corporate share capital by 1990, public bodies such as Petronas (the state oil company) and FeLDA were encouraged to purchase stock on behalf of the Malay community and hold it in trust (see Milne & Mauzy 1986, pp. 136–42, Lim 1983a, pp. 10–4, Mehmet 1986, Othman 1984, pp. 198–208). It should be stressed that although these policies and programmes were introduced in the 1970s to fulfil the objectives of the NEP, they are still very much part of the political and economic landscape; the NEP is a policy that remains central to the operation of the Malaysian political economy.

The New Economic Policy, poverty reduction, and social restructuring

Reduction of poverty

The Fifth Malaysia Plan states that the incidence of poverty in Peninsular Malaysia has declined from 49.3 per cent of households in 1970 to 18.4 per cent in 1984. In 1989 the figure was 17 per cent (Figure 6.1 and Table 6.3). On the face of it this is an impressive achievement, and analysts such as Pang Eng Fong (1983, p. 320) maintain that 'Malaysia's progress towards reducing poverty in the 1970s cannot be challenged'. At the same time however, and in contradiction of this, Mehmet argues that 'despite ample resources and rapid growth, the strategy of NEP trusteeship has failed to eradicate poverty, and indeed many of the adopted policies have tended to perpetuate and reproduce it' (Mehmet 1986, p. 157, see also Milne & Mauzy 1986, pp. 134–6). Why is there this discrepancy? Three factors can be highlighted in explanation.

First, there is the influence of exogenous factors. How far is the reduction a direct result of government action as, for example, Young, Bussink and Hasan stress in their book (1980) and how far is it determined by developments beyond government control? The precipitous fall in the international price of rubber in 1974 from M$2.80 to M$0.97 per kilogram of RSS No. 1 (rubber smoked sheet), and then its rise to over M$4.00 by early 1980, was highly influential in determining the income levels of smallholders in the rubber sector and the incidence of poverty there (Stubbs 1983).

Secondly, should poverty reduction be assessed in absolute or in proportional terms? If the former approach is taken, then as late as 1983 the number of households living in poverty was still comparable with the figures for 1970 (Figure 6.2); it is only as a proportion of the total number of households that significant reductions were being achieved (Figure 6.1). This becomes even more pertinent when the statistics on the urban poor are examined. For in 1983, the number of poor urban households was almost 100 000 – up from 86 000 in 1970 – and even in 1987 the figure was still

81 000 (Figure 6.2). Although this lends credence to the complaints from of the Chinese community that not enough was being done to reduce urban poverty, it is more likely that a transfer of rural poverty to urban areas was occurring as poor Malays moved into the towns and cities in search of work. This has intensified competition between job seekers in the towns, and because of the racial employment composition targets, coupled with the preference given to Malays in the public sector, it has generally been the non-Malays, primarily the poorer sections of Chinese society, who have fared worst (Pang Eng Fong 1983, p. 322).

The third and final factor, and one that will be returned to, is income inequality.[4] For although poverty has declined both absolutely and proportionally, income inequalities have either remained static or have widened (Mehmet 1986, pp. 151–3, Tan Tat Wai 1982, pp. 328–9, Shari & Jomo 1984, p. 331). Thus, those who have benefited most from a period of rapid economic growth have been those Malaysians, and especially those Malays, who were rich to begin with. It has also been argued that the failure to narrow income differentials, and the actually widening of them in intra-ethnic terms, is directly linked to the NEP (Mehmet 1986, p. 152). To support this view, some analysts have pointed to the experience of Singapore, where a non-ethnic-based development strategy has done far more to reduce poverty and income inequality (Pang Eng Fong 1983). However, although it is true that the benefits of Singapore's spectacular economic growth (see ch. 9) have been widely distributed, a direct comparison with Malaysia obscures the great differences between the two countries. In particular, Singapore does not have to contend with a backward rural sector nor deal with such deep-seated structural problems as the small size of landholdings. This is the cause of much of Malaysia's rural poverty and it cannot easily be solved through mere poverty alleviation measures (Mehmet 1986, pp. 17–42).

Social restructuring

The bare statistics presented in Table 6.3 seem to indicate that the NEP's targets are at least on the way to being achieved, if not necessarily in time to meet the 1990 deadline. Malay and Malay interests controlled 24 per cent of share capital in 1988, up from 2.4 per cent in 1970; income differentials between Malays and Chinese have narrowed appreciably; Malay enrolment in degree courses is significantly improved; the structure of employment is such that more Malays, relatively as well as absolutely, are involved in the secondary and tertiary sectors of the economy; and, reflecting this, a greater proportion of Malays are living in urban areas. However, this apparent restructuring of society and economy in favour of the Bumiputras and at the expense, particularly, of the Chinese, is not as clear cut or as simple as the statistics might indicate.

The two points that have most concerned scholars relate to the restructuring of ownership and incomes. For it has been argued that far from broadly redistributing wealth to the Bumiputras as a disadvantaged group, the NEP has merely concentrated it in the hands of a select and powerful Malay élite. Intra-ethnic income inequalities have widened during the course of the NEP (Mehmet 1986, p. 152, Tan Tat Wai 1982, p. 328) and corporate wealth has become concentrated among a small section of Malays. Of the 24 per cent of corporate wealth controlled by Bumiputras, 8 per cent is held by trust agencies such as MARA, the National Corporation (Pernas), the state economic development corporations (SEDCs) and the Development Bank of Malaysia (BPMB) (Government of Malaysia 1986, p. 107). The remaining 16 per cent is overwhelmingly in the hands of a small Malay élite (this also includes shares held by Bumiputras through unit trusts and co-operatives). The reason for this structure of ownership is clear: most Malays are too poor to purchase shares, and so in order to meet the NEP targets the government has had to encourage public agencies to purchase shares on behalf of the Bumiputra population, and hold them in trust. The concentration of income and corporate wealth (or at least its control) among a small group of rich and/or influential Malays (as in the bureaucratic élite that controls the shares held in trust) has led many authors to question the validity of the claims made for the NEP and to maintain that it is merely 'enriching certain individual Malay elites instead of realizing the redistributive goals of benefiting the Malay masses' (Yeu-man Yeung 1982, p. 95, and see Aznam & McDonald 1989c). From this has emerged an analysis of the Malaysian political economy that plays down the pluralist perspective and emphasizes a class-based one (e.g. Jomo 1984, 1986, 1987, Brennan 1985, Husin Ali 1984).

Malaysian society can be stratified along ethnic or class lines, and there are forces pulling individuals in both directions (Husin Ali 1984, p. 18). The former is most visible and has dominated Malaysian politics since independence. This has given rise to the perception that while the Chinese – as a monolithic and homogeneous bloc – dominate the economy, the Malays – similarly monolithic in character – dominate politics. In fact, the class-based analysts argue, a poor Malay has far more in common with a poor Chinese than he or she does with a rich Malay, and vice-versa. Thus the communal nature of Malaysian politics has served to mask the struggle between classes. Indeed, it is claimed that the true conflict in Malaysia is between three rival class factions, the Malay governing class, the non-Malay (Chinese) capitalist class, and the metropolitan bourgeoisie. Their struggle has merely been played out on a racial stage (Brennan 1985, p. 95). Some of the class theorists take this one step further, arguing that it not only masks internal class divisions, but also obscures the foreign domination of the country through the 'essentially comprador character of the bureaucrat bourgeoisie' (Jomo 1984, p. 169).

However, this characterization of the 'real' nature of Malaysian society has not gone unchallenged. Critics of it note that tensions are almost always ethnically expressed and that although this may be written off by some as 'false consciousness', the reality is that few Malaysians perceive their position and their role in class terms (Milne & Mauzy 1986, p. 77). It is also likely that if class does become an issue, it will not transcend race but will merely emerge in a racial framework so that co-operation between poor Malays and poor Chinese will remain limited (Haji Ahmad 1982, p. 98).

The New Economic Policy in Malaysia

A second area in which the success of the NEP has been questioned concerns the position of Malay managers and entrepreneurs. For although more businesses appear to be run and owned by Malays (Table 6.5), it is claimed that in many cases the Malay is merely a figurehead who facilitates the issue of government contracts, quotas, and licences. This is the so-called Ali Baba system in which Ali is the *de jure* Malay 'front man' while Baba is the *de facto* Chinese manager and owner (the word Baba refers to the Baba Chinese of Malacca) (Milne & Mauzy 1986, p. 138, and see Suryadinata 1985b, p. 22–3 with reference to Indonesia). This issue of control and ownership also extends to previously foreign-owned companies (note that it is foreigners who have lost the most corporate wealth since 1970). For control is not contingent upon ownership if the foreign company can maintain a monopoly on marketing and technology (Shari & Jomo 1984, p. 346).

In spite of these many arguments that question the efficacy and success of the NEP in meeting its stated objectives – even when the time factor is disallowed – it is undeniable that the policy has played a significant role in furthering the interests of Malays, particularly in or through the public sector but also in the private sector. More enter higher education, more are members of professional organizations, and relatively more are now engaged in employment in the secondary and tertiary sectors. It has been possible to bring these policies into play without seriously undermining the absolute wealth of the Chinese population largely because of the high rates of growth that the Malaysian economy has generally enjoyed since 1970 (see Table 9.1). However, Malaysia is exceptionally well-endowed in

Table 6.5 Malay and Chinese ownership of selected service industries, 1971 and 1981

| | 1971 | | 1981 | |
	Bumiputra	Chinese	Bumiputra	Chinese
Wholesale				
Percentage of establishments	2.5	78.5	8.2	81.8
Percentage of turnover	0.8	66.2	5.3	55.5
Retail				
Percentage of establishments	13.0	74.6	34.2	57.7
Percentage of turnover	3.0	81.2	11.5	74.6
Road transport operators				
Percentage of establishments	17.8	61.2	62.5	30.7
Percentage of revenue	17.3	60.9	42.2	37.2
Hotels and other lodgings				
Percentage of establishments	1.6	94.8	5.0	83.5
Percentage of revenue	3.6	68.5	8.6	34.3
Professional services				
Percentage of establishments	7.0	69.7	10.2	65.2
Percentage of revenue	4.4	57.0	17.8	53.6

Source: Government of Malaysia 1986, pp. 114–15.
Note: Bumiputra figures include both Bumiputra individuals and trust agencies.

124

terms of natural resources and this has allowed it the freedom to follow a redistributive strategy. It is highly unlikely that the Malaysian experience could be transferred to other countries facing similar problems. This is not to say that there are no costs involved for Malaysia, and indeed there is some weight to the argument that the NEP contains the seeds of its own failure. For the policy has served to damp down both domestic (i.e. Chinese) and foreign investment (Bowie 1988, pp. 56–7) and at the same time raise Malaysia's foreign debt. In so doing the NEP has slowed economic growth and no doubt contributed to the economic recession of 1985–6, when the policy was suspended.

This discussion of the NEP has focused largely on the policy itself rather than on its implications for the Chinese in Malaysia. In so doing, it might be felt that the discussion has drifted away from the central issue, the Chinese. However, it should be remembered that the NEP's raison d'être lies in the pluralist nature of the Malaysian political economy. Thus the promotion of Bumiputra interests, which are at the core of the NEP, and the (implicit) hindrance of Chinese interests are two sides of the same coin. Nevertheless, although the two are inextricably linked, it is necessary to examine more directly the position of the Chinese in Malaysian society, politics, and economy, and the Chinese perception of that position.

Chinese reactions to the New Economic Policy

The Chinese reaction to the introduction of the NEP was moderate and measured, largely because the Chinese community and their public figures recognize that their position as a minority, immigrant group affords them little political power that is not dependent upon the support of Malay politicians. Thus, the activities of the Malaysian Chinese Association (the MCA) – a member of the ruling coalition Barisan Nasional (the National Front, formerly the Alliance) – are constrained within limits that have been set by the United Malays National Organization (UMNO), the dominant (Malay) 'partner'. However, although the NEP as a policy cannot be challenged – doing so has been deemed seditious – there are two areas that particularly concern the Chinese.

The first involves the Industrial Co-ordination Act (ICA) and the powers that it gives to Malay bureaucrats in the allocation of quotas, licences, and contracts. This discriminates in favour of Bumiputra businessmen regardless of cost or the operation of market forces, provides numerous opportunities for graft and corruption, and can result in gross mismanagement. In 1986, a wholly owned subsidiary of Bank Bumiputra Malaysia (BBM), Malaysia's largest bank, lost so much money (M$2.5 billion) that it threatened to bankrupt the parent company. In the ensuing investigations it was found that the subsidiary, Bumiputra Malaysia Finance (BMF), had been grossly mismanaged and inadequately supervised by BBM, and that corruption and bribery had been endemic in its operation (see Cottrell 1986, pp. 151–3, Aznam & Seaward 1987, pp. 17–21). Of course corruption is nothing new in Malaysia or elsewhere in Southeast Asia, but since the institution of the NEP in the early 1970s the links between politics and business have become closer, and National Front politicians are in an unprecedented position to distribute largesse in the form of quotas, contracts, and licences (Clad 1989, pp. 43–63). The consequence is that senior politicians – even the Prime Minister himself – have been implicated in a series of scandals. One of the most recent examples concerns the M\$3.4 billion contract to complete the highway running from the Thai border to Singapore, the so-called North–South Highway project. This was initially awarded to United Engineers (Malaysia) Bhd (UE). However it was later revealed by the opposition politician Lim Kit Siang that UMNO had a financial interest in the contract. UE was found to be controlled by Hatibundi, a company in turn owned by UMNO (see Seaward 1987a, p. 76, 1987b, pp. 66–7, 1987c, pp. 44–5, Westlake 1987, pp. 62–4). Critics of the government argue, as an article on corruption in Malaysia in the *Far Eastern Economic Review* puts it, that 'unethical practices pervade every aspect of [Mahathir's] government', that there is 'nepotism and favouritism of political allies in awarding government contracts', and that there exists an 'alliance of political and business interests to siphon off the national wealth and the savings of unsuspecting investors' (Aznam & Seaward 1987, p. 17, and see Bowie 1988, pp. 63–4). The close links between politics and business also create far greater potential for poor economic decision-making. The construction of the Penang Bridge and the production of a 'Malaysian' car, the Proton Saga, are both pointed to as examples of political decisions that were taken with little consideration as to their economics and profitability. Chee Peng Lim (1988, p. 59) claims that the Proton Saga project lacks economic viability and has suffered from poor timing, a small domestic market, limited export potential, and high costs. He concludes by pleading that economic planning not be made on the basis of personal 'whims and fancies'.

There are also close parallels between the arguments in favour of the NEP and those that have been mobilized to present the case for the support of 'infant industries', both in terms of the forces that brought it into existence in the first place, and in terms of the problems that have resulted from it (see Chapter 9). The objective of the NEP was to raise the economic position of the Bumiputras relative to the non-Bumiputras by protecting and aiding them as a group, so that ultimately they would be able to compete on an equal footing. The result, however, has been that protection and assistance have become institutionalized and 'income and wealth distribution [skewed] in favour of non-competing groups who derive quasi-rents and other forms of unearned rewards from their influential and privileged status' (Mehmet 1986, p. 132).

The second area of concern centres on education and the allocation of university places to Malays and Chinese. In 1970, Malay enrolment in degree courses accounted for 39.7 per cent of places (up from 20 per cent in 1963/64) and Chinese enrolment for 49.2 per cent (Table 6.3). By 1985, the respective figures were 63.0 per cent and 29.7 per cent (Government of Malaysia 1986, p. 493). Places in higher education were becoming less easily available to the Chinese – who have traditionally held great store by educational attainment – and this at a time when the numbers of Chinese families wishing to enrol their children on courses was increasing. The Chinese attempt to establish a university to meet these demands, the Merdeka University project, was quashed by the government, which argued that it was contrary to the national education policy because the medium of instruction was to be Chinese rather than Malay (Loh Kok Wah 1984, pp. 97–104). Among the Chinese, education is perhaps the single issue over which sensitivities are greatest, yet the government has persistently promoted an education system based upon a Malay interpretation of society. Thus Malay is the medium of instruction in all state primary and secondary schools, and on most university courses. There has also been a gradual movement towards a greater Islamization of schooling, which is a particular worry for the Chinese (Milne & Mauzy 1986, pp. 94). One example of many instances of tension arising out of educational disagreements arose in 1987 and concerned the promotion of 100 teachers unable to speak Mandarin to the equivalent position of deputy head in Chinese primary schools. The great majority (some 86 per cent) of Malaysian Chinese parents send their children to such Chinese primary schools so that they can learn their 'mother tongue'. The move on the part of the government quickly escalated into a serious ethnic confrontation, with the Chinese fearing that the move was yet another step towards the imposition of a national language policy (Aznam 1987a, pp. 14–21, 1988, pp. 19–20).

The assimilation of the Chinese into Malay society

Unlike the Chinese in Thailand and Cambodia and, to a lesser extent, Indonesia, those in Malaysia have not been assimilated into the indigenous society. The Malays, Chinese, and Indians have maintained their separate identities, and although there has been some degree of acculturation – for example, many Chinese Malaysians use chilli in their cooking and Malays eat some Chinese foods – this has not occurred to the extent that pluralism has been diminished in any meaningful sense. As Tan Chee Beng (1984, p. 195) points out:

> the inter-ethnic encounter is not intensive and Chinese find it easier to chat with Chinese, and Malays with Malays. It is therefore common to find more Chinese in Chinese-operated coffee-shops, likewise the Malays in Malay-operated coffee-shops. Even in the same shop, members of the same ethnic group tend to cluster at the same tables.

The policies followed during the colonial period undoubtedly helped to prevent the assimilation of the Chinese. However, this does not adequately account for the enduring nature of pluralism. Many analysts have highlighted Islam as an impediment to integration (e.g. Tan Chee Beng 1984, p. 199, Winzeler 1985, pp. 116–17), some going so far as to state that it is 'the last and most impenetrable ethnic barrier' (Milne & Mauzy 1986, p. 72). Not only do the dietary prohibitions of Islam (alcohol, pork) constrain relations, but in addition a Muslim may not legally marry a non-Muslim before he or she has formally converted to Islam (Winzeler 1985, p. 116). And even when a Chinese embraces Islam, this is often still not sufficient to bridge the gulf between Malay and non-Malay, and the individual in question becomes a member of a special, separate class of Muslims and Malaysians (Milne & Mauzy 1986, p. 73). The sheer size of Malaysia's Chinese 'minority' also plays a part in limiting assimilation. There is, to some extent, security in numbers and unlike the Chinese in Indonesia, where Islam is also the religion of the indigenous people but where the Chinese constitute only 2.8 per cent of the population, the Chinese Malaysians have not been forced to conform through mere weight of numbers.

The size of Malaysia's Chinese minority has also been important in dictating the limits of government action. In Indonesia, it has been possible for the government to promote actively fairly draconian policies of assimilation, 'encouraging' Chinese Indonesians to take Indonesian names, send their children to Indonesian schools, and learn and use Bahasa Indonesia, the national language (Suryadinata 1985b, pp. 19–20, Lee Yong Leng 1980). Indeed, Indonesian efforts to limit the use of the Chinese language are such that the importation of publications in Chinese is banned (Suryadinata 1985b, p. 20) In Malaysia, however, the government has had to be rather more circumspect in its actions, and policies have been directed towards accommodation rather than assimilation. Since 1969, however, there has been a more concerted drive to promote a Malay national culture. Some Malays consider that this should ideally incorporate not only the Malay language and Malay culture, but also Islam. A more moderate view holds that although Malay culture should provide the basis for the Malaysian national culture it should also incorporate some non-Malay elements provided they are not in conflict with it (Tan Chee Beng 1987, pp. 108–9).

Since Malaysia is a plural society, it is not surprising that political parties should also be arranged and divided along ethnic lines. Although it was hoped in the run-up to independence that a political party cutting across racial groups could be created, this proved to be impossible. Currently, UMNO Baru (new UMNO), Semangat '46 (Spirit of '46) and the PAS represent Malay and Muslim interests; the Chinese are represented by the MCA, Gerakan and the DAP;[5] and the Malaysian Indian Congress (MIC) aims to meet the aspirations of the Indian community. The geographical distribution of the votes cast for the various parties in the August 1986 general election shows the extent to which politics is still communal in nature. In the Malay rural strongholds of Kedah, Perlis, Kelantan, and Trengganu, the DAP won not a single seat. In those constituencies where the Chinese make up 59 per cent of the population or more, the National Front, perceived by the Chinese to be Malay-dominated in spite of the fact that it contains two Chinese parties, won not a single seat (Seaward 1986c, pp. 14–15). Indeed the rhetoric of Malaysian politics is, if anything, becoming more ethnically chauvinist, with politicians of all ethnic groups continually playing on the fears of one group or another. Sometimes this is expressed in terms of the indigenous–non-indigenous dichotomy – that is Bumiputra–non-Bumiputra – but, and this applies in particular to Peninsular Malaysia, it is ultimately the Malay–Chinese divide that is of overriding significance. Even the pretence of 'national' politics appears to be at an end, and this has frozen, possibly even reversed, the forces of assimilation. As Loh Kok Wah (1984, p. 95) notes 'The fact that party politics in Malaysia is ethnically-based sets the stage for greater ethnic conciousness in general and for the forces of ethnic cohesion, specifically, to be greater'.

No doubt partly because of the limited contact between the two ethnic groups, the views that one holds of the other are highly entrenched. The Chinese are considered to be hard-working, diligent, crafty, and acquisitive by nature, characteristics that, in the Malay view, often manifest themselves in usurious and exploitative behaviour. The Malays are perceived by many Chinese to be lazy, indolent, and good-for-nothing. These caricatures of the Malays and Chinese not only tend to limit better understanding but have also too often been used for political expediency. If the Chinese are, by dint of their very Chineseness, likely to be money-grabbing, crafty, and by extension, exploitative; while the Malays are likely to be economically unsophisticated and vulnerable, then surely measures need to be enforced to control the former and to aid the latter? The best example of such a perspective comes in a book by Prime Minister Mahathir Mohamed published in 1970, *The Malay dilemma*. Drawing upon a rather environmentally determinist view of the Chinese and Malays, he argues that in Malaysia:

> No great exertion or ingenuity was required to obtain food. There was plenty for everyone throughout the year . . . Under these conditions everyone survived. Even the weakest and least diligent were able to . . . marry and procreate . . . Thus except for a few, [Malay] people were content to spend their unlimited leisure in merely resting or in extensive conversation with neighbours and friends.
>
> For the Chinese people life was one continuous struggle for survival. In the process the weak in mind and body lost out to the strong and the resourceful . . . By the time the Chinese began to emigrate in numbers to the islands and the peninsula of Southeast Asia, the effect of environment, heredity and other factors had already had their maximum effect. The people who left the shores of China were hardened and resourceful (Mahathir 1970, pp. 21–2, 24–5).

On the basis of this view of the Chinese and Malays and drawing upon other historical factors, Mahathir recommends that:

> Where necessary, laws must be promulgated in order to render effective whatever economic policy may be considered necessary. Harsh punitive measures should be meted out to those who impede the elevation of the Malays to an equality with the other races (Mahathir 1970, p. 60).

The Chinese and the NEP: prospects for the future

As the NEP was set to run over a twenty-year period, until 1990, there is the question of whether the policies associated with the programme will be continued after that date. In 1988 the Malaysian government established the National Economic Consultative Council (NECC) with a membership of 150 including Chinese, Indians, and Malays to formulate a replacement for the NEP (Aznam & McDonald 1989a). Their report will be issued in 1990. Already, however, speeches by Malay politicians including the Prime Minister make it clear that the essence of the programme will remain in force even if adaptations are made to meet changing economic and social conditions. In a widely quoted 1986 speech, UMNO member of parliament Datuk Abdullah Ahmad bluntly stated that: 'The NEP must continue to sustain Malay dominance in the political system in line with the contract of 1957. Even after 1990, there must be mechanisms of preservation, protection and expansion in an evolving system' (Seaward 1986a, pp. 77).

More worrying for the Chinese, he went on to warn that they should not question the objectives of the NEP, for this – a reference to the 1969 riots – would be to 'play with fire' (Seaward 1986a, p. 77). Although Abdullah's speech was one of the more blatant expressions by a Malay politician of the perceived need to maintain the status quo, there can be little doubt that his beliefs are widely held. In November 1988, for example, Prime Minister Mahathir stated that the NEP target of Bumiputra ownership or control of at least 30 per cent of corporate stock would not be abandoned after 1990 (Seaward 1988, p. 10). However, this is not to say that the policy is immutable. During the recession of 1985, when the economy contracted by 1.5 per cent to be followed by growth of only 2.1 per cent in 1986, some elements of the NEP were held in abeyance. For example, the stipulations regarding ownership of equity were relaxed in order to attract greater foreign investment (Seaward 1986b, 1986d). Restructuring society while the economy was rapidly growing – as it was throughout the 1970s and in to the 1980s – was a comparatively easy task, and even those groups that were losing in relative terms were still gaining absolutely. However, if the NEP were maintained during the economic recession, there would be sections of the population – namely the Chinese – who would lose absolutely. Rather than face the political and economic consequences of redistributing wealth at a time when the economy was no longer growing, Mahathir suspended many of the restructuring provisions of the NEP.

It was always recognized that the suspension of the NEP was to meet short-term economic objectives (although, admittedly, with possible political ramifications) and since 1986, with the return to rapid growth, the policy has been revived. As far as the Chinese are concerned, little has changed and many would argue that conditions are becoming increasingly difficult. The detention under the Internal Security Act (ISA) of over 100 opposition politicians and other activists towards the end of 1987 for racial agitation, coupled with the institution of further controls on press freedom, reinforced for many Chinese their powerlessness in the face of a Malay-dominated political system (see Aznam & Tasker 1987, pp. 14–15, Aznam 1987b, pp. 15–16). Some observers consider that higher rates of emigration of Malaysian Chinese to Australia and Canada, and an increased outflow of Chinese capital, are a response to those events (Tasker & Aznam 1987, pp. 21–2).

The overriding dominance of Chinese–Malay relations in the Malaysian political economy has obscured the progress that other ethnic groups have made, specifically the Indians and the indigenous tribal groups. The position of the latter has been discussed in greater detail in Chapter 4. However, it is arguably the Indian community that has benefited least under the NEP. Indians constitute 8 per cent of the total population yet own only 1.5 per cent of share capital, a figure that has remained static over the 20 years of the NEP (Aznam & McDonald 1989c, p. 29). In addition, although there are a handful of wealthy Indian businessmen and women, there exists a far larger number of poorly paid estate workers for whom income and conditions have improved little. The reason is clear: the Indian community enjoys neither the political dominance of the Malays, nor the economic power of the Chinese. As a small minority, obscured by the dominant issue of Chinese–Malay relations, their position has been accorded a low priority.

The ethnic issue continues to colour and dominate political activity in Malaysia. In spite of the fact that the NEP has now been in force for twenty years, the Malays still feel that they are economically deprived by comparison with the Chinese. Indeed, far from reducing the ethnic divisions and distinctions that characterized Malaysian society in 1971, the NEP has caused them to become institutionalized, making it even more difficult to talk of 'Malaysians' rather than 'Malays' and 'Chinese Malaysians'. Little can be said or done that is not seen in the light of the NEP and the wider issue of Malay–Chinese relations. So far as the Chinese themselves are concerned, they believe that they are being increasingly pressured by the Malay political majority. Today, the issues at stake are not just equality of incomes, education, and employment; but also Malay cultural dominance, reflected in the promotion of Bahasa Malaysia, Islam, and a Malay interpretation of Malaysia.

Notes to Chapter 6

1 Bumiputra is the term now used in government documents to refer to the indigenous population. The term means 'princes' or 'sons of the soil' and includes both Malays – who are numerically by far the dominant group – as well as other indigenous groups such as the tribal Dayaks.

2 Numerous authors have since argued that this 'liberal' citizenship policy was, in fact, discriminatory. The principal of *jus soli* (citizenship by birth), which was so important to the Chinese, was not made retroactive for non-Malays and many still feel that 'the perpetuation of Malay special privileges reduces their [the non-Malays] citizenship to second-class status' (Strauch 1981, p. 27, see also Cham 1977, pp. 204–8).

3 The Alliance was the ruling coalition dominated by the Malay party UMNO (United Malays National Organization) but also including the MCA (Malaysian Chinese Association) and the MIC (Malaysian Indian Congress).
4 Although the narrowing of income inequalities was not explicitly linked to the poverty alleviation targets, it can be viewed as a useful substitute given that the basis for measuring poverty remains disputed.
5 The DAP has tried ro present itself as a multiracial party. However, in reality it is an alternative opposition Chinese party.

7

Urbanization and primacy: Bangkok

Urbanization and primacy in Southeast Asia: an overview

Southeast Asia is one of the least urbanized regions of the world. According to World Bank statistics, 30 per cent of the region's population lived in urban areas in 1987. This compares with a figure of 57 per cent (weighted) for the entire middle-income grouping of economies (Table 7.1). However, although Southeast Asia is relatively under-urbanized it has, like most developing countries, exhibited a high rate of urban population growth. Between 1965 and 1980 the region's urban population grew at an annual average rate of 4.5 per cent, while between 1980 and 1987 the rate was 4.7 per cent. Urban population growth was significantly in excess of overall population growth throughout the period between 1960 and 1987 (Table 7.1). The urban structure of Southeast Asia has another feature worthy of note: the degree to which one city in each country dominates the urban

Table 7.1 Urbanization and the urban population of Southeast Asia

	Population (millions) 1987	Urban population as percentage of total (+ projected)			Percentage average annual growth of urban population		Percentage average annual growth of total population	
		1965	1987	2000	1965–80	1980–7	1965–80	1980–7
Brunei	0.2	—	76[1]	—	—	—	—	—
Indonesia	171.4	16	27	36	4.7	5.0	2.1	2.1
Malaysia	16.5	26	40	42	4.5	5.0	2.5	2.7
Philippines	58.4	32	41	49	4.0	3.8	2.8	2.5
Singapore	2.6	100	100	100	1.6	1.1	1.6	1.1
Thailand	53.6	13	21	23	4.6	4.9	2.7	2.0
Average[2]	—	20	30	37	4.5	4.7	2.4	2.2

Sources: World Bank 1989, Lee-Jay Cho and Bauer 1987, p. 16, Ginsburg 1988, p. 41.
Notes: 1) 1982 data. 2) Weighted relative to 1985/7 population and excluding Brunei.

133

hierarchy.[1] These cities are often referred to as 'primate cities'. In 1980 the primate capital cities of Southeast Asia, all capitals – Bangkok, Kuala Lumpur, Jakarta and Manila – accounted for 37 per cent of the total urban population of the the countries in question. Further, the rate of growth of the capital cities has considerably outpaced that of the urban population as a whole (Tables 7.1 and 7.2).

Urban primacy

The concept of the primate city was first developed by Jefferson in a short paper published in 1939. With reference to London, Paris and a number of other cities he noted that they were both considerably larger than the second cities of their respective countries and were also functionally dominant:

> The finest wares are to be found there, the rarest articles, the greatest talents, the most skilled workers in every science and art. Thither flows an unending stream of the young and ambitious in search of fame and fortune, and there fame and fortune are found. London is the kingdom's market for all that is superlative in intellectual and material productions. Its supereminence as a market runs parallel to its supereminence in size. It is the primate city of the United Kingdom . . . All over the world it is the Law of the Capitals that the largest city shall be supereminent, and not merely in size, but in national influence (Jefferson 1939, pp. 226–7).

Table 7.2 The primate cities of Southeast Asia

	Population (millions)[1]			Percentage of urban population in largest city[2]		Four city index of primacy[3]		Two city index of primacy[4]		Per-centage growth rate of primate city[5]
	1980	latest	2000	1960	1980	1960	1980	1960	1980	1970–80
Bangkok (Thailand)	4.7	5.7 (1988)	9.5	65	69	11.49	10.22	26.94	51.46	8.1
Manila (Philippines)	5.9	6.7 (1984)	11.1	27	30	3.23	3.44	—	—	4.1
Kuala Lumpur (Malaysia)	1.3	—	3.8	19	27	0.73	1.39	—	—	7.6
Jakarta (Indonesia)	6.5	7.9 (1985)	12.0	20	23	1.17	1.34	—	—	3.6

Notes: 1) Source: Jones 1988, p. 139. 2) Source: World Bank 1987. 3) The ratio of the population of the largest city to that of the next three largest. Source: Jones 1988, p. 143. 4) The ratio of the population of the largest city to that of the second largest. Source: Thienchay Kiranandana & Suwanee Suransiengsunk 1985, pp. 61–2. 5) Yeu-man Yeung 1988, p. 160.

Although methods of measurement vary (see Table 7.2), the concept of primacy is particularly applicable to Southeast Asia and there have been a succession of articles examining the 'great' cities of the region (e.g. Ginsburg 1976, 1988, Drakakis-Smith & Rimmer 1982, Yue-man Yeung 1988, London 1977, 1980). Table 7.2 shows the extent to which the capital cities of each country are numerically dominant. It should also be borne in mind, and this will be developed later in this chapter with reference to Bangkok, that they are also politically, economically, and culturally dominant. Indeed, their 'supereminence' is such that the primate cities are felt by some analysts to be parasitic, preying on the rest of their respective countries and extracting wealth and surplus value, and actually inhibiting the growth of the less developed hinterlands (see London 1977, 1980, Ginsburg 1988).

Components of urban growth

There are three components to Southeast Asia's rapid rate of urban growth. First, there is the natural increase (the excess of births over deaths) in the urban population. Second, there is a flow of rural migrants into urban areas. This has attained very great significance during periods of political instability. During the Emergency in Malaya for example, when the communist insurgency was at its most powerful, the rate of growth of the urban population averaged 5.8 per cent per year between 1947 and 1957 (Bidani 1985, p. 23). And third, there is the reclassification of rural areas as urban areas. This may arise either because of the expansion of city boundaries or from a redefinition of what constitutes an urban area. Kuala Lumpur, for example, more than doubled in size to 243 square kilometres when it became the Federal Territory in 1974 (Yue-Man Yeung 1988, p. 158).

At this point it is necessary to define two terms: urban growth and urbanization. The former is the increase in the size of the total urban population. The latter is the increase in the proportion of the total population living in urban areas. Thus, although natural increase in the urban population can contribute to urban growth, it rarely contributes to urbanization. It is rural–urban migration together with the reclassification of rural areas, that accounts for the process of urbanization. In addition, migrants – the majority of whom are of child-bearing age – contribute disproportionately to the high rate of natural increase because of their high fertility (Rogers & Williamson 1984, pp. 267–9). Jones (1988, p. 140) postulates that:

> It is reasonable to expect that, as rates of natural increase decline (as they are doing in most Southeast Asian countries), if rural–urban disparities persist and if economic growth is rapid (which is far less certain over the next decade in Southeast Asian countries), the relative contribution of rural–urban migration to the growth of cities will increase.

Before leaving this discussion of urban growth rates and urbanization it is necessary to consider what is meant by urban. This is because – and as the areal expansion of Kuala Lumpur in 1974 makes clear – rates of growth are highly dependent upon how the terms are defined, and the countries of the region do not report their urban populations uniformly. In 1957 Malaysia classified all gazetted areas with a population of over 1000 as urban; in 1970 this was changed to all gazetted areas with a population of over 10 000. In Indonesia, those places with urban characteristics, together with all municipalities and regency capitals, are considered urban. In Thailand, urban areas are equated with the administrative division of a municipality (Bidani 1985, p. 16, Thienchay Kiranandana & Suwanee Surasiengsunk 1985, pp. 34–7). These variations in definition mean that comparisons across the region should be undertaken with caution, and the statistics should only be used as broad indicators of scale.

Problems of urban growth

Although statistical comparison between the countries of Southeast Asia may be difficult, its primate cities are experiencing similar problems. These stem largely from the inability of city authorities to cope with the rate of urban growth. In most cases they lack the political and legislative authority to administer their cities successfully, and are at the same time dependent on the central government for revenue. This revenue is invariably lacking (see Drakakis-Smith & Rimmer 1982, pp. 20–1). The problems they face include a lack of adequate housing and the consequent proliferation of squatter settlements and slum communities; an overstretched transport system with resultant congestion; pollution; a shortage of employment opportunities, and the growth of underemployment and the informal sector; and an inability to provide a reasonable level of services (water, sanitation, rubbish disposal, electricity).

There are two countries that do not face the problems outlined in the previous paragraph, or at least face them to a far lesser degree. These are Singapore and Brunei (whose capital is Bandar Seri Begawan). Both countries are wealthy, and in Singapore's case there was a concerted political effort, reinforced with the necessary funds, to solve the urban problems that it faced at independence, particularly the need to provide adequate housing. So much so in fact, that in the 28 years between 1960 and 1988 the Housing Development Board (HDB) built a total of 642 000 'dwelling units'. Some 87 per cent of the Republic's population is now housed in dwellings constructed by the HDB (Ministry of Communications and Information 1989, and see Ching-ling Tai, 1988) (see Figure 9.1). The Singaporean government is also investing in a mass transit system with an estimated total cost of S$5 billion (due to be completed in 1992), and to control congestion has even introduced such innovative measures as an area licensing scheme. This cordons off the central city between 7.30 a.m. and 10.15 a.m. and allows entry only to those cars with special licences or to taxis with at least four passengers (Yeu-man Yeung 1988, p. 175). There has also been discussion of the introduction of a quota system to reduce the rate of increase of private cars (Balakrishnan 1990)

However, not only are Singapore and Brunei exceptions but it is also doubtful whether their experiences in urban planning are transferable to the other countries of the region. They are both wealthy and because they lack a large poor rural population have not had to deal with high rates of rural–urban migration. The developmental pressures and priorities of a city state such as Singapore are very different from those of a country in which the majority of the population live in the countryside and are engaged in agricultural pursuits. Although there are some lessons to be learnt, it should not be imagined that Jakarta, Bangkok, Kuala Lumpur, or Manila should or could directly follow Singapore's lead. Nevertheless, the governments of the other countries of the region are becoming increasingly concerned about the state of their urban areas and particularly about their capital cities. It is now widely felt that the planning of urban areas should be strengthened and pursued more assiduously, and that the process of urbanization itself should be controlled.

Planning, urban bias, and diseconomies of scale

The concern with the physical planning of the capital cities of Southeast Asia is reflected in the creation of single metropolitan authorities throughout the region (Table 7.3). These have been given the task of 'creating a new and more "rational" approach to urban management', and as a result a succession of master plans have been drawn-up (Drakakis-Smith & Rimmer 1982, pp. 21–2). In addition, however, there has been an attempt to control the growth of the capital cities by adopting decentralization policies. These have usually involved promoting the growth of intermediate or secondary cities, often by creating regional growth poles (Jones 1988, pp. 141–50). In the case of Jakarta, a rather more draconian measure was introduced in 1970 when the city was declared 'closed' to all new migrants. Before immigrants were issued with residence permits they had to produce proof of employment and accommodation, and deposit with the metropolitan authorities the 'equivalent of the return fare to their point of origin' (Yue-man Yeung 1988, p. 171).

Why is there such concern with the growth of the capital cities of Southeast Asia? In short, both national and city governments believe that they are too large,[2] and for two principal reasons. First, it is felt that the primate cities of the region are beginning to exhibit diseconomies of scale, such as excessive congestion, high land prices, and pollution. Second, it is considered that their growth is impeding the growth of secondary cities and stifling development in the countryside. Not only is this sometimes regarded as uneconomic, but it is also of political concern as it increases

Table 7.3 The creation of single metropolitan authorities in Southeast Asia

Jakarta	Special Region of the Capital City of Jakarta	1964
Bangkok	Bangkok Metropolitan Authority	1972
Kuala Lumpur	Federal Territory of Kuala Lumpur	1974
Manila	Metro-Manila Commission	1975

inequalities between urban and rural areas, especially between the capital city and the rest of the nation.

Although city size and efficiency are often discussed, there is very little empirical evidence to support the contention that the capital cities of Southeast Asia are experiencing diseconomies/disamenities of scale, or that their urban hierarchies are in a state of disequilibrium. Indeed, the little evidence that exists from other regions of the world appears to indicate that primate cities are growing faster than other urban centres for the simple reason that they remain the most profitable places for businesses to locate in and for migrants to travel to (see Potter 1985, pp. 116–20, Egan & Bendick 1986, pp. 209–11, Kelley & Williamson 1987, pp. 32–5, Tolley 1987, pp. 52–4, Rogers & Williamson 1984, pp. 275–9; Richardson 1989). As Jones (1988, p. 142) writes:

> The attempt to block big city growth [in Southeast Asia] by impo-
> sition of controls is a 'dead end street' approach that tends to distort
> natural forces and entails large social costs. It fails to recognise that
> diseconomies of metropolitan growth . . . if sufficiently serious, will
> affect private investment decisions. These market-based adjustments,
> if complemented by a strategy of eliminating [urban] biases . . . should
> avoid the need for draconian policies.

However, although the primate cities of the region may remain economi-cally efficient, their dominance is such that many planners, bureaucrats, and politicians feel that it is socially and politically imperative that their growth be controlled. A second point, and one that is hinted at in Jones's quote, is that the true 'efficiency' of the region's great cities is masked by 'implicit policies' that promote their growth. By this is meant those policies that are adopted for other reasons but that have the effect of promoting urbanization, and particularly capital city urbanization. It should be added that there also exist explicit policies that are intentionally aimed at generating urban growth. Such policies result in an 'urban bias'[3] that favours urban development and urban populations at the expense of farmers and the countryside (Jones 1988, pp. 145–7). These policies can include industrial incentives, the taxation of agriculture and the subsidization of staple foods, overvalued exchange rates, tax breaks for industry, and investment in – and subsidization of – urban services and infrastructure. How far urbanization has been accelerated as a result is almost impossible to say. Egan & Bendick (1986, p. 209) are of the opinion that: 'If urban bias had never existed in public policies, there is reason to believe that the majority of the urban development we observe today would still exist'.

Of all the cities of Southeast Asia, the primate city *par excellence* – indeed, perhaps the world's best example of a primate city – is Bangkok, the capital of Thailand. The population of the Bangkok metropolis in 1988 was 5 670 000, while that of Thailand's second largest city, Chiangmai, was under 250 000. Bangkok therefore had a population almost 23 times larger than the country's second city. It is likely, furthermore, that in reality the figure is even higher than the official data indicate, with most informed estimates putting Bangkok's population at somewhere between 7 million and 10 million.

Bangkok: primate city *par excellence*

Bangkok, or to give it its shortened Thai name Krungthep,[4] was established on the eastern banks of the Chao Phraya river in 1782 by King Rama I, the founder of the present Chakri dynasty. The site was chosen for defensive reasons, and protected from the marauding Burmese the city flourished as the political and economic focus of the kingdom of Siam (Smithies 1986). However, population growth was hardly spectacular, and on a number of occasions the city suffered from severe outbreaks of disease. Sternstein (1984, p. 48) writes, for example, that cholera sometimes 'reduced the resident population by a fifth or more in a few weeks'. From an initial population of some 50 000, Bangkok expanded in fits and starts to approximately 200 000 by 1900 (Figure 7.1). However, it should be emphasized that population estimates for these early years are gross approximations and are highly unreliable. Sivaramakrishnan and Green (1986, p. 96), and Donner (1978, p. 787) quote a population figure of 400 000 for the 1850s, while Sternstein (1984) is of the opinion that it was somewhere closer to 100 000. In general, many of the early estimates are inflated, perhaps because the eyewitnesses 'succumbed to a visual fallacy' of assuming that the entire area of the city was as densely built up as were the strips of land (and water) along the canals, which were the main arteries of communication (Sternstein 1984, p. 48) (see Figure 7.2).

Population growth began to accelerate at the turn of the 20th century, and between 1950 and 1980 was expanding at an annual rate in excess of 8 per cent per year in the built–up area, and at 5 per cent in the entire Greater Bangkok Metropolitan Area (Sternstein 1984, p. 46). By the early 1950s, the city's population had reached 1 million, by 1968 2.7 million, and by 1976 4.6 million. In 1988 it was 5.67 million (Figure 7.3). Bangkok has also expanded

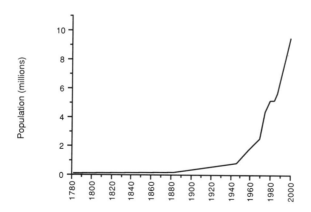

Figure 7.1 Population of Bangkok, 1782–2000

Figure 7.2 Bangkok *khlong* (canal): artery of communication and open sewer (photograph: Chris Dixon)

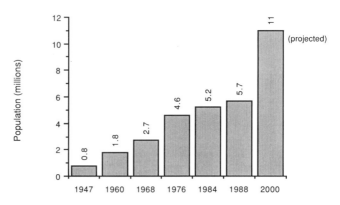

Figure 7.3 Population of Bangkok, 1947–2000

in area from 13.3 square kilometres in 1900, to 96.4 square kilometres by 1958. Today, the Bangkok Metropolitan Region encompasses some 1600 square kilometres (Figure 7.4). Assuming a medium tempo of growth, the Bangkok Metropolitan Region will have a projected population approaching 11 million by 2000 (Thienchay Kiranandana & Suwanee Surasiengsunk 1985, p. 74).

There are three components to the growth of Bangkok's population: natural increase, migration from the countryside and from other urban

Figure 7.4 Bangkok: expansion of urbanized area, 1900, 1958, and 1968 (adapted from Sivaramakrishnan & Green 1986)

areas, and the expansion of the city boundaries. A lack of data makes estimating the relative balance between these three components difficult. However, the Economic and Social Commission for Asia and the Pacific has estimated that between 1960 and 1970 the ratio of natural increase to migration to area annexation for all urban areas was 5:4:1, while for the period from 1970 to 1979 it was 4:3:3 (ESCAP 1982, p. 29). For Bangkok alone, it is likely that the share of net migration in urban growth has been even higher. One estimate for the period from 1970 to 1975 puts the figure at over 45 per cent (Medhi Krongkaew & Pawadee Tongudai 1984, p. 9), while another, spanning the years between 1972 and 1982, attributes 33 per cent of population growth to migration (Angel & Sopon Pornchokchai 1989, p. 137). One final point to make concerns the official definition of urban. As was noted in the introductory section of the chapter, urban areas in Thailand are currently equated with municipal areas. This includes all *nakorn* (city) municipalities, all *muang* (town) municipalities, and all *tambon* (commune) municipalities.[5] In 1984 there were 126 such municipalities in Thailand, only a small increase from the 117 that existed in 1947 (Thienchay Kiranandana & Suwanee Surasiengsunk 1985, p. 35, and see ESCAP 1982, pp. 23–4). However, this definition of urban excludes all those urban areas at the lower end of the urban hierarchy, the larger so-called sanitary districts. If these larger sanitary districts – an admittedly somewhat arbitrary division – are included in the definition of urban, then Thailand's 1984 urban population increases from 8.6 million to 12.7 million, and level of urbanization from 17.1 per cent to 25.1 per cent (Thienchay Kiranandana & Suwanee Surasiengsunk 1985, p. 49). This shows the extent to which the kingdom's urban population has been underestimated and illustrates the dangers of using national statistics as a basis from which to make comparisons across the Southeast Asian region.

The most interesting aspect of the figures for the components of urban growth in Thailand is the importance of migration. Rural Thais have always been fairly mobile, and they have been travelling to, and working in, Bangkok for many years (see Rigg 1989a). However, two developments have increased the flow of rural migrants. First, from the 1960s successive Thai governments have invested considerable resources in improving Thailand's road system. This has brought the rural population into closer contact with Bangkok and has made it fairly easy for them to travel there. Second, as farmland has become an increasingly scarce resource, and as disparities between Bangkok and the rest of the country have widened, so migration to the capital has become a more attractive proposition. Indeed, for some poor rural households it has become a necessity.

This rapid rate of growth has brought with it problems of inadequate housing, transport, services, and employment. It has also led to criticisms that the city is too large, that it is parasitic, and that its growth must be controlled. The remainder of this chapter will examine the problems and strains that Bangkok is currently facing, and will also address the issues of primacy and overurbanization.

Squatter and slum communities

The extent of the squatter 'problem'

The National Housing Authority (NHA) estimated that 551 420 persons (13 per cent of the city's population) were living in 410 slum and squatter settlements within the metropolitan area of Bangkok in 1981[6] (Figure 7.5) (Somsook Boonyabancha 1983, p. 255). However, this was only an estimate and other commentators believe that the squatter population was considerably higher. It is significant that the NHA figure excludes many 'mini' squatter settlements. A more detailed survey based on 1984 air photographs mapped a total of 1020 slum areas that supported an estimated population of 1.16 million (approximately 23 per cent of Bangkok's total population) (Angel & Sopon Pornchokchai 1989, pp. 137–8, Angel 1988). In spite of the fact that the slum population decreased in relative terms between 1974 and 1984, the absolute total rose from 139 326 to 160 147 housing 'units'. It seems clear that although officially Bangkok's 'poor' population only accounts for 5 per cent to 6 per cent of the total, significantly more are living in overcrowded communities where basic services and infrastructure are poor or entirely lacking (NESDB n.d.(b), p. 292).

Unlike the situation in many cities in the developing world, the squatter settlements of Bangkok are rarely illegal in the pure sense of the term. Approximately two-thirds of the squatter population live in houses built on privately owned land, and the landlords extract a land rent from their squatter residents. The remaining third reside on public land (Somsook Boonyabancha 1983, p. 257). Interestingly, although private landlords are understandably rarely willing to give their tenants rights of permanent occupation, it is those squatters living on public land who are at the greatest risk of eviction. Somsook Boonyabancha, for example, has calculated that two-thirds of families under the threat of eviction live on government-owned land, and in 1985 these numbered some 272 000, or over a quarter of the total squatter population (Somsook Boonyabancha 1983, p. 257, Angel & Somsook Boonyabancha 1988, p. 110). As can be seen in Figure 7.5, the settlements are dispersed throughout the city, and those established on public land generally tend to be rather larger than those on private land.

Conditions in the squatter settlements

Douglass (1984, p. 144) describes the conditions that the squatter residents of Bangkok have to endure in the following terms:

> In the slums . . . life is only livable because of the capacity of the human mind to become accustomed to the unthinkable. With no sanitation services, garbage is dumped next to the flimsy houses, breeding flies, rats, mosquitos and disease . . . All the slums are overcrowded, with whole families sleeping in a tiny room. Cooking, eating, chatting and the cacophony of existence spill by necessity from small rooms to the out-of-doors.

143

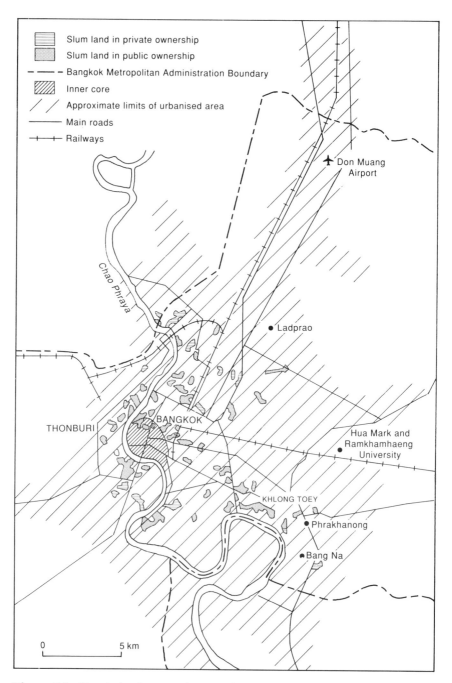

Figure 7.5 Bangkok: city map showing slum and squatter settlements

Legend:
- Slum land in private ownership
- Slum land in public ownership
- Bangkok Metropolitan Administration Boundary
- Inner core
- Approximate limits of urbanised area
- Main roads
- Railways

Don Muang Airport

Ladprao

Chao Phraya

THONBURI

BANGKOK

Hua Mark and Ramkhamhaeng University

KHLONG TOEY

Phrakhanong

Bang Na

0   5 km

The squatter settlements of Bangkok are a vivid reminder that even though some people may maintain that Thailand is on the verge of attaining the status of a newly industrializing country (see Chapter 9), there still remains a large poor population living at times in appalling conditions (see Figure 7.6). It also needs to be stressed, however, that the squatter residents of the city are not all equally poor, and there are great differences between the conditions in which they lead their lives. In Stokes's terms, there are both 'slums of hope' and 'slums of despair', and also, for that matter, 'families of hope' and 'families of despair' (Stokes 1962). This is clear in Thorbek's study of slum life in Khlong Toey slum, the largest in Bangkok (Figure 7.5). She notes that one family had a monthly income of over 20 000 baht (£500), and a large house with a record-player, refrigerator, freezer, television, and a motorcycle.[7] They also owned land in Bangkok as well as upcountry, and two of their children had been to university. The husband was even able to afford to support a second, 'minor' wife. In contrast, another household in the same vicinity was living, quite literally, from hand-to-mouth. Thorbek (1987, p. 43) describes their position from the perspective of the woman as follows:

The poorest woman in the slum lived in completely different circumstances [to the family described above]. She had come to Bangkok as a fourteen-year-old and had ended up as a prostitute at the harbour. She had been grossly exploited by a pimp while she was young. Now she lived in a hut with an adoptive son and a man who was badly addicted

Figure 7.6 Accumulation of rubbish beneath squatter huts (photograph: Chris Dixon)

to heroin . . . She had no regular income, but got free rice at the Prateep School. She often talked or worked a little with a couple of the other families who lived nearby and she survived on the odd meal she could share with them. She starved.

Official concern for squatters and squatter settlements

During the 1980s there emerged a heightened concern among officials for the plight of the squatter communities of Bangkok. No doubt this is partly because the Bangkok Metropolitan Administration is now an elected city government and is therefore more accountable to the population. The current governor of Bangkok, Chamlong Srimuang, is a strict Buddhist who lives a spartan existence himself, and crusades for the rights of the poor. It is significant that he enjoys considerable public support. The media have also taken a greater interest in the conditions that exist in squatter settlements and have played an important role in raising public awareness and pressuring government agencies into action (see Angel & Somsook Boonyabancha 1988, pp. 118–20). A final reason why the 1980s saw a rather more concerted effort on the part of the authorities to improve slums such as Khlong Toey is because the provision of adequate housing is seen to play an important economic function. It is not just a social service that is a drain on public funds. Construction provides employment for unskilled workers, it has strong backward and forward linkages to other sectors of the economy (e.g. building materials, house fixtures), and has a multiplier effect of approximately two (Becker 1988, p. 13–4).[8]

However, although a National Housing Authority (NHA) was formed as long ago as 1973 when four existing public bodies were amalgamated (Chawalit Nitaya & Ubonwan Ocharoen 1980, p. 84), the impact on the squatter population has been disappointing. The numbers living in slum communities are still high, and services and conditions usually remain poor. Initially an annual construction target of 20 000 to 24 000 low-income housing units was set. By 1977, four years into the building programme, a total of 3394 had been completed. The main problem facing the NHA was underfunding. The government agreed to provide a subsidy of 10 per cent of the NHA's capital each year, but beyond this the authority had to be self-financing. As a result, the NHA was forced either to pass its costs onto the residents of its estates, or go into debt. As it turned out, it did both. By 1977, the NHA had an accumulated debt of US$5.5 million and the rentals of flats were proving beyond the means of much of the poor population the authority was designed to serve (see Figure 7.7) (Sivaramakrishnan & Green 1986, pp. 111–13, Chawalit Nitaya & Ubonwan Ocharoen 1980, p. 85, Thorbek 1987, p. 29).

With these problems in mind, the NHA changed its strategy in 1977 and began to concentrate, with the support of the World Bank, on slum upgrading programmes, and sites and services projects. Three reasons for this change in strategy can be highlighted. First, it is cheaper; second it is explicitly targeted at the poor; and third, it was becoming more widely accepted that the squatter settlements of Bangkok were not worthless,

Figure 7.7 National Housing Authority development, Bangkok (photograph: Chris Dixon)

lawless communities that would only benefit from demolition. An NHA survey of 1975 found that 15 per cent of dwellings contained cottage industries, that the value of the buildings and existing infrastructure was some 1400 million baht, and that the slums were 'stable communities with middle-class aspirations, improving employment and substantial existing structures' (quoted in Chawalit Nitaya & Ubonwan Ocharoen 1980, p. 85). In 1980, 14 480 slum families had benefited from such programmes, and the Sixth Five Year Plan (1987–1991) aims to upgrade a further 20 000 slum units (Thorbek 1987, p. 29, NESDB n.d.(b), p. 297). However, this approach to the squatter 'problem' is also facing severe constraints, of which the most intractable is the land question.

The central problem is the grave shortage of affordable land that can be used to provide squatters with secure ownership. This is becoming more serious as Bangkok expands and as the pressures on land become greater. In 1985, 86 squatter communities, or over a quarter of squatter households, were facing the risk of eviction: 17 were needed for road construction, 16 for commercial developments, 14 for public buildings, 9 for residential developments, and 5 for other types of development (Angel & Somsook Boonyabancha 1988, p. 110). Of these 86 communities, 49 were actually evicted in 1985 and 1986, amounting to 5073 households (Angel & Sopon Pornchokchai 1989, p. 141). It should be obvious that without secure ownership substantial investment in improving conditions and upgrading services – either by the squatter households themselves or by the government – is economically risky. A final point to emphasize is that even though most communities that face eviction are on public land –

147

and particularly on land owned by the Crown Property Bureau – this does not make the problem any easier to solve. Paradoxically, it actually makes it harder. The Crown Property Bureau operates very much as a private company, and like other public bodies is 'faceless' and can act without regard to social obligations. In contrast, small private landlords often have an intimate relationship with their tenants and are culturally obliged to take account of their concerns. It is notable that most evictions from private land follow the death of the original landlord and a subsequent change in ownership (Somsook Boonyabancha 1983, p. 264). When landlords do decide to clear their land it occurs peacefully, and they usually pay compensation to their tenants either by 'stopping the collection of land rents a year or more prior to clearance, or through direct payments to departing families to enable them to relocate their houses elsewhere' (Angel & Sopon Pornchokchai 1989, p. 140). Two other reasons why squatters on public land are most at risk of eviction is because public lands tend to be concentrated in the city centre (where development pressures are greatest) and because most residents on private land have a rental agreement with their landlords.

One means of overcoming the land problem is by 'land sharing' (see Angel & Somsook Boonyabancha 1988, Jensen 1989). This involves the division of land between the squatters and the landlord, and represents a possible solution when there are conflicting claims. So far as the private landlord is concerned, it avoids confrontation and lengthy court proceedings. And when land is owned by a public agency it prevents negative press coverage. In recent years, households facing the risk of eviction have managed to organize themselves better, petition politicians, and gain the support of the press. Land sharing as a compromise solution is felt by some to be particularly appropriate to the Thai context. As Angel and Somsook Boonyabancha (1988, p. 120) maintain:

> There is a strong orientation in Thai culture to avoid open conflict, to settle arguments peacefully, to appeal to higher authority when adversaries cannot reach agreement, and to secure solutions that are evolutionary in nature and do not fundamentally upset the status quo.

Although efforts to improve conditions in Bangkok's slum and squatter settlements have taken on a new urgency, the problem will remain severe for the foreseeable future. Funds are lacking and co-ordination between the various government bodies involved is poor. Moreover, in spite of such imaginative solutions as land sharing, the shortage of suitable land at an appropriate price will remain acute (Tongchai Savasdisara et al. 1987, p. 17, NESDB n.d.(b), p. 261). But that said, Bangkok's low-income housing market is improving. The NHA is building a few 'core' houses for the very poor; the private sector is providing house-and-land packages for sale for between US$6000 and US$10 000 (sometimes requiring monthly payments of less than US$60), and there is also a low-cost house and flat rental market that makes units available for as little as US$12 per month (Angel & Sopon

Pornchokchai 1989, p. 142). The point is that many residents of Bangkok's slum and squatter communities would rather stay where they are. The alternatives are more expensive, they are less conveniently located, and they provide a better quality of housing than most slum residents require. In general, the existing private land rental system works well, and it should not be replaced, but improved. As Angel and Sopon Pornchokchai (1989, p. 145) write:

> In an important sense, present slum housing is cheap and attractive to low-income people, even though it may look hideous to outsiders. Any action to destroy this housing stock which does not consider its proper replacement with viable alternatives thus contributes to worsening the housing situation in Bangkok.

The provision of services, transport, and communications

Services

A linked but rather wider issue is the provision of services in Bangkok. In general, services are more widely available than they are in the rest of the country and they are also often provided at less than cost. The Sixth Development Plan (1987–91), for example, states that 4.78 million residents have access to piped water, 67 per cent of the total population of the city (NESDB n.d.(b), p. 261). Bangkok also consumes much of the country's electricity, has by far the greatest concentration of telephones, has a greater variety of educational establishments, and is well served by doctors, dentists, and pharmacists (Table 7.4). Even squatter settlements are relatively well served. One study of 38 squatter settlements reported that in every case there was electricity available, and that 90 per cent of the settlements also had access to piped water (although both services were often used illegally) (Roovers *et al.* 1989, p. 155). Sewerage is the least developed service. Only 2 per cent of the city's population is connected to Bangkok's limited sewerage system and most solid waste is collected from cesspits and septic tanks (Anat Arbhabhirama *et al.* 1987, pp. 213–15).[9] This is unlikely to change for some time, as it has been estimated that the construction of a city-wide sewerage system would cost a massive 36 671 million baht (1980 prices) (Anat Arbhabhirama *et al.* 1987, p. 215), equivalent to 33 per cent of total government expenditure in 1980 (NSO 1982, p. 66). It should be borne in mind that although the level of service provision is low compared with that of the capital cities of the developed world, it is very good when compared with the secondary towns and cities and with the rural areas of Thailand. For although Bangkok is in many respects a modern city (see Figure 7.8), Thailand is still a developing country.

Transport and communications

Bangkok's transportation system is an even bigger problem than its other services. Indeed, it is so overburdened that its inadequacies threaten to

Table 7.4 Services available in Bangkok and Thailand, 1986–7

	Bangkok	Whole kingdom	Percentage in Bangkok
Population	5 609 000	53 873 000	10.4
Hospital beds	16 461	84 438	19.5
Physicians	4 211	9 580	44.0
Dentists	878	1 468	59.8
Pharmacists	2 850	3 622	78.7
Maternal death rate (per 1000 population)	0.04	0.35	—
State institutes of higher education	8	14	57.1
Graduates (1985)	42 960	54 420	78.8
Telephone exchanges[1]	69	310	22.3
Main telephone stations	686 151	1 005 872	68.2
Line capacity	861 392	1 251 102	68.9
Cinemas	101	580	17.4
Cinema seats	103 152	401 304	25.7

Sources: NSO 1988a, 1988c, 1988d, 1989b.

Note: 1) Telecommunications data are for the Metropolitan Telecommunications Area. This encompasses the Bangkok Metropolis and the surrounding provinces of Nonthaburi, Pathumthani and Samut Prakan.

Figure 7.8 Sukhumvit Road, Bangkok (photograph: author)

undermine Thailand's economic development (Handley 1988c, p. 94). Road traffic congestion is among the worst in the world and at peak periods speeds can average less than 10 kilometres per hour (Figure 7.9) (Pendakur 1984, p. 34, Yeu-man Yeung 1988, p. 169). In addition, the city's port, Khlong Toey (which is Thailand's only major international port, handling some 70 per cent of trade), has been unable to cope with the increasing volumes of traffic associated with an export-led boom. In 1988, ships were having to wait four to five days to get a berth, and such were the delays that shippers threatened to increase rates (Handley 1988b, p. 95). This continuing congestion at Khlong Toey should be eased when the Laem Chabang deep-water port on Thailand's Eastern Seaboard is completed in 1991 (Figure 7.10, and see below). The reasons why Bangkok's transport system and port should be so overburdened are linked to the familiar issues of poor planning and co-ordination, and inadequate funding.

With respect to the city's roads, Viraphong Vachratith (1988, p. 19) quotes Thailand's planning agency, the National Economic and Social Development Board, as saying: 'Bangkok's road network has developed over the years with little planning and control. As a result, the network lacks structural coherence and, quite apart from capacity problems, serves traffic needs very inefficiently'. There is excessive division of responsibilities between at least five government agencies, and little co-ordination in planning and running the city's road network (Sivaramakrishnan & Green 1986, p. 113). Compounding this problem, expenditure on road construction in the capital has been minimal and Bangkok has one of the lowest proportions of road surface to total area in the world. The figure in the early 1980s was 9 per cent, compared with 22 per cent in London and 24 per cent in New York (Medhi Krongkaew & Pawadee Tongudai 1984, p. 39). Bangkok's public transport system is inadequate and in poor condition. For political reasons the Bangkok Mass Transit Authority (BMTA) has been forced to keep fares artificially low and its fleet of over 5000 buses is ageing and inadequately maintained. When bus fares were raised from 1.50 baht to 2.00 baht in 1981, such was the outcry from Bangkok's bus travellers that the government and the BMTA were forced to back down and reintroduce the old fare (Pawadee Tonguthai 1987, p. 190). At the time, fares in the countryside, where average incomes are considerably lower than they are in Bangkok, were already 2.00 baht. The National Economic and Social Development Board notes in the Sixth Five Year Plan that the BMTA has accumulated a 'huge' deficit due to inefficient management and what it euphemistically calls 'many other reasons' (NESDB n.d.(b), p. 261). Between 1977 and 1983 the BMTA made an accumulated loss of 3.8 billion baht (Pawadee Tonguthai 1987, p. 190). Recently, private buses have been introduced on some routes to compete with the BMTA and it is intended to reduce the Authority in size and privatize some sections of it (NESDB n.d.(b), p. 296).

Part of the blame for the state of Bangkok's transportation system must rest with the investment decisions taken by successive governments of

Figure 7.9 Traffic congestion in Chinatown, Bangkok (photograph: author)

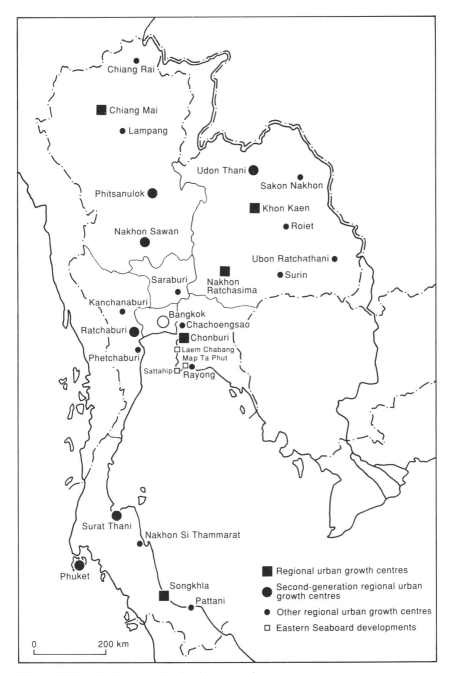

Figure 7.10 Thailand: regional urban growth centres

former Prime Minister Prem Tinsulanond (1980–8) on the advice of the NESDB (and in particular Snoh Unakul, the Secretary-General of the planning agency – see Handley 1989a, p. 71) . Throughout the 1980s the Thai government adopted a conservative fiscal policy and a strict ceiling on external borrowing was maintained. This partly explains the kingdom's current strong fiscal position, but it has also meant that investment in urgent infrastructural projects has been delayed. Prime Minister Chatichai Choonhavan, who replaced Prem in 1988, recognized that Thailand's growth was at risk of being constrained by the capital's infrastructural bottlenecks and so has now given the go-ahead to a number of long overdue projects. Among the most significant is the decision to build a second-stage expressway at a projected cost of US$1.12 billion, an elevated mass transit railway powered by induction motors at a cost of US$1.17 billion, and an elevated highway linking Don Muang Airport with the city centre at a cost of US$288 million (Paisal Sricharatchanya 1989a, p. 30, Viraphong Vachratith 1988, Handley 1988a, p. 66). All three schemes are aimed at improving road transport in the capital. In addition, in early 1989, the decision was taken to proceed with a US$157.5 million modernization programme for Thailand's telecommunications services which are similarly overstretched. Again, the motivation has been the fear that if the system is not improved then Thailand's continued economic growth could be at stake. In this case the decision was prompted 'by the growing concern that the country's dismal telecommunications services might deter foreign investors' (Handley 1989b, pp. 83–4).

Pollution, subsidence, and flooding

Pollution

Rapid growth, a dearth of planning controls, inadequate regulation, and a lack of funds have all contributed to the pollution of Bangkok. It was not until 1981 that national air-quality standards were imposed, and currently there are two networks of air monitoring stations in the capital, established in 1978 and 1983. As Table 7.5 shows, the major airborne pollutants are carbon monoxide and suspended particulates, levels of both of which regularly exceed the standards set by the National Environmental Board. The problem is most severe, as might be expected, in the vicinity of major roads and intersections, and the degree of air pollution is accentuated by the fact that there are no laws on the zoning of industrial and residential land use (Thorbek 1987, p. 28). However, far more serious than airborne pollution is water pollution. The khlongs (canals) on which Bangkok is built are used as drains by much of the population of the city and as a result usually have a dissolved oxygen content of zero. The Thai Development Research Institute's report on the Thai environment notes that the values of the biological oxygen demand (BOD5) of the khlongs of Bangkok are 'equivalent to sewage, rather than to those of normal water' (Anat Arbhabhirama *et al.* 1987,

Table 7.5 Pollution standards and levels of pollution in Bangkok

Pollutant	NEB standards	Levels recorded
Carbon monoxide (CO)	8 hour – 20 mg/m^3 24 hour – 50 mg/m^3	Exceeded at major intersections Improving because vehicles becoming more efficient, and increasing use of LPG and diesel fuels that emit less CO
Ozone (O$_3$)	1 hour – 0.2 mg/m^3	Standards not exceeded
Sulphur dioxide (SO$_2$)	Annual – 0.1 mg/m^3 24 hour – 0.3 mg/m^3	Standards not exceeded (maximum 24 hour 0.07 mg/m^3, 1981–4)
Total suspended particulates (TSP)	Annual – 0.1 mg/m^3 24 hour – 0.33 mg/m^3	Regularly exceeded (both 24-hour and annual geometric mean), rates generally getting worse
Lead	24 hour – 0.01 mg/m^3	Highest at roadsides and main intersections, but within NEB standards (a 1984 study in ten locations recorded 24-hour lead concentrations in the range 0.001–0.005 mg/m^3). Levels generally improving due to reduction in lead in petrol and increased use of LPG and diesel fuels

Source: Anat Arbhabhirama *et al.* 1987, pp. 193–211.

p. 220). The effluent that flows into the khlongs of the city in turn flows into the Chao Phraya River, which is also in danger of becoming biologically dead in much of its lower reaches. In addition, concentrations of heavy metals and pesticides, although not yet at critical levels, need to be continuously monitored (Anat Arbhabhirama *et al.* 1987, pp. 213–22).

Subsidence and flooding

A final problem, which is peculiar to Bangkok and does not afflict the other cities of Southeast Asia, is subsidence. Bangkok like Venice – a city to which it is often compared[10] – is literally sinking. The major cause of subsidence is the excessive pumping of ground water (up to 1.15 million cubic metres per day), compounded by the increasing weight of buildings constructed in the city (Yeu-man Yeung 1988, p. 170). In the eastern sections of Bangkok (Ladprao, Hua Mark, Phrakhanong, and Bang Na) the annual rate of land subsidence exceeds 10 centimetres, while in the central districts it ranges from 5 to 10 centimetres per year (Figure 7.8). In places (e.g. near Ramkhamhaeng University), Bangkok is now below sea level. The effects of subsidence can be seen in the greater frequency and intensity of flooding, which has been aggravated by the filling-in and obstruction of khlongs and smaller drainage channels. Although subsidence and flooding are now recognized to be severe problems, no long-term solution has yet been implemented.

The government and planning of Bangkok

The Bangkok Metropolitan Administration (BMA) was established as the autonomous city government of Bangkok in 1972. However, the responsibilities that fall to it are relatively few: solid waste management, road maintenance and construction, drainage, public health, and primary education. Other services are administered and provided by government agencies such as the National Housing Authority, the Bangkok Mass Transit Authority, and the Port Authority of Thailand. Although in theory the BMA functions as an autonomous body with considerable power, in reality it lacks the fiscal and administrative authority to act independently of the central government. Sivaramakrishnan & Green (1986, p. 116) write that: 'Although the BMA has a sizable staff, a substantial budget, and a modest range of functions, it remains a relic of the past municipal system . . . and is not the metropolitan government it should be'.

The overall planning of the Bangkok metropolis is unco-ordinated and ineffectual, reflecting the weakness of the BMA. The Greater Bangkok Plan (1960–90) has been reviewed twice (in 1968 and 1971) and yet neither plan has come close to implementation (Sivaramakrishnan & Green 1986, p. 107). In general, government agencies involved in the provision of urban services and infrastructure have their own budgets and follow their own plans and priorities. The BMA has no authority to co-ordinate the work of the other agencies in line with the metropolitan development plan (NESDB n.d.(a), p. 146, NESDB n.d.(b), p. 292). As a result, virtually every analysis concludes by emphasizing the duplicative and unco-ordinated nature of planning in the city.

Bangkok as parasitic: urban bias and diseconomies of scale

It has been observed on innumerable occasions that 'Bangkok is Thailand'. Although this is certainly an exaggeration, the capital does dominate the kingdom to a remarkable degree. Not only in terms of size and economic activity, but also in political terms, for the Thai state is very much a Bangkok-based state. It is for these reasons that London (1980, p. 113) finds that he is able to write that the capital of Thailand is a 'near-prototypical primate city' (see also Korff 1989).

It has already been observed that Bangkok's population is at least 23 times greater than the second city of Thailand.[11] And it is larger than life in many other respects. Bangkok has the highest concentration of universities, hospitals, doctors, industries, financial organizations, tele-phones and private cars (Tables 7.4 and 7.6). It generates 49 per cent of GDP, processes 95 per cent of imports and exports, and has a per capita monthly income over two times greater than the national average (Table

Table 7.6 Functional dominance of Bangkok

	Bangkok	Whole kingdom	Bangkok as percentage or multiple of whole kingdom
Population (1988)	5 717 000	54 961 000	10.4
Gross regional/domestic product (millions of baht, 1987)	605 165	1 234 031	49.0
Manufacturing	230 559	295 513	78.0
Electricity and water supply	17 440	31 859	54.7
Banking, insurance and real estate	32 100	48 672	66.0
Services	90 707	171 665	52.8
Average household monthly income (baht, 1986)	7 427	3 710	2 times
Motor vehicles registered	1 760 167	6 045 474	29.1
Passenger cars registered	570 000	789 459	72.2
Domestic telex services (Jan–June 1987)[1]	1 726 758	2 456 940	70.3
Divorce licences	11 666	33 344	35.0
Divorce rate (/1000)	1.77	0.69	2.5 times
Colour televisions per 100 private households	56	21	2.5 times

Sources: NSO 1987b, 1988a, 1988b, 1988c.
Note: 1) Units: length of service in minutes.

7.6). Bangkok is the functional core of Thailand, lying at the heart of the nation's transport network, housing the key centres of political and military decision-making, and dictating social and cultural life. To achieve wealth, power, and prestige, an individual invariably needs to live and work there. Whatever index or definition of primacy is used, Bangkok is undoubtedly one of the world's best examples of a primate city.

There are a number of questions and issues that flow from this. First, can such an unbalanced urban hierarchy be efficient? Second, what is the effect of such a concentration of political and economic power on Thailand's hinterlands? And third, what are the forces that have allowed such a degree of primacy to arise?

Bangkok as parasitic

The fact of Bangkok's primacy is impossible to refute. Difficulties arise, however, when its effects are investigated. To those analysts who see Bangkok as parasitic, the best evidence is found in the remarkable disparities between it and the rest of the kingdom, and particularly such underdeveloped regions as the Northeast. London (1977, p. 50) explains:

It is just a short step from contrasting those highly developed primate cities with their undeveloped hinterlands to assuming and asserting that the primate city actually acts as an obstruction to hinterland economic growth.

157

The notion of primate city parasitism has drawn on the wider theory of dependency. It is argued that Bangkok 'exploits' the rural hinterlands, extracting surplus value and forcing the countryside into a subordinate position characterized by its enduring underdevelopment. Cities, of course, cannot act of their own accord. It is the élite classes within the city who dominate and who in turn exploit the countryside. The point, of course, is that we should examine Bangkok in politico-economic terms 'with a main focus of concern being the role of power, group, or class interests, and public policymaking in creating and maintaining spatial inequalities' (London 1985, p. 208).

Urban bias

The pattern of Thailand's development since the 1960s has corresponded, broadly speaking, with Lipton's 'urban bias' model of economic development (Pawadee Tonguthai 1987, p. 185). From the publication of the First National Economic Development Plan (1961–6) onwards, resources have been preferentially allocated to industry and to the urban areas, and taxes and tariffs have favoured the modern sectors of the economy at the expense of agriculture and rural areas. The development of the countryside, and this was particularly the case until the mid 1970s, was neglected (London 1985).

There is a wide array of 'implicit policies' that can be highlighted to support the case for Thailand's urban bias in development. As has already been discussed, services in Bangkok are heavily subsidized by the state. The BMTA for example was losing an average of 546 million baht per year between 1977 and 1983 (Pawadee Tonguthai 1987, p. 190). In addition, the Board of Investment embraced import-substitution industrialization in the 1960s, and as part of this policy provided industries with tax concessions, cheap credit, and tariff protection. All served to subsidize industry. And as Bangkok and its environs has always been the logical place for industries to locate, it has led to the growth and the subsidization of the capital city. Of these implicit policies, however, the most extensively researched has been the rice premium, discussed in Chapter 3.

One of the rice premium's aims was to lower the price of rice in urban areas. To achieve this objective, rice producers were taxed to the extent that between 1955 and 1966 the premium represented a tax to the farmer of over 80 per cent (Bertrand 1980, Rigg 1987). During that time, the premium contributed between 11 per cent and 14 per cent of total government revenue. Although the rice premium is possibly the 'single most disputed and the most researched policy element in Thai economic history' (Holtsberg 1982, p. 172), no one questions the fact that it has seriously disadvantaged agricultural producers and benefited urban consumers. The rice premium, along with other implicit policies, has helped to encourage rural–urban migration, by making the opportunity costs of working in the city more attractive (Pawadee Tonguthai 1987, p. 189–90). Many of the workers in Bangkok's flourishing informal sector are rural migrants who have travelled to Bangkok either to find their fortunes or sometimes merely to survive through the long and unproductive dry season (Figure 7.11).

Diseconomies of Scale

The discussion above raises the question of whether such policies, which have helped to promote the urbanization of Thailand, are 'sensible'. This needs to be examined in economic and political terms. So far as the economic implications of the policies are concerned, there is little to go on. It is certainly the case that they have made urban areas, and particularly Bangkok, relatively more attractive. But how far rural–urban migration flows have increased as a result is unclear. Nor is it clear how far the capital is suffering from diseconomies of scale. It is claimed that capital costs are higher in Bangkok than in smaller, secondary cities, that negative externalities such as pollution and congestion are more serious, and that there are severe management diseconomies arising from the size of the bureaucratic infrastructure and its lack of responsiveness to consumer demand.[12] But even without the implicit policies favouring urban areas, it is likely that Bangkok would remain the most attractive place for industries to locate. However, although it is the economic implications of the policies discussed above that have generated the most attention, it is worth remembering that many have an equally important political raison d'être. They have been designed to placate the volatile urban population, and also to make the capital more attractive to potential foreign investors (Douglass 1984, p. 175). Moreover, the change in policy to emphasize the

Figure 7.11 The informal sector: a roadside fruit seller, Bangkok (photograph: author)

control of Bangkok's expansion, the decentralization of urban growth, and the allocation of greater resources to agriculture and rural areas, has been motivated primarily by political considerations.

Decentralization policies and the control of the growth of Bangkok

There is little evidence to suppose that Bangkok is experiencing diseconomies of scale, but policies to limit the city's growth, redirect migration flows to regional urban centres, and promote the growth of secondary cities are now firmly on the planning agenda. In fact, Khon Kaen in the Northeast was first identified as a growth pole as long ago as 1962 (Figure 7.10). Through the course of the Fourth (1977–81) to the Sixth (1987–91) Five Year Development Plans, these decentralization policies have received increasing attention. Currently, there are five regional urban growth centres, six second-generation regional urban growth centres, and 13 'other' regional urban growth centres (Figure 7.10) (NESDB n.d.(b), p. 317). The Sixth Plan states that it will 'continue to accommodate the policy of decentralizing prosperity to the regions' (NESDB n.d.(b), p. 289). In addition, there has been an attempt to encourage industries to locate on the outskirts of the Bangkok metropolis rather than in the city itself. The best example is the much vaunted Eastern Seaboard Project.[13]

The Eastern Seaboard Development Project (ESDB) has been presented by the NESDB as the solution to Bangkok's congestion (NESDB n.d.(b), p. 319). Development is concentrated around Map Ta Phut in Rayong province and Laem Chabang in Chonburi province, where the Thai government is in the process of building two deep-water ports (at Laem Chabang and at Sattahip outside Map Ta Phut), a network of new roads, railways and water pipelines, two new industrial estates, and six new reservoirs (Figure 7.10) (NESDB n.d.(b), pp. 319–25). Completion dates for some of the projects have been delayed because of funding problems, although it is anticipated that the core of the programme will be finished by 1991–2 (BBMR 1989, pp. 63–4).

In addition to the promotion of regional urban growth, rather more attention has been paid to improving conditions among the agricultural population. Land reform policies have been introduced, cheap credit made more widely available, the new rice technology has been more enthusiastically disseminated, and greater funds allocated to health care, education and community development. These policies have been partly designed to narrow differentials between rural and urban areas and so encourage the rural population to stay put. Ironically, such programmes have often increased the rural population's awareness of the disparities that exist and in this way have actually promoted migration to Bangkok and to other urban centres (ESCAP 1982, p. 67). The emphasis on rural development was also prompted by increasing security fears in peripheral areas. From the mid-1970s through to the early 1980s, the Communist Party of Thailand was gathering increasing support in the Northern, Northeastern and Southern regions, and in an attempt to reduce support for the insurgents the Thai government reversed its policy of neglecting rural areas and began to invest

160

substantial funds in rural and agricultural development (London 1985). As Vandenbosch and Butwell observed with reference to the Northeast, the administration was 'running scared in the wake of the known subversive threat in that part of the land' (1966, p. 219).

Summary

The cities of Southeast Asia make a visitor the most acutely aware of the poverty and disparities that continue to exist in the region. For it is in urban areas that the contrast between wealth and poverty, and luxury and squalor are most obvious. Squatter settlements exist alongside with modern, fully air-conditioned office blocks. BMW and Mercedes-Benz cars crowd the streets, as do beggars, prostitutes, and child workers. At the same time, the problems of congestion, inadequate housing, and pollution seem almost intolerable and the cities on the verge of collapse. This image, however, is in many respects a false one.

Wages in urban areas are invariably considerably higher than those in rural areas, and migrants travel to the cities of Southeast Asia to take advantage of them. And they rarely travel without prior knowledge of employment and often have somewhere to stay, either with a relative or with a fellow villager who has already become established in the city. In this sense migration does not occur on the off-chance of securing a job, and most migrants are fully aware of the job opportunities that await them. Although conditions in work and the level of services may be very low, they are often better than those that exist in many villages.

A second area of difficulty concerns whether the primate cities of the region are becoming so large that they have become economically inefficient, and are beginning to exhibit diseconomies of scale. Statements arguing the case for diseconomies of scale tend to have two weaknesses. First, they are highly impressionistic. There is very little empirical evidence to support the contention. And, second, urban economic efficiency is distorted by a range of implicit policies that promote (or inhibit) urbanization. Therefore, the forces at work are considerably distorted.

Notwithstanding these caveats, Bangkok and the other capital cities of Southeast Asia will continue to provide the most striking visual impression of the stresses of development and the difficulties of effective planning.

Notes to Chapter 7

1 See McGee 1967 for an early statement on primacy in the region.
2 In 1983, the United Nations conducted a survey of 126 developing countries to discover whether they considered their population distributions to be acceptable. 123 of the 126 (and the three others were all small island states) replied that they regarded them to be either partly of wholly inappropriate (Oberai 1987, p. 13).
3 The notion of 'urban bias' is associated most closely with the work of Lipton (see especially Lipton 1977). See also, however, Byres (1979) for a stinging attack on the 'myth' of urban bias.

4   The principal portion of the official Thai name of Bangkok is: *Krungthep-phramaha-nakhonbawon-rathanakosin-mahinthara-yutthayaa-mahadilok-phiphobnob-pharaat-raatchathaanii-buriiromudomsantisuk. . .* (Haas 1964, p. 15 – Thai-English Dictionary).

5   *Nakorn* municipalities are places having 50 000 or more inhabitants and a population density of more than 3000 per square kilometre; *muang* munici-palities are places with a population of between 10 000 and 50 000 inhabitants and with a population density of not less than 3000 per square kilometre; and *tambon* municipalities are places having urban characteristics which have been declared as small municipalities by official decree (Thienchay Kiranandana & Suwanee Surasiengsunk 1985, p. 35).

6   In Bangkok, the terms 'slum' and 'squatter' are used interchangeably.

7   In 1981 the average monthly income of a household in Bangkok was 5972 baht; in 1986 the figure had risen to 7427 (NSO 1987a, p. 79, 1988c). Another survey conducted among squatter households in the Bangkhen area of Bangkok found that monthly household incomes varied between 800 and 21 000 baht (Roovers *et al.* 1989, p. 156).

8   The increase in national income arising from an increase in investment expenditure in any industry. Thus, a multiplier effect of two implies that for every unit of investment in housing, national income will increase by two units.

9   This book has been republished, with a few alterations, by Oxford University Press (Anat Arbhabhirama *et al.* 1988).

10 It is often referred to as the 'Venice of the East'.

11 Bangkok has dominated Thailand's urban hierarchy since the late 18th century. Sternstein (1984, p. 67) believes, for example, that throughout the period from 1780 to 1900 the city was ten times the size of Siam's second most populous town, Chiangmai.

12 See Richardson 1989 for a general discussion of these factors.

13 There are also now plans to develop an industrial centre in the Southern region of Thailand (see Handley 1989c).

8

Natural resources in Southeast Asia: oil and gas development and the Indonesian economy

Introduction

With the exception of Singapore, the countries of Southeast Asia are rich in natural resources. These include large reserves of timber in Indonesia and Malaysia, tin in Thailand and Malaysia, copper and gold in the Philippines, and oil and gas in Malaysia, Brunei, and Indonesia. The exploitation of the region's natural resources has helped to fuel development and to generate valuable foreign exchange. In 1986, minerals, timber, and fishery products valued at almost US$19 billion were exported, amounting to more than 42 per cent of total exports. And if plantation crops and other agricultural products are included, then these figures rise to US$27.4 billion and 61 per cent respectively (Table 8.1). Indeed, such has been the degree of exploitation that in some instances the natural resources in question have been severely depleted. Thailand, for example, has made the transition from one of the world's largest exporters of tropical hardwoods to a net importer of timber in little more than ten years. Petroleum is the most important of Southeast Asia's natural resources, and has had the greatest impact on its economies. Oil and gas represent the largest single exports of Malaysia, Indonesia and Brunei; indeed in the last of these countries it accounts for 97 per cent of total exports by value. For the region as a whole, petroleum, natural gas, and petroleum products make up nearly 29 per cent of total exports (Table 8.1).

This chapter will examine the development of the petroleum industry in Indonesia. For, with the exception of Brunei, no other country of the region has derived so much apparent benefit from a single natural resource, and is so dependent upon it as is Indonesia on petroleum. However, the intention of this chapter is not merely to assess the development of the petroleum industry. It will also examine how oil and gas, and the wealth they have generated, have affected development in general. How has petroleum distorted the economy? What has it enabled the Indonesian government to achieve that otherwise would have been beyond its scope? How has it altered business practices in the country? And, more broadly, how much of a blessing has Indonesia's oil wealth turned out to be? These questions can never be fully answered, as there are many factors moulding and driving the development process.

Table 8.1 Southeast Asia: exports of natural resources, 1986

	Value (US$ millions)	Percentage of total exports
Brunei		
Crude oil	745	40.6
Liquified natural gas	970	52.9
Petroleum products	67	3.7
Total natural resource exports	1 782	97.2
Other exports	52	2.8
Total exports	1 834	100
Indonesia		
Petroleum	5 501	37.2
Natural gas	2 776	18.7
Plywood and sawn timber	1 363	9.2
Mining	253	1.7
Copper	171	1.2
Coal	31	0.2
Shrimps	285	1.9
Total natural resource exports	10 178	68.7
Plantation crop exports[1]	1 910	12.9
Other exports	2 717	20.3
Total exports	14 805	100
Malaysia		
Petroleum	2 080	15.1
Liquified natural gas	729	5.3
Saw logs	1 106	8.0
Sawn timber	499	3.6
Tin	250	1.8
Other minerals	104	0.8
Total natural resource exports	4 768	34.6
Rubber and palm oil	2 399	18.3
Other agricultural exports	470	3.4
Other exports	6 129	43.7
Total exports	13 766	100
Philippines		
Forest products	243	4.2
Lumber	154	2.7
Plywood	68	1.2
Mineral production	300	5.2
Copper concentrates	109	1.9
Gold	91	1.6
Iron ore agglomerates	76	1.3
Petroleum products	88	1.5
Fish (fresh and preserved)	207	3.6
Total natural resource exports	838	14.5
Plantation crops[2]	891	15.6
Other agricultural exports[3]	86	1.5
Other exports	3 905	68.4
Total exports	5 720	100

Table 8.1 continued

	Value (US$ millions)	Percentage of total exports
Thailand		
Tin	116	1.3
Fishery products	951	10.7
Tuna	289	3.3
Prawns and lobsters	169	1.9
Precious stones	314	3.5
Total natural resource exports	1 381	15.5
Plantation crops	867	9.8
Other agricultural exports	1 872	21.0
Other exports	4 773	53.7
Total exports	8 893	100
Singapore		
Total exports[1]	22 266	100
ASEAN Region		
Petroleum, natural gas and petroleum products	12 956	28.8
Other minerals	1 337	3.0
Timber and other forest products	3 211	7.1
Marine products and aquaculture	1 443	3.2
Total natural resources	18 947	42.1
Plantation crops	6 067	13.5
Other agricultural exports	2 428	5.4
Total natural resources, including agricultural exports	27 442	61.0
Total exports	45 018	100

Notes: 1) Coffee, spices and tea, rubber and palm oil. 2) Coconut products, sugar and sugar products, pineapples, bananas and coffee. 3) Fruits and vegetables, abaca fibres, tobacco, mangoes. 4) Singapore has a large refining and petrochemical industry. In 1986, exports of mineral fuels totalled $US4612 million. However, all of the feedstock was imported.

Sources: various.

Nevertheless, and as will become clear in the discussion, petroleum has played a major role in the shaping of the Indonesian economy, and time and again development priorities and strategies have been contingent upon the state of the petroleum industry.

The development of the petroleum industry in Indonesia

The early years (1871–65)

The use of petroleum in Indonesia pre-dates the arrival of Europeans in Southeast Asia. Reid (1988, p. 75) writes that natural flows of petroleum at Perlak in North Sumatra (Figure 8.1) provided lighting oil for many of the inhabitants of the area, and Acehnese chroniclers regarded it as 'such a natural wonder that [they] saw it as a sign of God's special blessing on

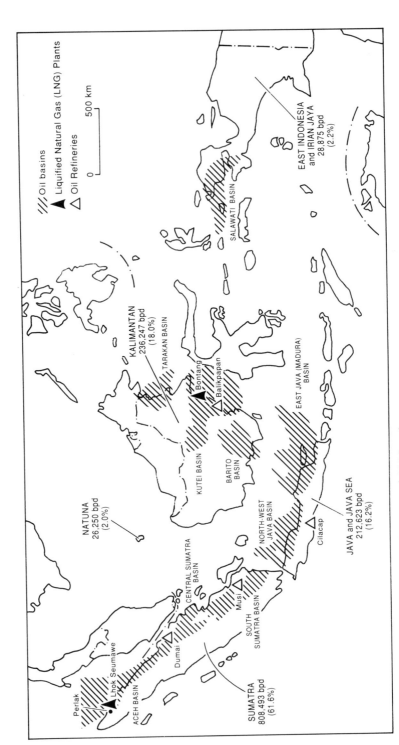

Figure 8.1 Indonesia: oil basins, refineries, and LNG trains

their country'. However, although the use of oil can be traced back several hundred years, commercial exploitation did not begin until the late 19th century. The first well was sunk in 1871 in North Sumatra, and by 1885 oil was being produced on a commercial basis. The Royal Dutch Company took over the first concession in 1890, and by the outbreak of the First World War annual production of crude oil had reached over 12 million barrels (US Embassy 1988, p. 22, Arndt 1983a, p. 136). This increased through the course of the 1920s and 1930s, and in 1938 production was some 55 million barrels (Figure 8.2).[1]

Not surprisingly, it took some time for the industry to recover from the ravages of the Second World War – at the end of which crude oil production had declined to 6 million barrels – and it was not until 1951 that pre-war levels of production were surpassed. The development of the large Central Sumatran Minas field by Caltex[2] further boosted production, and by 1960 it stood at 150 million barrels. However, although output grew at 8 per cent per year between 1950 and 1966, exploration was minimal. The economic nationalism of President Sukarno, and the real fear that the assets of foreign oil companies would be expropriated, restricted investment. Such was the investment climate that in 1965 Shell sold all its assets to the Indonesian government for US$110 million (Palmer 1978, p. 138).

The rebirth of pragmatism (1965–73)

This investment climate changed in 1966/67 with the introduction of the production-sharing contract (PSC) and a more liberal and welcoming attitude to foreign oil companies and investors. It is no accident that this change in attitude should have occurred shortly after Sukarno was replaced by Suharto as President of Indonesia in 1965. Suharto recruited a team of highly trained Indonesian technocrats (the so-called Berkeley Mafia) to advise him, and the resulting New Order was generally far more pragmatic in dealing with the economic problems that afflicted the

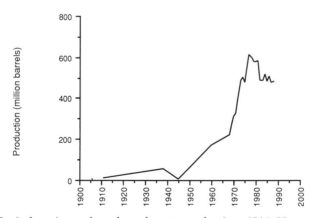

Figure 8.2 Indonesia: crude and condensate production, 1911–88

nation. It was recognized that foreign companies could make an important contribution to development, and should be encouraged to do so.

The PSC was one of the results of this liberalization of the economy, and since then it has formed the basis of Indonesia's petroleum development policy. The PSC was the brainchild of a medical graduate, Major-General Ibnu Sutowo, who was at that time head of the state-owned oil exploration, development, and refining company, Permina. When Permina was amalgamated in 1968 with another state-owned oil company Pertamin, to form Pertamina,[3] Ibnu Sutowo was appointed as its first president-director. The PSC is essentially a legal agreement between a contractor (usually a foreign oil company) and Pertamina, which represents the Indonesian government. Contract areas are granted on the understanding that the foreign company involved carries all the risks and costs of exploration. Costs are only recoverable from commercial production, and to begin with only to a maximum of 40 per cent of its agreed selling price ('cost oil').[4] The remaining 'profit oil' was then split (after tax) 65:35 for the first 75 000 barrels per day (bpd), and 67.5:32.5 for the remainder. When a field is declared commercial, a contract is signed that normally extends over a 30-year period from the date at which exploration began. At all times, however, ultimate management responsibility rests with Pertamina, and the oil in the ground, together with all facilities, is the property of the state oil company[5] (see Lukman & McGlinchey 1986, pp. 75–6, Palmer 1978, pp. 138–9, Subroto 1986).

With the introduction of the PSC and the generally more favourable investment climate, foreign oil companies – mostly Japanese and American

Figure 8.3 Oil rig in Sumatran tropical rainforest (courtesy of BBC Radio Vision)

– began to take up large contract areas (Figure 8.3). Exploration expenditure began to rise and additional fields in Sumatra and Kalimantan came into production (Table 8.2). Between 1968 and 1973, Indonesian oil output increased at an average annual rate of 17 per cent, rising from 220 million barrels per year at the beginning of the period, to 489 million barrels per year by the end (Figure 8.2). Approximately 90 per cent of output was produced from wells managed by foreign companies (Arndt 1983a, p. 138).

The oil boom (1973–82)

The oil price shock of 1973 heralded the beginning of Indonesia's oil boom. The Organization of Petroleum Exporting Countries (OPEC), to which Indonesia belongs, decided upon cartel action. In the space of a year the price of oil quadrupled, with the f.o.b. price of Minas crude increasing from US$2.93 in April 1972 to US$12.60 in July 1974 (Arndt 1983a, p. 138). As a result, Indonesian petroleum exports rose from US$900 million to US$5.2 billion between 1972 and 1974 (Figure 8.4). Government revenues from corporate tax on oil consequently increased from 199 billion rupiahs to 973 billion rupiahs (Figure 8.5).[6] The implications for Indonesia's development were enormous. Virtually overnight, the country's balance of payments crisis was at an end and the government had access to what must have seemed almost unlimited funds. The salaries of teachers were quadrupled, other civil servants found theirs doubled, and the development budget for 1974/75 was revised, with expenditure increased by more than 200 per cent (Arndt 1983a, p. 141, Robison 1987, p. 23). When, in 1979, the second oil shock saw prices double once again to reach over US$35 per barrel in 1981/82, foreign exchange earnings, government revenue, and development expenditure received another fillip. By the early 1980s, Indonesia's balance of payments surplus was almost US$4 billion (1980/81), foreign assets topped US$11 billion (1981/82), government revenue from the oil sector was US$8.6 billion (1981/82), and petroleum was contributing more than 80 per cent of total exports (Nasution 1984, Robison 1987, Lukman & McGlinchey 1986) (Table 8.2). With the increase in the price of oil, so expenditure on exploration also rose. This peaked in 1982 when US$1.72 billion was invested in oil exploration and approximately 250 exploration wells were sunk (US Embassy 1988, p. 33).

The oil price slump (1982–)

However, this oil bonanza was not to last. Plagued by global overproduction, the price of oil slumped from a peak of US$35 per barrel of Minas crude in 1981/82 to US$25 in 1985. By April 1986, although the official selling price of Sumatran Light (Minas) was US$28.53 per barrel, Pertamina was agreeing discounted prices of US$10 (= spot price) (Table 8.2). The effect of the price decline was accentuated by the fact that OPEC was forced to reduce the quotas allotted to each of its members in an attempt to

Table 8.2 Indonesia: selected economic indicators, 1969–88

	1969	1971	1973	1975	1977	1979	1981	1983	1985	1987	1988
Crude and condensate production (million barrels)	271	325	489	477	615	580	585	490	484	479	485
Natural gas production (billion SCF)	62	121	186	222	543	999	1124	1186	1580	1732	1851
Minas crude (US$ per barrel)[1]	1.6	2.3	3.6	12.7	13.6	17.7	35.0	29.5	28.6	17.6	16.7
Oil exports (US$ bn)[2]	0.4	0.5	1.4	5.1	7.3	9.6	18.2	13.6	9.1	6.2	4.4
Gas exports (US$ bn)[3]	—	—	—	—	0.9	1.2	2.6	2.6	3.9	2.6	2.2
Total oil/gas exports (US$ bn)	—	—	—	—	8.2	10.8	20.8	16.2	13.0	8.8	6.6
Oil/gas as percentage of total exports	17	19	21	74	68	67	82	76	68	50	38
Corporate oil tax (rupiahs, trillions)	0.05	0.11	0.35	1.25	1.95	4.26	8.63	9.5	11.1	10.1	9.5
Oil revenues as percentage of total domestic revenue	21	25	33	46	45	64	71	66	58	48	41
Exploration expenditure (US$ millions)	27	123	210	458	273	477	1456	1481	1177	583	728
Development expenditure (rupiahs, trillions)	0.12	0.20	0.45	1.40	2.16	4.01	6.94	9.90	10.9	9.5	12.3
Inflation (percentage)	10	2	31	19	11	20	9	12	4	9	8

Notes: 1) Government schedule of prices. 2) Crude and crude products. 3) LNG + LPG.
Sources: various.

boost demand. In consequence, Indonesia's exports of oil and condensate declined from 383 million barrels in 1981 to 295 million barrels in 1985 (Lukman & McGlinchey 1986, p. 85). Indonesia's fiscal situation was turned on its head. Foreign exchange earnings plummeted, government revenue declined, and the country's balance of payments moved into deficit (Figures 8.4 and 8.5, Table 8.2). The wages of civil servants were frozen, development expenditure declined, and other austerity measures were introduced (Arndt & Hill 1988). It has been estimated that for each one dollar fall in the price of oil, Indonesia lost approximately US$300 million

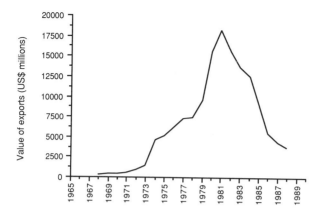

Figure 8.4 Indonesia: value of exports of crude and crude products, 1968–88

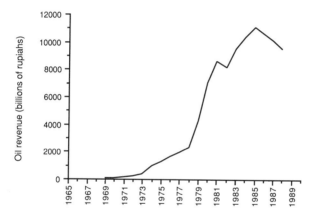

Figure 8.5 Indonesia: government oil revenue, 1969–88 (corporate oil tax)

in annual foreign exchange earnings. In addition, losses to the government intensify the lower prices fall, as a greater percentage of sales are taken up with meeting the costs of production (cost oil), leaving less profit oil from which the government derives its tax revenues (Lukman & McGlinchey 1986, pp. 70–1). Although the 1990 invasion of Kuwait by Iraq led to a significant strengthening in oil prices, the long-term trend is for Indonesia's oil revenues to continue to steadily decline. Exploration costs are rising, reserves are falling, and domestic consumption of oil is growing. Further, non-oil exports are expanding rapidly and becoming relatively more important.

The foregoing rather dense discussion of the development of Indonesia's petroleum industry is intended only to set the scene for the remainder of the chapter. The analysis will now turn to assess the impact of oil and gas on the wider economy.

Oil and Indonesia's development strategies

Development strategies before the oil boom (1945–73)

The first 20 years of Indonesia's independence (1945–65) are indelibly stamped with the ideology and beliefs of President Sukarno. Sukarno was part-populist, part-socialist. He harboured a deep distrust of capitalism and set about nationalizing many foreign-owned enterprises, restricting the activities of the Chinese business community, and creating a highly regulated economy in which the state played a dominant role. In 1959, for example, government-owned enterprises were awarded monopoly rights to import nine categories of goods that accounted for 75 per cent of total imports (Pangestu & Habir 1989, p. 227). Economic chaos ensued:

> By the end of the period [1965], the country experienced high rates of inflation [over 600 per cent], very low levels of trade, almost zero foreign exchange reserves, a domestic manufacturing sector operating at only an estimated 20–30 per cent capacity, and badly damaged economic and physical infrastructure (Pangestu & Habir 1989, p. 227).

In addition, unemployment may have been as high as 25 per cent, tax revenues were minimal, and there was a serious shortage of food, particularly rice (Gelb & Glassburner 1988, p. 200).

When Suharto became President in 1965, he was faced with an economy in disarray. With the support and encouragement of the newly appointed Berkeley mafia, he began to introduce more liberal policies. Foreign investment was again welcomed, some nationalized industries were returned to their previous owners, subsidies to state-owned enterprises were reduced, and the rupiah was devalued. Throughout this period from 1945 to 1973, the petroleum industry, although important, was not crucial to the functioning of the economy. Oil and oil revenues were less than 20 per cent of total exports and government revenue, and the industry did not have a conspicuous impact on development strategies.

The oil boom (1973–82)

The rise in oil prices and government revenue following the first oil shock of 1973 gave Suharto and his advisers far greater freedom in their choice of development strategy. For it was never clear that those in the government and the bureaucracy were entirely convinced of the efficacy of the free-market economics espoused by the World Bank and certain individuals in the planning agency, BAPPENAS.[7] The fiscal crisis of 1965 had forced the government to embrace more *laissez faire*, export-oriented, and austere economic policies. But it was not out of choice, and the oil boom provided an opportunity to return to the economic nationalism of the early years of Indonesia's development.

Government control over the economy increased again, and greater restrictions were placed upon the activities of foreign companies. It was stipulated that new foreign investment had to be in the form of joint ventures, the number of industries closed to foreign participation was increased, and tax incentives were reduced. The state also increased its stake in the economy, substantially expanding the range of activities in which it was engaged (Pangestu & Habir 1989, p. 229). In general terms, there was a return to import-substitution industrialization, with greater investment in, and protection of, infant domestic industries. Perhaps the best examples are P.T. Krakatau Steel and P.T. Nurtanio Aircraft Industry. The former received investments totalling a reported US$3.79 billion, while for the latter the 1987 figure was US$900 million (Robison 1987, p. 36, Nasir 1987b, p. 112). In addition, and less prominently, there were the funds available for irrigation, education, health, roads, energy, agriculture, and for investment in other areas of Indonesia's social and economic infrastructure. Of course, this is not to say that without the revenues from oil some of these investments would not have occurred. Indeed, Suharto had identified these as priority areas for investment some time before the first oil shock (Gelb & Glassburner 1988, pp. 203–4). But, as Arndt (1983a, p. 145) writes, 'the oil bonanza made all this very much easier and greatly quickened the pace'. Robison (1986, p. 172) sums up the period of Indonesia's oil boom as follows:

> For policy-makers in the period 1974/75–1981/82 the enormous sums made available to the state through oil company tax meant that the state could finance and directly invest in economic development, on a scale previously impossible, either through the creation of infrastructure, the provision of credit to national corporations and direct state investment in major resource, or through industrial projects. It is not an exaggeration to say that the state was awash with funds.

The oil slump (1982–)

Perhaps not surprisingly, the fall in oil prices and oil revenues from the early 1980s on played into the hands of the 'reformists'. Very broadly, their recommendations encouraged the government to take four steps to offset the effects of the oil-price slump. First, to introduce austerity measures; second, to try to increase non-oil revenue; third, to increase efficiency and cut down on waste in public sector enterprises; and, fourth, to deregulate the economy and encourage non-oil exports.

To save money, 48 public sector projects with a total cost of over US$20 billion were either cancelled, re-scheduled or opened up to alternative financing in 1983. The rephasing of four major industrial plants alone saved, for example, US$3 billion in foreign exchange expenditure budgeted for in the 1983/84 fiscal year (Nasution 1984, pp. 18–20). In addition, development expenditure was cut by 22 per cent in 1986/87 and a number of subsidies were reduced (Kaye 1986, p. 101). The rice support price paid to farmers was held constant, fertilizer and pesticide subsidies were reduced, the price of oil products was increased, and salaries of civil servants were frozen (Hobohm 1987, pp. 59–60, Nasution 1984, p. 24).

In addition to introducing austerity measures, the government embarked on an exercise to boost non-oil revenues. A new income tax law was introduced at the beginning of 1984, and a 10 per cent value-added tax (which has since been broadened) in April 1985. A range of lesser changes accompanied these major tax reforms. Departure tax, for example, was increased from 35 000 rupiahs to 150 000 rupiahs per household in 1982, and now stands at 250 000 rupiahs per individual. The changes constituted an effort to rationalize the tax system, improve the efficiency of tax collection, and strengthen tax administration – all with the object of increasing government revenue (see Hobohm 1987, pp. 57–9, Nasution 1984, pp. 24–5). To the same end, the government has tried to improve the efficiency of the public sector. The seriousness of the administration in this regard can best be seen in the appointment in 1985 of a Swiss trade inspection company (Société Générale de Surveillance – SGS) to oversee import procedures, thus removing responsibility from the notoriously corrupt and inefficient customs administration (see below) (Simandjuntak 1988, p. 385, Robison 1987, p. 33, Hill 1987, p. 15).

However, the most far-reaching change resulting from the fall in oil prices has been the government's decision to undertake an extensive programme of deregulation. The objective is to boost non-oil exports and reduce Indonesia's dependence upon petroleum. There is not space here to recite all the reforms that have been introduced. But they have included major deregulations of the banking sector in 1983 and 1988, reforms of import and export procedures in 1986, 1987, and 1988, and devaluations of the rupiah in 1983 and 1986. These steps have led to the lifting of credit controls, the removal of fixed interest rates, and the abolition of some import monopolies. In December 1986 President Suharto even went so far as to ask the Co-ordinating Economic Minister to examine all aspects of state enterprises and investigate the possibility of selective privatizations of state enterprises (see Simandjuntak 1988, Arndt & Hill 1988, Hobohm 1987, Sadli 1987, Hill 1987, pp. 20–5, Juoro 1989).

This is not to say that the reformists' battle is won. Once again, it has been the necessity to introduce reforms, because of the oil price decline, that has prompted the retreat from economic nationalism. There remain powerful elements in the government, the bureaucracy, and the business world who are resistant to the changes that have been introduced and who forcefully argue against any further reforms. Privatization, is anathema to these individuals on ideological grounds. It is alleged that even Suharto's family has financially benefited from the system as it exists and would have preferred it to remain largely intact. That part of the economy geared to the domestic market remains highly protected and inefficient, and many monopolies remain in place. Dismantling the edifice of protection will not be easy; the example of the Philippines where entrenched interest groups have managed to prevent any meaningful reform of the system must represent a compelling object lesson to reformists in Indonesia. Hobohm (1987, p. 68) believes that a classic Indonesian compromise has been wrought in trying to confront these competing forces:

> This compromise appears to have resulted in a decision to create two separate and largely independent sectors within the economy, one geared to the external and the other to the internal market, and each enjoying a different incentive structure. [The] pace and pattern of economic development . . . will depend in no small measure on how the relative balance of power between the two influential groups of 'technocrats' and 'economic nationalists' eventually settles.

And, it might have been added, on whether the price of oil recovers sufficiently to allow a return to state-led import-substitution industrialization.

The rise in oil prices in 1973 was not an unmixed blessing; not only did it influence the pattern of Indonesia's development – perhaps in some instances even dictating it – but it also placed considerable strains upon the economy.

The rise in oil prices: problems of adjustment and the 'Dutch disease'

The rise in oil prices brought serious inflationary risks. In theory at least, it should have been possible for the government to have invested the additional revenue abroad, or to have used it to pay for additional imports, and in these ways to have partly avoided the potentially inflationary effects of the massive increase in revenue. However, 'word soon spread throughout the bureaucracy that the time was ripe for initiating expenditure proposals and during late 1973 and early 1974 ambitious spending plans were drawn up' (McCawley 1980, p. 44). The result was that actual government expenditure during 1973/74 and 1974/75 exceeded budgeted expenditure by 'an enormous 35 per cent and 25 per cent respectively' (McCawley 1980, p. 44). Inflation rose from 6.6 per cent in 1972, to 31 per cent in 1973, and over 40 per cent in 1974 (Warr 1986, p. 35).

These rates were certainly disturbing to a government that had fought so hard to control the hyperinflation associated with the policies of President Sukarno. But, considering the degree of increase in government revenue – up 300 per cent between 1972 and 1974 – the rate of inflation was in fact fairly modest. As it turned out, events forced the government to spend considerable sums of the additional foreign exchange on imports. The failure of the rice harvest in 1972 meant that large quantities of rice and fertilizer had to be imported (at high prices because of the commodity boom), and there was also a US$1 billion outlay on imports linked to Indonesia's satellite and telecommunications programme (Arndt 1983a, pp. 140–1, Arndt 1984b, pp. 65–7, McCawley 1980, p. 44). Equally important, the 'Pertamina crisis' (see below) meant that the government had to pay off short-term loans of at least US$1 billion in 1975.

In the slightly longer term, the oil boom faced Indonesia with the task of how to deal with what has become known as the 'Dutch disease'. The term was allegedly coined by *The Economist* in November 1977 with reference to the impact of natural gas on the Dutch economy (Warr 1986). Very simply put, the increase in foreign exchange earnings associated, in Indonesia's case, with the oil boom, has two effects. First, it causes the domestic currency to appreciate, thus making imports cheaper and exports more expensive (although the exchange rate regime is also important in this regard). And, second, it is likely to cause inflation to rise and with it the costs of production. Taken together, these two effects decrease the competitiveness of domestic import-substituting and export-oriented industries. In the long term, the outcome is the undermining of the non-oil industrial sector, and with it growing dependence on petroleum exports (see Warr 1986, Arndt 1983a, pp. 142–4, Gelb *et al*.1988, pp. 21–8).

Indonesia certainly has suffered from a decline in the international competitiveness of its industrial sector. In this sense, it has exhibited the symptoms of the Dutch disease (see Pangestu 1986, Hill & Pang Eng Fong 1988, pp. 154–5). The International Monetary Fund's index of 'competitiveness', for example, shows that its competitiveness declined from 130 in 1972 to 82 in 1976 (Warr 1986, p. 37). Between 1973 and 1982, the value of non-oil exports only increased from US$1.9 billion to US$ 3.9 billion, while Indonesia's non-oil current account deficit rose from US$ 1.4 billion to US$ 14.2 billion (Robison 1987, p. 21). By 1981, oil and gas were contributing over 80 per cent of total exports (Warr 1986, p. 40). But, in comparison with some other oil-exporting countries, such as Nigeria and Trinidad, Indonesia has been only moderately afflicted by the Dutch disease. The government allocated considerable sums to create a domestic industrial base, however highly protected and inefficient it may have been, and manufacturing and agriculture have performed relatively well (see Gelb & Glassburner 1988, pp. 214–15). It has been the government's success in avoiding the worst effects of the disease that has provided the foundation for the current rapid increase in non-oil exports.

Rent-seekers, corruption, and the 'Pertamina crisis'

Rent-seekers and corruption

One of the side-effects of the oil boom was that it greatly increased the scope for corruption and 'rent-seeking' in a country that already had a reputation for excessive degrees of both. Rent-seekers are those businessmen who try to establish links with the government in order to 'become the recipients of the rent the government can confer by disposing of its resources, offering protection, or issuing authorization [or monopoly rights] for certain types of activities it regulates' (Yoshihara 1988, p. 68). As the Indonesian government became more closely involved in the economy, and placed more restrictions on business activity, so rent-seeking became almost indispensable to all companies. This meant establishing contacts with influential bureaucrats and politicians, and it is no accident that many monopolies were, and are, awarded to the relatives and associates of senior political figures (Hobohm 1987, p. 68, Robison 1986, pp. 323–70, Clad 1989, pp. 81–6).

Not only was there a proliferation of rent-seeking (or 'crony capitalism'), but corruption also became virtually endemic. The sums of money generated by the oil boom encouraged greater corruption and also imbued the government with a certain laziness in the management of its financial affairs (Robison 1986, p. 391–5, Arndt & Hill 1988, p. 108). It is noteworthy that it has taken the recent oil price slump to encourage a more concerted attempt to reduce corruption. Presidential Instruction No. 4 of 1985 (Inpres 4/1985), which reformed customs and excise procedures and led to the appointment of SGS to supervise import procedures, is the most radical example of this change in perspective. It took responsibility away from the Customs Department, a department so notoriously corrupt that it was estimated that shippers were having to pay over US$200 million each year in bribes, and where it cost US$1000 for an Indonesian to 'buy' even the lowest of positions, but where that investment could be repaid in a matter of weeks (Kaye 1985a, p. 119). 'Inpres 4 is a fascinating and significant development' notes Robison (1987, p. 34), 'It expresses the willingness of the state to sacrifice whole sections of the web of patronage and expropriation that constitute politico-bureaucratic power under the New Order where these interests pose fundamental threats to the broader economic fabric'.

The 'Pertamina crisis'

Pertamina, the state oil company, was established in 1968 under the leadership of Ibnu Sutowo.[8] The company was given control of all operations, and all royalties and government taxes paid by foreign oil companies were channelled through Pertamina. Rather than passing these revenues on to the Bank of Indonesia, Sutowo and his colleagues invested the funds in projects of their own choosing. Pertamina became regarded as virtually a 'state within a state', and by 1975 was one of the 200 largest corporations in the world (Glassburner 1976, pp. 1100). Investments included a steel mill, a fertilizer plant, oil tankers, hotels and offices, plantations, a telecommunications centre, and an airline. Many of these projects proved to be financially unsound. However, although elements in the government were highly critical of Sutowo's methods and the fact that Pertamina was virtually unaccountable, the company and its president-director retained the support of President Suharto and many Indonesians (Robison 1986, pp. 233–5). McCawley (1978, p. 5) writes:

> He [Ibnu Sutowo] closed contracts and got foreign investors out into the field; he had the image of 'riding the foreign investment tiger' but getting away with it. He attracted envy – and respect. Even Indonesians

who had sympathized with Sukarno's hostility to western capitalists could feel that if it really was necessary to sup with the devil, then at least this was the way to do it.

However, Sutowo's attempt at empire building was not to last. In 1972, the government insisted that state enterprises obtain government approval for all long-term overseas borrowings. In response, Pertamina turned to short-term finance that it managed to roll over until the beginning of 1975, when the company found that it was unable to meet its obligations. The government was forced to take over Pertamina's debts, which totalled more than US$10 billion. It was the necessity immediately to meet a portion of these debts (over US$1 billion) that negated some of the inflationary effects of the oil boom, a necessity that led Arndt (1984b, p. 67) to write that the Pertamina crisis, which in all other respects was a national disaster, was in this regard a 'blessing in disguise' (see also Arndt 1983a, p. 141, Gelb & Glassburner 1988, pp. 204–5). In 1976, General Ibnu Sutowo was dismissed 'with honour'. It is significant that Pertamina is now merely a government agent, and the entire accounting structure of the company has been altered so that there is no longer any chance tht it will behave like a state within the state.

A rather wider issue raised by the Pertamina crisis is whether the funds invested by the state have been put to good use, or have been squandered. In other words, has the import-substitution industrialization characteristic of the oil boom proved to be successful, or has it merely encouraged the growth of inefficient, loss-making industries?

Import–substitution industrialization: economic nationalism versus efficiency

As was noted in an opening section of this chapter, the oil boom led to a return to the state-led import-substitution industrialization (ISI) that was such a feature of the Sukarno period. In 1987 there were 214 state enterprises with assets of nearly 114 trillion rupiahs and sales of more than 32 trillion rupiahs, approximately one third of GDP (Pangestu & Habir 1989, p. 232). Their performance has generally been poor: they are highly protected, internationally uncompetitive, and receive large implicit subsidies (Robison 1987, pp. 34–44, Kaye 1985b, pp. 68–9). How inefficient they are no one knows, as it is impossible to gain access to the necessary information. Hill (1987, p. 20) believes that even officials in the Department of Finance are unaware of the profitability of state enterprises. Overall, return on assets is thought to be less than 3 per cent (Hill 1987, p. 22). The company that has received possibly the most attention is the state-owned aircraft corporation, P.T. Nurtanio.

P.T. Nurtanio, which is now simply referred to as IPTN (the acronym for Industri Pesawat Terbang Nusantara), was established in 1976 under the leadership of Dr B. J. Habibie, the Minister of Research and Technology, and with the full support of the President. Habibie argued, and continues to argue, that if Indonesia is to develop and achieve economic take-off, it must have its own high-technology industrial base. Significantly, IPTN is one of the few industries to have survived the austerity measures brought on by the oil price slump. The company is financed through the national budget and by Pertamina, and this makes it very hard to establish the quantity of funds allocated to the company, although IPTN insists that upto 1987 it had been US$900 million (Nasir 1987b, p. 112).

IPTN assembles helicopters and aeroplanes produced by CASA of Spain, Messerschmitt of Germany, Bell of the USA, and Aérospatiale of France. It also jointly manufactures with CASA the CN-235 (a twin-engined 30–40 seater). As of 1987, IPTN had produced 269 aircraft, and sales had risen from US$6.3 million in 1976, to US$67 million in 1985 (Hill & Pang Eng Fong 1988). Without doubt, Habibie has done a great deal in a relatively short time, and in an industry that requires high levels of skills and advanced equipment. However, many analysts doubt that this is an appropriate developmental road for Indonesia to take.

These sceptics point to the fact that all but four of the aircraft sold domestically were purchased by state-owned enterprises, while only eight aircraft have been sold overseas and only two of these were actually manufactured by IPTN (Nasir 1987a, p. 114). Second, the notion that the aircraft are Indonesian is to stretch a point. IPTN is mainly an assembler of imported components. Third, because, as Pertamina was until 1976, IPTN is largely unaccountable, it is difficult to estimate the rate of return on assets. Hill (1987, p. 22) believes that it may be just 0.1 per cent, an extremely low figure. Fourth, for a company that produces so little, IPTN absorbs a large proportion of Indonesia's limited pool of trained engineers. Over 2000 of its 13 000 employees are university graduates, most of whom might be better employed elsewhere (Hill & Pang Eng Fong 1988, p. 159).

In answer to these sceptics, Habibie would no doubt reply that they have missed the point. The criticisms do not take account of the new skills and technology that are being acquired, the increased technological independence that results, nor the spin-offs into other industries that will occur. Economic nationalists such as Habibie see oil revenues as an opportunity to bypass the early, low-technology, and low-skill stages of development and enter the development race at a level equal to that of the advanced Western countries. They argue that Japan, and now Korea, have successfully followed a path of state-led industrialization, and Indonesia is merely adopting their example.

The benefits of the oil boom

Although the oil boom resulted in greater wastage, and in a sometimes less than economically rational pattern of investment, it would be wrong to imagine that funds were entirely squandered. When account is taken of scandals such as the Pertamina crisis, corruption at a level that is possibly unsurpassed in the region, and the proliferation of inefficient and uncompetitive industries, it is sometimes too easy to overlook the productive uses to which Indonesia's oil wealth has been put. After all, non-oil GDP[9] (at current market prices) increased from 3378 billion rupiahs in 1971 to 57 391 billion rupiahs in 1983 (Robison 1987, p. 20).

The oil boom has provided Indonesia with the opportunity to build-up an impressive, albeit often protected, industrial base. Not surprisingly perhaps, much of this has centred on the oil industry. In 1974 the output of local oil refineries totalled 86 million barrels, and much of the country's crude output had to be shipped to Singapore for refining (Khong Cho Oon 1986, p. 108). By 1988, with the construction and expansion of refineries in Central Sumatra (Dumai), South Java (Cilacap), and East Kalimantan (Balikpapan) (Figure 8.1), output had risen to 247 million barrels (Bank Indonesia 1989, p. 168). Total installed capacity approaches 300 million barrels, sufficient to absorb approximately 60 per cent of production. The production of liquified natural gas (LNG) and liquified petroleum gas (LPG) has also been substantially expanded. Indonesia is now the world's largest exporter of LNG and controls 40 per cent of the total world market (US Embassy 1988, p. 49). Exports of LNG in 1988 amounted to US$2.2 billion (from a peak figure of US$3.9 billion in 1985), and have become the country's second most valuable export after oil (Table 8.2). Pertamina has a controlling interest in ten LNG 'trains', six located at Lhok Seumawe in Aceh, northern Sumatra, and four at Bontang in East Kalimantan (Figure 8.1). LPG production has also been expanded. Annual production has risen to approximately 800 000 tonnes, with exports peaking at 725 000 tonnes (US$145 million) in 1984 (US Embassy 1988, p. 62). Other downstream developments include a substantial expansion in Indonesia's petrochemical, and particularly agrochemical, industries. Urea production has reached 5.27 million tonnes per year, while ammonia output is 2.99 million tonnes (Goldstein 1989b, p. 53). Additional planned expansion into commodity plastics, and synthetic fibres and rubbers is intended to develop the country's downstream industries further by improving linkages between the oil industry and such activities as textiles and light manufacturing (Goldstein 1989a, 1989b). It has been these sorts of investments, both in the oil and non-oil sectors, that have provided the basis for the recent surge in non-oil exports, an issue that will be developed in the final section of the chapter.

Together with these investments, the wealth generated by the oil boom has also been channelled into 'social' projects, into agriculture, and into the development of a modern infrastructure. As Hill (1988, p. 24) notes, the 'massive surge in oil revenue during the 1970s enabled Jakarta to finance regional development and impose uniform . . . economic and social priorities throughout the sprawling archipelago'. The Elementary Schools Programme means that enrolment rates are high throughout the country (some 6000 schools were built each year), public health centres have been constructed, and sanitation improved (Arndt 1983a, p. 145). Oil revenues have also allowed the government to build and improve irrigation schemes, finance a rice-price support scheme, and heavily subsidize supplies of fertilizer and pesticides. By the early 1980s, the fertilizer subsidy, for example, amounted to more than US$500 million each year (Manning

1987b, p. 72). In so doing, Indonesia managed to achieve self-sufficiency in rice production by the early 1980s, a considerable achievement (Manning 1987b, p. 66). In addition, funds were available to finance such projects as the transmigration scheme, under which over 5 million poor and landless Indonesians have been settled in the Outer Islands (see Chapter 5), and to subsidize rice and kerosene so that some of the fruits of the oil boom could filter through to the poorest of consumers.

Implications of the oil price slump

Implications for the oil industry and for energy policy

The fall in oil prices, and the realization that petroleum will never provide such a windfall as it did during the ten-year period from the early 1970s to the early 1980s, has caused the Indonesian government to re-examine its energy policy.

Oil reserves are notoriously difficult accurately to gauge. However, various authorities estimate that remaining proven reserves at current prices and using current technology are 8 billion to 10 billion barrels; another 14 billion to 15 billion barrels of oil equivalent may also be recoverable from yet to be discovered fields (US Embassy 1988, p. 31). The top end of the unproven reserves estimates stands at 50 billion barrels (Hobohm 1987, p. 24). With production running at approximately 1.2 mbd, proven reserves are sufficient to last only 18 to 23 years. Confronted with forecasts such as these, and with the major producing fields reaching maturity, the Indonesian government has attempted to encourage greater exploration activity and enhance recovery from existing fields. It has tried to attain these two objectives by deregulating the industry and making investment by foreign oil companies more attractive. For example, a package of exploration incentives announced at the beginning of 1989 gives contractors who find oil in the 'frontier' areas of eastern Indonesia 25 per cent of production, as against 15 per cent elsewhere (Schwarz 1989, p. 73, see also FEER 1988, pp. 82–3). The government has also made it more attractive for companies to use enhanced recovery techniques so that production from mature wells is increased.

How successful these incentives will prove to be is hard to say. However, it is worth pointing out that exploration expenditure by petroleum companies declined from US$1.72 billion in 1982 (at the height of the oil boom) to US$0.58 billion in 1987 (US Embassy 1988, p. 33). In 1988 exploration expenditure was US$0.73 billion (Table 8.2). Moreover, new oil reserves have been discovered over the course of the 1980s at a rate of only 150 million barrels per year (Schwarz 1989, p. 73). Over the same period, annual production has averaged close to 500 million barrels.

In addition to providing more attractive exploration incentives, the Indonesian government has invested funds in the development of natural gas resources. Potential reserves of natural gas are estimated to be 109 trillion cubic feet, or sufficient for 70 years' production at current rates

(US Embassy 1988, p. 53). An added attraction of LNG is that the 10- to 20-year agreements concluded with Japan, South Korea and Taiwan guarantee a stable volume of sales over the long term. The importance of these agreements is that they have been linked to the construction of extensive (and expensive) gas liquification facilities. Without them the risks of development might have been too great. The contracts also have the added attraction of representing 'an island of relative tranquility in a sea of dangerously unstable oil markets' (Lukman & McGlinchey 1986, p. 73).

With declining oil revenues and the prospects of declining production, so the Indonesian government has changed its overall energy policy. In order that as much oil as possible is available for export, there has been a concerted attempt to diversify into alternative domestic energy sources. These include coal, hydropower, geothermal power, and nuclear power. For example, in an effort to promote the use of these alternative energy resources, as well as to discourage wasteful consumption, the domestic fuel subsidy has been progressively reduced since 1982, while subsidization of domestic consumers such as P.T. Krakatau Steel has come under review (see FEER 1990b, p. 83).

Implications for Indonesia's political order

This issue has already been touched upon. The move towards a more export-oriented development strategy, largely brought on by the decline in oil revenues, has great implications for the system of patronage that evolved during the period of state-led import substitution. If the market is to play a greater role in development, and if efficiency gains are to be achieved, then domestic capitalists – as well as bureaucrats and politicians – will lose their privileges and their monopolies. Just as the cadres and bureaucrats in the Soviet Union and the People's Republic of China have been resistant to the changes thrust upon them in the name of efficiency, so will those with vested interests in Indonesia. Nevertheless, the reality of the country's economic position demands that these reforms be introduced. As Robison (1987, p. 50) points out:

> Whereas the oil bonanza allowed for general economic growth and the sustenance of politico-bureaucrats and their capitalist clients, the decline in oil prices has meant that the vested interests of the entrenched political and economic forces run increasingly counter to the viability of the economy as a whole.

Implications for non-oil exports

The fall in oil revenue has brought into sharp perspective the dangers of Indonesia's dependence on oil and gas. Most alarmingly, the country's public debt service ratio (the cost of servicing the public debt as a percentage of exports) stands at 40 per cent. Not only has the government attempted to increase non-oil revenue by, among other things, reforming the tax system, but it has also paid special attention to the promotion of non-oil exports. The rupiah has been devalued twice in recent years, by 28 per cent in April 1983 and by 31 per cent in September 1986, in an effort to increase the competitiveness of the non-oil sector. The second devaluation, coupled with a limited degree of deregulation, does seem to have boosted non-oil growth. Over a two-year period between 1986 and 1988 non-oil exports grew by 40 per cent, with manufactured exports expanding by 28 per cent (Jayasuriya & Manning 1988, p. 132, and see Hill 1987, pp. 25–33). This rapid growth rate continued during 1989. Although three years of growth hardly represent irrefutable evidence of a new dawn, Jayasuriya and Manning (1988, p. 132) believe the figures suggest 'that the manufacturing sector could become the engine which powers the economy back to the high growth rates of the early 1980s'. Significantly, whereas in 1981 non-oil exports accounted for a mere 19 per cent of total exports, by 1989 the proportion had risen to 61 per cent (Schwarz 1990).

Summary

This chapter has discussed the implications of Indonesia's oil windfall of the 1970s. The quadrupling of prices between 1972 and 1973, and then their further doubling between 1979 and 1981, has often been presented in black and white terms: to Indonesia and the other oil exporting countries, the price rise was a bonanza; to the rest of the world, close to a disaster. However, this is a grossly restricted perspective. The initial rise in prices presented Indonesia with serious inflationary risks. In the slightly longer term, the appreciation of the rupiah faced the Indonesian administration with the risk that the non-oil sector might become increasingly uncompetitive (the 'Dutch disease') and helped to make the country overdependent on a single commodity. This dependence could be ignored while prices were buoyant, but the precipitous fall in oil prices in the mid-1980s has revealed the dangers inherent in such an unbalanced export profile.

But the implications of Indonesia's oil boom were not restricted to such macro-economic effects. The increase in revenue caused Indonesia's development strategy to change course, and for rent-seeking and corruption to become increasingly prevalent. The austerity of the early part of Suharto's presidency was no longer a necessity, and nor was the involvement of foreign companies. The state began to take a larger role in the economy, monopolies were given to domestic capitalists, and import-substitution industrialization became the dominant strategy. Inefficiency increased in tandem.

This is not to say, however, that Indonesia would have been better off if the oil bonanza had never occurred. The funds allowed the government to achieve development objectives that otherwise would have been impossible. The economy grew at an average annual rate of 7.5 per cent between 1973 and 1981, and the country advanced from being one of the least developed countries in the world (according to the World Bank) to the status of a 'middle income' country by 1981. A valuable economic infrastructure has been created, and Indonesia is in a good position to exploit the oil-price slump and develop a vibrant, and internationally competitive, non-oil industrial base.

Notes to Chapter 8

1 For an account of the early years of Indonesia's oil industry see Ooi Jin Bee, 1982.
2 Caltex had in fact set up a rig just before the Japanese occupation, and it was the Japanese (under the direction of an army corporal) who first struck oil (Richard Barry, personal communication).
3 The acronym for Perusahaan Pertambangan Minyak Nasional (National Oil Mining Company).
4 Cost oil is now up to a maximum of 80 per cent of the agreed selling price.
5 This even extends to the furniture in the houses of oil company executives.
6 The increase in profits for foreign oil companies as a result of the first oil shock also led the Indonesian government to renegotiate the PSC. The profit share ffor the state was increased from the original 65:35 split, to 85:15. In some cases it was even as high as 88:12 (Subroto 1986, p. 191, Lukman & McGlinchey 1986, p. 75).
7 The acronym for Badan Perencanaan Pembangunan Nasional (National Development Planning Board).
8 For various accounts of the Pertamina crisis see McCawley 1978, Glassburner 1976, Robison 1986, Palmer 1978.
9 'Non-oil GDP' is calculated by subtracting the mining sector, which is dominated by the oil and gas industries.

9

Export-oriented development: the Singapore experience in an ASEAN context

Introduction

During the last quarter of a century there has been a dramatic shift in the locus of world economic activity away from the developed countries of the West towards Asia and the Pacific. It is here that the most vibrant economies are located, and as commentators constantly reiterate, the coming century will be the era of the Pacific. The economic performance of Japan, and of the newly industrializing countries (NICs) of East Asia (South Korea, Taiwan, and Hong Kong), has contributed most to this reorientation. However, more recently the performance of a second tier of countries has gained increasing attention. These are the countries of ASEAN. In the period between 1965 and 1989 the economies of the countries of the ASEAN region (excluding Brunei) grew at an average annual rate of more than 6 per cent (weighted by population) and the World Bank now classifies all the ASEAN nations as 'middle income' (Table 9.1). Singapore, with a per capita income of more than US$8000 (1988), is already classified as a NIC (Figure 9.1), while Malaysia and Thailand are touted by many as soon to join the club. Even the Philippines, which has been severely afflicted by political instability and a consequent loss of business confidence during much of the 1980s, has recovered to a limited extent.

However, even a cursory survey of the countries of the region serves to illustrate their differences. They have diverse resource endowments, have had varied historical experiences, and are at different stages of development. Indonesia, extending over 1.9 million square kilometres, is a poor, agriculture-based economy with a population of more than 185 million. Singapore, by contrast, is a rich city state with 2.7 million inhabitants and a land area of only 620 square kilometres. This heterogeneity should constantly be borne in mind when evaluating their relative performances. Nevertheless, there is an increasing tendency to examine ASEAN not just as a political association, but also as a loose economic unit. This stems from two facts. First, ASEAN consists of a core group of relatively large, natural resource-rich economies that have much in common, at least superficially: Indonesia, Malaysia, the Philippines, and Thailand. This group is sometimes referred to as the ASEAN-4 and accounts for over 99 per cent of the population of the region. In addition to the ASEAN-4 two other countries need to be considered: Singapore and Brunei. Brunei is a

Table 9.1 Southeast Asian economies: performance and structure, 1965–90

	Thailand	Malaysia	Singapore	Indonesia	Philippines	Brunei
Growth of production (average annual percentage growth)						
GDP growth						
1965–80	7.4	7.3	10.2	7.9	5.9	—
1980–7	5.6	4.5	5.4	3.6	−0.5	6.9[1]
1988	10.5	8.7	11.0	3.8	6.7	−12[2]
1989	10.5	7.6	9.2	6.2	6.0	—
1990 (est.)	9–10	6.5	7–9	6.5–7	5–7	—
Sectoral growth 1965–80						
Agriculture	4.6	—	3.1	4.3	4.6	—
Industry	9.5	—	12.2	11.9	8.0	—
(Manufacturing)	10.9	—	13.3	12.0	7.5	—
Services	8.0	—	9.7	7.3	5.2	—
Sectoral growth 1980–87						
Agriculture	3.7	3.4	−3.9	3.0	1.8	—
Industry	5.9	5.8	4.0	2.1	−2.8	—
(Manufacturing)	6.0	6.3	3.3	7.8	−1.1	—
Services	6.4	3.8	6.4	5.6	−0.0	—
Structure of production (percentage)						
1965						
Agriculture	35	28	3	56	26	—
Industry	23	25	24	13	28	—
(Manufacturing)	14	9	15	8	20	—
Services	42	47	73	31	46	—
1987						
Agriculture	21	—	1	26	24	2
Industry	34	—	38	33	33	51
(Manufacturing)	28	—	29	14	25	—
Services	46	—	62	41	43	47
Sectoral allocation of the labour force (percentage)						
1965						
Agriculture	82	59	6	71	58	
Industry	5	13	27	9	16	
Services	13	29	68	21	26	
1980						
Agriculture	71	42	2	57	52	
Industry	10	19	38	13	16	
Services	19	39	61	30	33	
Structure of merchandise exports[3] (percentage)						
Primary commodities						
1965	95	94	65	96	95	—
1986	58	64	32	79	40	97
Manufactures						
1965	5	6	34	89	6	—
1986	42	36	68	22	61	3

Sources: Various.
Notes: 1) 1980–4. 2) 1986 data. 3) There are some rounding errors in this set of figures.

Figure 9.1 Singapore's central business district with HDB apartment blocks in foreground (photograph: Philip Stott)

small, extremely rich country with a per capita income of nearly US$13 000 (1987). Its wealth is founded on a single commodity, oil, which accounts for 97 per cent of export earnings. Singapore, by contrast, has built its wealth on the export of manufactured goods and, increasingly, on modern services. The second unifying element is the fact that in recent years the countries of the region, with the exception of Brunei, have chosen to follow a broadly similar development strategy. This strategy is known as export-led or, more accurately, export-oriented industrialization.

The following discussion will concentrate on the development of Singapore. This is because Singapore is often presented as a 'role model' for the other countries of the region. Of particular concern will be the implications of Singapore's experience for the ASEAN-4. It is worth noting that development is usually perceived to be a linear process in which countries pass through particular 'stages'. Thus Singapore is regarded by many as being merely one or two steps ahead of Indonesia, Malaysia, the Philippines, and Thailand.

ASEAN development: structural change and development

When the ASEAN-4 achieved self-government after the Second World War, their economies were agriculture-based, and primary commodities made up over 90 per cent of exports. Even as late as 1965, this characterization remained broadly accurate (Table 9.1). At this time, Singapore's economy was based upon entrepôt trade and services, which constituted 73 per cent of GDP.[1] Since the mid-1960s however, the ASEAN-4 and Singapore have undergone a process of continuing structural change. Between 1965 and 1980 industrial output in the countries of the region expanded annually at between 8 per cent and 12 per cent, with manufacturing spearheading the process. By contrast, agricultural production grew at less than 5 per cent per year. This pattern of growth has continued in the period since 1980 (Table 9.1). Associated with the change in the structure of production there has also occurred a sectoral and spatial shift in the labour force as workers have moved out of agriculture into industry and services, largely located in urban areas.

The initial growth of the economies of Southeast Asia, like those of most developing countries, was based upon import-substitution industrialization (ISI). This was even true of Singapore (Figure 9.1). At the time the climate of world opinion was one of 'export pessimism' and an inward-looking ISI strategy was advocated by the World Bank and by the majority of economists (e.g. Prebisch, Hirschman, and Nurkse). The logic underlying ISI was that an indigenous industrial base was only likely to evolve if infant industries were protected from foreign competition. Thus tariff barriers and quantitative quotas were put in place, and domestic production was encouraged to substitute for goods that were previously imported. The industries that developed in this protected environment mainly produced simple, non-durable consumer goods for domestic sale. Although ISI is now a widely maligned strategy, it should be emphasized that this early period of industrialization in Southeast Asia had its successes. It gave the countries of the region an opportunity to produce for the domestic market, provided local entrepreneurs with a chance to establish themselves, and allowed production and marketing skills to be acquired.

ISI is commonly thought of as consisting of two stages: an 'easy' first stage in which the production of non-durable consumer goods is roughly in line with the prevailing comparative advantage, and a much more difficult second stage in which consumer durables, and intermediate and capital goods are produced. These second stage goods require far greater investment, and production is often dependent on foreign technology and expertise. The restricted local market also means that there are limited economies of scale, and production costs rise accordingly. To protect these industries, governments must increase protection and distort further their economies. By the 1970s it was becoming clear to the ASEAN-4 that the limits of ISI were being reached and that a change in strategy was necessary if growth were to be sustained. There were a number of factors that led to this broad change in strategy.

First, and perhaps most persuasively, there was the performance of Singapore and the other NICs of East Asia: Hong Kong, South Korea, and Taiwan. By adopting an outward-looking strategy of export-oriented industrialization, these countries had managed to achieve consistently high rates of economic growth. Their example was a crucial lesson for the governments of the ASEAN-4, as it was for many economists. Second, ISI was constrained by the limits of the domestic market, and by the

1970s there was little slack left to ensure further growth. Third, the protection afforded to domestic infant industries, rather than providing an opportunity for an internationally competitive manufacturing base to become established, had merely encouraged the growth of small, inefficient and largely uncompetitive companies. It also encouraged the growth of rent-seeking or 'directly unprofitable profit-seeking' (see Chapter 8). As the domestic market became saturated there was therefore little possibility that surplus production could be marketed abroad without heavy subsidies. Fourth, the investment incentives associated with ISI, along with the overvaluation of the local currency, tended to favour capital-intensive methods of production while at the same time discouraging exports. This meant that the strategy had only a limited impact on levels of employment. Finally, the ISI strategy, rather than saving foreign exchange, was forcing the ASEAN-4 to import increasing quantities of capital and intermediate goods to service their import-substituting industries. As a result, both Thailand and the Philippines experienced severe balance of payments difficulties. These factors, complemented by a generally favourable external trading and investment environment, encouraged the ASEAN-4 to shift from ISI to an export-oriented industrialization (EOI) strategy (Figure 9.2)

Before turning to examine this shift in greater detail, and with particular reference to the case of Singapore, there are three further points that can usefully be made. First, ISI and EOI are not mutually exclusive. In every instance, elements of the ISI strategy have remained in place. What has

---

Singapore   ISI   EOI   Restructuring   Recession
1959 - - - - - - - - - - 1965 - - - - - - - - - - - - - - - 1979 - - - - - - - 1985 - - - - -

Thailand   ISI   EOI
1959 - 1972 - - - - - [1980] - - - - - - - - - - - -

Malaysia   ISI   EOI
1957 - - - - - - - - - - - - - 1968 - - [1971] -

Indonesia   ISI   EOI
1949 - [1973] - - - - - 1981 - - - - - - - - - -

Philippines   ISI   EOI
1949 - - - - - - - - - - - - 1967 - - - - - - - - [1972] -

EOI = Export-oriented industrialization

ISI = Import subsitution industrialization

Note: the periods designated only denote a change in emphasis from ISI to EOI.

The dates in square brackets indicate the date of establishment of the first EPZs.

Figure 9.2   Development strategies in Southeast Asia

occurred is a shift in emphasis towards EOI. Second, although ISI is now out of vogue, it is argued by some commentators that a period of ISI is a necessary precondition for EOI (see ILO 1980, p. 19). And third, although export-oriented industrialization is sometimes also referred to as export promotion, it is' important to bear in mind that EOI in the case of the ASEAN-4 involves the removal of barriers to exports, rather than any bias in favour of exports over import substitution. Essentially, an export-oriented strategy seeks the removal of distortions in the economy.

Singapore has achieved the highest rate of growth among ASEAN members and was the first to turn to EOI. The Republic is often portrayed as a 'free market' success story, and in embarking on EOI the ASEAN-4 have made it clear that they wish to emulate its success. Such has been the paradigm shift in favour of EOI, and against ISI, that some commentators apparently believe that there is little left to discuss. Wong (1987, p. 120), for example, writes: 'The general superiority of the outward-looking strategies, particularly in the context of the structural characteristics of these NICs, seems no longer in doubt'.

Singapore: the emergence of a NIC

Development and growth: 1959–79

When Singapore achieved self-government in 1959 it was beset with problems. Population growth was 4.4 per cent per year, unemployment stood at between 10 per cent and 15 per cent, poverty and industrial unrest were widespread, there was political turmoil, a flight of foreign and local capital, little manufacturing base to speak of, and the island's infrastructure was in decay (Grice & Drakakis-Smith 1985, p. 351, Heineberg 1988, p. 18–19). Prime Minister Lee Kuan Yew and his colleagues in the Peoples Action Party (PAP) initially opted to promote industrialization through a process of import substitution, a strategy given greater logic when Singapore joined with Malaya, British North Borneo (now Sabah), and Sarawak to form the Federation of Malaysia in 1963. However, in 1965 Singapore broke with Malaysia and with it gave up secure access to the larger Malaysian market. From that point onwards the government turned to export-oriented industrialization in order to achieve its aims. This decision was further reinforced in 1967 when the British government announced its intention of dismantling its military bases in Singapore, which at that time directly and indirectly accounted for between 23 per cent and 24 per cent of GNP (Rodan 1989, p. 87). Because of a lack of domestic entrepreneurs, technology, and capital, the Singapore government recognized that this reorientation could not be based upon domestic resources. Instead they turned to foreign investment and the involvement of foreign multinational companies (MNCs).

To attract foreign investment, the economy was liberalized and a series of incentives, some of which pre-date separation, were provided to MNCs. In 1959 the Pioneer Industries Ordinance and the Industrial Expansion

Ordinance were enacted to provide pioneer industries with tax exemptions for up to five years. In 1961, the Economic Development Board (EDB) was established to promote and guide industrialization. In 1967 the Economic Expansion Incentives Act was introduced, taxing the profits of companies exporting approved manufactured goods at 4 per cent for between 10 and 15 years rather than the usual 40 per cent. And in 1967 the Jurong Town Council (JTC) was set up to build low-cost industrial estates (Chong Li Choy 1986, pp. 59–60, Hakam 1985, p. 95, Chen 1983, pp. 9–10).

Complementing these measures, the government sought also to control wages and labour. It was recognized that MNCs would not be attracted to a country with the severe labour unrest that was characteristic of Singapore during the 1950s and early 1960s. In 1961 the government gave its support to the moderate National Trades Union Congress (NTUC) and became increasingly involved in and associated with the union movement. The Industrial Relations Ordinance of 1960 allowed for the swift resolution of industrial disputes and 'defined strikes as illegal after the Industrial Arbitration Court had taken cognizance of a dispute' (Chen 1983, p. 12). In these ways, and numerous others, the government managed to co-opt and institutionalize the unions. 'These political and legal moves achieved their aims. As Lim and Pang Eng Fong (1986, p. 11) point out: 'They de-politicised the labour movement, establishing *de facto* government control over unions, transferred bargaining power from workers to employers, and ushered in a period of labour peace that persists to this day' (see also Heyzer 1983, pp. 122–5).

In 1972 the government established the tripartite National Wage Council (NWC) on which the government, the NTUC, and the employers all have representatives. The NWC was set up with the intention of stabilizing wage increases and linking them to productivity, again with the objective of making Singapore an attractive location for foreign investors. Although the recommendations of the Council are not mandatory, they have been followed by the public sector and by most companies. In addition to these fiscal incentives the Singapore government dramatically improved the island's infrastructure, and provided a politically and economically secure and stable location in which MNCs could base their operations.

The response of MNCs to these incentives was dramatic. Cumulative foreign investment in manufacturing (gross fixed assets) rose from US$157 million at the end of 1965 to US$600 million in 1969; in 1971 it stood at US$1575 million (Figure 9.3). In 1975, wholly and majority foreign–owned manufacturing enterprises employed 52 per cent of workers in manufacturing, and accounted for 71 per cent of output, 63 per cent of value added, and 84 per cent of direct manufactured exports (Table 9.2). Much of this foreign investment was concentrated in the petroleum industry and originated in large part from the USA, the United Kingdom, and the Netherlands (in 1972 these three countries accounted for 61 per cent of cumulative foreign investment in manufacturing).

In response to this massive influx of foreign investment, Singapore's economy expanded rapidly. Annual GDP growth averaged 10.1 per cent between 1965 and 1979 (Figure 9.4). Expansion was initially concentrated

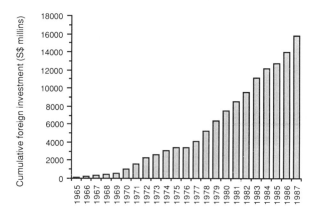

Figure 9.3 Singapore: cumulative foreign investment in manufacturing, 1965–87 (gross fixed assets)

Table 9.2 Role of foreign multinational companies in Singapore's manufacturing sector, 1975 and 1980

	Percentage of workers	Percentage of output	Percentage of value-added	Percentage direct exports	Percentage capital expenditure
1975					
Wholly foreign-owned	31.5	56.2	47.4	66.1	47.2
Majority foreign-owned	20.5	15.1	15.3	18.0	17.5
Combined	52.0	71.3	62.7	84.1	64.7
1980					
Wholly foreign-owned	39.9	58.7	54.1	71.5	61.3
Majority foreign-owned	18.5	15.0	13.3	13.2	13.3
Combined	58.4	73.7	67.4	84.7	74.6

Source: Pang Eng Fong 1985, p. 82.

in labour-intensive industries. However, Singapore's policy makers did not intend that the republic should remain a cheap wage location for foreign MNCs and in 1970 set about encouraging firms to upgrade, as well as trying to attract more capital-intensive and skill-intensive enterprises (Rodan 1989, p. 104.)[2] As a result the 1970s saw a diversification into electronics, precision equipment (e.g. watches and theodolites), transport and communications, and business-related services. Although Singapore was more adversely affected by the world recession of 1974–5 than many other countries, with manufacturing output actually falling by 7.3 per cent in 1975, in general terms this strategy of MNC-led, export-oriented industrialization was spectacularly successful. An advanced manufacturing

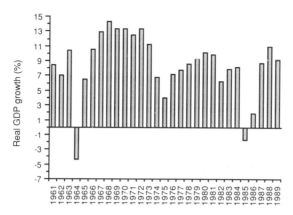

Figure 9.4 Singapore: real GDP growth, 1961–89

base was quickly established, full employment was achieved, real incomes rose rapidly, there was a constant overall balance of payments surplus, and the benefits of growth were widely distributed (see Figures 9.1 and 9.5).

Restructuring and the second industrial revolution: 1979-

THE SECOND INDUSTRIAL REVOLUTION
Notwithstanding these successes, however, towards the end of the 1970s the government felt that it was time to embark on a second bold restructuring of

Figure 9.5 Singapore: shop houses and skyscrapers (photograph: Philip Stott)

193

the economy (the first being the move from ISI to EOI in 1965). In essence this involved a more concerted, forced shift from labour-intensive into increasingly skill-intensive and capital-intensive industries and production methods. There were a number of domestic and international trends that encouraged the government to promote this change in emphasis (see Hakam 1985, p. 94, Mirza 1986, p. 59). First, other developing nations with far lower wage rates, among them the ASEAN-4, were beginning to compete with Singapore in labour-intensive industries. Second, the role of Singapore as a 'middleman', processing primary products such as oil and rubber from Malaysia and Indonesia, was in decline. These countries were developing their own refining and processing facilities, making Singapore's role redundant. Third, growing unemployment was forcing down wage rates in the developed nations, narrowing Singapore's wage advantage. Fourth, the development of new technology was eliminating the need for labour-intensive methods in some industries, encouraging MNCs to relocate back in their home countries. And fifth, it was appreciated that the use of cheap immigrant labour could only be a temporary solution to the labour shortages that Singapore was experiencing.

This second industrial revolution sought to overcome these impending problems by forcing enterprises to upgrade. The primary means by which this was to be achieved was through using the NWC to force wages up ahead of productivity. In the three years between 1979 and 1981, wages rose by between 42 per cent and 46 per cent (Rodan 1989, pp. 144–5). In addition, the government expanded the Skills Development Fund, established a Vocational and Industrial Training Board, further restricted the use of cheap immigrant labour, eased controls on the immigration of skilled professionals, and promoted investment in research and development.

THE 1985 RECESSION

Initially it appeared as if the second industrial revolution had enabled the ever dextrous Singapore economy to manage another successful reorientation (see for e.g. Mirza 1986, p. 59, Rodan 1987, p. 161). Growth of GDP, labour productivity and manufacturing value added were all buoyant. However, by the end of 1984 it was clear that the economy was going into recession. In 1985 the economy shrunk by 1.7 per cent, the profitability of foreign manufacturing firms declined by 70 per cent, 90 000 workers were laid off, and unemployment rose to over 4 per cent (Figure 9.4) (Chong Li Choy 1986, p. 62). The reason for the recession lay in a coincidence of negative internal and external factors (see Rigg 1988, pp. 345–9, Clad 1989, p. 127–31).

To begin with there was an international decline in the fortunes of two of Singapore's leading sectors: shipbuilding and ship repair, and oil refining. In addition, the policy of pushing wage rates ahead of productivity substantially increased unit labour costs, reducing profitability and causing the country to lose international competitiveness. Between 1980 and 1985, unit labour costs in manufacturing rose by 40 per cent in Singapore. In Taiwan, by contrast, they rose by 11 per cent, in South Korea by 1 per cent, while in Hong Kong they actually declined by 22 per cent (Holloway 1987a,

p. 55). The government's intention of encouraging firms to upgrade was also stymied by a dearth of trained personnel to spearhead the process.

RECTIFICATION AND RECOVERY

Facing the first contraction of the economy since the export-oriented strategy was embraced, the Singapore government announced the creation of an Economic Committee in March 1985 to examine the country's problems and prospects. The committee was placed under the leadership of the Prime Minister's son, Lee Hsien Loong, and its report, *The Singapore economy: new directions*, was released in February 1986 (Ministry of Trade and Industry 1986). The report offers a detailed analysis of the conditions that had led up to the recession, and in essence contains three main proposals. First, in order to re-establish Singapore's competitiveness among the Asian NICs, it was suggested that the high wage policy of the second industrial revolution should be reversed and manufacturers' costs reduced. Second, and in the longer term, the report presented the case for a reorientation of the economy away from manufacturing and increasingly into modern services. It is in these human capital-intensive activities that Singapore is now felt to have the greatest comparative advantage and it is significant that such service industries are also less dependent on foreign investment. And third, the report argued for a liberalization of the economy, foreseeing a reduced role for the government in managing the country's economic affairs. In large part the report's recommendations have been adopted by the government. Employers' costs were substantially reduced through a reduction in contributions to the Central Provident Fund from 25 per cent of wages to 10 per cent; corporate tax was reduced from 40 per cent to 33 per cent; there were reductions in a wide assortment of statutory board charges (e.g. 10 per cent to 50 per cent reductions in telephone and telex charges); wages were frozen in 1986 and 1987; and the NWC embarked on a comprehensive review of the wage system so as to ensure greater flexibility (see Rigg 1988, pp. 349–51, Rodan 1989, pp. 190–8, Bowring 1986, pp. 72–7, Low 1988b).

The economy responded quickly to these policy changes, and combined with a recovery in the international economy (e.g. strong US demand for electronics), they led to a resurgence in growth (Figure 9.4). However, although the government has shown how rapidly it can react to a reversal in economic fortunes, and also how effectively the business community can respond to those policy changes that have been introduced, the 1985 recession has wider implications. In the view of some commentators, the recession of 1985 marks a watershed in Singapore's development. It has 'shocked both policy-makers and the business community out of a feeling of self satisfaction born of success' and has led to a re-examination of issues that had previously been left unquestioned (Krause *et al.* 1987a, p. 217).

Notwithstanding the 1985 recession, and the re-examination of issues that it has stimulated, Singapore's success has made it a standard-bearer for those who advocate an outward-looking export-oriented strategy. Neoclassical economists such as Milton Friedman have claimed that Singapore's success is the product of the 'free market' and use its example to argue the case against state intervention (see Rodan 1989, pp. 25–30). Singapore and the NICs of East Asia are regarded as a role model not only by many analysts but also by the governments of the ASEAN-4 and other developing countries. Chen (1983, p. 4), for example, writes that the 'impressive achievements in social and economic development over the past two decades have made Singapore as a country one of the most outstanding models of development'. This perspective begs a number of important questions. First, is the view that Singapore represents a 'free market' success story entirely accurate? Second, have there been any undesirable implications, or repercussions, that have flowed from the development strategy that has been embraced? Third, is Singapore's experience transferable to the other members of ASEAN, and what lessons does it hold for the ASEAN-4? As Indonesia, Malaysia, the Philippines, and Thailand are currently embarking on similar strategies of export-oriented development, these questions are obviously particularly pertinent.

The role of the state in Singapore's development

The view of Singapore as the archetypal *laissez faire* economy could not be further from the truth. However, this is not to say that it is not a capitalist economy, but rather that its success has not been built upon the operation of the free market. The government has been highly interventionist and has very carefully, and very successfully for much of the time, stage managed Singapore's development.[3]

To begin with, and as already discussed, Prime Minister Lee and the PAP set out to control labour and wages. The institutionalization of the unions, to the extent that the union movement now sees its role as one of 'partnership' with the government, provides perhaps the most dramatic evidence of this. In addition, however, it controls the labour market by restricting the number of foreign workers allowed into the country, and regulates wage costs through the operation of the NWC. The most blatant, and least successful such intervention was the corrective wage policy of the second industrial revolution. More insidious so far as some observers are concerned, have been the population control policies that have been instituted, an element of social engineering that will be returned to a later in the discussion. The government has also established a Skills Development Fund to assist in training, and itself employs some 20 per cent of all workers (Lim 1983c, p. 756, Pang Eng Fong 1985, p. 67).

The second area of government intervention comes in the guise of state enterprises. In 1977, the government held approximately one-third of net fixed assets (Deyo 1981, p. 58), and in 1987 it had a stake in 450 firms with a total paid-up capital of S$5 billion (Holloway 1987b, p. 69, Clad 1989, p. 143). These include shipyards (one of the largest being Keppel Corporation Limited), an airline (Singapore Airlines), a shipping line (Neptune Orient Lines), and a Bank (the Development Bank of Singapore). All the enterprises are expected to be run commercially, and to make a profit. If they become unprofitable, they are allowed to go bankrupt. The government has tended to use these public enterprises to pioneer the restructuring of the economy, stimulating and canalizing both domestic and foreign private investment (Seah 1983, p. 152).

The Singapore government is also the sole supplier of infrastructure and of many services. Public monopolies provide all utilities, manage the port and airport, control television and radio, and supply education at all levels. The Housing and Development Board (HDB) established in 1959 provides housing for 87 per cent of Singapore's population, and by 1989 had constructed over 642 000 dwelling units since it began its building programme in 1960 (see Figure 9.1). Money to finance the HDB and many other investments has come in large part from the Central Provident Fund into which employers and employees make compulsory payments. Contributions have ranged from 10 per cent of wages in 1955 to 50 per cent by 1985. As of July 1988, employers were contributing 12 per cent (to a maximum of S$720 per month) and employees 24 per cent (to a maximum of S$1440 per month). The size of the CPF, which is in effect a fully funded welfare system, can be judged by the fact that by the end of 1988 it had 2.06 million members with S$32.5 billion to their credit. In 1988 alone net contributions amounted to S$4985 million and represented 24 per cent of gross national savings (Ministry of Communications and Information 1989). In total, Lim estimates that more than half of domestic income passes through government hands (Lim 1983c, p. 756). Finally, the government holds 75 per cent of all land.

For all the above reasons, although it is true that unlike the other countries of Southeast Asia Singapore has no national development plan, it would be entirely inaccurate to see the island's economy growing purely through market forces. As Lim (1983c, p. 761) rather colourfully, but not entirely fairly, observed in 1983, Singapore's success has been the result 'more of the Long Arm of state intervention than . . . of the Invisible Hand of the free market'. The point, of course, is that the government, at least up until 1985, had been very successful in its interventions. In addition, it should be emphasized that although it plays a leading role in the economy, it tends not to distort prices. It is this that most clearly distinguishes the Singapore experience from the ISI policies that were pursued by the ASEAN-4 during the 1960s and 1970s. In terms of simple averages of tariff rates, the Philippines in 1978 recorded the highest rate of protection at 44 per cent, followed by Indonesia (33 per cent), Thailand (29 per cent), Malaysia (15 per cent), and finally Singapore (6 per cent) (Ariff & Hill 1985, p. 80).

The 1985 recession stimulated the PAP to take some steps towards reducing the government's role in the economy and embarking on a degree of deregulation. Intervention and authoritarianism, although perhaps appropriate for the first 20 years of Singapore's development, are now felt to be increasingly inappropriate as the government attempts to transform the country into an advanced information and service centre. As Finance Minister Richard Hu observed in an interview in 1987:

> The government has, during the early stages of the economy, had to take a lead to get the economy going. Now we have to move on

to a different level of development, different industries – smaller, entrepreneurial – where I think the private sector must play a far larger role (FEER 1987, p. 70).

For this and other reasons, the government is relaxing the regulatory environment and privatizing some state-owned industries. The NWC has adopted more flexible guidelines, the CPF is to give investors more responsibility in determining how their funds are invested, and plans to privatize 41 government-linked companies (e.g. Singapore Airlines) are already under way (Low 1988b, pp. 258–9). These changes also extend to the education system and housing programme, which are both undergoing reforms so as to introduce greater autonomy and flexibility. In addition, Low (1988a, 1988b, p. 259) believes that the government has adopted a more open, consultative style and is becoming generally less overbearing in its approach.

Implications of state-led dependent development

In much of the literature on Singapore's economic progress, and especially that issuing from Singapore itself, there has been little analysis of the possible negative implications of the development strategy that has been followed. This should be balanced against some of the more critical analyses, however, which have sometimes failed fully to acknowledge the success that the government has had in building a vibrant economy and improving living standards.

The greatest area of concern regarding Singapore's foreign investment driven, export-oriented strategy is the dependency that it may have engendered. As Rodan (1989, p. 113) has argued, 'there is an externally-imposed precariousness about participation in this structure over which even the most astute policy-makers in world export bases such as Singapore have very little control'. These fears seemed well-founded in 1985 when a fall in regional and international demand for Singapore's products played a significant part in bringing on the recession of that year. Although this dependence on external developments is partly a result of growing global interdependence and the small size of Singapore's domestic market, the government's development strategy has also been directly responsible. Foreign trade amounts to 3.69 times GDP, higher than Hong Kong (2.32), Taiwan (0.99) and South Korea (0.66), the other export-oriented Asian NICs (Asia Yearbook 1990, pp. 8–9).

The threat of growing protectionism in both the developed and the developing world has added to the worry that Singapore may become increasingly vulnerable to developments beyond its control. In 1988, the USA withdrew the benefits of the Generalized System of Preferences (GSP) from Singapore, and also from Hong Kong, South Korea, and Taiwan. In 1989, it went further, labelling Japan as an 'unfair trader' under the provisions of the Omnibus Trade and Competitiveness Act (better known as Super 301), and reportedly only left South Korea and Taiwan off the list because of some market-opening measures on their part (Chanda 1989, pp. 99–100). Krause (1987b, p. 73) is of the opinion that protectionism is becoming 'systematic' in the world economy, and non-tariff barriers are increasingly used to restrict imports (Rodan 1989, p. 197). As Singapore's success to date has been built on a relatively open international trading environment, the prospect of increasing protectionism raises questions as to whether such a strategy will be equally productive in the future.

In a rather different vein, it has been argued that Singapore's strategy of state-led development has been necessarily authoritarian in character. At independence, Lee Kuan Yew expressed the view that Singapore, small and lacking in resources, would have to be disciplined if it were to survive and to flourish. This ideology of survival stressed a number of related values that Rodan (1989, p. 90) has listed as discipline, resilience, achievement-orientation, adaptability, patriotism and self-sacrifice. At times the ideology has led to infringements of workers' rights and civil liberties, restrictions on press freedoms, the manipulation of the political system, and the imprisonment and allegedly harsh treatment of political prisoners. It has also led to a degree of what critics of the PAP's paternalistic and authoritarian methods have termed 'social engineering' (see Wilkinson 1988). This involves attempting to control the number of children parents should have, what language they should speak, where they should live, and what they should study (Grice & Drakakis-Smith 1985, pp. 356–7). In 1984, for example, Prime Minister Lee expressed concern at the far higher levels of fecundity among women with no education than among those with university qualifications. Believing intelligence to be hereditary, he argued that the nation's economic and social future was in jeopardy. As a consequence the government introduced a series of measures to encourage women graduates to have more children (Rodan 1989, pp. 184–6).

This issue of the authoritarian and paternalistic nature of Singapore's development, and also that of the other Asian NICs, is an almost impossible issue to confront with objectivity. Supporters of the PAP's approach believe that, given the insecurity of Singapore's position at separation in 1965, it was essential that the government encourage a degree of discipline and self-sacrifice. They further point out that paternalism, and the subordination of the individual in the interests of society as a whole, has a strong basis in Confucian ethics and East Asian culture (Sikorski 1985, pp. 183–5). To Singapore's critics, however, these are merely excuses employed to disguise the government's increasingly repressive actions and attitudes. A second question is whether authoritarianism is a necessary precondition for successful export-oriented growth. It is argued that during the early difficult stages of development it is essential that there be continuity of purpose, and the discipline to adopt economic policies that might involve some short-term sacrifices (see ILO 1980, pp. 9–22, Kohli 1986). Although seductive, in the end the debate is sterile, sheds little light, and has few lessons for the other developing countries of the world. Finally, it is also worth noting that Singapore's success has been inspired by one man: Prime Minister Lee Kuan Yew. Although he is still relatively young – Lee was 65 in 1988 – arrangements have already been made for his succession, possibly in late 1990. The question, however, is whether Singapore's new Premier (probably Goh Chok Tong) will have the same authority and direction of purpose as Lee, and will be able to continue to guide the country successfully.

The transfer of Singapore's experience to the ASEAN-4

As the ASEAN-4 have now all embarked on development strategies that broadly fall within the EOI mould, it is obviously relevant to ask whether Singapore's experience is transferable to the other countries of the region.

Singapore is clearly very different from the ASEAN-4. It is a small Chinese city state, with no poor rural hinterland. From the outset, therefore, resources could be concentrated in the city, rather than having to be dispersed to a countryside where the potential for industrialization was limited. Singapore also benefited from an advantageous location on the Malacca Straits, and at independence had a relatively efficient infrastructure and educated workforce. Rather more controversial is the claim that Singapore and the other NICs have certain cultural advantages. These have their roots in Confucian values that stress hard work, diligence, submission to authority, thrift and the value of education (see Wong 1987, pp. 127–31).

In addition to these advantages, analysts such as Harris (1986) and Rodan (1985, 1989) claim that Singapore benefited from 'historical specificity'. In their view, the republic opted for its strategy of foreign investment-driven, export-oriented industrialization just at a time when the world's markets were at their most open, and when foreign MNCs were searching actively for countries in which to locate (Rodan 1985, pp. 180–3). The ASEAN-4, as they pursue the same path, are faced with rather different circumstances. Markets in general are less accessible, and technological advances (e.g. in robotics) have negated the attractiveness of developing countries as low wage locations. Automation (mechatronics) of some assembly and quality control processes, for example, has made the production of textiles and electronic components less labour-intensive. As a result MNCs have begun to consider relocating production back in the markets of the developed world, a trend that also circumvents the problems of growing protectionism (see Hakchung Choo & Ifzal Ali 1989, p. 19). A final point that has been raised about other developing countries' ability to emulate the NICs concerns 'crowding out'. It is felt that if the ASEAN-4, along with other developing countries, pursue similar policies then the markets of the developed world will become swamped, increasing competition and encouraging protectionism. Thus it is felt that although there may be room for four NICs, there is not room for 40. For those who subscribe to this view, Singapore's strategy of EOI 'was feasible because of opportune historical conditions, *not because this strategy made universal sense* [emphasis added]' (Rodan 1989, p. 208).

Elements of the above argument that Singapore's experience cannot easily be replicated by the ASEAN-4 are convincing. However, there are also some important factors that are either glossed over or entirely ignored. The first point concerns the difference between historical specificity (the tyranny of the unique) and opportunity. Supporters of historical specificity maintain that those who see universal validity in the EOI strategy are guilty of reductionism and an ahistorical approach to Singapore's success (e.g. Rodan 1985, p. 180). But they in turn fail to accept that history throws up many opportunities, and also to recognize that the NICs themselves have very different resource bases, histories, and systems of government (see Browett 1985, pp. 799–801). Since late 1985, for example, the appreciation of the yen has encouraged Japanese manufacturers to locate their production facilities offshore. This has led to a massive influx of Japanese investment in Southeast Asia. Net Japanese direct investment in Thailand, for example, increased from 1798 million baht per year in the period 1981–5, to 3046 million baht in 1986. In 1988 it reached 14 612 million baht (Somsak Tambunlertchai 1989, pp. 101–2). Thus, although particular historical circumstances can never be repeated, similar opportunities do arise. Indeed, they will always exist, and it is only a case of managing them. The impressive export-led growth of the Thai economy is a case in point.

The second point, which is possibly so obvious as to be often left unremarked upon, is that economies continually evolve. As the ASEAN-4 begin to develop a labour-intensive export base, so the NICs are also undergoing a process of structural change and are moving into increasingly skill-intensive and capital-intensive industries. It is significant that in 1988 foreign investment by the four Asian NICs in the ASEAN-4 (defined in terms of projects approved) exceeded that of Japan. In total, it amounted to US$3.7 billion and represented 31 per cent of total foreign investment in Indonesia, Malaysia, the Philippines, and Thailand (Holloway 1989, p. 71).[4] Those who doubt whether the NIC experience can be repeated neglect this dynamism, and also the degree of diversity that exists within single categories of industries labelled 'labour-intensive' or 'capital-intensive'. As such they present a picture that is both too static and too monolithic.

Given the above, what lessons, if any, does Singapore's success have for the ASEAN-4? James *et al.* (1987), together with others, such as Chaponniere (1985), accept that special conditions are important in understanding the success of the NICs but contend that 'the key is the outward-looking development strategies adopted by these countries' (James *et al.*1987, pp. 17–18). Thus they believe that Singapore's experience is relevant to the ASEAN-4, and see their impressive recent economic growth as being linked to the shift they have undertaken from ISI to EOI, and the attractive investment climate that has been created. In addition, however, there must be a consistent commitment to EOI. Pang Eng Fong (1985, pp. 88–9) notes the dangers that economic nationalism, disorderly government intervention, and short-termism can have in distorting an export-oriented strategy. Thus, equally important in ensuring success is the quality of government and of policy implementation, two aspects of development that must be allied with an export-oriented strategy. As Lim and Pang Eng Fong (1986, p. 107) point out:

> In general, the chief lesson of Singapore's development experience for other countries is that an efficient, honest and forward-looking

state apparatus, unencumbered by doctrinaire political or economic philosophy, and ever-responsive to changes in market forces, can effectively mobilise a country's people and resources to make the most of those prevailing market forces.

The ASEAN-4: NICs in the making?

In the 1970s and 1980s, the governments of Indonesia, Malaysia, the Philippines, and Thailand have all followed Singapore's example and embraced a shift in development strategy from ISI to EOI (Figure 9.1).[5] To reiterate, the pressures that encouraged this change in strategy consisted of a combination of growing deficits in trade and balance of payments, compounded by the realization that the first, 'easy' stage of ISI was coming to an end. These countries' domestic markets for locally produced consumer goods were becoming saturated and the protection that producers had enjoyed from foreign competition ensured that little of the excess output could be profitably exported. The spectacular success of the export-led industrialization policies followed by Singapore and the other NICs must also have played a role. That the shift from ISI to EOI should have been delayed for so long is a reflection of the influence wielded by domestic capitalists and, in the cases of Indonesia and Malaysia, the wealth generated by oil and gas (see Chapter 8). Once again it should be pointed out that irrespective of this policy reorientation towards EOI, many of the measures protecting import-substituting industries have remained in place, and the two strategies are pursued simultaneously. In Thailand, for example, the effective rates of protection on manufactured goods for the domestic market (excluding food, beverages, and tobacco) actually increased from 44 per cent in 1971, when export promotion was first officially endorsed, to approximately 90 per cent at the end of the 1970s (Linnemann *et al.* 1987, p. 298).

As in the case of Singapore, a factor that has facilitated the move into export-oriented industrialization has been foreign investment. Agencies such as the Boards of Investment in Thailand and the Philippines (BOI), the Malaysian Industrial Development Authority (MIDA), and Indonesia's Capital Investment Coordinating Board (BKPM – Badan Kordinasi Penanaman Modal), have all increased incentives to foreign investors and streamlined their procedures. In addition, all four countries have established export processing zones (EPZs) in which foreign manufacturers can locate free of import duties and with the additional attraction of added investment and export incentives (Figure 9.2). Moreover, manufacturers in EPZs are often less constrained by minimum wage and other employment regulations. There has, in turn, been a significant increase in foreign direct investment (FDI) in the ASEAN-4 (Table 9.3). In 1988 this averaged over US$850 million for each of the countries of the region, with the largest flows originating from Japan and the USA (Naya 1987).

The impressive recent growth record of the ASEAN-4 has led to a debate as to whether they are a second tier of NICs. *Newsweek*, *The Economist* and

Table 9.3 Foreign direct investment in Southeast Asia, 1965–88 (US$ millions per year)

	1965–71[1]	1972–6	1977–80	1981–4	1985–7	1988
Indonesia	48.5	198.7	230.9	218	338	542
Malaysia	69.5	317.5	603.5	1180	527	611
Philippines	−8.3	55.3	52.9	76	149	936
Singapore	61.5	487.6	920.7	1317	775	1066
Thailand	43.6	87.2	101.7	306	202	1092

Sources: Naya 1987, p. 71, IMF 1989b, IMF 1989c.
Notes: 1) In the cases of Indonesia, Malaysia, and Singapore the figures are for the years 1967–71.

the *Far Eastern Economic Review* have all run articles labelling Thailand and Malaysia as candidates, or prospective candidates, of this exclusive club (*Newsweek* 1988, pp. 6–12, *Economist* 1989, p. 15, FEER 1989b, pp. 96–100). Some of the factors militating against their progression to NIC status have already been discussed: the rise in protectionism, crowding-out, and historical specificity.[6] In addition, however, it needs to be asked what exactly we mean by the term 'newly industrializing country' or, as the World Bank has now rather unhelpfully decided to term them, 'newly industrializing economies'. The label is much used, but little defined.

Among the features that have been variously noted as characteristic of NICs are an export-oriented development strategy, rapid growth and diversification in manufactured exports, rapid structural change, a developed manufacturing sector, a per capita income in excess of US$1000 combined with a wide dispersal in its distribution, a per capita income in excess of US$2000, a poor natural resource endowment, a disciplined labour force, and overt foreign domination (Chen 1985, pp. 131–4, Rodan 1989, p. 1, Ariff & Hill 1985, p. 231, Balakrishnan 1989, p. 96, Browett 1985, p. 789, *Economist* 1989). If we are to accept that all of these characteristics are prerequisites for attaining the status of a NIC, then not one of the ASEAN-4 is close to joining. This wealth of indicators says more about the attempts to isolate the NICs as special cases than it does about whether their experience – broadly defined as rapid, industry-based, export-oriented growth – can be replicated by other developing countries. Nevertheless, and more usefully, the discipline involved in attempting a definition does raise issues that are worthy of further discussion.

First, each of the ASEAN-4 has a relatively large, and often poor, agricultural population. Although there may have occurred a structural shift into industry and services, the bulk of the population still remains in agriculture (see Chapter 3). The incorporation of these people into the growth process is possibly the major challenge facing Indonesia, Malaysia, the Philippines, and Thailand. From the capital cities of Southeast Asia, the region may appear to be vibrant and modern. However, whereas per capita incomes in Bangkok averaged 23 400 baht in 1986, the figure for the poor Northeast was only 5918 baht, a quarter of that in the city (NSO 1987a, pp. 80–1). Bangkok may therefore have the attributes of a NIC, but it does not apply to large areas of the countryside, where incomes are low, services lacking, health poor, communications difficult, and where poverty is widespread. An important feature of the growth of the Asian NICs is that it has been accompanied by a wider dispersal in income. It is also worth noting that Thailand's infrastructure – and this includes Bangkok as well as the countryside – is poorly developed, and must be improved and expanded.

Yoshihara (1988, pp. 111–18) takes a rather different tack and argues that not only are the ASEAN-4 far from becoming NICs, but also that Singapore is not a NIC. He makes this claim on the basis of Southeast Asia's 'technologyless industrialization' (see also Krirkkiat Phipatseritham & Yoshihara 1989, Clad 1989). He notes that unlike Japan, Taiwan, and South Korea, the countries of Southeast Asia are wholly dependent on imported technology and have few domestic capitalists of their own who can compete in the export markets of the world.[7] Southeast Asian manufacturers may be able to assemble components, but they cannot make them. In Thailand's case, the low quality of industrial entrepreneurship, the absence of a coherent government policy to promote industrialization, and the importance of the primary sector are among the various factors highlighted to explain the kingdom's weak technological base (Krirkkiat Phipatseritham & Yoshihara 1989). Yoshihara (1988, p. 118) concludes:

> Thus none of the ASEAN countries can join the NICs on their own because they lack their own technological bases. Their industrialization has been largely 'technologyless' because they failed to commit themselves to progress in science and technology.

For this reason, and also because growth has been largely confined to the tertiary sector, because it is dominated by Chinese capital, and because it is characterized by rent-seeking, Yoshihara (1988, pp. 3–4) believes that the Southeast Asian region is an example of 'ersatz' capitalism.

The prospects for Southeast Asian development

The ASEAN-4 face a very different world trading environment from that which existed when the NICs embarked on their strategy of EOI. However, this is not a sufficient reason to indulge in a new bout of export pessimism. As the recent performances of Indonesia, Malaysia, and Thailand demonstrate, there remains considerable scope for export-led growth. Nevertheless, there do exist a handful of potential constraints to expansion.

First, there is the issue of developed world protectionism. This is a serious threat to growth, and the countries of Southeast Asia are already finding their entry into the markets of the First World hampered by quotas, tariffs, and non-tariff barriers (see Ariff & Hill 1985, pp. 99–116, World

Bank 1987, pp. 133–53). A recent example involves the US decision to cut the benefits that Thailand receives under the Generalized System of Preferences in retaliation for the failure of the Thai authorities to give sufficient protection to intellectual property rights (particularly as they apply to computer software).[8] However, two points need to be set against this widely voiced fear of a resurgence in protectionism. To begin with, the climate of intellectual opinion has swung firmly in favour of EOI, open markets, and free trade. This should help to mitigate against wide-ranging protectionist measures. And, second, the countries of Southeast Asia do not rely on a single market. Therefore restrictions in one market can be offset to a degree by growth in another. This is becoming increasingly relevant as trade between developing countries (South–South trade) grows in importance, and as the NICs themselves begin to import labour-intensive manufactured goods from the ASEAN-4 and elsewhere.

A second potential constraint to growth lies in the continued tendency among the ASEAN-4 to intervene excessively in their economic affairs. As Chapter 8 illustrates, given the opportunity many governments would rather increase the level of state involvement in their economies than decrease it. The attractions of economic nationalism remain strong. It was only the failure of ISI, and the growing balance of payments deficits that accompanied this failure, that forced the governments of the ASEAN-4 to opt for a more open, export-oriented strategy. Should conditions change, they may be tempted to resort once again to more interventionist policies. This would distort prices, discourage foreign investment, decrease competitiveness, and lead inevitably to bad policy making.

How these threats to export-oriented growth are weighted is crucial in determining the tenor of any assessment of Southeast Asia's economic prospects. Such an assessment would also involve playing the dangerous game of futurology. In *Southeast Asia in the 1980s: the politics of economic crisis*, Robison, Hewison, and Higgott doubt the viability of EOI for the countries of the region. They write (1987a, pp. 10–12):

> Pressures to move from ISI to EOI strategies were therefore contradicted not only by political and economic interests vested in ISI and by ideological attachment to economic nationalism, but also by a growing realisation that the EOI route was less viable than supposed by the ideologues of the IMF and the World Bank . . . the major Southeast Asian countries are caught in a bind, unable to sustain the existing ISI structures and facing real difficulties in moving into the sphere of EOI.

Since their book was published, however, the actions of the governments of the ASEAN-4 have demonstrated their willingness partly to confront vested political and economic interests. Events have also shown that there does remain considerable scope for export-oriented growth. As the NICs have upgraded and their industrial structure has changed, so the ASEAN-4 and other developing countries have been provided with an opportunity to move increasingly into the production and export of labour-intensive manufactures. Sensible domestic policies, coupled with a favourable inter-national trading environment, should ensure that the countries of the region take advantage of this opportunity. If this occurs, and there is good reason to be optimistic, then the growth of the ASEAN-4 will lead to a further fragmentation of the Third World, and this simple threefold division will become even less easy to sustain.

Notes to Chapter 9

1 The high level of primary exports in Table 9.1 reflects re-exports of processed primary products such as petroleum and rubber.
2 For example, through the Economic Expansion Incentives (Amendment) Act of 1970 which restricted eligibility for benefits under the 1967 Act, and by a tightening of the labour market (Rodan 1989, p. 104).
3 For various accounts of the role of the state in development see Lim 1983c, Rodan 1989, Pang Eng Fong 1985, Lim & Pang Eng Fong 1986, Seah 1983, Krause 1987c.
4 In Malaysia in 1989, foreign investment approved by the Malaysian Industrial Development Authority totalled US$3.2 billion. Of this, 40 per cent (US$1.3 billion) originated from Taiwan, Singapore and Hong Kong alone (Tsuruoka 1990b, p. 34).
5 For a brief discussion see Robison, Higgott and Hewison 1987, pp. 4–10, Ariff & Hill 1985, pp. 19–25.
6 See Clad 1989, pp. 96–124 for a pessimistic assessment of Thailand's export-led 'boom'.
7 Clad (1989, pp. 24–5) writes: 'Free market Southeast Asia enters the closing years of this century largely bereft of new ideas . . . and watching in resentful fascination as market dynamism fashioned elsewhere widens the gap between the region's unchanged role as a *receiver* of technology and the West's (and Northeast Asia's) authentic, technological competence'.
8 Thailand has lost GSP benefits on US$165 million of exports to the USA out of a total of US$600 million that comes under the GSP.

10

Regional co-operation in Southeast Asia: the Association of Southeast Asian Nations

Introduction

The Association of Southeast Asian Nations (ASEAN) was established in August 1967 following the signing of the Bangkok Declaration by the foreign ministers of Indonesia, the Philippines, Singapore and Thailand, and the Deputy Prime Minister of Malaysia. In 1984, after it gained full sovereignty in its external affairs, Brunei became the sixth member of ASEAN.

ASEAN is often perceived to have been a remarkable success. It has managed to survive over 20 turbulent years, has created a cohesive image for itself, and has done much to further the interests of its member countries in the international arena. These are no mean achievements, especially when placed against the experiences of other regional organizations in Asia, Africa, and Latin America. Hal Hill (n.d., p. 82), for example, writes that 'as a political and economic association Asean has been without doubt the most successful in the developing world'. However, a body of opinion holds that when the rhetoric is pushed to one side – and there was a great deal on the occasion of the Association's twentieth anniversary in 1987 – little of substance remains (e.g. Clad 1989, pp. 215–36). This chapter aims to explore the extent to which ASEAN has furthered the cause of regional co-operation, and to decide whether we are justified in talking of an ASEAN regional identity.

Antecedents: the Association of Southeast Asia and Maphilindo

ASEAN was not the first attempt to create a regional grouping in Southeast Asia. There were two antecedents: the Association of Southeast Asia (ASA), and Maphilindo. ASA was established in 1961, and comprised Malaya, the Philippines, and Thailand. Its aims were to promote friendly consultation, collaboration, and assistance in the economic, social, cultural, scientific, and administrative fields (Suriyamongkol 1988, pp. 46–7). However, ASA was quickly accused by Indonesia of being a pro-Western and anti-communist alliance (Rajendran 1985, p. 15). Its effectiveness was also restricted by its limited membership, and when Malaysia and the Philippines broke off diplomatic relations in 1964–5 in a dispute over sovereignty claims to the East Malaysian state of Sabah (formerly North Borneo), virtually all prospects for any significant degree of co-operation disappeared (Suriyamongkol 1988, p. 48). Although ASA officially remained in existence until 1967, it was effectively inactive from 1964 onwards.

Maphilindo was established in 1963 and, as its name suggests, comprised Malaysia, the Philippines, and Indonesia. The grouping had no institutional framework, and only embraced very broad principles of co-operation. Indeed, it was much more a forum for regional consultation. The fact that Maphilindo grew out of a desire by President Macapagal of the Philippines to create a 'Greater Malay Federation' had the disadvantage of limiting its membership (Rajendran 1985, p. 16). There were also serious differences between the three countries even prior to the creation of Maphilindo (Irvine 1982a, p. 10), and when President Sukarno adopted a policy of confrontation towards Malaysia in 1963 (the so-called *Konfrontasi*) the grouping began to dissolve, finally disintegrating in 1966 (Shee Poon-Kim 1977, p. 754, Suriyamongkol 1988, p. 46).

However, although ASA and Maphilindo can hardly be characterized as success stories, they did provide a legacy on which ASEAN could build. First, ASA's diplomatic framework was incorporated into ASEAN's structure, as were many of its aims. Second, Maphilindo provided the foreign policy stance of non-alignment. Third, the shortcomings and ultimate failure of both Maphilindo and ASA forcibly illustrated the dangers that political differences could pose to any regional organization. But the most important legacy left to ASEAN was the habit of consultation and the concept of Southeast Asian subregionalism.

The formation of ASEAN

During the mid-1960s there were a number of developments, both internal and external to the Southeast Asian region, that paved the way for the formation of ASEAN. In October 1965 Suharto replaced Sukarno as President of Indonesia and immediately decided to bring the 'Confrontation' with Malaysia to an end. Similarly, when Marcos was elected to the Philippine Presidency in November 1965 he began to de-emphasize the Philippine claim to Sabah (Irvine 1982a, p. 10). As a result, relations between both pairs of countries markedly improved. In addition, tensions between Singapore and Malaysia eased between 1965 and 1967 as the two countries recovered from Singapore's decision to leave the Federation of Malay States in 1965.

However, although internal developments created a favourable environment in which a regional organization could be created, it was external developments that arguably provided the stimulus that led to ASEAN's formation. For, during the 1960s, the countries of Southeast Asia became increasingly concerned about the security of the region. To begin with, there were growing fears that the People's Republic of China might try to 'export' revolution and provide support to domestic insurgency groups (Rajendran 1985, p. 17, Suh 1984, p. 58). Certainly, the attempted coup in Indonesia in 1965 was widely felt to have been promoted by China. At the same time, the United Kingdom had announced that it was withdrawing its forces from Malaysia and Singapore (Suh 1984, pp. 57–8), and there were also growing worries that the USA might scale down its presence in the region as domestic public opinion turned against the involvement of US servicemen in the escalating conflict in Indochina (Chan Heng Chee 1986, pp. 113–14).[1] These external developments all served to impress upon the non-communist countries of Southeast Asia the need to take a more active role in the maintenance of their security. Indeed, the organization was primarily a product of security fears and weaknesses. It was not a product of a desire just to promote greater regional economic, social, and cultural co-operation.

Original aims and objectives

The Bangkok Declaration of 1967, work on which had commenced in 1966, gives little indication that the political and security considerations discussed above were important in its formulation. Ostensibly, ASEAN was established to 'promote active collaboration and mutual assistance on matters of common interest in the economic, social, cultural, technical, scientific and administrative fields' (ASEAN Declaration reproduced in Suriyamongkol 1988, p. 239). Mindful, no doubt, of the accusation that ASA was an anti-communist alliance, the signatories of the Bangkok Declaration wished to make the document as uncontroversial as possible.

This is not to say that there were no disagreements over the wording of the Declaration. An initial stumbling block concerned the statement to be made regarding the presence of foreign military bases on ASEAN soil. Indonesia wished to incorporate a fairly 'hard' statement, stressing their temporary nature; the Philippines, which considered the US military presence at Clark Air Field and Subic Bay Naval Base to be necessary for its own security, was concerned not to alienate the USA (Irvine 1982a, pp. 12–13). The result was a compromise statement:

Affirming that all foreign bases are temporary and remain only with the expressed concurrence of the countries concerned and are not intended to be used directly or indirectly to subvert the national independence and freedom of States in the area or prejudice the orderly processes of their national development (Bangkok Declaration reproduced in Suriyamongkol 1988, p. 238).

Of the forms of co-operation that the Bangkok Declaration embraced, it was economic co-operation that was regarded as being the most important. Irvine (1982a, p. 13) quotes Tun Ismail of Malaysia as saying that it is 'axiomatic that economic co-operation is often the most durable foundation upon which political and cultural cooperation can be built'. In spite of statements such as this, however, the Bangkok Declaration set no guidelines, no time schedule, and did not provide a framework through which co-operation, of whatever type, could be achieved. The Declaration was an open-ended statement of good intentions and an affirmation of partnership and peace. ASEAN has no formal charter and, for the first nine years, had no Secretariat (Wong 1985, p. 81).

The progress of ASEAN

Since 1967, ASEAN's development can usefully be divided into three phases. The first phase spans the 1967–75 peroid; the second, from 1975 to 1979; and the third from 1979 onwards. As will become clear in the discussion, in each of these phases ASEAN was responding primarily to developments in the international arena.

Phase 1: The difficult early years (1967–75)

The first eight years of ASEAN's existence was a period in which little tangible was achieved. Scarcely a year after the signing of the Bangkok Declaration, the Sabah dispute between Malaysia and the Philippines had resurfaced, and for an eight-month period the activities of the Association were effectively suspended (Irvine 1982a, p. 19). The dispute was felt to be so serious that the establishment of a rival organization was even mooted (Shee Poon-Kim 1977, p. 757). At the end of 1968, relations were strained still further when two Indonesian marines who had been found guilty of sabotage and murder during the *Konfrontasi* were hanged in Singapore (Chan Heng Chee 1986, p. 115).

In view of impediments such as these, it is not surprising that the cause of Southeast Asian regionalism appeared to be in limbo. Admittedly some progress was made – a number of committees dealing, for example, with food and agriculture, communications, tourism, and commerce and industry were set up – but there was virtually no concrete progress in regional economic or political co-operation (see Castro 1982, pp. 74–7). But this underestimates the significance of the first phase of ASEAN's existence. It should be remembered that when the five members met in Bangkok, there still existed deep divisions between them. Indeed, some commentators believe that the surprising fact was that the Association was ever established (Tasker 1987a, p. 106). As Shee Poon-Kim (1977, p. 753) writes:

> the ASEAN countries form a group of distinct heterogeneous communities that differ greatly in their political, social, and economic structures, cultural ethos and ruling elite philosophies. These differences have often been so fundamental that they have predetermined attitudes towards regional cooperation.

This first undistinguished and undramatic phase of ASEAN's development was a period in which the member countries grew together. The habit of consultation became inculcated, greater mutual trust was developed, their world views became rather more harmonious, and an ASEAN identity began to evolve. These achievements are loose and ill-defined, and possibly as a result are underplayed, but without such a period the organization might well have found the stresses of working together too great (see Irvine 1982b, pp. 37–8, Antolik 1982, pp. 316–17). This has certainly been the case with many other attempts at regional co-operation in the developing world. It is noteworthy that the nature of the Bangkok Declaration – open-ended and without specific objectives – helped in this regard, as it set no targets and placed the organization under little pressure to produce 'results'.

Phase II: growing pressures for co-operation (1975–9)

In 1975 the USA finally withdrew from South Vietnam and the government in Saigon fell to the victorious forces of the communist North. This was quickly followed by the fall of anti-communist governments in Cambodia and Laos. For ASEAN, these changes in the geopolitics of the region marked the beginning of a period of great uncertainty (Simon 1983, p. 307). For although in public ASEAN appeared happy that the conflict in Indochina had finally come to an end, and messages of goodwill and good relations were transmitted to the Vietnamese government, there is no doubt that as a group its members were deeply worried (Irvine 1982a, pp. 31–3). Vietnam had the largest and most powerful army in the region, and there was little sign that its leaders were favourably disposed towards the market-economy, Western-oriented countries of ASEAN (Rajendran 1985, pp. 36–42).

The communist victories in Indochina encouraged, possibly even forced, the members of ASEAN to strive to co-operate more closely. In spite of differing assessments of the Vietnamese threat, each of the member nations felt that it was imperative that a united response be made. This culminated in the Bali Summit of February 1976, a watershed in ASEAN's development. Three important documents were signed at the Summit: the Treaty of Amity and Cooperation, the Declaration of Concord, and a Joint Press Communiqué. The first was a statement of broad principles for co-operation, the second outlined a programme of action, and the third, the details of that programme (Suriyamongkol 1988, pp. 105–7, 243–54). The Bali Summit resulted in a slightly less veiled statement concerning the security and political interests of the member nations. However, that said, ASEAN ostensibly still remained an economic and socio-cultural association, not a political one (Drummond 1986, p. 35). In addition to its move on security, the summit laid the foundations for intensified economic cooperation. This took the form of pledges to supply one another with basic commodities (particularly oil and rice), to build 'ASEAN Industrial Projects' in each country, and to exchange preferential tariffs (Castro 1982, Irvine 1982b, Suriyamongkol 1988, pp. 98–107). The important point, however, is that these agreements would not have been accomplished so quickly had it not been for the changes in Indochina. External political developments, albeit with serious internal ramifications, had the effect of galvanizing a comatose ASEAN into action.

As if to emphasize that the Association now meant business, an ASEAN Secretariat was established shortly after the Summit had ended (Wong 1985, p. 83).

Phase III: the achievement of maturity (1979–)

In 1979, a second development in Indochina again forced ASEAN to reappraise itself. On Christmas Day 1978, Vietnamese forces invaded Cambodia. By January 1979 they had ousted the Khmer Rouge and installed a puppet regime under Heng Samrin. ASEAN – and in particular the front-line state, Thailand – was appalled. The presence in Cambodia of more than 200 000 battle-hardened Vietnamese soldiers (members of the largest army in Southeast Asia), put Thailand on the edge of a conflict that threatened the integrity of ASEAN. There were real fears that Vietnam, which had signed a defence treaty with the Soviet Union and joined COMECON, might invade the kingdom of Thailand (Irvine 1982b, pp. 65–7). ASEAN became, in effect, an informal security grouping, and the polarization of the region, which had been in the offing since 1975, was finally firmly established. Weatherbee (1989, p.185) describes the effect of the invasion on the members of ASEAN:

> The westward military thrust into Kampuchea by the Vietnamese gave concrete expression to the foreboding and looming menaces that had informed the ASEAN security managers since the communist victories in Indochina in 1975. No matter how complex the factors may have been in Hanoi's decision to invade, it was a dramatic demonstration to a worried ASEAN of the willingness of its potential adversary to use force in pursuit of its external political objectives. The perception was that the first Southeast Asian 'domino' had fallen to aggressive Vietnamese expansionism.

ASEAN reacted swiftly and decisively. An ad hoc meeting of its foreign ministers was convened a week after Pol Pot had been driven from Phnom Penh, and a statement deploring the invasion and calling for an immediate withdrawal was released. This response might seem unremarkable, but it is important to realize that ever since 1975 ASEAN had gone out of its way not to provoke Vietnam. The increasing numbers of Vietnamese boat people (seaborne refugees) arriving in ASEAN waters in 1978, for example, had elicited only a weak response and Tasker (1987a, p. 107) claims that the Association's foreign ministers 'were visibly nervous about making any pointed criticism of Hanoi'. The invasion of Cambodia changed this state of affairs. ASEAN became increasingly critical of Vietnam, political and security co-operation – formerly a taboo topic – was openly discussed, and the Association managed to organize a highly effective international response to the invasion. Once again, an external threat had acted as a catalyst for greater co-operation.

This brief history of ASEAN since its formation in 1967 tells us little about the substance of regional political and economic co-operation.

Rhetoric is no substitute for action, and the remainder of this chapter will examine the extent to which ASEAN has produced tangible results.

Trade and industrial co-operation

When ASEAN was established, its most important ostensible aim was to foster greater regional trade and industrial co-operation. During the period since 1967, the pressures encouraging such economic co-operation have grown in intensity. In particular, the member states have become concerned about the rise of trade protectionism in the developed world, and the emergence and strengthening of other regional trade associations (see Chapter 9). With reference to the latter issue, the creation of a single European market in 1992 and the conclusion of a Free-Trade Agreement between the USA and Canada are both sources of current concern (see Rowley 1989, p. 53). The European Community has even recently queried ASEAN's status as an association of developing countries (Aznam 1990). These fears and pressures finally bore fruit at the historic Bali Summit during which ASEAN made a long-term commitment to full regional trade liberalization. To that end, a number of instruments have been adopted of which four stand out: the agreements on Preferential Tariff Arrangements, ASEAN Industrial Projects, ASEAN Industrial Cooperation, and ASEAN Industrial Joint Ventures.

Trade co-operation: preferential tariff arrangements

The agreement on Preferential Tariff Arrangements (PTAs) was signed in Manila in February 1977.[2] It operates through four mechanisms: long-term quantity contracts which give priority supply to ASEAN nations during times of international shortage, purchase finance support at preferential rates for products of ASEAN origin, preference in government procurement, and the exchange of tariff preferences. It was also agreed that non-tariff barriers should be liberalized on a preferential basis. Of these measures, the decision to reduce tariffs is easily the most important.

Initially, Preferential Tariff Arrangements (PTAs) were extended on a product-by-product basis, with each country agreeing to offer a minimum of 50 items quarterly. This was later increased to 150, so that in total some 3000 items were being offered each year. The preference adopted either took the form of a five-year freeze in the tariff rate, or a cut in that rate. As Table 10.1 indicates, not only has the number of items included on the PTA list risen continually since 1977, so that by 1986 it included some 19 000 products, but the depth of the tariff cut has been increased from an initial 10 per cent, to a maximum margin of preference (MoP) of 50 per cent.

This may appear to represent an impressive attempt at regional trade liberalization. However, there are three reasons to doubt its impact upon regional patterns of trade. First, the products on the list are minutely classified.[3] An example is the decision by Thailand to cut its tariff on

Table 10.1 ASEAN: the development of preferential trading arrangements, 1978–86

	Products subject to PTA	Tariff cut (percentage)
1978	71	10
1980	6188	20
1981	6581	25 (max.)
1982	8529	25 (max.)
1984	18 933	50 (max.)
1986	18 907	50 (max.)

Sources: Meyanathan and Haron n.d., p. 25, Castro 1982, p. 83, Wells 1983, p. 159, Wong 1985, p. 88.

Note: Sources give different figures for the number of products subject to PTAs. The above is a collation of the data from various sources.

eight categories of pig bristle (*Economist* 1986, p. 75). Secondly, some of the items included on the PTA list are not even produced by the countries of the Association. Two famous examples are the generous decision by the Philippine government to reduce it tariffs on snow ploughs, and by the Indonesian government on nuclear reactors (Wong 1985, p. 88). And thirdly, many of the items included are of the 'zero-binding' type in which the preferential treatment takes the form of holding tariffs at zero for a minimum of five years.[4]

In an effort to get around these problems, it was proposed in 1980 that PTAs be extended on an across-the-board basis. This was initially limited to items with a total yearly traded value (in 1978) of less than US$50 000 which would benefit from a MoP of 20 per cent. This ceiling was raised to US$500 000 in 1982, then to US$1 million, US$2.5 million, and finally to US$10 million by 1984. In addition, the minimum tariff reduction was increased to 25 per cent, with a maximum figure of 50 per cent. This does appear to overcome the problems associated with the product-by-product approach. However, once again, there are reasons to doubt the efficacy of these measures in boosting intraregional trade. Three particular problems stand out.

First, each country is able to draw up a 'national exclusion list' on which it can place 'sensitive' products. This includes more than 6800 items, and the tendency has been for governments to include any product that they feel is vulnerable to competition. It is estimated that excluded items represent as much as 25 per cent of all trade in the case of the Philippines, 39 per cent in Malaysia, 54 per cent in Indonesia, 63 per cent in Thailand, and 2 per cent for Singapore (Awanohara 1987b, p. 106). Brunei has a liberal trade policy and would have a figure similar to that of Singapore. Secondly, although tariffs may be reduced, non–tariff barriers (NTBs) remain in place. Indeed, some analysts are of the opinion that it is NTBs rather than tariff barriers that do most to impede international flows of trade (e.g. Sanchez 1987, p. 3). In ASEAN, these barriers range from lengthy customs procedures, to strict quality and safety standards (Sanchez 1987, p. 6, Ooi Guat Tin n.d., p. 58–60). Thirdly, in order to qualify for a tariff reduction, businessmen must show that at least 50 per cent of the value of the good has been locally added (60 per cent in the case of Indonesia). Because of the time involved, it has been reported that many businessmen do not even bother to fill in the necessary forms (*Economist* 1986, p. 75). Crone (1988, p. 34) summarized the reaction of ASEAN government's to the PTA as follows: 'Each country has attempted to protect its domestic producers, preserve future options, and still comply with the letter of the agreement by allowing politically or economically insignificant goods to be "freed"'.

These constraints to greater intraregional trade among the ASEAN countries were seriously addressed at the ASEAN summit held in Manila in December 1987. It was decided there that within five years (i.e. by 1992) 50 per cent of all intra-ASEAN trade by value should be included under the PTA arrangements and that this should account for 90 per cent of traded items. To achieve this end, it was further proposed that the exclusion lists be reduced to 10 per cent of the number of traded items (to 2700 items from the current 6800), that the exemption be restricted to 50 per cent of the value of ASEAN traded goods (to take account of products that have a high traded value, such as oil), and that the margin of preference be increased to a minimum of 25 per cent. It was also decided that NTBs would be frozen, and then gradually reduced (Clad 1987, p. 9, Crone 1988, p. 47). The effects of these decisions have yet to be seen.

Reflecting this failure to introduce an effective means of promoting greater trade co-operation, the level of intraregional trade as a proportion of total ASEAN trade has actually marginally decreased in the 22 years of the Association's existence (Figure 10.1). In 1967, 18.3 per cent of total trade in the region was classified as intraregional. In 1988, the figure was 16.9 per cent. It has been estimated that only 2–5 per cent of the value of intra-ASEAN trade comes under the PTA arrangements, and that its effect on trade has been minimal (Awanohara 1987b, p. 106, Crone 1988, p. 34). The reasons for such impediments to greater trade co-operation will be returned to later in the chapter.

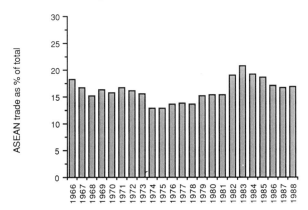

Figure 10.1 Intra-ASEAN trade as percentage of total ASEAN trade, 1966–88

Industrial co-operation: ASEAN Industrial Projects

At the Bali Summit, it was decided that industrial co-operation should be encouraged through the construction of a series of ASEAN Industrial Projects (AIPs).[5] The logic of the scheme centred on market size: it was argued that while the domestic markets of the member states were too small for many types of industry to be economically viable, the regional market was large enough to make their construction and operation profitable (Wong 1985, p. 89). With the world economy in a state of some turmoil following the oil price rise of 1973, regional industrial co-operation appeared as a particularly attractive proposition to the ASEAN governments (Suriyamongkol 1988, pp. 113–17)

In March 1976, shortly after the Bali Summit, the economy ministers of the ASEAN countries met in Kuala Lumpur to agree on the details of the AIP scheme. Both Indonesia and Malaysia proposed that they build urea plants, Singapore a diesel engine project, the Philippines a superphosphates complex, and Thailand a soda ash plant (Table 10.2). The projects were to require an investment of between US$250 million and US$300 million, with the host country controlling 60 per cent of the equity and the other member states 10 per cent each. On completion, the output of each project would secure preferential access to the markets of other ASEAN countries. The scheme received a significant boost when Prime Minister Fukuda of Japan visited the region in 1977 and offered US$1 billion in soft loans to help finance the projects (Chee Peng Lim n.d., p. 98).

Prospects for the scheme were not bright right from the start. As early as May 1977, Singaporean officials were conceding that the projects might have to be deferred, and it was even suggested that a second set of smaller, less capital-intensive AIPs be substituted (Suriyamongkol 1988, p. 153). Because of its doubts about the viability of the scheme, the Singapore government

Table 10.2 ASEAN industrial projects

	Original proposal	Subsequent proposals
Singapore	Diesel engine plant (abandoned)	Factory producing hepatitis B vaccine
Thailand	Soda ash plant (abandoned)	No substitute
Philippines	Superphosphate plant (abandoned)	Pulp and paper plant (abandoned) Copper fabricating plant (abandoned)
Indonesia	Urea project (completed, January 1984, Aceh, Sumatra)	
Malaysia	Urea project (completed, 1985, Bintulu, Sarawak)	

Source: Suriyamongkol 1988.

decided in 1980 to reduce its equity participation in the other countries' projects to 1 per cent. Singapore also dropped its plans to build a diesel engine factory because of competition in the other member countries. In its place the administration proposed the construction of a US$4 million pharmaceutical plant producing hepatitis-B vaccine (*Economist* 1986, p. 75). In fact, only two of the AIPs originally proposed have been built: Indonesia opened its urea plant in Aceh (North Sumatra) at the beginning of 1984 (Suhartono 1986, p. 512), and the Malaysian urea plant located in Bintulu (Sarawak) came on stream in October 1985 (*Economist* 1986, p.75).[6] Both the Philippines and Thailand have abandoned their proposed AIPs (Table 10.2).

There are two main reasons for the lack of success of the AIP scheme. First, the original AIP package was put together in great haste, before the viability of each project had been assessed accurately. Subsequent feasibility studies, insisted on by the Japanese, showed that the projects would be unprofitable even in a regional market the size of ASEAN. For example, it was estimated that the Philippine superphosphate fertilizer project would have production costs per ton of fertilizer of between US$308 and US$379, while prevailing world prices in 1977 were approximately US$180 (Chee Peng Lim n.d., p. 104). Secondly, the assurances of a guaranteed regional market for the output were not forthcoming (Suriyamongkol 1988, p. 153). It was for this second reason that Singapore effectively withdrew from the scheme. National interests held sway over regional industrial co-operation.

Industrial co-operation: ASEAN Industrial Complementation

As the prospects for the AIPs dimmed, so ASEAN turned its attention towards industrial complementarity as a means of furthering regional industrial co-operation. Again, the logic behind the scheme lay in market share, resource pooling, and economies of scale. Horizontal integration was to be promoted, with companies in different countries of the region specializing in components of a single product or product range. The companies involved would then enjoy exclusive production rights for a specified period (two years for existing products and three years for new products) and preferential access to the markets of the other ASEAN member states (Huang Yuezhen 1987, *Economist* 1986, p. 75, Chee Peng Lim n.d., pp. 98–9). In October 1980, a Basic Agreement of ASEAN Industrial Complementation was signed and the ASEAN Chamber of Commerce and Industry (ASEAN-CCI) was given the task of identifying possible areas of complementarity (Wong 1985, p. 91). Certain stipulations were made: any ASEAN Economic Complementation package (AIC) must involve at least four member countries, and it must be approved by both the ASEAN-CCI and the governmental organizations involved (Chee Peng Lim n.d., p. 98).

By 1982, 30 AIC packages had been provisionally formulated by the ASEAN-CCI. Of these, only two have been approved by the ASEAN Economic Ministers (Chee Peng Lim n.d., p. 99). One involves the production of automobile components, and the other automobile parts (Wong 1985, p. 90). Neither proposal has had any significant effect on regional trade (Chee Peng Lim n.d., p. 109, Awanohara 1987b, p. 107). The failure of the scheme can be linked to two problems: First, it was overly complex and cumbersome. The scheme required the participation of at least four of the five member states, as well as the involvement of the private sector, two of the ASEAN economic committees and the ASEAN economic ministers (Chee Peng Lim n.d., p. 98, Wong 1985, p. 92). Co-ordination and the building of a consensus between the member countries proved to be virtually impossible. The second problem lay with Singapore's objections to the proposal that firms engaged in the scheme should enjoy exclusive production rights and tariff privileges (*Economist* 1986, p. 75, Awanohara 1987b, p. 107). Singapore felt that this would only encourage inefficient and uncompetitive industries, and would be harmful to its own interests (Huang Yuezhen 1987, p. 125).

One important outcome of Singapore's objections to the AIC scheme (and also to the AIPs) was a redefinition of ASEAN consensus. Prime Minister Lee Kuan Yew asked that if a country had no objections to a proposal going ahead, but itself wished to abstain from involvement, then this should be permitted (Castro 1982, p. 86). The formula was termed the 'five minus one' principle (now, six minus one) and is accepted in all negotiations concerning economic, but not political, co-operation (Awanohara 1987b, pp. 106–7).

Industrial co-operation: ASEAN Industrial Joint Ventures

In the wake of the failure of the AIC scheme, and no doubt in frustration, ASEAN turned its attention to yet another proposal to promote regional industrial co-operation: ASEAN Industrial Joint Ventures (AIJVs). First discussed in 1981, the idea was finally approved in 1983. To qualify, it was initially decided that all that was required was that two firms, from at least two ASEAN countries, should form a joint venture owning a stake of not less than 51 per cent in the new company. The joint venture would then benefit from a 50 per cent tariff cut in the markets of the participating countries (later raised to 75 per cent). At the ASEAN summit of December 1987, it was further decided that the MoP should be deepened to 90 per cent and that non–ASEAN partners should be allowed to control a maximum of 60 per cent of the equity in the AIJVs (Clad 1987, p. 9).

The AIJV scheme has several advantages over the the AIP and AIC proposals. First, a joint venture can go ahead with the agreement of only two member countries. Second, the projects are assessed and financed by the private sector. Third, the projects tend to be smaller, less complex, and carry less risk. And, fourth, no cumbersome institutional machinery, such as that associated with the AIC scheme, is required. However, although AIJVs should be far easier to establish, only nine have so far been approved, two of which are government-sponsored (Clad 1987, p. 9–10, Awanohara 1987b, p. 107, Crone 1988, p. 44). Huang Yuezhen (1987, p. 125) writes that the failure of the scheme was because of 'deep-seated problems reflecting rigidities in structure, administration and interpretation'. For although AIJVs grew out of a desire, enthusiastically promoted by Singapore, to give greater influence to the private sector in the promotion of regional industrial co-operation, there still remain differences of opinion between the member governments on investment, market access, and market-sharing (Suriyamongkol 1988, p. 229).

Impediments to economic co-operation

As should have become clear in the preceding discussion, progress in the promotion of regional economic co-operation has been slow and limited. This has been recognized by the leaders of the ASEAN countries:

> In the field of economic and trade cooperation, the achievement [of ASEAN] has been mediocre or worse (Prime Minister Mahathir of Malaysia in February 1985, quoted in Drummond 1986, p. 37)

> After 19 years of existence, Asean should already be evaluating the impact of regional economic cooperation; instead it is endlessly discussing how to get it off the ground. [This lack of progress] threatens to render meaningless our continued association (President Aquino of the Philippines in July 1986, quoted in Clad 1986, p. 15).

Why has the cause of regional economic co-operation advanced so little in Southeast Asia? It is possible to point to four areas of explanation: the structure of the economies of the member states, ASEAN's institutional structure and *modus operandi*, the dominance of national over regional priorities, and the success of the ASEAN economies.

The structure of the ASEAN economies

Analysts have repeatedly stressed that the reason why regional economic co-operation in ASEAN is so limited is because the economies of the member countries are competitive rather than complementary (Tan n.d., p. 66, Meyanathan & Haron n.d., p. 26, Suriyamongkol 1988, pp. 36–7, *Economist* 1986, p. 74, Drummond 1986, p. 38). With the exception of Singapore, ASEAN members specialize in the export of primary products to the developed world, and in many cases find that they are in competition with one another in the international marketplace. Singapore is the exception and, significantly, accounted for 47 per cent of all intra-ASEAN trade in 1988 (Table 10.3). Paradoxically, however, the differences between the economic structures and levels of development of the member states also restrict co-operation. For it has proved extremely difficult to design and implement schemes for regional economic co-operation that will benefit each country equally, and reaching a consensus has often been impossible (Meyanthan & Haron n.d., p. 26).

ASEAN's institutional structure and modus operandi

ASEAN operates on the basis of consensus (or on the slightly adapted six minus one principle). This has no doubt contributed to its solidarity,

Table 10.3 ASEAN trade flows, 1988

Exports ($US millions)

From To	Brunei	Indonesia	Malaysia	Singapore	Thailand	Philippines
Brunei	—	4	56	414	21	0.3
Indonesia	1	—	280	?	86	25
Malaysia	1.1	184	—	5 332	473	117
Singapore	101	1 656	4 081	—	1 224	221
Thailand	152	151	417	2 144	—	123
Philippines	32	87	315	519	59	—
Total ASEAN	287	2 082	5 149	8 409	1 863	486
Total exports	1 987	19 376	21 125	39 322	15 992	7 034

Imports ($US millions)

To From	Brunei	Indonesia	Malaysia	Singapore	Thailand	Philippines
Brunei	—	1	1	112	168	35
Indonesia	5	—	284	?	172	161
Malaysia	61	300	—	6 431	413	247
Singapore	456	896	2 186	—	1 505	353
Thailand	23	96	504	1 186	—	56
Philippines	0.4	36	135	263	190	—
Total ASEAN	545	1 329	3 110	7 992	2 448	852
Total exports	1 256	13 489	16 567	43 869	16 292	8 662

Source: IMF 1989a.

but also means that negotiations are characteristically long and convoluted (Wong 1985, p. 85, Alagappa n.d., pp. 196–7). Agreement is achieved only after much procrastination, and then on the basis of the lowest common denominator (Indorf 1987, p. 87).

ASEAN's institutional structure is also an impediment to regional economic co-operation.[7] Most major decisions are taken at yearly foreign ministers' meetings. Between these meetings, the interests of the Association are managed by the Standing Committee, which rotates each year between the ASEAN capitals. The committee consists of the foreign minister of the host country, the five ambassadors of the other member states, and the six ASEAN directors–general (Chan Heng Chee 1986, pp. 116–21). In addition to the Standing Committee there are a number of other ASEAN bodies that function only periodically. The most important for the promotion of regional economic co-operation is the ASEAN Economic Ministers Meeting, which is held twice a year (Alagappa n.d., pp. 183–4). This institutional structure has three implications: first, it means that national interests are likely to prevail over regional interests as there is no individual representing the interests of the Association. Second, the peripatetic nature of the Standing Committee means that it is 'inefficient and lacking in continuity and expertise' (Alagappa n.d., p. 188). And, third, there are difficulties of co-ordination because there is no integrated decision-making structure.

Dominance of national over regional priorities

National interests invariably predominate over regional interests. Or, rather, the short term predominates over the long term. As Villegas (1987, p. 123) notes: 'Most of the ASEAN leaders are well aware of the benefits of closer economic cooperation . . . but they are afraid to face the political consequences of economic adjustment and dislocation in the short run'. This has meant that whenever a decision has had to be taken that might harm the domestic producers of an ASEAN state, the government of that country has acted to minimize the effect. This can be best seen in the attempts to circumvent the PTA scheme.

The success of the ASEAN economies

The final point to raise in explanation of the modest progress of ASEAN economic co-operation concerns the success of member states' economies. Between 1965 and 1989 GDP was expanding at an average annual rate of over 6 per cent (see Table 9.1). With a relatively good performance in all the ASEAN economies except the Philippines, which recorded a negative 'growth' rate of 0.5 per cent between 1980 and 1987, there is little incentive to promote greater regional economic co-operation. Should there be a worsening in performance or a tightening of the extra-regional trade environment, this complacency could quickly change.

Political and security co-operation

If economic co-operation has achieved so little, how is it possible for Hill to label ASEAN as the most successful regional organization in the developing world? His comments refer to the Association's success in the political and security spheres.

In the opening section of this chapter it was noted that although political and security co-operation was de-emphasized in the Bangkok Declaration, it was just these concerns that led to the creation of ASEAN in 1967, and also to its 'reactification' after the Bali Summit of 1976. In view of this, it should be unsurprising that many analysts feel that it is in the spheres of political and security co-operation that the Association has achieved most.

The first point to reiterate is that ASEAN members are far more united today than was the case in 1967. They have a broadly similar world view and, more importantly, have acquired the habit of settling their differences through negotiation rather than confrontation. ASEAN has become a forum in which bilateral relations can be maintained on a regular basis, and the habit of consultation is now firmly instituted. The best examples of improved intraregional relations and closer political co-operation can be found in security co-operation and ASEAN's relationship with the outside world.

Security co-operation

Although ASEAN is not a military alliance, military ties between the member states have grown stronger during the last 20 years, and particularly since the victory of the North Vietnamese in 1975 and Vietnam's invasion of Cambodia at the end of 1978. Ostensibly, ASEAN has followed a policy of non-alignment, and has attempted to avoid being overtly incorporated into either the US or Soviet spheres of influence (Simon 1988, p. 67). To this end Malaysia called in 1971 for the neutralization of Southeast Asia and proposed that the region be declared a Zone of Peace, Freedom and Neutrality (ZOPFAN) free from interference by external powers (Irvine 1982a, pp. 23–9). Malaysia's proposal was endorsed in the Kuala Lumpur Declaration of 1971 (Saravanamuttu 1984, p. 186). However, neutralization for the countries of ASEAN is more image than substance. As Simon (1987, p. 76) has noted: 'ASEAN's 1971 endorsement of Malaysia's ZOPFAN proposal has proven an effective diplomatic device for projecting a regional image of neutrality while maintaining the guarantees of friendly external powers'.

The Philippines still has US bases on its soil, Thailand and the USA have close military links, and Singapore and Malaysia still belong to the Five Powers Defence Agreement together with the United Kingdom, Australia, and New Zealand. There are also bilateral security arrangements between the Untied Kingdom and Brunei (Simon 1988, pp. 85–6). The latest manifestation of ZOPFAN is the 1984 proposal (revived in 1987 by Indonesia) that Southeast Asia be declared a Nuclear Weapons Free Zone (NFZ) (Indorf 1987, p. 89, Simon 1988, p. 97). It is likely, however, that the NFZ proposal will also remain only a diplomatic device.

The problem is that in spite of a growing together over the past 20 years, ASEAN still has no common threat perception (Khong Kim Hoong & Abdul Razak Abdullah 1987). In the view of Indonesia, the People's Republic of China still represents the major threat to stability in the region.[8] As a result, Indonesia regards Vietnam as a valuable counterweight to China. Malaysia is also wary of Chinese intentions, but in addition is concerned about Soviet and Vietnamese expansionism. And in spite of being a strong proponent of neutralization, it regards the presence of US forces as necessary to balance the increasing Soviet military presence in Southeast Asia.[9] The Philippines, rather more distant from events in Indochina and with long-established military ties to the USA, has been reluctant to adopt any explicit policy of non-alignment and neutralization. Singapore and Brunei meanwhile, are both firm supporters of the US military presence in the region and are wary of both Chinese and Soviet intentions; Brunei also maintains close military links with the United Kingdom. Thailand, as the front line state that has faced the most immediate threat from the Vietnamese forces that invaded Cambodia in 1978–9, has maintained its traditional military links with the United States as well as cultivating its ties with China. Indeed, in March 1987, China agreed to supply Thailand with battle tanks (T69s) and other hardware (Paisal Sricharatchanya 1987, pp. 15–16). Although these relationships are obviously fluid, and particularly in the current climate of East–West relations, the point is that ASEAN countries are still not in agreement about the sources of external threats.

ASEAN members have, however, concluded bilateral and trilateral defence and security agreements with one another. In fact, the only countries without any form of military co-operation are Malaysia and the Philippines, which have still to settle finally their sovereignty dispute over Sabah (Simon 1988, p. 80). Joint naval, air, and army exercises are undertaken, intelligence is exchanged, there are close ties between military staffs, and there has even been recent discussion concerning the standardization of military equipment, and joint procurement and storage of spare parts (Chan Heng Chee 1986, pp. 134–5, Simon 1988, pp. 82–3, Suh 1984, pp. 64–9). Such links have laid the basis for more overt military co-operation should a threat to regional security arise.

ASEAN's external relations

Arguably even more impressive than the military and security arrangements between ASEAN members is the degree of co-operation in extra-regional affairs. This is best exemplified in the response to the Vietnamese invasion of Cambodia in 1978–79. In dealing with the invasion, and in its dealings with the countries of Indochina in general, ASEAN has shown an impressive degree of unity of purpose.

Since 1979, ASEAN has adopted a two-pronged strategy towards the Vietnamese occupation of Cambodia. On the one hand, ASEAN members have attempted to isolate Vietnam economically, diplomatically, and politically; and on the other, they have sought to pressure the country militarily. Through international lobbying ASEAN has succeeded in denying international recognition of the Vietnamese-backed Cambodian government in Phnom Penh. Such has been its success in this regard that the majority voting in favour of the ASEAN-sponsored Coalition Government of Democratic Kampuchea (CGDK) in the United Nations General Assembly continually rose between 1981 and 1986 from 77 (53 per cent in favour, 26 per cent against) to 115 (72 per cent in favour, 13 per cent against) (Jackson 1984, p. 242, Indorf 1987, p. 92).[10] The vote in 1989 taken after the claimed withdrawal of Vietnamese troops from Cambodia, recorded the highest ever number of votes in favour of the CGDK – 124 to 17 with 12 abstentions. As a result of Vietnam and Cambodia's subsequent international isolation they have been deprived of membership of the World Bank, Asian Development Bank, the International Monetary Fund, and of virtually all non-humanitarian aid and assistance from Western countries. The second element of ASEAN's strategy has been achieved through encouraging support for the forces of the three rebel factions that comprise the CGDK. The Chinese have provided large quantities of weaponry, channelled through Thailand, to the forces of the Khmer Rouge, while Sihanouk and Son Sann – leaders respectively of the National United Front for an Independent, Neutral, Peaceful and Cooperative Cambodia (FUNCINPEC) and the Khmer People's National Liberation Front (KPNLF) – have received support from ASEAN, the West and particularly from that USA. The rebel armies have also been able to use the refugee camps the line the Thai–Cambodian border to rest their forces, and as reservoirs of recruits. Without this support, orchestrated to a significant degree by ASEAN, it is hard to imagine that the war in Cambodia could have continued for so long. It has been in its response to the Vietnamese occupation of Cambodia that ASEAN had been both at its most decisive and its most unified.

In its dealings with the outside world, ASEAN has often found that the whole is greater than the sum of the parts. As an association with a total population of over 325 million and considerable economic potential, it can command respect and influence in international forums. For example, ASEAN is a 'dialogue partner' with the European Community, Japan, the USA, Canada, Australia, and New Zealand, and also sometimes responds as a group in international organizations such as GATT (General Agreement on Tariffs and Trade) (Indorf 1987, pp. 92–3, Wong 1985, p. 96). Furthermore, ASEAN has the ability to attract foreign ministers from major powers (such as former US Secretary of State George Shultz in 1986) to its annual conferences (Drummond 1986, p. 40). These formal and regular contacts have increased ASEAN's access to and influence over the major economic powers, and may also have increased levels of assistance.

ASEAN regional co-operation: an assessment

As this chapter has shown, ASEAN's record in industrial and trade co-operation has been poor. ASEAN leaders admit as much. Even the Chairman of the Group of Fourteen on ASEAN Economic Co-operation and Integration has written that it 'is a record of protracted negotiations, exasperation and frustration' (Seong n.d., p. 6). However, it would be wrong to conclude from this that the Association has failed. Since ASEAN was formed, a group of countries that initially had little to unite them have forged 'a political community of shared values and outlook, shared vulnerabilities, and a sharpened appreciation of interdependence in the struggle for peace and security' (Chan Heng Chee 1986, p. 111). They have done much to create an ASEAN 'consciousness', and to provide at least the Southeast Asian élites with a sense of regional identity to add to the generally already strong sense of national identity. Indeed, it is even possible to argue that the Southeast Asian region should now be equated with ASEAN, and that the Association has forged a new regional identity that excludes Burma and the countries of Indochina.

Although ASEAN has been a success in the rather nebulous sense that a resilient regional identity has been created, on the occasion of the Association's twentieth anniversary in 1987 it was widely felt that a crossroads has been reached (e.g. Hill n.d., p. 83, Awanohara 1987a, p. 104). If ASEAN was to develop as a regional organization then some new, bolder, initiatives had to be set in train that would lead to more tangible results. The December 1987 summit resulted in only rather limited proposals to promote further the cause of regional economic co-operation, and the goals set out were little different from those embraced at the Bali summit of 1976. As Crone (1988, p. 49) has noted, the meeting set out to change the pace of progress towards further economic co-operation, but it did not alter the trajectory. The heads of state present were seemingly more concerned with demonstrating their support for President Corazon Aquino of the Philippines, who had just replaced Ferdinand Marcos and whose position was insecure (Tasker 1987b, pp. 8–9, Clad 1987, pp. 9–10, Wong 1989). Nevertheless, it is useful to indulge in a little futurology. What are the prospects for greater economic co-operation, and could ASEAN grow to incorporate other countries of the region, or perhaps itself be incorporated into a larger, Pacific-wide organization?

Southeast Asian regionalism: prospects for the future

An ASEAN common market

The most concrete proposals for the further development of ASEAN economic co-operation have been put forward by Hans Rieger in a paper first presented at the end of 1986 and entitled *Towards the making of an ASEAN Common Market* (Rieger n.d.). Rieger recognizes that the countries of the region have very different trade regimes and industrial structures. He argues that if any progress is to be made in regional economic co-operation, then these difference must be taken into account. He maintains, furthermore, that such a rational approach to economic co-operation needs also to accept three preconditions. First, that any decision must be achieved on the basis of consensus; second, that each national government will only approve a proposal if it perceives that the net *national* benefits outweigh the net *national* costs; and third, that ASEAN governments will be more concerned about immediate benefits and costs rather than future ones (Rieger n.d., p. 73).

With this in mind, Rieger has proposed that 'a customs union of the larger Asean countries (Indonesia, Malaysia, the Philippines and Thailand) [be combined] with a free trade area comprising this customs union and the other Asean countries (Singapore and Brunei)' (Rieger n.d., p. 76). The larger four countries would agree on a common external tariff that would be as close as possible to the country with the lowest current external tariff wall (Malaysia). They would then trade freely between themselves. The two smaller countries would meanwhile maintain their own, lower, external tariff wall and form a free trade area linking themselves with the customs union, but only for goods of ASEAN origin. The logic of the proposal is that such an arrangement would allow Singapore and Brunei to maintain their fairly liberal external trade regime, while also protecting the industries of the other ASEAN countries from excessive competition. However, there are problems with the proposal and it should only be regarded as a suggestion as to how greater intraregional trade co-operation might be achieved.

Three points need to be emphasized: first, the proposals do not address the basic problem that the ASEAN economies are competitive rather than complementary. Even if ASEAN were to become a hybrid common market, its members' trading interests will still primarily lie outside the region (Tan n.d., p. 68). Second, and as Hill (n.d., p. 86–7) notes, it is still unclear whether the countries wish to take this route to greater co-operation. It is worth remembering that their success to date has been built upon greater extraregional trade. And third, even the four large countries of the Association have very different trade regimes and it would be surprising if they could agree on a common tariff wall.

A Pacific Basin Community?

If the prospects for significantly greater economic co-operation remain poor, what of the chances that ASEAN might become incorporated in a larger Pacific-wide regional grouping? Since the late 1970s there has been a great deal of discussion about the viability of a Pacific Community, or Pacific Basin Community, with the impetus for such a grouping coming largely from Japan and Australia (Soesastro 1983, Wanadi 1986).[11] This culminated in November 1989 when the foreign and economic ministers of the six ASEAN countries, together with those of the USA, Japan, Canada, Australia, South Korea, and New Zealand gathered in Canberra to lay the groundwork for the creation of an Asia-Pacific Economic Co-operation forum (APEC). The forum's aim is to increase regional trade, enhance investment and technology transfer between developed and developing countries, and to achieve these objectives by endorsing the principles of free trade. Although the developments are exciting, however, not all the ASEAN nations are equally enthusiastic about APEC: for while Singapore and Thailand are highly interested, Indonesia is rather more circumspect in its support. That said, it is not the intention – and it must be emphasized that APEC is still only a concept – that APEC should replace ASEAN. They would have different functions and memberships, and would fill different roles (FEER 1989a).

An expanded ASEAN?

Another possibility is that ASEAN itself might expand its membership. After all, Brunei did become the sixth member in 1984. The fourth article of the Bangkok Declaration revealingly states that: 'the Association is open for participation to all States in the South-East Asian Region subscribing to the aforementioned aims, principles and purposes' (quoted in Suriyamongkol 1988, p. 240).

This begs the question as to what constitutes the 'South-East Asian region'. At times it has seemed as though a fairly broad, and inclusive, definition has been embraced incorporating countries as far afield as Sri Lanka, Taiwan,

Fiji and other Pacific states, Australia and New Zealand (Indorf 1987, p. 95, Crone 1988, pp. 45–6). At other times, ASEAN has given the impression of being an exclusive club. Interestingly, when Sri Lanka tried to gain admission in 1981, ASEAN's Standing Committee rejected the application on the grounds that it was 'outside the geographic area' (Indorf 1987, p. 97). Papua New Guinea has the greatest chance of being admitted in the short to medium term (Anggoro 1986). It expressed a desire to join in 1986 and again in 1987, has the advantage of geographical proximity, and is also broadly similar to the current members in terms of political outlook and its approach to economic development.

The last two points cannot be applied to the countries of Indochina. Nevertheless, their inclusion in ASEAN makes the greatest geographic sense, and although the political and economic differences that divide the three 'Southeast Asias' (ASEAN, Burma, and Indochina) remain deep, there has been a degree of convergence during the latter half of the 1980s. To begin with, Burma, Cambodia, Laos, and Vietnam have all adopted rather more reformist, pragmatic economic policies. The collectivization of agriculture has been slowed down and in some cases reversed, and the private ownership of land legalized. Private enterprises have been tolerated and even encouraged, and foreign investment and joint ventures have been welcomed.[12] In addition to these economic reforms, there has also been limited political convergence between the countries of ASEAN and Indochina. Most significant, at the end of September 1989 Vietnam, under pressure from the Soviet Union and mindful of the demands that the occupation was having upon attempts to reinvigorate its economy, withdrew most of its forces from Cambodia (Tasker & Heibert 1989).

The shift from confrontation to conciliation in the region has, at one and the same time, raised the possibility that ASEAN may, in the longer term, expand its membership to include Cambodia, Laos, Vietnam, and perhaps even Burma. Conversely, however, since Vietnam's occupation of Cambodia was the galvanizing force behind ASEAN's greatest show of solidarity, its withdrawal may lead to a loss of subregional resilience as the members of the Association enter a period of reduced regional tension.

Notes to Chapter 10

1 Lee Yong Leng goes so far as to say that it 'was clear by 1967 that the United States of America was losing the war in Vietnam' (1978, p.28).
2 For various accounts of the PTA system see: Ooi Guat Tin n.d., Meyanathan & Haron n.d., Wells 1983, pp. 159–60, Wong 1985, pp. 87–9, Tan n.d.).
3 Products are classified according to the seven-digit BTN classification code. Thus, one product may represent a number of 'items' on the PTA list (e.g. 84.12.110 Domestic sprayers [plastic], 84.21.120 Domestic sprayers [aluminium], 84.21.190 Domestic sprayers [others]) (Tan n.d., p. 64).
4 Tan reports that for 'some countries, the proportion of zero-binding tariff preference items for some product groups was as high as 98 per cent' (n.d., p. 64).

5   The most detailed account of the ASEAN Industrial Projects is Suriyamongkol's book *Politics of ASEAN economic co-operation* (1988).

6   Both these plants have been losing money. They suffered from 'cost overruns [the Indonesia plant cost $US410 million], difficulties in reaching marketing arrangements in the face of global excess supply, and the need for low-priced natural-gas feedstock to make the product price competitive' (Awanohara 1987b, p. 106).

7   See Alagappa (n.d.) for a good summary of ASEAN's institutional framework.

8   In August 1990 the Chinese Premier Li Peng visited Jakarta to restore diplomatic relations, severed following the attempted coup by the Indonesian Communist Party (PKI) in 1965 and in which China had allegedly been implicated. The restoration of diplomatic relations should see a gradual easing of Indonesian suspicions of China and Indonesia's ethnic Chinese minority.

9   The Soviets have had use of extensive military facilities at Cam Ranh Bay in Vietnam since 1979. This has markedly increased the ability of the Soviet Union to project its influence in the region (Simon 1988, pp. 35–40).

10 The CGDK was not formed until 1982 when the three anti-Vietnamese groups led by Khieu Samphan, Prince Norodon Sihanouk and Son Sann – and with pressure from ASEAN and China – signed an agreement forming the CGDK under the presidency of Sihanouk. The 1981 UN vote was won by the genocidal government of Pol Pot's Democratic Kampuchea.

11 There are already some Pacific-wide organizations. For example, the Pacific Economic Co-operation Conference (PECC) and the business oriented Pacific Basin Economic Council (PBEC).

12 The Laotian government terms its equivalent of *perestroika, Chin tanakan may* or 'new thinking', whille in Vietnam it is termed *doi moi* or 'renovation'.

11

Setting an agenda for the future

This book has attempted to build up an understanding of modern South-east Asia through a discussion of various themes in the region's human geography. There are inevitably elements that will have been glossed over, and in some cases omitted entirely. However, it is hoped that the book has provided at least a framework through which the region can be interpreted. The main processes of change have been addressed, as have the primary challenges and the principal characteristics of the area. Nevertheless it is useful, in summary, to lay out what might be loosely termed an 'agenda for the future'. As is so often the case, it is sometimes difficult to separate pattern from chaos, and the transitory from the essential. The following brief discussion will set out those elements that, in the view of the author, will face the countries and governments of ASEAN with the greatest challenges in the next decade. It should be stressed, however, that this list is not exhaustive, and numerous other areas of concern could be highlighted. Six overlapping priority areas stand out: nation-building, efficiency and corruption, skills and education, infrastructure, environment, and the 'agricultural transition'.

Nation-building

First, and notwithstanding the considerable progress that has already been made, each of the countries of the region must continue to 'nation-build'. Not in the crude sense of homogenizing a population, but in the sense of ensuring that all groups – religious, political, cultural, and ethnic – feel that they have a stake in their respective countries. This includes easing Malay–Chinese rivalries, the sensitive incorporation of tribal groups, and greater political pluralism. Unsurprisingly, perhaps, during the early years of independence the rights of minorities (of all types) were often ignored, and in some cases actively suppressed. The emphasis was on maintaining security and 'unity'. However, the countries of the region have in the main now attained a degree of political maturity and economic progress that places their governments in a position to permit greater freedom of expression and action. This can already be seen in a loosening of controls in some areas. Thailand, for example, is gradually becoming increasingly democratic, while the Indonesian government has become rather more open in its dealings with the former Portuguese colony of East Timor. This is not to say that the tide of change is entirely one way. Many commentators

229

have identified a trend towards growing authoritarianism in Singapore, and would also highlight continuing extensive human rights abuses in the Philippines. Indeed the communist New People's Army in the Philippines fields a force of some 23 000 – 25 000 men and women who are active in 65 of the country's 73 provinces. This serious and countrywide insurgency has its roots in poverty, exploitation, inequality, and corruption. Although with the exception of the Philippines the communist insurgencies that were such a feature of the region from the early postwar years through to the 1980s are virtually moribund, there still remains a need to incorporate further marginalized households who often live on the peripheries – geographical, religious, ethnic, economic, political – of the state.

Reduction of corruption and the promotion of efficiency

The second priority area encompasses the reduction of corruption and the promotion of efficiency. The countries of ASEAN are all embarking on export-oriented strategies of industrialization and this makes it necessary for them to compete in the international arena. Corruption and rent seeking need to be reduced if the countries of the region are to maintain their high rates of growth. The failure of the Philippine economy has been due in significant part to the 'crony capitalism' that was such a feature of the Marcos period and has continued into the Aquino presidency. Contracts were awarded to politically well-connected businessmen, inefficient and influential domestic producers were protected from internal and foreign competition, and corruption became virtually endemic. The story, albeit perhaps in a less extreme form, has been the same in Brunei, Indonesia, Malaysia, and Thailand. Although it is difficult to confront entrenched interest groups, and to take away their privileges, this will become increasingly necessary as the countries of ASEAN progress and become more tightly integrated into the global economy. Domestic capitalists may have been more than willing to play the game of rent seeking, but foreign investors and multinationals – upon whom future growth is becoming increasingly contingent – are unlikely to be so understanding.

Skills and education

Third, and related to the llast point, it is clearly important that levels of education be substantially improved. If Thailand, Malaysia – and rather further into the future, the Philippines and Indonesia – are to join Singapore as newly industrializing countries (NICs), then training, skills, and education in general will attain a far higher profile. Inevitably, other developing countries with lower wage rates will begin to compete with ASEAN in labour-intensive manufactures, and in ressponse it will be necessary to upgrade into skill-intensive and capital-intensive industries (as Singapore has already done) where training and education are at a premium. At the beginning of 1990 Thailand's Prime Minister, Chatichai Choonhavan, was reported as saying that whereas 3000 engineers graduated from Thailand's ten engineering schools each year, the country needed 10 000 (Tasker 1990).

230

This shortage of skilled and trained workers is reflected in rising wages and in growing manpower shortages in some industries. The problem, however, is not just one of numbers; the Philippines has a greater proportion (some 26 per cent) of its college-age population in higher education than does the United Kingdom (Tiglao & Scott 1989). Quality is also important. Many schools produce poorly trained graduates who are ill-equipped to enter the modern industrial economy. It is the case that they are sometimes poorly equipped even to enter the agricultural sector. Learning is still too often by rote, teachers are poorly paid, and syllabuses are poorly tuned to modern demands. In higher education there is also what might be termed an enduring patron–client hierarchy in which talented younger scholars are constrained by their elders in what they do and in how they do it.

The inadequacies of Southeast Asia's educational system are reflected in the region's 'technologyless industrialization'. Authors such as Yoshihara (1988) and Clad (1989) stress the skills issue, noting that there does not exist the indigenous research and development to fuel a truly Southeast Asian based economic miracle. Clad quotes one scientist as saying that Thailand has still yet to produce its first PhD in physics, and in the main the region's rapid growth has been highly dependent upon imported technology.

Infrastructure

Another potential constraint to economic growth relates to the creation of an adequate infrastructure. Indonesia, Malaysia, the Philippines, and Thailand (Singapore and Brunei have relatively well-developed infrastructures) have tended to delay infrastructural investments until problems have already become serious. With the economies of the region projected to grow annually at between 5 per cent and 10 per cent, this lack of farsightedness is beginning to confront some of the countries with serious infrastructural bottlenecks. Thailand in particular is beginning to face the prospect that its poorly developed and overstretched infrastructure may begin to hinder growth. Traffic congestion in Bangkok (and in the other primate cities of the region) is appalling, telecommunications facilities are poorly developed, energy shortfalls are beginning to pose a potential problem, and skilled workers to fuel the export-led boom are in increasingly short supply. There is already some evidence, for example, that companies intending to invest in Thailand have looked elsewhere because of difficulties of transportation and communications.

Even Malaysia, the wealthiest of the natural resource-rich countries of the region, is facing the prospect of severe infrastructural bottlenecks. Japan's Overseas Economic Cooperation Fund (OECF) believes that, at current rates of growth, Malaysia's road, water, and electricity systems will reach capacity by 1993. Power failures are already beginning to affect some electronics firms, and as in the case of Thailand the implication is that foreign investment – which totalled M$2.68 billion from Japan alone in 1989 – might be diverted elsewhere (Tsuruoka 1990a).

Solving these problems requires adequate investment and, perhaps above all, adequate planning of investment. The development of an efficient infrastructure has been hindered by extensive corruption and cronyism. Not only has this meant that the funds allotted have been ineffectually spent, but also that the resulting developments have too often been poorly designed and built. Clad (1989, p. 44), for example, makes the point that the contract for the Malaysian North–South Highway project (discussed in Chapter 6) went to a financially beleaguered, but well-connected company lacking in the necessary experience to undertake such a massive project.

Environmental protection

A fourth element of this 'agenda for the future' centres on environmental protection. Just as the rights of minorities were sometimes ignored in the early years of independence, so too was the environment. Again, this is hardly surprising. The demands of promoting economic growth left little room for environmental concerns. However, there is an increasing feeling in the region that economic progress and the protection of the environment need not be in opposition. Allied to this, there is a greatly heightened awareness among some groups that the natural environment is a valuable resource worth protecting. Partly as a result, governments and politicians are beginning to take an interest in the environment, and not just as a source of raw materials. Perhaps the best example of this growing environmental awareness can be seen in the cancellation in March 1988 of the Nam Choan dam project in Thailand. This remarkable decision, remarkable in the Thai context at least, was made because of active campaigning by various groups at all levels in Thai society. Concerns focused on the impact the dam would have on the contiguous Huai Kha Khaeng and Thung Yai wildlife sanctuaries, which would have been partly flooded by its reservoir. Notwithstanding the convincing environmental (and other) arguments, the Thai government ultimately made its decision on the basis of the political costs that they would have to bear. It is important, if environmentalism is not just to become a transitory movement of the late 1980s and 1990s (as it was of the 1960s), that governments in the region become convinced of the social and economic benefits of protecting and nurturing the environment.

The agricultural transition

I have termed the final priority area, rather opaquely, the agricultural transition. Until after the end of the Second World War Southeast Asia remained a region where land – apart from a few densely populated areas such as the island of Java – was abundant. Agricultural systems, and this applied as much to wet rice as to shifting cultivation, were extensive and used land relatively inefficiently. However, evolving resource realities in modern Southeast Asia dictate that farmers in many areas intensify their use of land. This can already been seen in rising yields. The increase in output per unit of land has not, however, been sufficient to prevent the creation of a growing population of rural landless and land-poor. Some of these dispossessed rural inhabitants have sought work on the land of other farmers, but many are also drifting to frontier and urban areas. Those who have moved to the frontiers in farmland expansion and have cleared forest for agriculture (the best example being the *kaingineros* of the Philippines) have found that they have come into conflict with other upland groups and also with the need to protect the forest. Even more of the dispossessed have moved to urban areas, particularly the capital cities of the region. Here they have struggled to find work, swelled the populations of squatter and slum communities, and added to the already serious strains on urban infrastructures. The process (it should not be viewed as inherently a 'problem') needs to be managed from both ends. In the countryside, the intensification of agricultural production should be supported and promoted, as should rural industrialization. In the urban areas there must be a more concerted effort to provide jobs for migrants. Because their roots lie in the countryside, and because their sojourn in the city appears to be temporary, there has been a tendency to play down the problem. It needs to be accepted that the changing resource context in the countryside, and in particular the relationship between people and land, is not one merely of degree, but one of kind.

Southeast Asia and the Pacific century

The ASEAN region consists of countries that are among the most economically vibrant in the world. Their generally rapid rates of growth have contributed to the talk of a Pacific century and they are often held up as role models for other developing countries. Like all stereotypes, such a characterization is grossly simplistic. The Philippines is suffering from grave political and associated economic troubles, Indonesian industry remains inefficient and highly protected, and Singapore's success has rendered the country vulnerable to external international disturbances. Nevertheless, stereotypes and generalizations are also often based upon grains of truth, and this is no less true of the ASEAN countries of Southeast Asia. In contrast to many countries in South Asia, Africa, and Latin America, there is confidence and optimism about the future. Businessmen, politicians, bureaucrats – even farmers and workers – feel that the present augurs well for the future. This is reflected in the explanations that are employed to account for the serious problems that the region still continues to face. Relatively rarely – and again this contrasts with the situation in other developing areas – are colonialism, neocolonialism, the role of multinationals, dependency, and First World exploitation raised in explanation. Governments and populations in the region are far more likely to highlight their own inadequacies first. This tendency to be self-critical, yet nevertheless to view the future with optimism, should place the countries of the region in a favourable position to exploit the opportunities that may arise in the years to come.

Recommended reading

Chapter 1 Southeast Asia: physical and historical threads

Emmerson, D. K. (1984)
Fisher, C. (1966)
Lockwood, J. G. (1976)
Nieuwolt, S. (1977)
Whitmore, T.C. (ed.) (1981)
Whitmore, T.C. (1984)
Whitmore, T.C. (ed.) (1987)

Chapter 2 Colonization, decolonization, and the impact of the colonial period in Southeast Asia

Bastin, J. and Benda, H. (1968)
Hall, D. G. E. (1968)
Keyes, C. (1977)
Osborne, M. (1979)
Reid, A. (1988)
Steinberg, D. J. (ed.) *et al.*
Tate, D. J. M. (1979)

Chapter 3 Rice cultivation, the Green Revolution, and agrarian change in Southeast Asia

Barker, R. *et al.* (1985)
Booth, A. (1988)
Bray, F. (1986)
Hart, G. P. (1986)
Hayami, Y. and Kikuchi, M. (1981)
Lipton, M. with Longhurst, R. (1989)
Nørlund, *et al.*(eds) (1986)
Rigg, J. D. (1989b)
Scott, J. C. (1976)
Scott, J. C. (1985)

Chapter 4 Development and environment: the impact of development on the forest dwellers of East Malaysia and the Philippines

Cramb, R. A. and Reece,
  R. H. W. (eds) (1988)
Dove, M. R. (1985)
Eder, J. F. (1987)
Hong, E. (1987)
King, V. T. (1988a)

Chapter 5 Land settlement in Southeast Asia: the Indonesian transmigration programme

Arndt, H. W. (1983b)
Colchester, M. (1986b)
Hardjono, J. (1977)
Hardjono, J. (1986)
Hardjono, J. (1988)
Otten, M. (1986a)
Secrett, C. (1986)

Chapter 6. Immigrant communities and plural societies: the New Economic Policy and the Chinese in Malaysia

Brennan, M. (1985)
Husin Ali, S. (ed.) (1984)
Jomo K. S. (1984)
Jomo K. S. (1986)

Lim, L. Y. C. (1983b)
Mehmet, O. (1986)
Milne, R.S. and Mauzy, D. K. (1986)
Pang Eng Fong (1983)

Chapter 7 Urbanization and primacy: Bangkok

Angel, S. and Sopon
  Pornchokchai (1989)
Costa, F. J., *et al.*
  (eds) (1988)
Fuchs, R. J., *et al.*
  (eds) (1987)

Jones, G. W. (1988)
London, B. (1980)
Sternstein, L. (1984)
Thorbek, S. (1987)

Chapter 8 Natural resources in Southeast Asia: oil and gas development and the Indonesian economy

Arndt, H. W. (1983a)
Arndt, H. W. (1984b)
Arndt, H. W. and Hill, H. (1988)
Gelb, A. with Glassburner, B.
  (1988)

Lukman, N. and McGlinchey, J. M.
  (1986)
McCawley, P. (1978)
Robison, R. (1987)

Chapter 9 Export-oriented development: the Singapore experience in an ASEAN context

Ariff, M. and Hill, H. (1985)
Clad, J. (1989)
Grice, K. and Drakakis-Smith, D.
  (1985)
Harris, N. (1986)
Krause, L. B. *et al.* (eds)
  (1987a), (1987b) and (1987c)

Lim, L. Y. O. (1983c)
Mirza, H. (1986)
Rigg, J. D. (1988)
Robison, R. Hewison, K. &
  Higgott, R. (1987)
Rodan, G. (1989)

Chapter 10 Regional co-operation in Southeast Asia: the Association of Southeast Asian Nations

Broinowski, A. (ed.) (1982)
Drummond, S. (1987)
Indorf, H. H. (1987)
Noordin Sopiee *et al.*
  (eds) n.d.
Pfennig, W. and Suh, M. M. B.
  (eds) (1984)

Simon, S. W. (1987)
Simon, S. W. (1988)
Suriyamongkol, M. L. (1988)
Wong, J. (1985)
Wong, S. C.M. (1989)

References

Abdoellah, O. S. 1987. Comparative 'adaptive strategies' of transmigrants in Indonesia: a case study of Barambai, South Kalimantan. In *Human ecology of health and survival in Asia and the South Pacific*, T. Suzuki & R. Ohtsu (eds), 73–91 Toyko: University of Tokyo Press.

Abraham, C. 1986. Manipulation and management of racial and ethnic grou in colonial Malaysia: a case study of ideological domination and control. In *Ethnicity and ethnic relations in Malaysia*, R. Lee (ed.), 1–27. Monograph Series on Southeast Asia, Center for Southeast Asian Studies, Northern Illinois University.

Aggarwala, N. 1984. Moving millions of people to sparsely populated areas: the case of Indonesia, *Courier*, **84**, 73–6.

Alagappa, M. n.d. Asean institutional framework and modus operandi: recommendations for change. In *Asean at the crossroads: obstacles, options and opportunities in economic co-operation*, N. Sopiee, Chew Lay See & Lim Siang Jin (eds), 183–230. Kuala Lumpur: Institute of Strategic and International Studies.

Alexander, J. & P. Alexander 1982. Shared poverty as ideology: agrarian relationships in colonial Java. *Man*, **17**, 597–619.

Anat Arbhabhirama, Dhira Phantumvanit, J. Elkington & Phaitoon Ingkasuwan 1987. *Thailand: natural resources profile*. Bangkok: Thailand Development Research Institute.

Anat Arbhabhirama, Dhira Phantumvanit, J. Elkington & Phaitoon Ingkasuwan 1988. *Thailand: natural resources profile*. Singapore: Oxford University Press.

Anderson, J. N. 1987. Lands at risk, people at risk: perspectives on tropical forest transformations in the Philippines. In *Lands at risk in the Third World: local-level perspectives*, P. D. Little, M. M. Horowitz & A. E. Nyerges (eds), 249–67. Boulder, Colo.: Westview Press.

Angel, S. 1988. 'Where have all the people gone?' Urbanization and counter-urbanization in Thailand. *Journal of the Siam Society* **76**, 245–59.

Angel, S. and Somsook Boonyabancha 1988. Land sharing as an alternative to eviction: the Bangkok experience. *Third World Planning Review* **10** (2), 107–26.

Angel, S. and Sopon Pornchokchai 1989. Bangkok slum lands: policy implications of recent findings. *Cities* **6** (2), 136–46.

Anggoro, J. K. 1986. The issue of PNG's membership of ASEAN. *Indonesian Quarterly* **14** (4), 455–61.

Antlov, H. 1986. Tradition and transition: harvest and social change in rural Java. In *Rice societies: Asian problems and prospects*, I. Nørlund, S. Cederroth & I. Gerdin (eds) 151–70. London: Curzon Press

Antolik, M. 1982. The cautious consolidation of ASEAN. *Contemporary Southeast Asia* **4** (3), 316–29.

Apin, T. 1987. The Sarawak timber blockade. *Ecologist* **17** (4/5), 186–8.

Ariff, M. and Hill, H. 1985. *Export-oriented industrialisation: the ASEAN experience*

Sydney: Allen & Unwin.

Arndt, H. W. 1983a. Oil and the Indonesian economy. *Southeast Asian Affairs 1983*, 136–50. Singapore: Institute of Southeast Asian Studies.

Arndt, H. W. 1983b. Transmigration: achievements, problems, prospects. *Bulletin of Indonesian Economic Studies* **19** (3), 50–73.

Arndt, H. W. 1984a. Little land many people. . . *Far Eastern Economic Review*, 1 November 40.

Arndt, H. W. 1984b. The oil bonanza and poverty. In H.W. Arndt, *The Indonesian economy: collected papers*, 61–71. Singapore: Chopmen Publishers.

Arndt, H. W. 1986. Transmigration to Irian Jaya. In *Between two nations: the Indonesian–Papua New Guinea border and West Papua nationalism*, R. J. May (ed.), 161–74. Bathhurst, Australia: Robert Brown & Associates.

Arndt, H. W. and H. Hill 1988. The Indonesian economy: structural adjustment after the oil boom. *Southeast Asian Affairs 1988*, 106–19. Singapore: Institute of Southeast Asian Studies.

Asia yearbook 1981, Hong Kong: Review Publishing.

Asia yearbook 1990, Hong Kong: Review Publishing.

Audley-Charles, M. G. 1981. Geological history of the region of Wallace's line. In *Wallace's line and plate tectonics*, T. C. Whitmore (ed.), 24–35. Oxford: Clarendon Press.

Audley-Charles, M. G. 1987. Dispersal of Gondwanaland: relevance to evolution of the angiosperms. In *Biogeographical evolution of the Malay Archipelago*, T. C. Whitmore (ed.), 5–25. Oxford: Clarendon Press.

Awanohara, S. 1987a. An alternative to politics. *Far Eastern Economic Review*, 3 December, 104.

Awanohara, S. 1987b. Will Asean open the door to itself? *Far Eastern Economic Review*, 3 December, 104–7.

Aznam, S. 1987a. The language of politics. *Far Eastern Economic Review*, 29 October, 14–21.

Aznam, S. 1987b. Taming the tame. *Far Eastern Economic Review*, 10 December 15–16.

Aznam, S. 1988. Speaking of unity. *Far Eastern Economic Review*, 11 February, 19–20.

Aznam, S. 1990. Terms of trade. *Far Eastern Economic Review*, 1 March, 55

Aznam, S. & H. McDonald 1989a. Ethnic economics. *Far Eastern Economic Review*, 22 June, 28–9.

Aznam, S. & H. McDonald 1989b. Poverty amid plenty. *Far Eastern Economic Review*, 22 June, 32.

Aznam, S. & H. McDonald 1989c. The corporate cake. *Far Eastern Economic Review*, 22 June, 29–31.

Aznam, S. & N. Seaward 1987. A question of trust. *Far Eastern Economic Review*, 2 April, 17–21.

Aznam, S. & R. Tasker 1987. The double-edged sword. *Far Eastern Economic Review*, 19 November, 14–15.

Babcock, T. 1986. Transmigration: the regional impact of a miracleeeeee cure. In *Central government and local development in Indonesia*, C. MacAndrews (ed.), 157–189. Singapore: Oxford University Press.

Balakrishnan, N. 1989. The next NIC. *Far Eastern Economic Review*, 7 September, 96–8.

Balakrishnan, N. 1990. Autocratic solution. *Far Eastern Economic Review*, 22 February, 30.

Bank Indonesia 1989. *Indonesian financial statistics*, **22**, Jakarta.

Barbier, E. 1989. Cash crops, food crops and sustainability: the case of Indonesia. *World Development* **17** (6), 979–89.

Barker, R. 1985. The Philippine Rice Program – lessons for agricultural development. In *More than the grains: participatory management in the Rice Sufficiency Programme 1967–1969*, R. M. Salas (ed.), 193–211. Tokyo: Simul Press.

Barker, R., Herdt, R. W., & Rose, B. 1985. *The rice economy of Asia*. Washington, DC: Resources for the Future.

Barlow, C. 1985. Indonesian and Malayan agricultural development, 1870–1940. *Bulletin of Indonesian Economic Studies* **21** (1), 81–111.

Bastin, J. & Benda, H. J. 1968. *A history of modern Southeast Asia: colonialism, nationalism, and decolonization*. Englewood Cliffs, NJ: Prentice-Hall.

BBMR 1989. The Eastern region. *The Bangkok Bank Monthly Review* **30** (2), 58–66.

Becker, T. 1988. Housing Asia's millions. *Asian Development Bank Quarterly Review*, October, 12–15.

Bertrand, T. 1980. *Thailand: case study of agricultural input and output pricing*, World Bank Staff Working Paper No. 385, Washington, DC: World Bank.

Bidani, N. D. 1985. Demographic characteristics of the urban population in Southeast Asia. In *Urban society in Southeast Asia, Volume 1: social and economic issues*, Gerald H. Krause (ed.), 15–42. Asian studies monograph series. Hong Kong: Asian Research Service.

Binswanger, H. P. 1984. *Agricultural mechanization: a comparative historical perspective*. World Bank Staff Working Paper No. 673. Washington DC: World Bank.

Blaikie, P. 1985. *The political economy of soil erosion in developing countries*. London: Longman.

Blaikie, P. & H. Brookfield 1987. Retrospect and prospect. In *Land degradation and society*, P. Blaikie & H. Brookfield (eds), 239–50. London: Methuen.

Bodley, J. H. 1982. *Victims of progress*. Palo Alto, Calif.: Mayfield Publishing (2nd edn).

Booth, A. 1985. Accommodating a growing population in Javanese agriculture. *Bulletin of Indonesian Economic Studies* **21** (2), 115–45.

Booth, A. 1988. *Agricultural development in Indonesia*. Sydney: Allen & Unwin.

Boserup, E. 1965. *The conditions of agricultural growth: the economics of agrarian change under population pressure*. London: Allen & Unwin.

Botafogo, J. G. 1985. Development and environment: a reply to *The Ecologist*. *Ecologist* **15** (5/6), 207–9.

Bowie, A. 1988. Redistribution with growth? The dilemmas of state-sponsored economic development in Malaysia. *Journal of Developing Societies* **4** (1), 52–66.

Bowring, P. 1986. New market road. *Far Eastern Economic Review*, 27 March, 72–7.

Bray, F. 1986. *The rice economies: technology and development in Asian societies*. Oxford: Basil Blackwell.

Brennan, M. 1985. Class, politics and race in modern Malaysia. In *Southeast Asia: essays in the political economy of structural change*, R. Higgott and R. Robison (eds.), 93–127. London: Routledge & Kegan Paul.

Broinowski, A. (ed.) 1982. *Understanding ASEAN*. London: Macmillan

Brookfield, H. 1972. Intensification and disintensification in Pacific agriculture: a theoretical approach. *Pacific Viewpoint* **13** (1), 30–48.

Brookfield, H. 1988. 'Sustainable development' and the environment. *Journal of Development Studies* **25** (1), 126–35.

Brosius, J. P. 1983. The Zambales Negritos: swidden agriculture and environmental change. *Philippine Quarterly of Culture and Society* **11**, 123–48.

Browett, J. 1985. The newly industrializing countries and radical theories of development. *World Development* **13** (7), 789–803.

Budiardjo, C. W. 1986. The politics of transmigration. *Ecologist* **16** (2/3), 111–16.

Bugo, H. 1988. Economic development since independence: performance and prospects. In *Development in Sarawak: historical and contemporary perspectives*, R. A. Cramb & R. H. W. Reece (eds), 49–55. Monash Paper on Southeast Asia No. 17, Centre of Southeast Asian Studies, Monash University.

Bunnag, J. 1973. *Buddhist monk, Buddhist layman: a study of urban monastic organization in Central Thailand*. Cambridge: Cambridge University Press.

Bunting, A. H. 1988. The humid tropics and the nature of development. *Journal of Biogeography* **15**, 5–10.

Byres, T. 1979. Of neo-populist pipe-dreams: Daedalus in the Third World and the myth of urban bias. *Journal of Peasant Studies* **6** (2), 210–44.

Cadeliña, R. V. 1988. A comparison of Batak and Ata subsistence styles in two different social and physical environments. In *Ethnic diversity and the control of natural resources in Southeast Asia*, A. T. Rambo, K. Gillogly & K. L. Hutterer (eds), 59–81. Michigan Papers on South and Southeast Asia No. 32. Ann Arbor: University of Michigan.

Castro, A. 1982. ASEAN economic co-operation. In *Understanding ASEAN*, A. Broinowski (ed.), 70–91. London: Macmillan.

Caufield, C. 1985. *In the rainforest*. London: Heinemann.

Cederroth, S., and I. Gerdin 1986. Cultivating poverty: the case of the Green Revolution in Lombok. In *Rice societies: Asian problems and prospects*, I. Nørlund, S. Cederroth & I. Gerdin (eds), 124–50. Scandanavian Institute of Asian Studies. London: Curzon Press.

Cham, B. N. 1977. The 'racial bargain' in West Malaysia. In *Development and under-development in Southeast Asia*, G. P. Means (ed.), 198–217. McMaster University Printing Services: Canada.

Chambers, R. 1984. Beyond the Green Revolution: a selective essay. In *Under-standing Green Revolutions: agrarian change and development planning in South Asia*, essays in honour of B. H. Farmer, T. P. Bayliss-Smith & S. Wanmali (eds), 362–79. Cambridge: Cambridge University Press.

Chambers, R. 1987. *Sustainable livelihoods, environment and development: putting poor rural people first*. Discussion Paper No. 240, Institute of Development Studies, University of Sussex.

Chan Heng Chee 1986. ASEAN: subregional resilience. In *Security interdependence in the Asia Pacific region*, J. W. Morley (ed.), 111–43. Lexington, Mass.: Lexington Books.

Chanda, N. 1989. Bark worse than bite. *Far Eastern Economic Review*, 8 June, 99–100.

Chaponniere, J. R. 1985. Industrial development in Singapore and South Korea: a challenge to development economics? *Contemporary Southeast Asia* **7** (2), 127–47.

Chattip Nartsupha 1986. The village economy in pre-capitalist Thailand. In *Back to the roots: village and self-reliance in a Thai context*, S. Phongphit (ed.), 155–65. Bangkok: Culture and Development Series 1. Bangkok: Rural Development Documentation Centre.

Chawalit Nitaya & Ubonwan Ocharoen 1980. Case study: Bangkok, Thailand. In *Policies towards urban slums: slums and squatter settlements in the ESCAP region*,

Madhu Sarin (ed.), 78-92. Bangkok: United Nations.

Chee Peng Lim 1988. The Proton Saga – no reverse gear! The economic burden of the Malaysian car project. In *Mahathir's economic policies*, Jomo (ed.), 48–62. Kuala Lumpur: Insan.

Chee Peng Lim n.d. Asean co-operation in industry: looking back and looking forward. In *Asean at the crossroads: obstacles, options and opportunities in economic co-operation*, N. Sopiee, Chew Lay See & Lim Siang Jin (eds), 91–138. Kuala Lumpur: Institute of Strategic and International Studies.

Chen, E. K. Y. 1985. The newly industrializing countries in Asia: growth experience and prospects. In *Asian economic development: present and future*, R. A. Scalapino, S. Sato & J. Wanadi (eds), 131–60. Institute of East Asian Studies, University of California, Berkeley.

Chen, P. S. J. 1983. Singapore's development strategies: a model for rapid growth. In *Singapore development policies and trends*, P. S. J. Chen (ed.), 3–25. Singapore: Oxford University Press.

Ching-ling Tai 1988. *Housing policy and high-rise living: a study of Singapore's public housing*, Singapore: Chopmen.

Chong Li Choy 1986. Singapore's development: harnessing the multinationals. *Contemporary Southeast Asia* **8** (1), 56–69.

Chovanes, A. B. 1986. On Vietnamese and other peasants. *Journal of Southeast Asian Studies* **17** (2), 203–35.

Clad, J. 1986. Rising sense of drift: foreign ministers agree Asean has reached a plateau. *Far Eastern Economic Review*, 10 July, 15.

Clad, J. 1987. Full of good intentions: slow progress on economic cooperation. *Far Eastern Economic Review*, 24 December, 9–10.

Clad, J. 1988. The timber tycoon and his influential friends. *Far Eastern Economic Review*, 24 November, 48–9.

Clad, J. 1989. *Behind the myth: business, money and power in Southeast Asia*. London: Unwin Hyman.

Clad, J. & M. D. Vitug 1988. The politics of plunder. *Far Eastern Economic Review*, 24 November, 48–50.

Clammer, J. R. 1986. Ethnic processes in urban Melaka. In *Ethnicity and ethnic relations in Malaysia*, R. Lee (ed.), 47–72. Monograph Series on Southeast Asia, Center for Southeast Asian Studies, Northern Illinois University.

Coedes, G. 1968. *The Indianized states of Southeast Asia*, Honolulu: East-West Center Press.

Colchester, M. 1986a. Banking on disaster: international support for transmigration. *Ecologist* **16** (2/3), 61–70.

Colchester, M. 1986b. The struggle for land: tribal peoples in the face of the transmigration programme. *Ecologist* **16** (2/3), 99–110.

Colchester, M. 1986c. Unity and diversity: Indonesian policy towards tribal peoples. *Ecologist* **16** (2/3), 89–98.

Colchester, M. 1987. Native protests stifled in Malaysian government crack-down. *Ecologist* **17** (4/5), 189.

Colchester, M. 1989. *Pirates, squatters and poachers: the political ecology of dispossession of the natives of Sarawak*. London: Survival International.

Collier, W. L. 1981. Agricultural evolution in Java. In *Agriculture and rural development in Indonesia*, G. E. Hansen (ed.), 147–73. Boulder: Westview Press.

Collier, W. L., Gunawan Wiradi & Soentoro 1973. Recent changes in rice harvesting methods: some serious social implications. *Bulletin of Indonesian Economic Studies* **9** (2), 36–45.

Collier, W. L., Soentoro, Gunawan Wiradi & Makali 1974. Agricultural technology and institutional change in Java. *Food Research Institute Studies* **13** (2), 169–94.

Conklin, H. C. 1957. *Hanunóo agriculture: a report on the integral system of shifting cultivation in the Philippines.* FAO Forestry Development Paper No. 12. Rome: Food and Agricultural Organization of the United Nations.

Coppel, C. A. 1980. China and the ethnic Chinese in Indonesia. In *Indonesia: the making of a nation,* J. A. C. Mackie (ed.), 729–734. Research School of Pacific Studies, Australian National University, Canberra.

Coppel, C. A. 1983. *Indonesian Chinese in crisis,* Kuala Lumpur: Oxford University Press.

Costa, F. J. et al. (eds) 1988. *Asian urbanization: problems and processes.* Berlin: Gebruder Borntraeger.

Cottrell, R. 1986. The Carrian connection. *Far Eastern Economic Review,* 20 March, 151–3.

Courtenay, P. P. 1981. The plantation in Malaysian economic development. *Journal of Southeast Asian Studies* **12** (2), 329–48.

Courtenay, P. P. 1987. Letter from Malacca. *Far Eastern Economic Review,* 10 September, 102.

Coutts, P. J. F., J. P. Wesson, S. Galuego, & D. Dinopol 1981. A summary report of the fifth Australian archaeological expedition to the Philippines, 1980. *Philippine Quarterly of Culture and Society* **9** (2), 77–110.

Cramb, R. A. 1988. The commercialization of Iban agriculture. In *Development in Sarawak: historical and contemporary perspectives,* R. A. Cramb and R.H.W. Reece (eds), 105–134. Monash Paper on Southeast Asia No. 17, Centre of Southeast Asian Studies, Monash University.

Cramb, R. A. & G. Dixon 1988. Development in Sarawak: an overview. In *Development in Sarawak: historical and contemporary perspectives,* R. A. Cramb & R. H. W. Reece (eds), 1–19. Monash Paper on Southeast Asia No. 17, Centre of Southeast Asian Studies, Monash University.

Cramb, R. A. and Reece, R. H. W. (eds) 1988. *Development in Sarawak: historical and contemporary perspectives,* Monash paper on Southeast Asia no. 17, Centre of Southeast Asian Studies, Monash University.

Crone, D. 1988. The ASEAN summit of 1987: searching for new dynamism. *Southeast Asian Affairs 1988.* Singapore: Institute of Southeast Asian Studies.

Cross, M. 1987. Solving the world's food problem. *New Scientist,* 16 April, 45.

Dalrymple, D. G. 1986. *Development and spread of high-yielding rice varieties in developing countries.* Washington DC: Agency for International Development.

Daud, F. 1985. Some patterns of ethnic relations in Malaysia. *Asian Profile* **13** (2), 117–28.

De Koninck, R. & W. D. McTaggert 1987. Land settlement processes in Southeast Asia: historical foundations, discontinuities and problems. *Asian Profile* **15** (4), 341–56.

Demaine, H. 1978. Magic and management: methods for ensuring water supplies for agriculture in South East Asia. In *Nature and Man in South East Asia,* P. A. Stott (ed.), 49–67. London: School of Oriental and African Studies.

Department of Statistics 1989. *Monthly digest of statistics* (Singapore) **27,** 12.

Deuster, P. 1981. West Sumatra and South Sulawesi. In *Agricultural and rural development in Indonesia,* G. E. Hansen (ed.), 79–94. Boulder, Colo.: Westview Press.

Deyo, F. C. 1981. *Dependent development and industrial order: an Asian case study* New York: Praeger.

deYoung, J. E. 1966. *Village life in modern Thailand.* Berkeley: University of California Press.

References

Donner, W. 1978. *The five faces of Thailand: an economic geography*. London: Hurst.

Donner, W. 1987. *Landuse and environment in Indonesia*. London: Hurst.

Dorall, R. F. & M. A. E. Regpala 1984. Dams, pines and tribes: reflections on frontier development in the Philippines. In *Environment, development and natural resource crisis in Asia and the Pacific*, 253–76. Penang: Sahabat Alam Malaysia.

Douglass, M. 1984. *Regional integration on the capitalist periphery: the Central Plains of Thailand*. Research Report No. 15, Institute of Social Studies, The Hague.

Dove, M. R. 1985. *Swidden agriculture in Indonesia: the subsistence strategies of the Kalimantan Kantu'*. Berlin: Mouton.

Drakakis-Smith, D. W. & P. J. Rimmer 1982. Taming 'the wild city': managing Southeast Asia's primate cities since the 1960s. *Asian Geographer* **1** (1), 17–34.

Drummond, S. 1986. National policies, regional co-operation and the cohesion of ASEAN. *Southeast Asian Journal of Social Science* **14** (1), 35–44.

Ecologist 1986. Open letter to Mr. Clausen, retiring President of the World Bank, and Mr. Conable, President elect. *Ecologist* **16** (2/3), 58–60.

Economist 1986. Taking ASEAN seriously. *Economist*, 15 February, 74–5.

Economist 1989. The fifth tiger. *Economist*, 28 October, 15.

Eder, J. F. 1987. *On the road to tribal extinction: depopulation, deculturation and adaptive well-being among the Batak of the Philippines*. Berkeley: University of California Press.

Eder, J. F. 1988. Hunter-gatherer/farmer exchange in the Philippines: some implications for ethnic identity and adaptive well-being. In *Ethnic diversity and the control of natural resources in Southeast Asia*, A. T. Rambo, K. Gillogly and K. L. Hutterer (eds), 37–57. Michigan Papers on South and Southeast Asia No. 32, University of Michigan, Ann Arbor.

Egan, M. L. & M. Jr Bendick 1986. The urban–rural dimension in national economic development. *Journal of Developing Areas* **20**, 203–22.

Emmerson, D. K. 1984. 'Southeast Asia': What's in a name? *Journal of Southeast Asian Studies* **15** (1), 1–21.

Endicott, K. M. 1984. The economy of the Batek of Malaysia: annual and historical perspectives. *Research in Economic Anthropology* **6**, 29–52.

ESCAP 1982. *Migration, Urbanization and Development in Thailand*. Comparative study on migration, urbanization and development in the ESCAP region, Country Report No. 5, Bangkok: Economic and Social Commission for Asia and the Pacific.

Feder, E. 1983. *Perverse development*. Quezon City: Foundation for Nationalist Studies.

Feder, G. 1987. Land ownership security and farm productivity: evidence from Thailand. *Journal of Development Studies* **24** (1), 16–30.

FEER (1987). The government's role, (an interview with Finance Minister Richard Hu). *Far Eastern Economic Review*, 8 January, 70–2.

FEER (1988). Priming the oil drillers. *Far Eastern Economic Review*, 15 September, 82–3.

FEER (1989a). Asia-Pacific community: expanding the rice bowl. *Far Eastern Economic Review*, 16 November, 10–19.

FEER (1989b). Malaysia: do you sincerely want to be a NIC? *Far Eastern Economic Review*, 7 September, 96–100.

FEER (1990a). Malaysia's Indians in the race. *Far Eastern Economic Review*, 7 June, 15–21.

FEER (1990b). Pertamina given go-ahead to stop price discounting. *Far Eastern*

Economic Review, 15 February, 83.

Fisher, C. A. (1966). *South-east Asia: a social, political and economic geography*. London: Methuen (2nd edn).

Fuchs, R. J., G. W. Jones & E. M. Pernia (eds) 1987. *Urbanization and urban politics in Pacific Asia*. Boulder, Colo.. Westview Press.

Fujisaka, S. 1986a. Change and development in the Philippine uplands. In *Man, agriculture and the tropical forest: change and development in the Philippine uplands*, S. Fujisaka, P. E. Sajise & R. A. del Castillo (eds), 1–11. Bangkok: Winrock International Institute for Agricultural Development.

Fujisaka, S. 1986b. Pioneer shifting cultivators, upland ecosystem, and 'social forestry' policy in the Philippines. *Philippine Sociological Review* **34** (1–4), 26–36.

Fukui, H. 1978. Paddy production technology: present and future. In *Thailand: a rice-growing society*, Y. Ishii (ed.), 246–71. Monograph of the Center for Southeast Asian Studies, Kyoto University. Honolulu: University Press of Hawaii.

Furneaux, R. 1965. *Krakatoa*. London: Secker & Warburg.

Furnivall, J. S. 1948. *Colonial policy and practice: a comparative study of Burma and Netherlands India*. New York: New York University Press.

Furnivall, J. S. 1980. Plural societies. In *Sociology of South-East Asia: readings on social change and development*, H.-D. Evers (ed.), 86–96. Kuala Lumpur: Oxford University Press.

Geertz, C. 1963. *Agricultural involution: the process of ecological change in Indonesia*. Berkeley: University of California Press.

Geertz, C. 1967. Form and variation in Balinese village structure. In *Peasant society: a reader*, J. M. Potter, M. N. Diaz and G. M. Foster (eds), 255–78. Boston: Little, Brown.

Gelb, A. and associates 1988. *Oil windfalls: blessing or curse?* New York: Oxford University Press.

Gelb, A. with B. Glassburner 1988. Indonesia: windfalls in a poor rural economy. In *Oil windfalls: blessing or curse?*, A. Gelb and associates, 197–226. New York: Oxford University Press.

George, W. 1987. Complex origins. In *Biogeographical evolution of the Malay Archipelago*, T. C. Whitmore (ed.), 119–31. Oxford: Clarendon Press.

Ginsburg, N. 1976. The great city in South-East Asia. In *Changing South-East Asian cities: readings on urbanization*, Y. M. Yeung & C. P. Low (eds), 2–7. Singapore: Oxford University Press.

Ginsburg, N. 1988. Reflections on primacy: cases from Asia. In *Asian urbanization: problems and processes*, F. J. Costa, A. K. Dutt, L. J. C. Ma & A. G. Noble (eds), 39–45. Berlin: Gebruder Borntraeger.

Glaeser, B. (ed.) 1987. *The Green Revolution revisited*. London: Allen and Unwin.

Glassburner, B. 1976. In the wake of General Ibnu: crisis in the Indonesian oil industry. *Asian Survey* **16** (12), 1099–112.

Glover, I. G. 1979. Prehistoric plant remains from Southeast Asia, with special reference to rice. In *South Asian archaeology 1977*, Vol. 1, M. Taddei (ed.), 7–37. Naples: Istituto Universitario Orientale.

Goldsmith, E. 1985a. Is development the solution or the problem? *Ecologist* **15** (5/6), 210–19.

Goldsmith, E. 1985b. Worshipping at the altar of economic pragmatism. *Ecologist* **15** (4), 146–8.

Goldstein, C. 1989a. Complex problems. *Far Eastern Economic Review*, 30 March, 52–3.

Goldstein, C. 1989b. The sum of the parts. *Far Eastern Economic Review*, 30 March, 53–5.

Government of Malaysia 1971. *Second Malaysia Plan 1971–1975*. Kuala Lumpur: Government Press.

Government of Malaysia 1976. *Third Malaysia Plan 1976–1980*. Kuala Lumpur: Government Press.

Government of Malaysia 1981. *Fourth Malaysia Plan 1981–1985*. Kuala Lumpur: National Printing Department.

Government of Malaysia 1986 *Fifth Malaysia Plan, 1986–1990*. Kuala Lumpur: National Printing Department.

Grandstaff, T. B. & S. W. Grandstaff 1987. Choice of rice technology: a farmer perspective. In *Community management: Asian experience and perspectives*, D. C. Korten (ed.), 51–61. West Hartford, Conn.: Kumarian Press.

Grice, K. & D. Drakakis-Smith 1985. The role of the state in shaping development: two decades of growth in Singapore. *Transactions of the Institute of British Geographers* **10** (3), 347–59.

Guinness, P. 1982. Transmigrants in South Kalimantan and South Sulawesi. In *Population resettlement programs in Southeast Asia*, G. W. Jones & H. V. Richter (eds), 63–71. Development Studies Centre Monograph No. 30, Australian National University, Canberra.

Gullick, J. 1981. *Malaysia: economic expansion and national unity*. London: Ernest Benn.

Haas, M. R. 1964. *Thai-English student's dictionary*. Stanford: Stanford University Press.

Hadi, S. & Y. B. Lung 1988. Swidden cultivation among the Tunjung of East Kalimantan with particular emphasis on socio-economic factors. *Sarawak Museum Journal* **60**, 111–48.

Haji Ahmad, Z. 1982. The political structure. In *The political economy of Malaysia*, E. K. Fisk & H. Osman-Rani (eds), 88–103. Kuala Lumpur: Oxford University Press.

Hakam, A. N. 1985. Deliberate restructuring in the newly industrializing countries of Asia: the case of Singapore. *East Asia: International Review of Economic, Political and Social Development* **3**, 93–108.

Hakchung Choo & Ifzal Ali 1989. The newly industrializing economies and Asian development: issues and options. *Asian Development Review* **7** (2) 1–25.

Hall, D. G. E. 1968. *A history of South-East Asia*. London: Macmillan (3rd edn).

Hall, K. R. 1985. *Maritime trade and state development in early Southeast Asia*. Honolulu: University of Hawaii Press.

Handley, P. 1988a. Above the madding crowd. *Far Eastern Economic Review*, 8 December, 66.

Handley, P. 1988b. Ports clog, roads jam. *Far Eastern Economic Review*, 29 September, 94–6.

Handley, P. 1988c Thailand hits the wall. *Far Eastern Economic Review*, 29 September, 94–5.

Handley, P. 1989a. A planner quits. *Far Eastern Economic Review*, 4 May, 71.

Handley, P. 1989b. Progress by numbers. *Far Eastern Economic Review*, 23 March, 83–4.

Handley, P. 1989c. Seeding the South. *Far Eastern Economic Review*, 30 March, 56–7.

Handoko, B. S. 1983. Productivity, farmsize and employment in rice production in Java and Bali, Boston University PhD, Ann Arbor, Mich.: University Microfilms International.

Hanson, A. J. 1981. Transmigration and marginal land development. In *Agriculture and rural development in Indonesia*, G. E. Hansen (ed.), 219–35. Boulder, Colo.: Westview Press.

Hardjono, J. 1977. *Transmigration in Indonesia*. Kuala Lumpur: Oxford University Press.

Hardjono, J. 1986. Transmigration: looking to the future. *Bulletin of Indonesian Economic Studies* **22** (2), 28–53.

Hardjono, J. 1988. The Indonesian transmigration program in historical perspective. *International Migration* **26** (4), 427–39.

Harris, N. 1986. *The end of the Third World: newly industrializing countries and the decline of an ideology*. Harmondsworth, Middlesex: Penguin.

Hart, G. P. 1986. *Power, labor and livelihood: processes of change in rural Java*. Berkeley: University of California Press.

Hayami, Y. 1981. Induced innovation, Green Revolution, and income distribution: comment. *Economic Development and Cultural Change* **30** (1), 169–76.

Hayami, Y. 1984. Assessment of the Green Revolution. In *Agricultural development in the Third World*, C. K. Eicher & J. M. Staatz (eds), 389–96. Baltimore: John Hopkins Press.

Hayami, Y. & A. Hafid 1979. Rice harvesting and welfare in rural Java. *Bulletin of Indonesian Economic Studies* **15** (2), 94–112.

Hayami, Y. & M. Kikuchi 1981. *Asian village economy at the crossroads: an economic approach to institutional change*. Tokyo: University of Tokyo Press.

Headland, T. N. 1986. Why foragers do not become farmers: a historical study of a changing ecosystem and its effect on a Negrito hunter-gatherer group in the Philippines, PhD thesis, University of Hawaii. Ann Arbor, Mich.: University Microfilms International.

Heineberg, H. 1988. Singapore – from the British colonial base to the up-and-coming 'Chinese' city state. *Applied Geography and Development* **31**, 15–36.

Heng Pek Koon 1988. *Chinese politics in Malaysia: a history of the Malaysian Chinese Association*. Singapore: Oxford University Press.

Herdt, R. W. 1987. A retrospective view of technological and other changes in Philippine rice farming, 1965–1982. *Economic Development and Cultural Change* **35** (2), 329–49.

Heyzer, N. 1983. International production and social change: an analysis of the state, employment and trades unions in Singapore. In *Singapore development policies and trends*, P. S. J. Chen (ed.), 105–28. Singapore: Oxford University Press.

Higgot, R. & R. Robison (eds) 1985. *Southeast Asia: essays in the political economy of structural change*. London: Routledge & Kegan Paul.

Higham, C. 1989. *The archaeology of mainland Southeast Asia from 10,000 BC to the Fall of Angkor*. Cambridge: Cambridge University Press.

Hill, H. 1987. Survey of recent developments. *Bulletin of Indonesian Economic Studies* **23** (3), 1–33.

Hill, H. 1988. Ensuring regional growth now the oil boom is over. *Far Eastern Economic Review*, 1 September, 24–5.

Hill, H. n.d. Challenges in Asean economic cooperation: an outsider's perspective. In *Asean at the crossroads: obstacles, options and opportunities in economic co-operation*, N. Sopiee, Chew Lay See & Lim Siang Jin (eds), 81–9. Kuala Lumpur: Institute of Strategic and International Studies.

Hill, H. & Pang Eng Fong 1988. The state and industrial restructuring: a comparison of the aerospace industry in Indonesia and Singapore. *ASEAN Economic Bulletin* **5** (2), 152–68.

Hill, R. D. 1977. *Rice in Malaya: a study in historical geography*. Kuala Lumpur: Oxford University Press.

Hirsch, P. 1987. Deforestation and development in Thailand. *Singapore Journal of Tropical Geography* **8** (2), 129–38.

Hirsch, P. 1989. The state in the village: interpreting rural development in Thailand. *Development and Change* **20** (1), 35–56.

Hobohm, S. 1987. *Indonesia to 1991: can momentum be regained?* Special Report No. 1077, London: The Economist Intelligence Unit.

Holloway, N. 1987a. Guidelines for flexibility. *Far Eastern Economic Review*, 1 January, 54–5.

Holloway, N. 1987b. The rise of the entrepreneur. *Far Eastern Economic Review*, 8 January, 68–71.

Holloway, N. 1989. The numbers game. *Far Eastern Economic Review*, 16 November, 71.

Holtsberg, C. 1982. Rice pricing policy. In *Basic needs and government policies in Thailand*, P. Richards (ed.), 161–81. Singapore: Maruzen Asia.

Hong, E. 1987. *Natives of Sarawak: survival in Borneo's vanishing forest*. Malaysia: Institut Masyarakat.

Hose, C. 1988 *Natural man: a record from Borneo*, Singapore: Oxford University Press (first published 1926).

Huang Yuezhen 1987. The continuing myth of Asean integration. *Far Eastern Economic Review*, 7 May, 124–5.

Hugo, G. J., T. H. Hull, V. J. Hull & G. W. Jones 1987. *The demographic dimension in Indonesian development*. Singapore: Oxford University Press.

Hull, T. H. & G. L. Dasvarma 1988. Fertility trends in Indonesia 1967–1985. *Bulletin of Indonesian Economic Studies* **24** (1), 115–21.

Hunter, G. 1966. *South-East Asia: race, culture and nation*. London: Oxford University Press.

Hurst, P. 1987. Forest destruction in South East Asia. *Ecologist* **17** (4/5), 170–4.

Husin Ali, S. 1984. Social relations: the ethnic and class factors. In *Ethnicity, class and development: Malaysia*, S. Husin Ali (ed.), 13–31. Kuala Lumpur: Persatuan Sains Sosial Malaysia.

Husin Ali, S. (ed.) 1984 *Ethnicity, class and development: Malaysia*, Kuala Lumpur: Persatnan Sains Sosial Malaysia.

Husken, F. 1979. Landlords, sharecroppers and agricultural labourers: changing labour relations in rural Java. *Journal of Contemporary Asia* **9** (2), 140–51.

ILO 1980. *Export-led industrialisation and employment: proceedings of a symposium.* Asian Employment Programme (ARTEP), Bangkok, publication of the International Labour Office, Geneva.

IMF 1989a. *Direction of trade statistics yearbook, 1989*. Washington DC: International Monetary Fund.

IMF 1989b. *International Financial Statistics* **XLII** (1).

IMF 1989c. *International Financial Statistics* **XLII** (8).

Indorf, H. H. 1987. ASEAN in extra-regional perspective. *Contemporary Southeast Asia* **9** (2), 86–105.

Ingram, J. C. 1971. *Economic change in Thailand, 1850–1970*. Stanford: Stanford University Press.

Irvine, R. 1982a. The formative years of ASEAN: 1967–1975. In *Understanding ASEAN*, A. Broinowski (ed.), 8–36. London: Macmillan.

Irvine, D. 1982b. Making haste less slowly: ASEAN from 1975. In *Understanding ASEAN*, A. Broinowski (ed.), 37–69. London: Macmillan.

Ishii, Y. 1978. History and rice growing. In *Thailand: a rice growing society*, Y. Ishii (ed.), 15–39. Monographs of the Center of Southeast Asian Studies, Kyoto University. Honolulu: University Press of Hawaii.

Jackson, J. C. 1968. *Sarawak: a geographical survey of a developing state.* London: University of London Press.

Jackson, K. D. 1984. Indochina: war without end. In *ASEAN security and economic development*, K. D. Jackson & M. H. Soesastro (eds), 238–50. Research Papers and Policy Studies 11, Institute of East Asian Studies, University of California, Berkeley.

James, W. E., S. Naya, & G. M. Meier 1987. *Asian development: economic success and policy lessons.* International Center for Economic Growth. Madison, Wis.: University of Wisconsin Press.

Jayasuriya, S. & C. Manning 1988. The pitfalls of Indonesia's non-oil economic growth. *Far Eastern Economic Review*, 8 September, 132–4.

Jefferson, M. 1939. The law of the primate city. *Geographical Review* 29 (2), 226–32.

Jeffries, B. 1989. Call of the wild. *Far Eastern Economic Review*, 19 January, 38–9.

Jensen, L. 1989. A Thai alternative to slum clearance. *World Development* 2 (1), 14–16.

Jomo, K. S. 1984. Malaysia's New Economic Policy: a class perspective. *Pacific Viewpoint* 25 (2), 153–72.

Jomo, K. S. 1986. *A question of class: capital, the state and uneven development in Malaya.* Oxford: Oxford University Press.

Jomo, K. S. 1987. Economic crisis and policy response in Malaysia. In *Southeast Asia in the 1980s: The politics of economic crisis*, R. Robison, K. Hewison and R. Higgott (eds), 113–48. Sydney: Allen & Unwin.

Jones, G. W. 1979. Indonesia: the transmigration programme and development planning. In *Migration and development in South-East Asia: a demographic perspective*, R. J. Pryor (ed.), 212–21. Kuala Lumpur: Oxford University Press.

Jones, G. W. 1988. Urbanization trends in Southeast Asia: some issues for policy. *Journal of Southeast Asian Studies* 19 (1), 137–54.

Jones, G. W. & H. V. Richter 1982. Introduction. In *Population resettlement programs in Southeast Asia*, G. W. Jones & H. V. Richter (eds), 3–8. Development Studies Centre Monograph No. 30, Australian National University, Canberra.

Juoro, U. 1989. Indonesia's invisible hand. *Far Eastern Economic Review*, 16 November, 70–1.

Kampoon Boontawee 1988. *Child of the Northeast.* Bangkok: Duang Kamol (English translation).

Kaye, L. 1985a. A change of customs. *Far Eastern Economic Review*, 25 April, 118–20.

Kaye, L. 1985b. Substitute for imports but not for efficiency. *Far Eastern Economic Review*, 14 November, 68–9.

Kaye, L. 1986. The unkindest cut. *Far Eastern Economic Review*, 16 January, 101–2.

Kebschull, D. 1986. *Transmigration in Indonesia: an empirical analysis of motivation, expectations and experiences*, Hamburg: Verlag Weltarchiv.

Kelley, A. C. & J. G. Williamson 1987. What drives city growth in the developing world? In *The economics of urbanization and urban policies in developing countries*, G. S. Tolley & V. Thomas (eds), 32–45. Washington DC: World Bank.

Keyes, C. F. 1977. *The golden peninsula: culture and adaptation in mainland Southeast Asia.* New York: Macmillan.

Khong Cho Oon 1986. *The politics of oil in Indonesia: foreign company-host government relations.* Cambridge: Cambridge University Press.

Khong Kim Hoong & Abdul Razak Abdullah. 1987. Security co-operation in

References

ASEAN. *Contemporary Southeast Asia* **9** (2), 129–39.

King, V. T. 1986. Land settlement schemes and the alleviation of rural poverty in Sarawak, East Malaysia: a critical commentary. *Southeast Asian Journal of Social Science* **14** (1), 71–99.

King, V. T. 1988a. Models and realities: Malaysian national planning and East Malaysian development problems. *Modern Asian Studies* **22** (2), 263–98.

King, V. T. 1988b. Why is Sarawak peripheral? Paper presented at the Syposium on the Peripheral Areas and Minority Groups of South-East Asia, University of Hull, 20–22 April 1988.

Klausner, W. J. n.d. *Reflection on Thai culture, collected writings of William J. Klausner*. Bangkok: Suksit Siam.

Kohli, A. 1986. Democracy and development. In *Development strategies reconsidered*, J. P. Lewis and V. Kallab (eds), 153–82. New Brunswick: Transaction Books.

Korff, R. 1989. Urban or agrarian? The modern Thai state. *Sojourn* **4** (1), 44–53.

Krause, L. B., Koh Ai Tee & Lee (Tsao) Yuan 1987a. Challenges facing Singapore. In *The Singapore economy reconsidered*, L. B. Krause, Koh Ai Tee and Lee (Tsao) Yuan (eds), 217–30. Singapore: Institute of Southeast Asian Studies.

Krause, L. B. 1987b. Industrialization of an advanced global city. In *The Singapore economy reconsidered*, L. B. Krause, Koh Ai Tee and Lee (Tsao) Yuan (eds), 54–77. Singapore: Institute of Southeast Asian Studies.

Krause, L. B. 1987c. The government as an entrepreneur. In *The Singapore economy reconsidered*, L. B. Krause, Koh Ai Tee and Lee (Tsao) Yuan (eds), 107–26. Singapore: Institute of Southeast Asian Studies.

Krirkkiat Phipatseritham & K. Yoshihara 1989. Thailand: industrialization without development. *East Asian Cultural Studies* **28** (1–4), 91–100.

La Loubère, S. de 1969. *The Kingdom of Siam*. Oxford in Asia Historical Reprints. Kuala Lumpur: Oxford University Press (first published 1961).

Lambert, D. H. 1985. *Swamp rice farming: the indigenous Pahang Malay agricultural system*. Boulder, Colo.: Westview Press.

Lando, R. P. n.d. *Fish in the waters and rice in the fields: cropping systems, agricultural development, and making a living in two North Thai villages*, Bangkok: USAID.

Lee Yong Leng 1978. Supranationalism in Southeast Asia: the case of ASEAN. *Journal of Tropical Geography* **46** (June), 27–36.

Lee Yong Leng 1980. Language and national cohesion in Southeast Asia. *Contemporary Southeast Asia* **2** (3), 226–40.

Lee Yong Leng 1982. *Southeast Asia: essays in political geography*. Singapore: Singapore University Press.

Lee-Jay Cho & Bauer J. G. 1987. Population growth and urbanization: what does the future hold? In *Urbanization and urban policies in Pacific Asia*, R. J. Fuchs, G. W. Jones & E. M. Pernia (eds), 15–37. Boulder, Colo.: Westview Press.

Leifer, M. 1986. Obstacles to peace in Southeast Asia. In *Into the Pacific era: Southeast Asia and its place in the Pacific*, H. Matsumoto & N. Sopiee (eds), 7–14. Proceedings of the Global Community Forum '84 Malaysia. Kuala Lumpur: Institute of Strategic and International Studies.

Leifer, M. 1987. *ASEAN's search for regional order*. Faculty Lecture 12, Faculty of Arts and Social Sciences, National University of Singapore, Singapore.

Leigh, M. 1979. Is there development in Sarawak? Political goals and practice. In *Issues in Malaysian development*, J. C. Jackson and M. Rudner (eds), 339–74. Kuala Lumpur: Heinemann.

Leigh, M. 1988. The spread of Foochow commercial power before the New Economic Policy. In *Development in Sarawak: historical and contemporary perspectives*, *rural labour markets in Asia: studies based on farm-level data*, S. Hirashima & M. Muqtada (eds), 151–75. Asian Employment Programme (ARTEP). New Delhi: ILO.

Liefrinck, F. A. 1969. Rice cultivation in northern Bali (1886–1887). In *Bali: further studies in life, thought and ritual*, J. van Baal *et al.* (eds). The Hague: W. van Hoeve Publishers Ltd.

Lim, D. (1983a). The political economy of the New Economic Policy in Malaysia. In *Further readings on Malaysian economic development*, D. Lim (ed.), 3–22. Kuala Lumpur: Oxford University Press.

Lim, L. Y. C. 1983b. Chinese economic activity in Southeast Asia: an introductory review. In *The Chinese in Southeast Asia: volume 1, ethnicity and economic activity*, L. A. Peter Gosling & Linda Y. C. Lim (eds), 1–23. Singapore: Maruzen Asia.

Lim, L. Y. C. 1983c. Singapore's success: the myth of the free market economy. *Asian Survey* 23 (6), 752–64.

Lim, D. 1986. East Malaysia in Malaysian development planning. *Journal of Southeast Asian Studies* 17 (1), 156–70.

Lim, L. Y. C. and Pang Eng Fong 1986. *Trade, employment and industrialisation in Singapore*. Geneva: International Labour Office.

Limlingan, V. S. 1986. *The overseas Chinese in ASEAN: business strategies and management practices*. Manila: Vita Development Corporation.

Linnemann, H., Dijck, van Pitou & H. Verbruggen 1987. *Export-oriented industrialization in developing countries*. Published for the Council for Asian Manpower Studies, Manila by Singapore University Press.

Lipton, M. 1977. *Why poor people stay poor: a study of urban bias in world development*. London: Temple Smith.

Lipton, M. 1987. Development studies: findings, frontiers and fights. *World Development* 15 (4), 517–25.

Lipton, M. & R. Longhurst 1985. *Modern varieties, international agricultural research and the poor*. CGIAR, study paper no. 2. Washington D.C: The World Bank.

Lipton, M. with R. Longhurst 1989. *New seeds and poor people*. London: Unwin Hyman. Hyman.

Lockwood, J. G. 1976. *The physical geography of the tropics: an introduction*. Kuala Lumpur: Oxford University Press.

Logan, J. R. 1847. The present condition of the Indian Archipelago. *The Journal of the Indian Archipelago and Eastern Asia* 1, 1–21.

Loh Kok Wah 1984. The socio-economic basis of the ethnic consciousness: the Chinese in the 1970s. In *Ethnicity, class and development: Malaysia*, S. Husin Ali (ed.), 93–112. Kuala Lumpur: Persatuan Sains Sosial Malaysia.

London, B. 1977. Is the primate city parasitic? the regional implications of national decision making in Thailand. *The Journal of Developing Areas* 12, 49–67.

London, B. 1980. *Metropolis and nation in Thailand: the political economy of uneven development*. Boulder, Colorado: Westview Press.

London, B. 1985. Thai city-hinterland relationships in an international context: development as social control in Northern Thailand. In *Urbanization in the world economy*, M. Timberlake (ed.), 206–30. Orlando, Florida: Academic Press Inc.

Lopez, M. E. 1987. The politics of lands at risk in a Philippine frontier. In *Lands at risk in the third world: local-level perspectives*, P. D. Little, M. M. Horowitz and A. Endre Nyerges (eds), 230–48. Boulder, Colorado: Westview Press.

Low, L. 1988a. Privatization in Singapore. In *Privatisation in less developed countries*, P. Cook and C. Kirkpatrick (eds), 259–80. Brighton, Sussex: Wheatsheaf Books.

Low, L. 1988b. The Singapore economy in 1987. *Southeast Asian Affairs 1988*, 253–65. Singapore: Institute of Southeast Asian Studies.

Luechai Chulasai, Suwarat Bhekasut & Thongchai Shusuwan 1986. Family labour, hired labour and employment linkages in rural Thailand. In *Hired labour and rural labour markets in Asia: studies based on farm-level data*, S. Hirashima and M. Muqtada (eds), 151–75. New Delhi: Asian Employment Programme (ARTEP), ILO.

Lukman, N. & J. M. McGlinchey 1986. The Indonesian petroleum industry: current problems and future prospects. *Bulletin of Indonesian Economic Studies* **22** (3), 70–92.

MacAndrews, C. 1978. Transmigration in Indonesia: prospects and problems. *Asian Survey* **18** (5), 458–72.

MacAndrews, C. 1982. Land settlement policies in Southeast Asia. In *Population resettlement programs in Southeast Asia*, G. W. Jones & H. V. Richter (eds), 9–23. Development Studies Centre Monograph No. 30, Australian National University, Canberra.

Mahathir, bin Mohamad 1970. *The Malay dilemma*. Kuala Lumpur: Federal Publications.

Majid, Z. 1983. Malaysia. In *Swidden cultivation in Asia, Volume 2, country profiles*, 157–238. Bangkok: UNESCO.

Makil, P. Q. 1984. Forest management and use: Philippine policies in the seventies and beyond. *Philippine Studies* **32** (first quarter), 27–53.

Malthus, T. R. 1970. *An essay on the principle of population and a summary view of the principle of population*. Harmondsworth, Middlesex: Penguin (first published 1798).

Manning, C. 1987a. Irian Jaya's migrants gain economic clout. *Far Eastern Economic Review*, 30 April, 40–1.

Manning, C. 1987b. Public policy, rice production and income distribution: a review of Indonesia's rice self-sufficiency program. *Southeast Asian Journal of Social Science* **15** (1), 66–82.

Manning, C. 1987c. Transmigration is seen as a solution to poverty. *Far Eastern Economic Review*, 30 April, 42–3.

Mantra, I. B. 1985. Population mobility in Indonesia: past and future. In *Urbanization and migration in ASEAN development*, P. M. Hauser, D. B. Suits & N. Ogawa (eds), 167–87. Tokyo: National Institute for Research Advancement.

Masing, J. 1988. The role of settlement in rural development. In *Development in Sarawak: historical and contemporary perspectives*, R. A. Cramb & R. H. W. Reece (eds), 57–68. Monash Paper on Southeast Asia No. 17, Centre of Southeast Asian Studies, Monash University.

McCawley, P. 1978. Some consequences of the Pertamina crisis in Indonesia. *Journal of Southeast Asian Studies* **9** (1), 1–27.

McCawley, P. 1980. Indonesia's new balance of payments problem: a surplus to get rid of. *Eknomi dan Keuangan Indonesia (Economics and Finance in Indonesia)* **28** (1), 39–58.

McGee, T. G. 1967. *The Southeast Asian city: a social geography of the primate cities of Southeast Asia*. London: Bell.

Mears, L. A. 1984. Rice and food self-sufficiency in Indonesia. *Bulletin of Indonesian Economic Studies* **20** (2), 122–38.

Medhi Krongkaew & Pawadee Tongudai 1984. *The growth of Bangkok: the economics of unbalanced urbanization and development*. Discussion Paper No. 90, Faculty of Economics, Thammasat University, Bangkok.

Mehmet, O. 1986. *Development in Malaysia: poverty, wealth and trusteeship*. London: Croom Helm.

Meyanathan, S. & I. Haron n.d. Asean trade co-operation: a survey of the issues. In *Asean at the crossroads: obstacles, options and opportunities in economic co-operation*, N. Sopiee, Chew Lay See & Lim Siang Jin (eds), 13–53. Kuala Lumpur: Institute of Strategic and International Studies.

Milne, R. S. 1970. 'National ideology' and nation-building in Malaysia. *Asian Survey* **10** (7), 563–73.

Milne, R. S. & D. K. Mauzy 1986. *Malaysia: tradition, modernity and Islam.* Boulder, Colo.: Westview Press.

Ministry of Communications and Information 1989. *Singapore 1989.* Singapore: Information Division.

Ministry of Trade and Industry 1986. *The Singapore economy: new directions.* Report of the Economic Committee. Republic of Singapore.

Mirza, H. 1986. *Multinationals and the growth of the Singapore economy.* London: Croom Helm.

Monbiot, G. 1989. The transmigration fiasco. *Geographical* **61** (5), 26–30.

Morely, R. J. & J. R. Flenley 1987. Late Cainozoic vegetational and environmental changes in the Malay archipelago. In *Biogeographical evolution of the Malay Archipelago*, T. C. Whitmore (ed.), 50–9. Oxford: Clarendon Press.

NESDB n.d.(a). *The Fifth National Social and Economic Development Plan (1982–1986).* Bangkok: National Economic and Social Development Board, Office of the Prime Minister.

NESDB n.d.(b). *The Sixth National Social and Economic Development Plan (1987–1991).* Bangkok: National Economic and Social Development Board, Office of the Prime Minister.

NSO 1982. *Statistical summary of Thailand 1982.* Bangkok: National Statistical Office, Office of the Prime Minister.

NSO 1987a. *Key statistics of Thailand 1987.* Bangkok: National Statistical Office, Office of the Prime Minister.

NSO 1987b. *Quarterly Bulletin of Statistics* **35** (2/3). Bangkok: National Statistical Office, Office of the Prime Minister.

NSO 1988a. *Key statistics of Thailand 1988.* Bangkok: National Statistical Office, Office of the Prime Minister.

NSO 1988b. *Quarterly bulletin of Statistics* **36** (2). Bangkok: National Statistical Office, Office of the Prime Minister.

NSO 1988c. *Statistical handbook of Thailand 1988.* Bangkok: National Statistical Office, Office of the Prime Minister.

NSO 1988d. *Statistical yearbook: Thailand, number 35, 1987–88.* Bangkok: National Statistical Office, Office of the Prime Minister.

NSO 1989a. *Key Statistics of Thailand 1989.* Bangkok: National Statistical Office, Office of the Prime Minister.

NSO 1989b. *Statistical handbook of Thailand 1989.* Bangkok: National Statistical Office, Office of the Prime Minister.

NSO 1989c. *Statistical yearbook: Thailand, number 36, 1988–89.* Bangkok: National Statistical Office, Office of the Prime Minister.

Nasir, A. 1987a. An artificial jewel. *Far Eastern Economic Review*, 11 June, 114–16.

Nasir, A. 1987b. Hi-tech, low yield. *Far Eastern Economic Review*, 11 June, 110–13.

Nasution, A. 1984. The Indonesia economy: problems of adjustment to global recession and lower oil prices. *Indonesian Quarterly* **12** (1), 16–31.

Naya, S. 1987. Economic performance and growth factors of the ASEAN countries. In *The ASEAN success story: social, economic and political dimensions*, L. G. Martin (ed.), 47–87. Hawaii: East–West Center.

Newsweek 1988. Asia's emerging superstar. *Newsweek*, June 27, 6–12.

Ngau, H., T. J. Apoi & Chee Yoke Ling 1987. Malaysian timber: exploitation for whom? *Ecologist* **17** (4/5), 175–9.

Nicolaisen, I. 1986. Pride and progress: Kajang response to economic change. *Sarawak Museum Journal* **36** (57), 75–113.

Nieuwolt, S. 1977. *Tropical climatology: an introduction to the climates of the low latitudes*. London: John Wiley.

Nørlund, I., S. Cederroth & I. Gerdin (eds) 1986. *Rice societies: Asian problems and prospects*. London: Curzon Press.

Nye, P. H. & D. J. Greenland 1960. *The soil under shifting cultivation*. Technical communication No. 51, Commonwealth Bureau of Soils, Commonwealth Agricultural Bureaux, Farnham Royal, UK.

Oberai, A. S. 1987. *Migration, urbanisation and development*. Paper No. 5, World Employment Programme, International Labour Office, Geneva.

Oey, M. 1982. The transmigration program in Indonesia. In *Population resettlement programs in Southeast Asia*, G. W. Jones & H. V. Richter (eds), 27–51. Canberra: Australian National University.

Oldeman, L. R. & M. Frère, 1982 *A study of the agroclimatology of the humid tropics of Southeast Asia*. Rome: Food and Agriculture Organization.

Ooi Guat Tin n.d. Asean preferential trading arrangements: an assessment. In *Asean at the crossroads: obstacles, options and opportunities in economic co-operation*, N. Sopiee, Chew Lay See & Lim Siang Jin (eds), 56–61. Kuala Lumpur: Institute of Strategic and International Studies.

Ooi Jin Bee 1976. *Peninsular Malaysia*. London: Longman.

Ooi Jin Bee 1982. *The petroleum resources of Indonesia*. Kuala Lumpur: Oxford University Press.

Ooi Jin Bee 1987. *Depletion of the forest resources in the Philippines*. Field Report Series No. 18, Institute of Southeast Asian Studies, Singapore.

Osborne, M. 1979. *Southeast Asia: an introductory history*. Sydney: Allen & Unwin.

Othman, A. Bin 1984. Growth, equality and poverty in Malaysia, 1957–1980. Unpublished PhD thesis, Boston University. Ann Arbor, Mich.: University Microfilms International.

Otten, M. 1986a. *Transmigrasi: myths and realities, Indonesian resettlement policy, 1965–1985*. International Work Group for Indigenous Affairs (IEGIA) Document No. 57, Copenhagen.

Otten, M. 1986b. 'Transmigrasi': from poverty to bare subsistence. *Ecologist* **16** (2/3), 71–6.

Owen, N. G. 1987. The paradox of nineteenth century population growth in Southeast Asia: evidence from Java and the Philippines. *Journal of Southeast Asian Studies* **18** (1), 45–57.

Paisal Sricharatchanya 1987 'Friendship' arms sales. *Far Eastern Economic Review*, 19 March, 15–16.

Paisal Sricharatchanya 1989a. Power to the people. *Far Eastern Economic Review*, 19 January, 30–1.

Paisal Sricharatchanya 1989b. Too little, too late. *Far Eastern Economic Review*, 12 January, 40.

Palmer, I. 1977. *The new rice in Indonesia*. Geneva: UN Research Institute for Social Development.

Palmer, I. 1978. *The Indonesian economy since 1965: a case study of political economy*. London: Frank Cass.

Panayotou, T. 1984. *USAID development strategy in relation to Thai agriculture and rural employment*. Bangkok: Agricultural Development Council and the Harvard Institute for International Development.

Pang Eng Fong 1983. Race, income distribution and development in Malaysia and Singapore. In *The Chinese in Southeast Asia: volume 1, ethnicity and economic activity*, L. A. P. Gosling & L. Y. C. Lim (eds), 316–35. Singapore: Maruzen Asia.

Pang Eng Fong 1985. Foreign investment and the state in a newly-industrializing country: the experience of Singapore. *East Asia: International Review of Economic, Political and Social Development* **3**, 61–92.

Pangestu, M. 1986. The effects of an oil boom on a small oil exporting country: the case of Indonesia. PhD thesis, University of California at Davis. Ann Arbor, Mich.: University Microfilms International.

Pangestu, M. & A. D. Habir, 1989. Trends and prospects in privatization and deregulation in Indonesia. *ASEAN Economic Bulletin* **5** (3), 224–41.

Pawadee Tonguthai 1987. Implicit policies affecting urbanization in Thailand. In *Urbanization and urban policies in Pacific Asia*, R. J. Fuchs, G. W. Jones & E. M. Pernia (eds), 183–92. Boulder, Colo.: Westview Press.

Pearce, D., A. Markandya & E. B. Barbier 1989. *Blueprint for a green economy*. London: Earthscan.

Pearse, A. 1977. Technology and peasant production: reflections on a global study. *Development and Change* **8**, 125–59.

Pearse, A. 1980. *Seeds of plenty, seeds of want: social and economic implications of the Green Revolution*. Oxford: Clarendon Press.

Pelzer, K. J. 1983. *Pioneer settlement in the Asiatic tropics: studies in land utilization and agricultural colonization in Southeastern Asia*. Westport, Conn.: Greenwood Press (first published 1945).

Pendakur, V. S. 1984. *Urban Transport in ASEAN*. Research Notes and Discussion Paper No. 43, Institute of Southeast Asian Studies, Singapore.

Pérez-Sainz, J .P. 1983. Transmigration and accumulation in Indonesia. In *State policies and internal migration: studies in market and planned economies*, A. S. Oberai (ed.), 183–227. London: Croom Helm.

Perry, D. H. 1985. The economics of transmigrant farming. *Bulletin of Indonesian Economic Studies* **21** (3), 104–17.

Pfennig, W. & M. B. Suh (eds) 1984. *Aspects of ASEAN*. Munich: Weltforum Verlag.

Phya Anuman Rajadhon 1955. The water throwing. *Journal of the Siam Society* **42** (2), 23–30.

Phya Anuman Rajadhon 1961. *Life and ritual in old Siam: three studies of Thai life and customs*. (t. and ed. by William J. Gedney). New Haven, Conn.: Hraf Press.

Pluvier, J. 1974. *South-East Asia from colonialism to independence*. Kuala Lumpur: Oxford University Press.

Popkin, S. L. 1979. *The rational peasant: the political economy of rural society in Vietnam*. Berkeley: University of California Press.

Potter, R. B. 1985. *Urbanisation and planning in the Third World: spatial perceptions and public participation*. London: Croom Helm.

Purcell, V. 1965. *The Chinese in Southeast Asia*. London: Oxford University Press (2nd edn).

Raffles, T. S. 1978. *The History of Java*. Volume 1. Oxford in Asia Historical Reprints. Kuala Lumpur: Oxford University Press (first published 1817).

Rai, N. K. 1982. From forest to field: a study of Philippine Negrito foragers in transition. PhD thesis, University of Hawaii. Ann Arbor, Mich.: University Microfilms International.

Rajendran, M. 1985. *ASEAN's foreign relations: the shift to collective action*. Kuala Lumpur: Arenabuku sdn. bhd.

Rambo, A. T. 1982. Orang asli adaptive strategies: implications for Malaysian natural resource development planning. In *Too rapid rural development: perceptions and perspectives from Southeast Asia*, C. MacAndrews & Chia Lin Sien (eds), 251–99. Athens, Ohio: Ohio University Press.

Rambo, A. T. 1984. No free lunch: a reexamination of energetic efficiency of swidden agriculture. In *An introduction to human ecology research on agricultural systems in Southeast Asia*, A. T. Rambo & P. E. Sajise (eds), 154–63. University of the Philippines: Los Baños.

Rambo, A. T. 1988. People of the forest. In *Key environments: Malaysia*, Earl of Cranbrook (ed.), 273–88. Oxford: Pergamon Press.

Ramsay, A. 1985. Population pressure, mechanization, and landlessness in Central Thailand. *Journal of Developing Areas* **19** (3), 351–68.

Reed, W. A. 1904. *Negritos of Zambales*. Ethnological Survey Publications (Department of Interior), Vol. II, part 1. Manila: Bureau of Public Printing.

Reid, A. 1988. *Southeast Asia in the age of commerce, 1450–1680, Volume One: the lands below the winds*. New Haven, Conn.: Yale University Press.

Reid, A. 1990. An 'age of commerce' in Southeast Asian history. *Modern Asian Studies* **24** (1), 1–30.

Richards, P. 1985. *Indigenous agricultural revolution*. London: Hutchinson.

Richardson, H. W. 1989. The big, bad city: mega-city myth? *Third World Planning Review* **11** (4), 355–72.

Rieger, H. C. n.d. Towards an Asean common market: a concrete proposal. In *Asean at the crossroads: obstacles, options and opportunities in economic co-operation*, N. Sopiee, Chew Lay See & Lim Siang Jin (eds), 72–80. Kuala Lumpur: Institute of Strategic and International Studies.

Rigg, J. D. 1985. The role of the environment in limiting the adoption of the new rice technology in Northeastern Thailand. *Transactions of the Institute of British Geographers* **10** (4), 481–94.

Rigg, J. D. 1986a. Innovation and intensification in Northeastern Thailand: Brookfield applied. *Pacific Viewpoint* **27** (1), 29–45.

Rigg, J. D. 1986b. The Chinese agricultural middleman in Thailand: efficient or exploitative? *Singapore Journal of Tropical Geography* **7** (1), 68–79.

Rigg, J. D. 1987. Forces and influences behind the development of upland cash cropping in Northeast Thailand. *Geographical Journal* **153** (3), 370–82.

Rigg, J. D. 1988. Singapore and the recession of 1985. *Asian Survey* **28** (3), 340–52.

Rigg, J. D. 1989a. *International contract labor migration and the village economy: the case of Tambon Don Han, Northeastern Thailand*. Papers of the East-West Population Institute, No. 112. Honolulu: East–West Center.

Rigg, J. D. 1989b. The new rice technology and agrarian change: guilt by association? *Progress in Human Geography* **13** (3), 374–99.

Robison, R. 1986. *Indonesia: the rise of capital*. A publication of the Asian Studies Association of Australia. Sydney: Allen & Unwin.

Robison, R. 1987. After the gold rush: the politics of economic restructuring in Indonesia in the 1980s. In *Southeast Asia in the 1980s: the politics of economic crisis*, R. Robison, K. Hewison & R. Higgot (eds), 16–51. Sydney: Allen & Unwin.

Robison, R., R. Higgot & K. Hewison 1987a. Crisis in economic strategy in the 1980s: the factors at work. In *Southeast Asia in the 1980s: the politics of economic crisis*, R. Robison, K. Hewison & R. Higgott (eds), 1–15. Sydney: Allen & Unwin.

Robison, R., K. Hewison & R. Higgot (eds) 1987b. *Southeast Asia in the 1980s: the politics of economic crisis*. Sydney: Allen & Unwin.

Rodan, G. 1985. Industrialisation and the Singapore state in the context of the new international division of labour. In *Southeast Asia: essays in the political economy of structural change*, R. Higgott & R. Robison (eds), 172–94. London: Routledge & Kegan Paul.

Rodan, G. 1987. The rise and fall of Singapore's 'Second Industrial Revolution'. In *Southeast Asia in the 1980s: the politics of economic crisis*, R. Robison, K. Hewison & R. Higgott (eds), 149–76. Sydney: Allen & Unwin.

Rodan, G. 1989 *The political economy of Singapore's industrialization: national state and international capital*, Basingstoke: Macmillan.

Rogers, A. & J. G. Williamson 1984. Migration, urbanization and Third World development: an overview. In *Migration, urbanization, and spatial population dynamics*, A. Rogers (ed.), 261–80. Boulder, Colo.: Westview Press.

Roovers, H. with P. Bergsma, J. Schokkenbroek, W. van Turnhout & H. Willemsen, 1989. Alternatives to eviction of klong settlements in Bangkok. *Third World Planning Review* **11** (2), 151–74.

Rowley, A. 1989. Carving up world trade. *Far Eastern Economic Review*, 15 June, 53.

Sadli, M. 1987. Indonesia's economy needs restructuring. *Indonesian Quarterly* **15** (2), 166–70.

Sajise, P. E. 1986. The changing upland landscape. In *Man, agriculture and the tropical forest: change and development in the Philippine uplands*, S. Fujisaka, P. E. Sajise & R. A. del Castillo (eds), 13–41. Winrock International Institute for Agricultural Development, Bangkok.

Sanchez, A. 1987. Non-tarrif barriers in ASEAN–Japan and intra-ASEAN trade. *ASEAN Economic Bulletin*, July, 1–8.

Saravanamuttu, J. 1984. ASEAN security for the 1980s: the case for a revitalised ZOPFAN. *Contemporary Southeast Asia* **6** (2), 186–96.

Sarawak Study Group 1989. Logging in Sarawak: the Belaga experience. In *Logging against the natives of Sarawak*, INSAN (ed.), 1–28. Institute of Social Analysis, Petaling Jaya, Malaysia.

Savage, V. R. 1984. *Western impressions of nature and landscape in Southeast Asia*. Singapore: Singapore University Press.

Schwarz, A. 1989. Oiling the wheels. *Far Eastern Economic Review*, 9 March, 73–5.

Schwarz, A. 1990. Economic monitor: Indonesia. *Far Eastern Economic Review*, 15 February, 74.

Schweizer, T. 1987. Agrarian transformation? rice production in a Javanese village. *Bulletin of Indonesian Economic Studies* **23** (2), 38–70.

Schweizer, T. 1989. Economic individualism and the community spirit: divergent orientation patterns of Javanese villages in rice production and the ritual sphere. *Modern Asian Studies* **23** (2), 277–312.

Scott, J. C. 1976. *The moral economy of the peasant: rebellion and subsistence in Southeast Asia*. New Haven, Conn.: Yale University Press.

Scott, J. C. 1985. *Weapons of the weak: everyday forms of peasant resistance*. New Haven, Conn.: Yale University Press.

Scott, M. 1989. The disappearing forests. *Far Eastern Economic Review*, 12 January,. 34–8.

Seah, L. 1983. Public enterprise and economic development. In *Singapore development policies and trends*, P. S. J. Chen (ed.), 129–59. Singapore: Oxford University Press.

Seaward, N. 1986a. Balancing the redress. *Far Eastern Economic Review*, 25 September, 76–8.

Seaward, N. 1986b. Recovery takes priority over restructuring. *Far Eastern Economic Review*, 25 September, 78–9.

Seaward, N. 1986c. Statistics obscuring the true poverty line. *Far Eastern Economic*

Review, 25 September, 80–1.

Seaward, N. 1986d. Welcome back to foreign investors. *Far Eastern Economic Review*, 25 September, 82.

Seaward, N. 1987a Allegations of corruption, *Far Eastern Economic Review*, 22 October, 76.

Seaward, N. 1987b. Delays on the road. *Far Eastern Economic Review*, 28 May, 66–7.

Seaward, N. 1987c. Politics takes its toll. *Far Eastern Economic Review*, 30 July, 44–5.

Seaward, N. 1988. Malaysia's NEP policies to continue after 1990. *Far Eastern Economic Review*, 8 December, 10.

Secrett, C. 1986. The environmental impact of transmigration. *Ecologist* **16** (2/3). 77–88.

Selvadurai, S. 1979. *Agriculture in Peninsular Malaysia*. Bulletin No. 148, Ministry of Agriculture, Kuala Lumpur.

Seong, Dato' Paul Leong Khee n.d. Asean: choosing our destiny. In *Asean at the crossroads: obstacles, options and opportunities in economic co-operation*, N. Sopiee, Chew Lay See & Lim Siang Jin (eds), 5–10. Kuala Lumpur: Institute of Strategic and International Studies.

Shand, R. T. 1987. Income distribution in a dynamic rural sector: some evidence from Malaysia. *Economic Development and Cultural Change* **36** (1), 35–50.

Shari, I. & K. S. Jomo 1984. The New Economic Policy and 'national unity': development and inequality 25 years after independence. In *Ethnicity, class and development: Malaysia*, S. Husin Ali (ed.), 329–55. Kuala Lumpur: Persatuan Sains Sosial.

Sharp, L. & L. M. Hanks 1978. *Bang Chan: social history of a rural community in Thailand*. Ithaca, NY: Cornell University Press.

Shee Poon-Kim 1977. A decade of ASEAN, 1967–1977. *Asian Survey* **17** (8), 753–70.

Sidhu, M. S. & G. W. Jones 1981. Population distribution in Peninsular Malaysia: historical trends and contemporary issues. In *Population dynamics in a plural society: Peninsular Malaysia*, M. S. Sidhu & G. W. Jones (eds), 1–28. Kuala Lumpur: University of Malaya Co-operative Bookshop.

Sikorski, D. 1985. Development versus idealism: can Singapore reconcile the conflict? *Contemporary Southeast Asia* **7** (3), 172–92.

Simandjuntak, D. S. 1988. Indonesia's economic development: recovery after deregulation. *Indonesian Quarterly* **16** (4), 377–404.

Simon, S. W. 1983. Davids and Goliaths: small power – great power security relations in Southeast Asia. *Asian Survey* **23** (3), 302–15.

Simon, S. W. 1987. ASEAN's strategic situation in the 1980s. *Pacific Affairs* **60** (1), 73–93.

Simon, S. W. 1988. *The future of Asian-Pacific Security Collaboration*. Lexington, Mass.: Lexington Books.

Sivaramakrishnan, K. C. & L. Green 1986. *Metropolitan management: the Asian experience*. New York: Oxford University Press.

Skinner 1957. *Chinese society in Thailand: an analytical history*. Ithaca, NY: Cornell University Press.

Smith, A. 1930. *An inquiry into the nature and causes of the wealth of nations*. London: Methuen (first published 1776).

Smithies, M. 1986. *Old Bangkok*. Singapore: Oxford University Press.

Soesastro, H. 1983. ASEAN and the political economy of Pacific cooperation. *Asian Survey* **23** (12), 1255–69.

Somsak Tambunlertchai 1989. Economic prospects and external economic relations of Thailand. *Asian Development Review* **7** (2), 88–112.

Somsook Boonyabancha 1983. Causes and effects of slum eviction in Bangkok. In *Land for housing the poor*, S. Angel, R. W. Archer, S. Tanphiphat & E. A. Wegelin (eds), 254–80. Singapore: Select Books.

Sopiee, N. Chew Lay See & Lim Siang Jin (eds) n.d. *Asean at the crossroads: obstacles, options and opportunities in economic co-operation.* Kuala Lumpur: Institute of Strategic and International Studies.

Sørensen, P. 1986. On the problem of early rice in Southeast Asia. In *Rice societies: Asian problems and prospects*, I. Nørlund, S. Cederroth & I. Gerdin (eds), 267–79. Studies on Asian Topics No. 10. London: Curzon Press.

Spencer, J. E. 1966. *Shifting cultivation in Southeastern Asia.* Berkeley: University of California Press.

Steinberg, D. J. (ed.) with D. P. Chandler, W. R. Roff, J. R. W. Smail, R. H. Taylor, A. Woodside & D. K. Wyatt, 1987. *In search of Southeast Asia: a modern history.* Honolulu: University of Hawaii Press.

Sternstein, L. 1984. The growth of the world's pre-eminent 'primate city': Bangkok at its bicentenary. *Journal of Southeast Asian Studies* **15** (1), 43–68.

Stokes, C. 1962. A theory of slums. *Land Economics* **38**, 187–97.

Stott, P. 1978. Nous avons mangé la forêt: environmental perception and conservation in mainland South East Asia. In *Nature and Man in South East Asia*, P. A. Stott (ed.), 7–22. London: School of Oriental and African Studies.

Strauch, J. 1981. *Chinese village politics in the Malaysian state.* Harvard, Mass.: Harvard University Press.

Stubbs, R. 1983. Malaysia's rubber smallholding industry: crisis and the search for stability. *Pacific Affairs* **56** (1), 84–105.

Subroto 1986. Indonesia's energy policies in national and global perspectives. *Indonesian Quarterly* **14** (2), 190–206.

Suh, M. B. M. 1984. Political cooperation among ASEAN countries. In *Aspects of ASEAN*, W. Pfennig & M. M. B. Suh (eds), 55–90. Munich: Weltforum Verlag.

Suhartono, R. B. 1986. ASEAN approach to industrial co-operation. *Indonesian Quarterly* **14** (4), 505–21.

Sungsidh Piriyarangsan 1983. *Thai bureaucratic capitalism: 1932–1960.* Bangkok: Chulalongkorn University Social Research Institiute.

Suratman & P. Guinness 1977. The changing focus of transmigration. *Bulletin of Indonesian Studies* **13** (2), 78–101.

Suriyamongkol, M. L. 1988. *Politics of ASEAN economic co-operation: the case of the ASEAN industrial projects.* Singapore: Oxford University Press.

Suryadinata, L. 1985a. *China and the Asean states: the ethnic Chinese dimension.* Singapore: Singapore University Press.

Suryadinata, L. 1985b. Government policies towards the ethnic Chinese: a comparison between Indonesia and Malaysia. *Southeast Asian Journal of Social Science* **13** (2), 15–28.

Tambiah, S. J. 1970. *Buddhism and the spirit cults in North-East Thailand.* Cambridge: Cambridge University Press.

Tan, G. n.d. Asean preferential trading arrangements: an overview. In *Asean at the crossroads: obstacles, options and opportunities in economic co-operation*, N. Sopiee, Chew Lay See & Lim Siang Jin (eds), 63–9. Kuala Lumpur: Institute of Strategic and International Studies.

Tan, Y. K. 1981. *The land and the agricultural organisation of Peninsular Malaysia: A historical interpretation.* Monograph No. 13, Centre for Development Studies, University College of Swansea, University of Wales.

Tan Chee Beng 1984. Acculturation, assimilation and integration: the case of the

Chinese. In *Ethnicity, class and development: Malaysia*, S. Husin Ali (ed.), 189–211. Kuala Lumpur: Persatuan Sains Sosial Malaysia.

Tan Chee Beng 1987. Ethnic relations in Malaysia in historical and sociological perspectives. *Kajian Malaysia* 5 (1), 99–119.

Tan Tat Wai 1982. *Income distribution and determination in West Malaysia*. Kuala Lumpur: Oxford University Press.

Tanabe, S. 1978. Land reclamation in the Chao Phraya delta. In *Thailand: A rice-growing society*, Y. Ishii (ed.), 40–82. Monographs of the Center for Southeast Asian Studies, Kyoto University. Honolulu: University Press of Hawaii.

Tasker, R. 1987a. Fear of Indochina helps forge cohesion. *Far Eastern Economic Review*, 3 December, 106–7.

Tasker, R. 1987b. 18-minute solidarity. *Far Eastern Economic Review*, 24 December, 8–9.

Tasker, R. 1990. Must try harder. *Far Eastern Economic Review*, 8 March, 28–9.

Tasker, R. & S. Aznam 1987. Voting with their feet. *Far Eastern Economic Review*, 26 November, 21–3.

Tasker, R. & M. Heibert 1989. A test of arms. *Far Eastern Economic Review*, 28 September, 20–1.

Tate, D. J. M. 1979. *The making of modern South-East Asia, volume two: the Western impact, economic and social change*. Kuala Lumpur: Oxford University Press.

Thienchay Kiranandana & Suwanee Surasiengsunk 1985. *Population policy background paper study on economic consequences of urbanization in Thailand, 1987–2001*. Bangkok: Thai Development Research Institute.

Thorbek, S. 1987. *Voices fromm the city: women of Bangkok*. London: Zed Books.

Tiglao, R. & M. Scott 1989. On the down grade. *Far Eastern Economic Review*, 6 July, 37–44.

Tolba, M. K. 1987. *Sustainable development: constraints and opportunities*. Guildford: Butterworth Scientific.

Tolley, G. 1987. Market failures as bases of urban problems. In *The economics of urbanization and urban policies in developing countries*, G. S. Tolley & V. Thomas (eds), 49–59. Washington, DC: World Bank.

Tongchai Savasdisara, W. E. J. Tips & Sunanta Suwannodom 1987. *Residential satisfaction, mobility and estate management in private lower-cost housing estates in Thailand*. Final report of the Belgian low-cost housing project. Research Monographs No. 13, Division of Human Settlement Development, Asian Institute of Technology, Bangkok.

Trewartha, G. T. 1981. *The earth's problem climates*. Madison: University of Wisconsin Press (2nd edn).

Tsuruoka, D. 1990a. Jam tomorrow. *Far Eastern Economic Review*, 5 April, 46–7.

Tsuruoka, D. 1990b. Pick a project. *Far Eastern Economic Review*, 1 February, 34–5.

Turton, A. 1988. Ideological commodity production. In *'Sociology of developing societies': Southeast Asia*, J. G. Taylor & A. Turton (eds), 207–10. Basingstoke: Macmillan Education.

Uhlig, H. 1984. Spontaneous and planned agricultural settlement – a general view of the present clearing-colonization in the ASEAN countries of South East Asia. In *Spontaneous and planned settlement in Southeast Asia: forest clearing and recent pioneer colonization in the ASEAN countries and two case studies on Thailand*, H. Uhlig (ed.), 6–118. Hamburg: Institute of Asian Affairs.

References

US Embassy 1988. The petroleum report. Indonesia, Embassy of the United States of America, Jakarta (unpublished).

Vandenbosch, A. & R. Butwell 1966. *The changing face of Southeast Asia.* Lexington: University of Kentucky Press.
Vatikiotis, M. 1987. Resettlement rethink. *Far Eastern Economic Review*, 29 October 1987, 28.
Vatikiotis, M. 1989. Resettlement squeeze. *Far Eastern Economic Review*, 30 November, 34–5.
Villegas, B. M. 1987. The challenge to ASEAN economic co-operation. *Contemporary Southeast Asia* **9** (2), 120–8.
Viraphong V. 1988. Unsnarling Bangkok traffic. *Bangkok Bank Monthly Review* **29** (1), 18–26.

Wanadi, J. 1986. Asean and Pacific Basin economic co-operation. In *Into the Pacific era: Southeast Asia and its place in the Pacific*, H. Matsumoto & N. Sopiee (eds), 25–32. Kuala Lumpur: Institute of Strategic and International Studies.
Warford, J. & Z. Partow 1989. Evolution of the World Bank's environmental policy. *Finance and Development* **26** (4), 5–8.
Warr, P. G. 1986. *Indonesia's other Dutch disease: economic effects of the petroleum boom.* Working Papers in Trade and Development No. 86/2, Department of Economics and National Centre for Development Studies, Australian National University, Canberra.
Watabe, T. 1978. The development of rice cultivation. In *Thailand: a rice-growing society*, Y. Ishii (ed.), 3–14. Monographs of the Center of Southeast Asian Studies, Kyoto University. Honolulu: University Press of Hawaii.
Watabe, T. 1985. Origins and dispersal of rice in Asia. *East Asian Cultural Studies* **24** (1–4), 33–9.
Weatherbee, D. K. 1989. ASEAN defense programs: military patterns of national and regional resilience. In *Security, strategy and policy responses in the Pacific Rim*, Y. Whan Kihl & L. E. Grinter (eds), 189–220. Boulder, Colo.: Lynne Rienner Publishers.
Wells, R. J. G. 1983. Intraregional cooperation in ASEAN. *Southeast Asian Economic Review* **4** (3), 155–64.
Westlake, M. 1987. Highway protests gain momentum. *Far Eastern Economic Review*, 10 September, 62–4.
Wharton, C. R. 1969a. The Green Revolution: cornucopia or Pandora's Box? *Foreign Affairs* **47** (3), 464–76.
Wharton, C. R. 1969b. Subsistence agriculture: subsistence and scope. In *Subsistence agriculture and economic development*, C. R. Wharton (ed.), 12–20. Chicago: Aldine.
Whitmore, T. C. (ed.) 1981. *Wallace's line and plate tectonics.* Oxford: Clarendon Press.
Whitmore, T. C. 1984. *Tropical rain forests of the Far East.* Oxford: Clarendon Press.
Whitmore, T. C. (ed.) 1987. *Biogeographical evolution of the Malay Archipelago.* Oxford: Clarendon Press.
Whitmore, T. C. 1989. Southeast Asian tropical forests. In *Tropical rain forest ecosystems*, H. Leith & M. J. A. Werger (eds), 195–218. Amsterdam: Elsevier Science Publishers.
Wilkinson, B. 1988. Social engineering in Singapore. *Journal of Contemporary Southeast Asia* **18** (2), 165–88.
Winzeler, R. L. 1985. *Ethinic relations in Kelantan: a study of the Chinese and Thai as ethnic minorities in a Malay state.* East Asian Social Science Monographs.

Singapore: Oxford University Press.

Wolf, E. R. 1967. Closed corporate peasant communities in Mesoamerica and Central Java. In *Peasant societies: a reader*, J. M. Potter, M. N. Diaz and G. M. Foster (eds), 230–46. Boston: Little, Brown.

Wong, J. 1985. ASEAN's experience in regional economic cooperation. *Asian Development Review* **3** (1), 79–98.

Wong, J. 1987. The Asian NICs towards year 2000: growth and adjustment. In *Asian and Pacific economy: towards the year 2000*, papers and proceedings of a conference held in Beijing, November 1986, Fu-chen Lo (ed.), 115–154. Kuala Lumpur: Asian and Pacific Development Centre.

Wong, S. C. M. 1989. ASEAN co-operation: problems and prospects. *Indonesian Quarterly* **17** (1), 69–80.

World Bank 1987. *World development report 1987*. New York: Oxford University Press.

World Bank 1988. *Indonesia: the transmigration program in perspective*. Washington, DC: World Bank.

World Bank 1989. *World Development Report 1989*. New York: Oxford University Press.

World Commission on Environment and Development 1987. *Our common future*. Oxford: Oxford University Press.

Yip Yat Hoong 1969. *The development of the tin mining industry in Malaya*. Kuala Lumpur: University of Malaya Press.

Yoshihara, K. 1988. *The rise of ersatz capitalism in South-East Asia*. Singapore: Oxford University Press.

Young, K., W. C. F. Bussink & P. Hasan, 1980. *Malaysia: growth and equity in a multiracial society*. Baltimore: Johns Hopkins University Press.

Yue-man Yeung 1982. Economic inequality and social injustice: development issues in Malaysia. *Pacific Affairs* **55** (1), 94–101.

Yue-man Yeung 1988. Great cities of Eastern Asia. In *The metropolis era, volume 1: a world of giant cities*, M. Dogan & J. D. Kasarda (eds), 154–86. Newbury Park, Calif.: Sage.

Index

Note: subjects relating to specific countries are listed under those countries.